THE GREAT COUNTRY INNS OF AMERICA COOKBOOK

More Than 400 Recipes from Morning Meals to Midnight Snacks

FOURTH EDITION

James Stroman, Jennifer Wauson, Kevin Wilson

Illustrations by Elizabeth Rietz

WOODSTOCK, VERMONT

Copyright © 2006 by James Stroman, Jennifer Wauson &
Kevin Wilson

Fourth Edition

Library of Congress Cataloging-in-Publication Data has
been applied for.

ISBN-13: 978-0-88150-706-5

Jacket photograph © Kindra Clineff
Inn illustrations in text by Elizabeth Rietz
Book design by Eugenie S. Delaney

Published by The Countryman Press,
P.O. Box 748, Woodstock, Vermont 05091

Distributed by W. W. Norton & Company, Inc.,
500 Fifth Avenue, New York, NY 10110

Printed in the United States of America

10 9 8 7 6 5 4 3 2

CONTENTS

INTRODUCTION

THERE ARE CERTAIN CONSTANTS about country inns, like the basic elements of simplicity and charm in a picture-postcard setting, that promise a cozy respite from travel. Imagine a robust fire crackling on the hearth, the aromas of fine foods wafting from the kitchen through the rambling structure, and an innkeeper who knows how to make you feel at home as soon as you step over the resident feline lying across the doorway. These are the characteristics of the old-style hostelries that lure thousands of visitors from bustling, big-city environs. Travelers from across the country fill the rosters of these historic country inns.

If you have to ask why people choose country inns over standard hotels, you probably wouldn't enjoy the special ambience. Indeed, these old-style places aren't for everyone. The hike to the third floor, if that's where your room happens to be, can be a chore for those accustomed to elevators. Many rooms have no telephone or television. But for the traveler enamored of things past and appreciative of homey pleasures, these inns offer wonderful retreats. They are the places to savor the classic style of country life. From the vintage structure—many of historical import—to the gregarious nature of the innkeeper, to delectable cuisine—be it gourmet or homemade-breads for breakfast—every element of the country inn experience is appealing.

Our thanks to the many innkeepers from Maine to California to Alaska to Hawaii who have so generously shared with us their exciting recipes, and have so graciously allowed us to share them with you.

THE INNS AND THEIR RECIPES

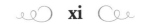

BREAKFAST

The Seven Sisters Inn

820 SE Fort King Street
Ocala, Florida 34471
352-867-1170
www.sevensistersinn.com

BUILT IN 1888, THIS QUEEN Anne–style Victorian bed-and-breakfast has been lovingly restored to its original stately elegance with beautiful period furnishings. The Inn was judged "Best Restoration Project" and is listed on the National Register of Historic Places. Faux paintings and murals, plus carved doors from Indonesia, begin an artistic expedition that reaches the four corners of the globe. World travelers can experience lighthouses of Cape Cod, a Safari Bengal room, gilded treasures and Egyptian artifacts, stone spa showers, a sultan's bed from mysterious India, fabrics imported from Paris, and the Zen-like harmony of the Orient. Jacuzzis, Victorian soaking tubs, spa showers, fireplaces, and heated towel bars are available in most rooms. Gourmet breakfast and afternoon tea are included.

*The Great Country Inns
of America Cookbook*

Amaretto-Banana Crepes

CREPES

½ cup whipping cream, chilled
2 tablespoons Kahlua or amaretto liqueur
¼ cup whipping cream
1 tablespoon melted butter
2 large bananas
4 ounces fine-quality semisweet chocolate, chopped

Keep crepes warm and on hand, ready to fill. First combine chocolate and ¼ cup cream in small bowl over simmering water. Stir occasionally until completely melted. In the meantime, cut bananas into small pieces—you should have about 2 cups. Stir chocolate mixture until smooth and remove from heat. Stir in the liqueur and finally add banana pieces, continuing to stir until smoothly mixed.

Spoon 3 tablespoons filling onto less attractive side of each crepe, gently spread to within ½-inch of each edge. Roll up crepe tightly like a cigar. Arrange seam side down in buttered baking dish in single layer. Brush crepes with the melted butter. Bake crepes 5 to 6 minutes or until hot. Meanwhile, whip ½ cup cream in a chilled bowl until soft peaks form. Slice another banana for garnish. Serve crepes hot. Spoon a little whipped cream onto or next to each crepe; finally add 2 or 3 thin banana slices, if using as a garnish.

Yield: 8 petite or 4 generous servings

Apple Breakfast Lasagna

- 1 (9-ounce) package frozen French toast (6 slices)
- 1 pound ground breakfast sausage, browned and drained
- 2 cups extra-sharp Cheddar cheese, grated
- 1 (20-ounce) can apple pie filling
- 1 cup granola

Preheat oven to 350°F.

Thaw French toast slices on a greased cookie sheet until thoroughly warmed. Layer sausage, cheese, apple pie filling, more cheese, then granola on each slice of French toast. Bake until cheese is melted and layers have warmed, about 10 to 15 minutes. Cut each slice into two pieces and serve hot.

Yield: 6 servings

The Skelton House B&B
97 Benson Street
Hartwell, Georgia 30643
706-376-7969
www.theskeltonhouse.com

THE SKELTON HOUSE B&B combines history and elegance while embracing contemporary comforts and grace. The gardens here are enjoyed by guests who browse, sit, or savor their early morning cups of coffee. Attorney Jim Skelton and his wife, Jessie, built their elegant Victorian home on Benson Street in Hartwell in 1896, laying the roots for a home for their family, which grew to include 10 children. The charm, grace, and hospitality of the original Skelton family and their grand home has been retained by this generation of Skeltons, as their recently restored home begins its new life as a bed-and-breakfast.

Hobbit Hollow Farm

3061 West Lake Road
Skaneateles, New York 13156
1-800-374-3796
www.hobbithollow.com

HOBBIT HOLLOW FARM has been painstakingly restored inside and out to recreate the casual comfort of an elegant country farmhouse. Hobbit Hollow serves a full farm breakfast as part of the room price. Overlooking Skaneateles Lake, it is situated on 320 acres of farmland with trails and ponds as well as private equestrian stables. Spend time contemplating the lake on the east verandah. Enjoy afternoon tea or coffee and watch the light play on the water in the soft wash of dusk. Rediscover what it means to be truly relaxed in a setting of tranquility. This is the perfect spot for a quiet, romantic getaway.

Apple-Cinnamon Quiche

1	medium apple (preferably tart), peeled and sliced
2	tablespoons butter
1	unbaked 9- or 10-inch piecrust
1	tablespoon sugar
1	teaspoon cinnamon
1	cup grated sharp Cheddar cheese
4	large eggs
1½	cups whipping cream

Preheat oven to 375°F.

Sauté apple slices in butter for 5 minutes. Layer the apple in the piecrust, then sprinkle it with the sugar, cinnamon, and cheese. In a medium bowl lightly whisk together eggs and cream and pour over apple mixture. Bake for 35 minutes or until a knife comes out clean.

Yield: 6 servings

Apple-Maple Crepes

CREPES

2 **eggs**
1½ **cups milk**
¼ **teaspoon salt**
1 **cup flour**
2 **tablespoons butter**

Mix all ingredients and let rest for 30 minutes. To cook, pour ⅓ cup of batter in a hot black crepe pan, flip, remove when done, and fill with a portion of the filling.

FILLING

5 **Granny Smith apples, cored, peeled, and sliced**
3 **tablespoons butter**
⅔ **cup brown sugar**
Grated zest from 1 orange
¼ **cup raisins**
⅓ **cup dark maple syrup**
cornstarch

Combine the first six ingredients and sauté until apples start to soften. Reserve liquid and add cornstarch until it thickens. Stuff the crepes. Spoon reserved liquid on top. Serve with choice of accompaniments.

Yield: 3 crepes

Brass Lantern Inn
717 Maple Street
Stowe, Vermont 05672
802-253-2229
www.brasslanterninn.com

ROM THE COZY FIREPLACES and soothing whirlpool tubs to the country quilts and spectacular mountain views, this charming and authentic Vermont bed-and-breakfast inn defines romance. Even during the busiest seasons, the inn's nine spacious and well-appointed guest rooms promise an intimacy not found in larger lodging accommodations.

Everything served is prepared fresh daily—including the breads and desserts—using only Vermont Seal of Quality products and produce. Each afternoon and into the evening enjoy complimentary coffee, tea, hot chocolate, and home-baked goodies by a crackling fire in the living room or out on the patio as the sun slips behind Mt. Mansfield, Vermont's highest peak.

Brackenridge House

A Bed and Breakfast Inn
230 Madison
San Antonio, Texas 78204
210-271-3442
1-800-221-1412
www.brackenridgehouse.com

BRACKENRIDGE HOUSE IS an intimate bed-and-breakfast, comfortably furnished with family quilts and antiques. It will remind you of Grandmother's house, only better—you don't have to make your bed, clean your plate, or clear the table. Ascend the staircase, greeted by classical music from the parlor, where you may drink coffee, enjoy a pre-breakfast snack, read, or converse with guests. In the formal dining room the table is set with crystal and china. A three-course gourmet breakfast is served, beginning with a fruit selection, proceeding to a main course that includes a breakfast meat, then finishing with a dessert, all accompanied by juice and your beverage of choice.

*The Great Country Inns
of America Cookbook*

Artichokes and Eggs

- 2 (10-ounce) cans condensed cream of chicken soup
- 1 tablespoon chopped onion
- ¼ cup sherry
- 1 small can sliced mushrooms, drained
- 2 cans artichoke hearts, drained and quartered
- 8 hard-cooked eggs, quartered
- 8 slices Old English or American cheese

Preheat oven to 400°F.

In a bowl, combine soup, onion, sherry, and mushrooms. Mix well. Arrange artichoke hearts and eggs in a 3-quart casserole. Add soup mixture and top with cheese slices. Bake for 25 to 30 minutes or until cheese is lightly browned.

Yield: 8 servings

Aunt Pittypat's
Pumpkin Pancakes

- 1 cup milk
- 1 tablespoon olive oil
- 1 large brown egg
- 1 tablespoon brown sugar
- ½ teaspoon cinnamon
- ⅛ teaspoon ginger
- ⅛ teaspoon nutmeg
- ¼ cup cooked and puréed pumpkin (or use canned)
- ½ teaspoon vanilla extract
- 1 cup pancake mix (we use Aunt Jemima original)

Mix in a blender the milk, olive oil, and egg. Add sugar, spices, pumpkin, and vanilla. Add this mixture to pancake mix. Whisk until blended. Grill (we use Puritan oil). Serve with maple syrup.

Yield: 12 pancakes

Gone with the Wind
Bed and Breakfast
14905 West Lake Road
Branchport, New York 14418
607-868-4603
www.gonewiththewind
onkeukalake.com

THIS STATELY STONE MANSION on a rolling hillside a hundred feet above the clear water of Keuka Lake in the Finger Lakes region of New York was opened in April of 1989. Since that time Linda and Robert Lewis, innkeepers/owners, have been guiding and serving thousands of guests. Most guests walk the many trails on the 14 acres, swim the waters of the private cove, or just enjoy the tranquilizing effect of gazebo gazing as the sounds and ripples bring relaxation. Everyone enjoys chatting around the breakfast tables while they relish breakfasts of fruit, home-baked Rhett's rhubarb coffee cake, one of Aunt Pittypat's many flavors of pancakes, or Ashley's stuffed French toast.

Inn at Sunrise Point

P. O. Box 1344
Camden, Maine 04843
207-236-7716
www.sunrisepoint.com

A PAMPERING SEASIDE haven, this bed-and-breakfast inn, recommended by Andrew Harper Best Hideaways, offers spectacular ocean views and all the luxuries you can expect from a four-diamond property. The inn is set within a secluded, 4½-acre oceanfront hideaway, just minutes from picturesque Camden. Sleep soundly in the wonderful sea air, comforted by the gentle murmur of waves outside your window. Awaken to the breathtaking sight of the sunrise across Penobscot Bay before enjoying a complimentary gourmet breakfast in the inn's bright conservatory or ocean room.

Baked Apple-Cinnamon Toast

	Sliced sweet bread (raisin cinnamon, apple, or challah)
2	**tablespoons butter**
5	**apples**
½	**cup brown sugar**
1	**tablespoon plus 1 teaspoon cinnamon**
¼	**cup applesauce**
⅛	**cup brandy**
	Raisins (optional)
12	**eggs**
2	**cups milk**
1	**teaspoon sugar**
	Extra slices of sautéed apple

Butter a 9 x 13-inch pan. Cover bottom with one layer of sweet bread. Melt butter in skillet. Add apples and sauté. Add brown sugar, brandy, 1 tablespoon of cinnamon, applesauce, brandy, and raisins (if you use raisin bread, you might want to skip the extra raisins). Cook for about 10 minutes. Pour apple mixture over bread. Cover mixture with a second layer of bread. In a large bowl, beat together eggs, milk, 1 teaspoon cinnamon, and sugar. Pour over bread until totally covered. You might need to add more egg mixture if not completely covered. Refrigerate overnight.

Preheat oven to 375°F. Bake for approximately 1 hour. Serve with a couple of sautéed apple slices on each helping.

Yield: 12 servings

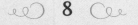

Baked Mushroom Frittata

- 2 tablespoons butter
- 2 cups white mushrooms, cleaned and sliced
- 1 pound fresh pork breakfast sausage
- 12 eggs
- ½ cup sour cream
- 1 cup milk or half-and-half
- 1 teaspoon salt
- 1 teaspoon black pepper
- 2 cups grated medium or sharp Cheddar cheese

Preheat oven to 350°F. Spray a 9 x 13-inch pan with cooking spray. In frying pan lightly sauté mushrooms in butter. Transfer to small bowl and wipe frying pan clean. Brown sausage meat, breaking it up into small pieces. Drain browned meat on paper towels. In large bowl, combine eggs, sour cream, milk, salt, and pepper. Mix well and beat slightly. Add mushrooms, sausage, and cheese, and mix gently to incorporate all ingredients. Bake for 55 minutes or until puffed up and golden brown. Let sit for 5 minutes. Cut into pieces for serving.

Yield: 6 servings

The Orchard Inn Bed and Breakfast

1207 Pecks Canyon Road
Yakima, Washington 98908
509-966-1283
www.orchardinnbb.com

The Orchard Inn Bed and Breakfast is delightfully located in a 4-acre, hillside cherry orchard with walking paths, minutes from downtown Yakima and Washington wine country. Guests relax in peaceful rooms with custom-made queen beds, private baths, and jetted tubs. The separate bed-and-breakfast entrance offers a cozy living room with a fine library of books on travel, wine, cuisine, fishing, and music, plus novels and German-language books. Enjoy a gourmet breakfast served in the Italian, German, or pergola (in season) dining areas. Celebrate your special occasion or just treat yourself to the perfect getaway, for both business and leisure travelers.

La Posada de Taos

309 Juanita Lane
P. O. Box 1118
Taos, New Mexico 87571
505-758-8164
www.laposadadetaos.com

*L*A POSADA DE TAOS bed-
and breakfast is a
historic adobe inn just
two blocks from the Taos Plaza. Relax
in front of your fireplace after a day on
the slopes. Unwind in your private
Jacuzzi (all rooms have private baths).
Enjoy a hearty breakfast in the morning
and home-baked snacks in the
afternoon. From dramatic sunrises to
stargazing nights, romantic moments
abound at La Posada. This century-old
adobe home, the first bed-and-
breakfast in Taos, captures the
elegance and charm, the quiet and
calm, the slower and simpler world of
the Southwest. Take a sunset walk
down narrow streets lined with stately
cottonwood trees and adobe homes or
relax on your veranda surrounded by
beautiful gardens that soothe your
spirit.

Baked Blintz

- 1 (8-ounce) package cream cheese
- 1 cup cottage cheese
- 5 eggs
- 1/3 cup plus 1 tablespoon sugar
- 1 teaspoon vanilla extract
- 1/2 cup butter, melted
- 1 cup flour
- 2 teaspoons baking powder
- 1 cup plain yogurt
- 1/2 cup sour cream
- 1/2 cup orange juice
- 4 tablespoons topping (jam or fresh berries)

Preheat oven to 375°F. Spray a 13 x 9-inch pan with cooking spray.

In a bowl, combine the cream cheese, cottage cheese, 1 egg, 1 tablespoon of sugar, and vanilla. Mix with a hand mixer until well blended. In another bowl, combine melted butter, 1/3 cup sugar, 4 eggs, flour, baking powder, yogurt, sour cream, and orange juice. Mix with a hand mixer until well blended. Pour half of egg and flour mixture into prepared pan. Spread all of cottage cheese mixture over egg mixture. Top with remaining egg and flour mixture. Bake for 40 to 50 minutes or until lightly browned. Cut into squares and serve with a dollop of topping.

Yield: 8 servings

*The Great Country Inns
of America Cookbook*

Belgian Waffles

2 cups all-purpose flour

2 teaspoons baking powder

2 tablespoons confectioners' sugar

1 tablespoon vegetable oil

2 cups milk

3 eggs, separated

2 teaspoons vanilla extract

Pinch of salt

Fruit of your choice

Whipped cream

In a large bowl, combine flour, baking powder, confectioners' sugar, oil, milk, and egg yolks. In another bowl, beat egg whites until they stand in soft peaks, then fold into batter (do not overmix). Using a 4-ounce ladle, pour $1/8$ of the mixture into a hot waffle iron and bake for about 2 minutes. Repeat with remaining batter. Top with fruit and whipped cream. Serve hot.

Yield: 8 waffles

The Glynn House Inn
59 Highland Street
Ashland, New Hampshire 03217
603-968-3775
www.glynnhouse.com

THE GLYNN HOUSE INN IS A restored Victorian New Hampshire bed-and-breakfast, set on a quiet, tree-lined street of Ashland. The inn is just a short walk from one of the area's best-known restaurants and White Mountain activities. The Glynn House Inn is only a short drive from major metropolitan areas, but a world away in every other aspect. The calming waters of the beautiful Lake Winnipesaukee and Squam Lake offer serenity in a tranquil setting. The Glynn House is the ideal choice for a romantic weekend or vacation getaway.

Alma del Monte

372 Hondo Seco Rd.
P.O. Box 617
Taos, New Mexico 87571
505-776-2721
www.almaspirit.com

*A*LMA DEL MONTE IS A modern hacienda that wraps you in romance, luxury, and privacy. Casual elegance and warm hospitality await guests behind the hand-carved doors of this inviting bed-and-breakfast. *Alma* means "spirit" with Spanish, and you can refresh your spirit in the fresh mountain air, pure artesian well water, and amazing endless skies that are the hallmarks of Taos, New Mexico. Guests rave about Alma's signature organic breakfast offerings. Every morning brings a three-course extravaganza of taste, texture, and color. Wake to birdsong and the sun rising over Taos Mountain. Watch the sun disappear behind Pedernal Mountain as the sky turns fiery. Experience the serenity of Taos's wide-open spaces. Make a wish upon the Milky Way.

Breakfast Cobbler with Oatmeal Cookie Crust

5 tablespoons butter
1 cup sugar
1 large egg white
1 teaspoon vanilla extract
1 cup all-purpose flour
¾ cup regular rolled oats (uncooked)
¾ teaspoon ground cinnamon or cardamom
Fruit of your choice
Whipped cream

Preheat oven to 350°F.

Beat butter and sugar with an electric mixer until creamy. Add egg white and vanilla, beat until blended. Stir in flour, oats and cinnamon. Crumble crust mixture over fruit filling. (Any fruit thickened as for pie filling.) Bake until topping is well browned, about 1 hour. Serve hot or cold. Garnish with a dollop of whipped cream. This cobbler is excellent with peaches, apricots, nectarines, and apples.

Yield: 8 servings

Breakfast Delight

- 1 can cream of onion soup
- 1 can Cheddar cheese soup
- 32 ounces frozen hash-brown potatoes
- 3 ounces cream cheese, softened

Preheat oven to 400°F. Grease a 9 x 13-inch pan.

Mix all ingredients together in large bowl. Pour into pan. Bake for 40 minutes.

Yield: 10 to 14 servings

1851 Historic Maple Hill Manor
2941 Perryville Road
Springfield, Kentucky 40069
859-336-3075
www.maplehillmanor.com

THE 1851 HISTORIC MAPLE Hill Manor is one of Kentucky's finest bed-and-breakfasts. Its colorful past includes stories of an antebellum plantation, use as a Confederate hospital, the childhood home of Phil Simms (former New York Giants quarterback), a popular dinner hall, and a children's home. Today it is a nationally recognized bed-and-breakfast. This working farm is set on 14 tranquil acres in the heart of Kentucky's scenic Bluegrass region. The home is considered one of the best preserved antebellum homes in the Commonwealth. Guests awaken to the delightful strains of chamber music and the wafting aromas of freshly brewed coffee and hot-from-the-oven muffins. The day begins with a specially prepared breakfast served on fine china in the dining room.

Magnolia Springs Bed & Breakfast

14469 Oak Street
Magnolia Springs, Alabama 36555
1-800-965-7321
www.magnoliasprings.com

THE MAGNOLIA SPRINGS BED & Breakfast is located halfway between the pristine, white sandy beaches of the Gulf of Mexico and the Eastern Shore, which sits on historic Mobile Bay. Magnolia Springs is a picturesque place and one of the few remaining places to receive mail by boat. From relaxing on the beaches to golf, shopping, and great fishing, Magnolia Springs has what you are looking for. You can stroll along oak-lined streets, fish, and relax on the porch to absorb the beautiful surroundings.

Breakfast Pizza

½	pound sausage
1	(8-ounce) package crescent rolls
2	cups hash browns
	Salt and pepper
6	eggs, beaten
¼	cup milk
1½	cups of Mexican cheese (4-cheese blend)
3	tablespoons grated Parmesan cheese

Preheat oven to 375°F.

In a skillet, cook sausage and drain. Separate crescent rolls, spread in a pizza pan, and seal the edges. Spoon sausage over dough and sprinkle hash browns over it. Salt and pepper to taste. In a bowl, combine eggs and milk and pour over mixture on pizza pan. Sprinkle Mexican cheese on top, followed by Parmesan cheese. Bake for 25 minutes.

Yield: 6 servings

Cheddar Omelet

- 2 tablespoons melted butter
- 6 ounces grated sharp Cheddar cheese
- 9 eggs
- ½ cup plain yogurt
- ½ cup milk
- ½ teaspoon salt
- ½ teaspoon basil (use fresh chopped purple basil leaves in season and garnish serving plate with a basil sprig)

Preheat oven to 350°F.

Melt butter in bottom of 8 x 8-inch baking dish. Sprinkle cheese over bottom of dish. In a bowl whisk together the eggs, yogurt, milk, salt, and basil until smooth. Pour over cheese and butter. Bake for 45 to 50 minutes.

Yield: 4 to 5 servings

The Inn at Harbour Ridge
6334 Red Barn Road
Osage Beach, Missouri 65065
573-302-0411
www.harbourridgeinn.com

THE INN AT HARBOUR RIDGE was designed and built specifically as a bed-and-breakfast. It was furnished casually for the comfort of all who seek quiet, peaceful accommodations with a private atmosphere and a bit of whimsy. The inn is the perfect spot for: a romantic weekend getaway, a few days of vigorous shopping at the Factory Merchants Outlet Mall, an antique treasure expedition, or just an escape from everyday living. The inn is located on an acre of countryside surrounded by towering oak trees and lovely landscaped gardens overlooking Lake of the Ozarks. Renew your spirit, refresh your soul at the Inn at Harbour Ridge.

Oak Knoll Inn

2200 East Oak Knoll Avenue
Napa Valley, California 94558
707-255-2200
www.oakknollinn.com

OAK KNOLL INN IS ONE OF THE most luxurious bed-and-breakfast inns in Napa Valley. The 600 acres of Chardonnay vines that surround the inn ensure guests the greatest luxury of all—quiet. "At Oak Knoll Inn, we start breakfast with a fruit course. While chocolate tacos may sound decadent, the dark, crisp chocolate tortilla provides a nice textural and flavor contrast to the sweetness of wonderful fresh California fruit. Topped with a fresh fruit sorbet—what could be better!"—Innkeeper Barbara Passino

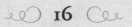
Chocolate Tacos

1 cup flour
1 cup sugar
6 tablespoons good-quality unsweetened cocoa
½ cup skim milk
6 small egg whites
½ cup oil (either vegetable or Old Hussy olive oil)
3 teaspoons vanilla extract
½ teaspoon salt

Beat all ingredients until smooth. Cover and chill at least 2 hours or overnight.

Heat a nonstick skillet over moderately high heat. Pour in a little less than ¼ cup of batter and tilt pan quickly to spread batter into an even circle. Once the edges look dry (2 or 3 minutes), flip it and cook another minute or two on the other side. If you have a taco rack, put soft tortillas in it to firm up, or drape them over a rack.

Fill each taco with your favorite fresh fruit, such as: strawberries (grind a tiny amount of fresh black pepper over them, or if they are not especially sweet, slice and sprinkle with balsamic vinegar and let sit for an hour before serving), raspberries, blueberries, blackberries, chopped mango, kiwi, or sliced peaches (grate some nutmeg over them).

Serve with a coordinated fruit sorbet, garnished with a mint sprig and an edible flower.

Yield: 20 servings.

Cinnamon-Baked Grapefruit

- 1 ruby red or pink grapefruit
- 1 teaspoon butter
   Cinnamon and sugar mixture
- 2 cherries

Preheat oven to 350°F.

Cut grapefruit in half and score each section. Sprinkle each half with cinnamon-sugar mixture. Place butter in center of each half. Place a cherry in center of each half. Bake for 15 minutes. Let grapefruit sit for 5 to 10 minutes before serving.

Yield: 2 servings

The Ivy
Bed & Breakfast

The Ivy Bed and Breakfast
331 North Main Street
Warrenton, North Carolina 27589
1-800-919-9886
252-257-9300
www.ivybedandbreakfast.com

THE IVY IS A LUXURIOUS, beautifully restored Queen Anne home in the old Warrenton historic district, offering the very best of the New South— beauty, charm, and hospitality in a romantic setting. The owners, Ellen and Jerry Roth, are a truly warm couple who love to pamper their guests with traditional Southern hospitality. If you are interested, they might even give you a cooking lesson that includes Ellen's Southern or Cajun cuisine. The inn is located near Lake Gaston and Kerr Lake, a short drive from Richmond or Raleigh. It's just a leisurely stroll to quaint downtown antique and specialty shops, the popular Hardware Café restaurant, historic churches, and the courthouse square. Guest rooms are named after the ladies of the house who lived there during its history.

Newport House
Bed & Breakfast

710 South Henry Street
Williamsburg, Virginia 23185
757-229-1775
www.newporthousebb.com

ERE IS WILLIAMSBURG'S most historically authentic bed & breakfast. Newport House was built to museum standards in 1988 from the 1756 design by famous architect Peter Harrison (1716–1775). It is furnished totally in the period with English and American antiques and reproductions (over a dozen of them designed by Harrison). Bed & breakfasts in this area are limited to 2 rental rooms each, which means that the owners can concentrate on providing luxury and personal service to their guests. Each spacious bedroom contains two-poster canopy beds, and even the blankets and carpets are historically authentic. John and Cathy Millar are the owners. A full breakfast served in the formal dining room usually includes delicious dishes made from authentic colonial recipes, with fruit and honey from The Millars' own garden, and an interesting historical seminar by John.

18

Colonial Jonnycakes

An authentic 18th-century recipe

- 2 cups white cornmeal (at Newport House, we use the authentic variety from Carpenter's Grist Mill, Wakefield, Rhode Island)
- 2 cups dark rum (we recommend the authentic Black Seal Rum from Bermuda)
- ½ cup half-and-half
- 1 teaspoon salt
- 1 tablespoon sugar
- 1 tablespoon molasses
  Hot water as needed

Mix ingredients (minus some of the water), stirring with a spoon. It will take about 30 minutes of sitting for the liquid to sink into the cornmeal enough, so you will know how much water to add to make the batter have the consistency of runny mashed potatoes. Pour onto greased griddle preheated to 375 to 400°F, forming pancakes about 2 to 3 inches in diameter. Cook 60 to 75 seconds on each side or until medium brown color. Serve with butter and a variety of Caribbean toppings, such as molasses, lime curd, pineapple preserve, nutmeg jam, or guava jelly.

Yield: 4 to 6 servings, 6 to 9 Jonnycakes each

Egg and Vegetable Puff

6 eggs, beaten
2 cups milk
1 cup Bisquick
1 onion, chopped
  Sundried tomatoes, mushrooms, or other vegetables,
    cut in bite-sized pieces
1 (8-ounce) package shredded Colby or Cheddar cheese

Preheat oven to 350°F. Grease a 9 x 13-inch casserole dish.

In a bowl, stir together eggs, milk, and Bisquick. Sauté
vegetables and stir into egg mixture. Add cheese. Pour into
casserole. Bake for 40 to 50 minutes.

Yield: 8 servings

**Brook Farm Inn
Bed and Breakfast**
15 Hawthorne Street
Lenox, Massachusetts 01240
1-800-285-7638
www.brookfarm.com

AT BROOK FARM INN, A breakfast buffet awaits you in the morning, and English tea with homemade scones is served each afternoon. The hospitality is unsurpassed. Located just down the hill and around the bend from Lenox center, Brook Farm welcomes you to the grace of its Victorian past and the comfort of the present. Lovingly furnished, this 130-year-old home, now a bed-and-breakfast inn, offers its guests comfort and tranquility in a completely smoke-free environment, surrounded by the beauty of the Berkshires and a tradition of poetry and literature.

Captain Tom Lawrence House—1861

A Cape Cod Bed and Breakfast Inn
75 Locust Street
Falmouth, Massachusetts 02540
508-548-9178
www.CaptainTomLawrence.com

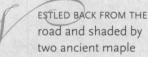

NESTLED BACK FROM THE road and shaded by two ancient maple trees, the Captain Tom Lawrence House is an intimate inn for those who appreciate fine accommodations and warm hospitality in a beautiful and historic setting. The house, with its circular stairway, hardwood floors, and high ceilings, remains much as it was when Captain Tom Lawrence lived there more than a century ago. Guests are invited to experience the elegance and history of this fine home, where every effort is made to provide the comfort and hospitality that is a hallmark of New England tradition. Breakfast is thoughtfully planned and prepared by your hosts, Anne Grebert and Jim Cotter. You will enjoy fresh fruit and a variety of creative entrées such as whole-wheat Belgium waffles served with seasonal fruit syrups, the inn's specialty.

Eggs Adare

4 strips cooked bacon, crumbled
   Cheddar cheese, grated
4 eggs
   Splash of milk
   Salt and pepper
   Fresh parsley or other herbs, chopped
2 toasted English muffins or slices of toast

Preheat oven to 250°F.

Lightly spray two 1-cup ramekins with cooking spray. Sprinkle bacon in bottom of each. Top with grated cheese. Prepare scrambled eggs using the eggs, milk, salt and pepper to taste, and herbs. Spoon eggs into ramekins. Bake for 10 minutes to set the eggs. When ready to serve, turn over onto half an English muffin or a slice of toast.

Yield: 2 servings

Eggs in a Nest with Red Pepper Chutney

5-inch flour tortillas
3 **eggs**
2 **tablespoons flour**
2 **tablespoons cream**
Salt and pepper
1 **cup total onions, bell peppers (any color),**
 and mushrooms
 smoked Gouda, shredded
 Bacon, ham pieces or cooked sausage (optional).

Preheat oven to 350°F.

To prepare the egg nests: Butter the tortillas on both sides. Push into large cupcake tins to form a small nest. Bake 5 minutes to form nests. Beat together eggs, flour, cream, and salt and pepper. Set aside. Sauté onions, peppers, and mushrooms in a frying pan. Place a portion of the veggie mixture in each nest. Top with the cheese. Add crumbled bacon, ham pieces, or cooked sausage if not serving vegetarians. Top with egg mixture. Bake until set, about 15 minutes.

RED PEPPER CHUTNEY

1 **(12-ounce) jar sweet red peppers**
 Lemon juice
1 **teaspoon cumin**
½ **teaspoon salt**
 Black pepper to taste

While baking the egg nests, make the chutney. Combine all the chutney ingredients in a saucepan. Heat slowly. Let set. Spoon the chutney onto a serving plate and place an egg nest on top. Garnish with sour cream. Repeat with remaining egg nests and chutney.

Yield: 8 servings

Point Pleasant Inn and Resort
333 Poppasquash Road
Bristol, Rhode Island 02809
401-253-0627
www.pointpleasantinn.com

THE POINT PLEASANT INN and Resort is located on Poppasquash Point, on a hillside overlooking Bristol Harbor. The inn is an English country manor house that offers a rare look at life from the pages of romance novels. Guest suites offer luxury accommodations, spectacular water and garden views, Italian linens, down comforters, and fireplaces. The home was built by Commodore Charles Bristed Rockwell as a mooring for his famous racing yacht, the *Belisarius*. The yacht is now on display at the Herreshoff Museum in Bristol.

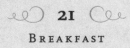

The Gables
Wine Country Inn

4257 Petaluma Hill Road
Santa Rosa, California 95404
707-585-7777
www.thegablesinn.com

THE GABLES WINE COUNTRY Inn is the perfect bed-and-breakfast for your next visit to the California wine country. The Gables is a beautifully restored Victorian mansion right in the center of California's spectacular Sonoma wine country. The inn sits on three lush green acres with magnificent vineyard and valley views. An easy one-hour drive north of San Francisco, it provides easy access to more than 200 wineries. Friendly, knowledgeable innkeepers provide unparalleled, personalized service to assure that guests enjoy their Sonoma wine country vacation to the fullest and return again and again.

Scrambled Eggs
with Goat Cheese
and Shiitake Mushrooms

3   tablespoons unsalted butter
6   ounces shiitake mushrooms, stems removed,
      caps thinly sliced
      Salt and freshly ground pepper
8   large eggs, beaten well
3   tablespoons snipped chives
3   ounces mild fresh goat cheese, crumbled (about ⅓ cup)

In large nonstick skillet, melt 2 tablespoons of the butter. Add mushrooms, season with salt and pepper and cook over moderate heat, stirring occasionally, until softened and lightly browned, about 5 minutes. In a bowl, season eggs with salt and pepper. Melt remaining tablespoon of butter in the skillet with the mushrooms; add eggs. Cook over moderately low heat without stirring until bottom is barely set, about 30 seconds. Add the chives and cook, stirring occasionally, until eggs form large soft curds. Remove from heat and sprinkle on cheese; let stand until softened, about 30 seconds. Gently fold the cheese into the eggs.

Yield: 4 servings

*The Great Country Inns
of America Cookbook*

English Muffin Bread
with Vegetable Egg Bake

BREAD

- 6 cups all-purpose flour
- 2 tablespoons yeast
- 1 tablespoon sugar
- ¼ teaspoon baking soda
- 2½ cups very warm water
- Cornmeal

Preheat oven to 350°F.

To make the bread: Combine 3 cups of the flour, yeast, sugar, and baking soda and sift into large bowl. Add the water. Beat until mixed thoroughly. Add remaining 3 cups of flour and mix until all flour is absorbed into the ball of dough. Spray two 8-inch loaf pans with nonstick spray and dust with cornmeal. Divide dough between loaf pans, flatten, and cover with clean cloth or paper towel until raised. Bake for 30 minutes.

VEGETABLE EGG BAKE

- 1 small zucchini, sliced
- 2 small carrots, sliced
- 1 medium onion, chopped
- 1 small green pepper, chopped
- 2 stalks celery, chopped
- 1 medium tomato, chopped
- 12 egg whites
- 4 egg yolks
- ⅓ cup fat-free sour cream
- ¼ cup Parmesan cheese, grated

Recipe continued on next page

**Gillum House
Bed & Breakfast**
35 Walnut Street
Shinnston, West Virginia 26431
304-592-0177
1-888-592-0177
www.Gillumhouse.com

THE GILLUM HOUSE HAS A great front porch with a comfortable glider and lots of books to choose from. Stroll on the rail trail or bike it. For more activities, just tell host Kathleen Panek your interests, and she will give clear directions for your personal tour—concierge service without the high price. Awaken to the aroma of baking each morning of your stay, as Kathleen makes muffins, adapted to be very low fat or fat-free (sugar-free muffins are also available) for a healthy, delicious breakfast. Enjoy a different mouth-watering entrée each morning.

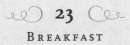

Preheat oven to 350°F.

Spray a medium skillet with nonstick spray. Add the vegetables and water, cover, and cook on low heat until the vegetables are softened. Drain and transfer to an 8 x 8-inch glass pan (acceptable for serving) that has been sprayed with nonstick spray. Combine the egg whites and egg yolks in a large bowl. Add the sour cream and cheese and whisk until blended. Add to the vegetables and stir just enough to mix. Bake for 30 minutes. Cut into pieces and serve immediately.

The English Muffin Bread and Vegetable Egg Bake can be baked at the same time and served together. Serve immediately with butter, jellies, apple butter, and/or honey.

Yield: 4 servings

Featherbed Eggs

Note: This is a custard-like egg dish, very light and fluffy.
It should be made at least six hours before baking.

- **6 slices bread, buttered**
- **1½ cups grated cheese (Cheddar, Gouda, Jack or any melting cheese)**
- **1½ cups milk**
- **6 eggs, slightly beaten**
- **Salt and pepper**

Arrange the slices of bread in a single layer in a shallow baking dish. Sprinkle lightly with salt and pepper to taste. Sprinkle the cheese evenly over the bread. Combine milk and eggs in a bowl, stir until blended, and pour over the bread and cheese. Cover and refrigerate for six hours.

DO NOT PREHEAT OVEN. Place the chilled baking dish in oven and set at 350°F. Turn on the oven and bake for about 1 hour or until the custard is puffy and lightly golden.

Variation: Omit the cheese and substitute thinly sliced ham and apple slices.

Yield: 4 servings

The Hoyt House
804 Atlantic Avenue
Fernandina Beach, Florida 32034
904-277-4300
www.hoythouse.com

IN A MAGNIFICENTLY restored 1905 Queen Anne mansion, 10 elegant guest rooms await you on coastal Amelia Island, Florida. Graceful wraparound porches, lazy ceiling fans, and tall bay windows warmly welcome visitors to Hoyt House, a grand mansion of yesteryear in the heart of the historic district of Fernandina Beach. A gourmet chef's breakfast, bikes, and beach chairs and towels are included with your comfortable guest room, and we invite you to enjoy complimentary afternoon snacks and evening wine. The Hoyt House is well known for old-world hospitality and elegant service. Golf, world-class tennis, classic-car shows, music festivals, antiques, early twentieth century architecture, a lighthouse, national parks and beaches, horseback riding, kayaking, fishing, boating, and bird watching await you on Amelia Island.

Good Medicine Lodge

537 Wisconsin Avenue
Whitefish, Montana 59937
406-862-5488
www.goodmedicinelodge.com

S ITUATED IN WHITEFISH, Montana, and in the heart of America's greatest outdoor-recreation region, Good Medicine Lodge is only a few turns from the Big Mountain, a short hike from Glacier National Park, a paddle away from Whitefish River and Lake, and a nine iron from the Flathead Valley's nine golf courses. The six spacious rooms and three suites, most with balconies and mountain views, have private baths, vaulted wood ceilings, and custom-made lodgepole pine or iron beds. Breakfast each morning includes fresh baked muffins, breads or cobblers, cereals, granola, yogurt, a variety of egg dishes, waffles or pancakes, coffee, tea, and juice.

Flathead Frittata

2 tablespoons vegetable oil
⅔ cup diced potatoes
⅔ cup chopped onion
⅓ cup diced summer squash
⅔ cup diced zucchini
⅔ cup diced red bell pepper
⅓ cup sliced mushrooms
1 dash salt and pepper (or to taste)
8 large eggs
½ cup milk
2 teaspoons dried basil or 2 tablespoons fresh
⅔ cup grated Parmesan cheese

Preheat oven to 350°F.

Heat oil in large skillet. Add potatoes, onion, squash, zucchini and bell pepper; sauté until almost tender. Add the mushrooms and sauté another 2 minutes. Salt and pepper to taste. Transfer the vegetables to a well-buttered 9 x 9-inch baking dish. Whisk the eggs and milk together in small mixing bowl. Stir in basil and pour egg mixture over the vegetables. Bake for 30 minutes. Remove from oven and top with cheese. Return to oven for 5 to 6 minutes or until cheese is melted.

Yield: one 9 x 9-inch frittata

French Toast

2 cups brown sugar

1 stick margarine or butter

2 tablespoons corn syrup

6 to 8 slices French bread (at least 1 inch thick)

1 (8-ounce block) cream cheese

2 cups milk

5 large eggs

1 teaspoon vanilla extract

1/3 cup confectioners' sugar

2 1/2 to 2 3/4 cups pecans or walnuts

In an 8 x 2 x 13-inch baking dish, melt the margarine. Add the brown sugar and corn syrup and mix well. Sprinkle pecans on sugar/butter mixture. Spread each slice of French bread heavily with cream cheese and place with cream cheese side down on the mixture in baking dish. Mix together milk, eggs and vanilla and pour over bread in dish. Cover and refrigerate overnight.

Preheat oven to 375°F. Bake for about 45 minutes until puffed and lightly browned. Remove from oven and cool slightly. Dust lightly with confectioners' sugar and serve.

Yield: 6 to 8 servings

Dowell House, Circa 1870
1104 South Tennessee Street
McKinney, Texas 75064
972-562-2456
www.dowellhouse.com

Dowell House has been pampering guests since 1990. Located in a spacious, Federal/Classical-style home built in 1870, where much of the original "Benji" movie was filmed, Dowell House has a rich history and an elegant ambiance to share with you. Step back into an era when life was genteel and slow. Linger over a full, fresh breakfast served with china, crystal, and silver in the formal dining room. Relax and have that second cup of coffee or sip tea in the sunroom or on the shady deck. Explore McKinney's old town square with its many art galleries, antique and crafts shops. Drive along quaint streets lined with early 20th century homes, or enjoy one of the many historical museums and sites in the area, yet be close to the many fine restaurants and shopping facilities in the metropolitan Dallas/Fort Worth area.

Joske House
Bed and Breakfast
241 King William
San Antonio, Texas 78204
210-271-0706
www.Joske.com

*T*HE JOSKE HOUSE IS A grand, 5,300-square-foot, nineteenth-century home built by San Antonio mercantilist Alexander Joske. The latest renovation, completed in 1990, removed none of the original parquet floors, chandeliers, paneling, or stained glass, but added many modern comforts such as air conditioning. The location that Mr. Joske chose, the corner of Beauregard and King William, is very convenient for touring San Antonio today. You can leave the house, stroll around the venerable historic district out into Southtown, where galleries and popular restaurants abound, or sample the ample amenities of all of downtown San Antonio. All are within a short walk. Only half a block from San Antonio's crown jewel, the Riverwalk.

Frittata Joske

2	tablespoons extra-virgin olive oil
3 or 4	small blue, yellow, or red potatoes
4 or 5	asparagus spears
4	whole eggs
4	egg whites
1/3	cup medium picante sauce
1/2	cup Cheddar cheese

Preheat oven to 475°F.

Cut potatoes into small bite-size pieces. Place olive oil in a cast-iron skillet. Add potatoes and sauté for about 10 minutes. Break asparagus into small pieces, using only the most tender parts. Add to olive oil and potatoes. Continue cooking for 6 to 8 minutes. In separate bowl, combine eggs and egg whites and beat until frothy. Fold picante sauce and cheese into beaten eggs. Add egg mixture to potatoes. Bake until lightly brown and set. Serve with fresh fruit and whole-wheat muffins for a light breakfast or with bacon, refried beans, and corn tortillas for a more hearty meal.

Yield: 2 servings

The Great Country Inns of America Cookbook

Gingered Grape and Orange Bake

2½   pounds seedless grapes (a mix of green and purple)
1   large orange
½   cup sugar
¼   cup flour
½   teaspoon ground ginger
½   teaspoon salt
1   tablespoon butter
    Milk
    Sugar
3   ready-made frozen puff-pastry squares, lightly softened

Preheat oven to 350°F.

Stem and wash grapes. Finely grate orange rind. Peel orange, slicing off and discarding white membrane. Use sharp knife to cleanly section orange. Discard any seeds. Mix grapes, orange rind, and orange sections. Set aside.

Mix together the sugar, flour, ground ginger, and salt. Stir into the grape and orange mixture. Spoon fruit and flour mixture into a greased pie plate. Dot with butter. Cut each pastry square into 4 squares. You will have 12 squares. Arrange them on top of fruit mixture. They will overlap slightly. Using a pastry brush, brush squares with a little milk. Sprinkle top with a little sugar. Bake for 30 minutes. This dish can be soggy. Carefully drain excess liquid after cooking.

Yield: 8 servings

Five Gables Inn
Murray Hill Road
P. O. Box 335
East Boothbay, Maine 04544
207-633-4551
www.fivegablesinn.com

MIKE AND DE KENNEDY are the owners/innkeepers in this wonderful hillside inn, which affords stunning views of Linekin Bay. Built in 1896, it has enjoyed a long tradition of hospitality. Fifteen of its 16 rooms have an ocean view. A wraparound veranda with plenty of comfortable seats is the perfect spot to view the magnificent bay and distant islands. The dining room offers Mike Kennedy's gourmet creations. Chef Kennedy is a graduate of the Culinary Institute of America. He shares a favorite with us here.

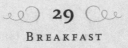

Chichester-McKee House
800 Spring Street
Placerville, California 95667
530-626-1882
info@innlover.com

D. W. CHICHESTER BUILT this gracious home for his wife, Caroline, in 1892. Lovingly restored in 2000, this beautiful country inn is currently owned by Doreen and Bill Thornhill. Beneath the Victorian dining room was once a pioneer gold mine. Guests will marvel at the wood and stained glass. It is an inspiration to come into this charming home, to find warm hospitality, and to remember a visit to an earlier time. A delightful breakfast is served in the dining room. The menu changes daily and features main-course egg specialties such as ham and asparagus crepes, eggs benedict, or Doreen's quiche. Bill's blend of coffee, fine tea, hot chocolate, juice, fruit dish, and baked pastries are included.

Ham And Asparagus Crepes with Cheese Sauce

CREPES

1 **cup milk**
3 **eggs**
²/₃ **cup flour**

Combine ingredients in blender. Heat an 8-inch pan to medium high. Pour batter in pan and roll around to cover pan. Cook until bubbles appear and edges start to turn brown. Flip over and cook other side a few seconds.

12 **thin slices Black Forest ham**
4 **slices Muenster cheese**
3 **cans asparagus**

SAUCE

3 **tablespoons melted butter**
3 **tablespoons flour**
1 **cup milk**
1 **cup grated sharp Cheddar cheese**
Dash of white pepper

Microwave butter, flour, and milk and whip with a wire whisk until smooth. Add grated Cheddar cheese and a touch of white pepper.

Preheat oven to 325°F. Lay crepes flat. Place a thin slice of ham, ⅓ slice of cheese, and two or three asparagus spears on each crepe. Roll up filled crepe and place in a 9 x 13-inch pan. Cover with foil. Bake for 30 minutes. Remove foil and brown the last 5 minutes. Serve two on a place with cheese sauce.

Yield: 12 crepes

Ham and Cheese Quiche

- 1 prepared piecrust
- 5 eggs
- 1 tablespoon finely diced onion
- 2 tablespoons diced red bell pepper
- ½ teaspoon tarragon
- 1 teaspoon prepared mustard
- 4 ounces shredded sharp white cheese
- ⅔ cup diced ham
- ⅓ cup plain yogurt
- ½ cup milk

Preheat oven to 350°F.

Place uncooked piecrust in pie plate. In a bowl, mix remaining ingredients and pour into piecrust. Bake for approximately 45 minutes, until lightly browned.

Yield: 4 to 6 servings

Tunnel Mountain Bed and Breakfast
Route 1, Box 59-1
Elkins, West Virginia 26241
304-636-1684
www.bbonline.com/wv/tunnel/

TUNNEL MOUNTAIN BED AND Breakfast is a charming three-story fieldstone home nestled on the side of Tunnel Mountain (part of Cheat Mountain), on five private wooded acres surrounded by scenic peaks, lush forests, and sparkling rivers. Named for the 1890 railroad tunnel that passes under the hillside, this bed-and-breakfast is a romantic country retreat. The interior is finished in pine and rare wormy chestnut woodwork. Tastefully decorated throughout with antiques, collectibles, and crafts, it extends a warm and friendly atmosphere where guests can feel at home. Just down the road from Tunnel Mountain Bed and Breakfast is the 998,000-acre Monongahela National Forest, which offers wonderful hiking and cross-country skiing opportunities.

1879 Merriman Manor
Bed & Breakfast

362 North College Street
U.S. Highway 127
Harrodsburg, Kentucky 40330
859-734-6289
merrimanmanor@bellsouth.net

*T*HIS 1879 VICTORIAN HOME has lovely craftsmanship and unique spacious- ness, from the main hall to the guest rooms. Savor the architecture of this fine home, located in Kentucky's first permanent settlement. The huge front gable gives the home a Queen Anne look. However, the four massive columns supporting the front porch are classical. Inside in the parlor, the mantel and adjacent archways are from the earlier Federal-period home, believed to have been in the first house on the property and then incorporated into this "new" home when it was built in 1879. Guests will enjoy breakfast in the formal dining room.

Hash-Brown Potato Casserole

- 1 tablespoon canola oil
- 1 (20-ounce) package hash-brown potatoes with onions and peppers
- ½ package hash-brown potatoes (plain)
- 1 can cream of mushroom soup
- ¾ cup half–and-half
- 1 teaspoon crushed red pepper
- 1 small can sliced mushrooms
- 1 package shredded sharp Cheddar cheese

In a large nonstick pan add oil and hash brown potatoes. Then stir in soup, half-and-half, crushed pepper, and mushrooms. Cook for approximately 10 minutes until slightly warmed throughout. Stir in cheese. Remove from heat and pour into 13 x 9-inch casserole. Cover and refrigerate overnight.

Preheat oven to 350°F. Cover casserole with foil and bake about 20 minutes. Remove foil and then let brown for 25 minutes.

Yield: 10 to 12 servings

Herb Cheese Frittatas

- 1 tablespoon butter
- 1 tablespoon plus 1 teaspoon chopped onion
- ¼ cup finely cubed ham
- 1 tablespoon plus 1 teaspoon herbed feta cheese, crumbled
- 4 eggs, stirred
- ¼ cup milk
- Dash of salt and pepper

Preheat oven to 350°F if baking today.

Grease 4 ramekins. Melt the butter in a skillet and sauté onion until translucent. Add ham and sauté for 3 minutes. Divide onion/ham mixture among ramekins. Sprinkle cheese into each ramekin. In a bowl, mix eggs, milk, salt, and pepper. Pour into each ramekin. Refrigerate overnight or bake for about 20 minutes. Test with a knife. Remove from ramekin and put on platter.

Yield: 4 servings

Ant Street Inn
107 West Commerce Street
Brenham, Texas 77833
1-800-805-2600
www.antstreetinn.com

THE ANT STREET INN BED-and-breakfast offers the finest in Southern hospitality and warmth, and the elegance of a first-class hotel. Centrally located in Brenham between Houston and Austin, the Ant Street Inn is an inviting destination for a relaxing overnight stay while traveling for business or pleasure. Relax in rocking chairs on the back veranda overlooking the courtyard garden, enjoy some of the many shops and restaurants in the historic Ant Street district, or dine in the inn at the Capital Grill while enjoying your favorite beer or wine. A scrumptious breakfast at the Capital Grill is included. The friendly people at the Ant Street Inn promise to make your stay comfortable and enjoyable.

Grant Corner Inn

122 Grant Avenue
Santa Fe, New Mexico 87501
505-983-6678
www.grantcornerinn.com

*H*ERE IS AN EXQUISITE colonial-manor inn in the heart of Santa Fe. With an ideal location just two blocks from the historic plaza, Grant Corner Inn is nestled among intriguing shops and galleries. Built in the early 1900s as a home for the Windsors, a wealthy New Mexican ranching family, the inn boasts charming guest rooms, each appointed with antiques and treasures from around the world.

Huevos con Esparragos

- 6 tablespoons (¾ stick) unsalted butter
- 10 fresh mushrooms, sliced
- 1 tablespoon finely chopped fresh parsley
- ½ clove garlic, minced
- ¼ cup all-purpose flour
- 2 cups milk
- ½ teaspoon salt
- 2 cups asparagus tips, steamed until tender-crisp
- 6 hard-cooked eggs, sliced
- 2 tablespoons fresh bread crumbs
- 1 cup (¼ pound) grated Monterey Jack cheese

Preheat oven to 350°F. Generously grease 2-quart glass baking dish.

In small sauté pan melt 2 tablespoons of the butter. Sauté mushrooms 1 minute, then add parsley and garlic; sauté another 2 minutes. Set aside. In medium saucepan melt remaining 4 tablespoons butter. Stir in flour and cook 4 minutes over low heat. Gradually add milk, stirring to smooth; add salt. Bring cream sauce to a boil; stir in asparagus tips, cover, and remove from heat.

Beginning and ending with cream sauce, layer prepared pan alternately with sauce, egg slices, and mushrooms. Sprinkle casserole with bread crumbs and cheese and bake for about 15 minutes, or until top of casserole is browned.

Yield: 6 servings

Lagniappe Quiche

- 1 preformed piecrust
- 1 tablespoon butter
- 1 small onion, finely chopped
- 1 cup cooked rice
- ½ cup diced ham
- ½ package frozen crawfish tails (thawed)
- 1 teaspoon Tony Chachere's Cajun Seasoning (or to taste)
- ½ teaspoon tarragon
- ½ teaspoon basil
- 5 eggs
- 1¼ cups half-and-half
- 2 tablespoons honey mustard
- 2 cups shredded cheese, mixed varieties

Preheat oven to 450°F.

Place piecrust in a 10-inch quiche dish and prick across the bottom with a fork. Bake for 5 minutes. Remove from oven; carefully prick piecrust again with a fork and bake for another 5 minutes. Reduce oven temperature to 350°F.

In a large saucepan, melt the butter over medium heat, add onions and sauté until tender. Add rice, ham, crawfish tails, cajun seasoning, tarragon, and basil. Mix together and cook 5 minutes or until heated through. In a medium-size bowl beat eggs then add half-and-half and honey mustard. Mix until blended. Spread 1 cup of the cheese on the piecrust, then add the rice mixture and spread evenly. Pour the egg mixture over the rice and gently mix together, taking care not to disturb the cheese. Bake for 25 to 30 minutes or until the quiche doesn't jiggle in the middle. Spread the remaining cup of cheese over the top and bake for an additional 5 minutes. Slice as you would a pie and serve hot.

Yield: 1 pie

Calloway Corners Bed & Breakfast

19778 Highway 371
P. O. Box 199
Calloway Corners, Louisiana 71073
318-377-2058
1-800-851-1088
www.callowaycornersbb.com

EMPTY FOR MANY YEARS, THIS house became the birthplace of the fictitious Calloway sisters, Mariah, Jo, Tess, and Eden, and was used on the cover of each of the first four Harlequin Romance novels. After meeting the authors in 1989, Jeanne Woods (the previous owner) decided to use the series' name for the bed-and-breakfast. In 1993, Harlequin coordinated a re-release for the books with a contest for readers, the winner getting a weekend for two at Calloway Corners along with a cash prize. While Harlequin was putting the finishing touches on the contest, the required administrative procedures were put in place to make Calloway Corners a "real" town.

Eagle Harbor Inn

9914 Water Street; P. O. Box 588
Ephraim, Wisconsin 54211
920-854-2121
1-800-324-5427
www.eagleharbor.com

*H*ERE IS A TRADITIONAL inn, intimate and welcoming. It offers early twentieth-century warmth in nine distinctly decorated rooms, all with private baths, and a sumptuous full breakfast.

To quote hosts Nedd and Natalie Neddersen: "Dear Friends, We look forward to meeting you personally and sharing our very special retreat with you and your family. We'll greet you with a glass of cool lemonade or hot mulled cider, a welcoming smile, and any assistance needed in planning your stay." Often called a hidden treasure, this intimate inn beckons your discovery.

Mediterranean Eggs

1	unbaked pie shell
	Shredded Cheddar cheese, as desired
1	small onion, diced
1	bunch fresh asparagus, chopped
1	tomato, cut into 6 wedges
6	eggs
1	cup heavy cream
	Fresh chopped thyme and oregano
	Salt and pepper

Preheat oven to 350°F.

Layer pie shell with onion, cheese, and asparagus. In a bowl, mix together egg and cream. Add thyme, oregano, salt, and pepper to taste. Pour into pie shell. Arrange tomato wedges on top in a wheel format. Bake for 1 hour and 20 minutes. Slice and enjoy.

Yield: 6 servings

Mexican Eggs

- 1 fresh tortilla
- 2 slices cooked bacon
- 1/3 cup low-fat refried black beans
- 1/2 cup shredded cheese, Mexican or mix of Cheddar and Jack cheeses
- 2 eggs, poached in enchilada sauce (pick the level of spice mild to hot)
  (Note: 1 can of enchilada sauce can poach about 8 eggs)
- 1/4 cup diced fresh tomatoes
  Sliced black olives
- 2 tablespoons sour cream

Warm the tortilla preferably over a gas flame until it just begins to toast and puff. Spread the center 1/3 of the tortilla with refried beans. Place one strip of bacon on either side of the beans. Top with half the cheese. Place in a warm oven to keep the tortillas warm and to gently melt the cheese while you poach the eggs.

In a flat pan with a cover, bring a can of prepared enchilada sauce to a boil, reduce to a simmer. Place eggs in the enchilada sauce to poach them gently, covered, about 4 minutes, until they reach desired doneness. Place eggs and some sauce on the prepared tortilla. Top with more cheese, tomatoes, olives, and a dollop of sour cream. Enjoy!

Yield: 1 serving

Casa de San Pedro
8933 South Yell Lane
Hereford, Arizona 85615
520-366-1300
www.bedandbirds.com

CASA DE SAN PEDRO IS LOCATED just 90 miles southeast of Tucson and 20 miles southeast of Sierra Vista in the San Pedro River Valley. For those interested in southeastern Arizona birding, Casa de San Pedro is centrally located, permitting easy day trips to other birding "hot spots" such as Madera Canyon, Patagonia, Empire Cienega, Garden Canyon, Miller Canyon, and Ramsey Canyon. The inn is adjacent to the San Pedro Riparian National Conservation Area and is situated on 10 acres bordering the San Pedro River. The broad grasslands in the valley and the cottonwood and willow trees along the river provide a constant supply of food, shelter and water for wildlife. Scenic mountain and riparian hiking and cycling trails are plentiful.

Poland Spring Resort

41 Ricker Road
Poland Spring, Maine 04274
207-998-4351
www.polandspringinns.com

OLAND SPRING RESORT HAS everything you'll need to enjoy an active or inactive vacation. At Poland Spring you'll meet some of the nicest people anywhere, and enjoy plentiful food and great entertainment. Poland Spring is more than a country inn. It has beautiful grounds, lovely buildings, and many outdoor as well as indoor activities. Poland Spring Resort has three inns and ten cottages, surrounded by a beautiful golf course. Like an old-time country inn, all of the food is fresh, wholesome, and, most of all, delicious. Breakfast and supper are served buffet style.

Orange Baked French Toast

	French toast bread (sliced thick)
¾	**cup flour**
2¼	**cups milk**
9	**eggs**
1½	**tablespoons sugar**
1	**teaspoon orange extract or zest**
¾	**teaspoon vanilla extract**
	Pinch of salt
1	**cup mandarin oranges**
1	**cup orange marmalade**

Line 9 x 13-inch pan with French toast bread. In a bowl, whisk together flour, milk, eggs, sugar, extracts, and salt. Pour over bread. Refrigerate overnight.

Preheat oven to 350°F. Arrange oranges over bread. Bake for 30 to 40 minutes. Smother with marmalade and serve.

Yield: 6 to 9 servings

Pecan-Pumpkin Waffles

2½ cups all-purpose flour
4 teaspoons baking powder
1 teaspoon salt
¾ teaspoon ground cinnamon
¼ teaspoon ground nutmeg
3 eggs, separated
1¾ cups milk
½ cup melted butter
½ cup cooked pumpkin
¾ cup chopped pecans
Confectioners' sugar (optional)
Maple syrup

In large mixing bowl, stir together flour, baking powder, salt, cinnamon, and nutmeg. In a bowl, beat egg yolks. Stir in milk, melted butter, and pumpkin. Stir this mixture into dry ingredients. In another bowl, beat egg whites until stiff, then fold into batter. Pour batter onto hot waffle iron and sprinkle with pecans. Serve with dusting of confectioners' sugar and maple syrup.

Yield: 8 waffles

McCleery's Flat
121 East Patrick Street
Frederick, Maryland 21701
301-620-2433
1-800-774-7926
http://www.fwp.net/mccleerysflat

McCLEERY'S FLAT, CIRCA 1876, is a French Empire–style townhome that offers European hospitality catering to sophisticated of travelers and business people who select a bed-and-breakfast as a first choice, not a last resort. Registered as a Historic Landmark by the Frederick County Historic Landmark Association, the establishment's past, setting, stately interior, and luxurious breakfasts are intended to draw those looking for a special traveling experience with a strong dose of easy elegance. For Civil War enthusiasts, the battlegrounds of Antietam, Gettysburg, and South Mountain are just around the corner. Guests can stroll along the tree-lined walks of historic downtown or step into the past with a horse-and-carriage ride. Also close by is bicycling or hiking in the Catoctin Mountains, along the famous C&O Canal, or on a portion of the Appalachian Trail. Beautiful rolling farmlands fill the countryside, complete with picturesque sunsets. The inn's rooms will enchant you, its breakfasts will delight you.

Puffs

**The Edward Harris
House Inn**

35 Argyle Street
Rochester, New York 14607
585-473-9752
www.edwardharrishouse.com

CONVENIENTLY LOCATED IN AN
urban village setting between
East and Park Avenues in
Rochester, the Edward Harris House
offers vacationers and business
travelers alike the relaxation of
neighborhood living with the convenience of a city location. The inn and
guest rooms are as individual as you
are. Several of the guest rooms have
working fireplaces; all rooms have
ultra plush bedding and fluffy down
comforters. Newly renovated en suite
private baths have towel warmers, hair
dryers, and plush robes in the winter.

¼ cup butter (for the pan)
¾ cup flour
3 eggs
1½ cups milk
½ cup sugar
¼ teaspoon salt
  Brown sugar
  Sour cream
  Fruit

Preheat oven to 425°F.

Place the butter in a pan and put in oven. Place flour in mixing
bowl. Add and beat the eggs, milk, sugar, and salt until smooth.
When the butter melts and starts to bubble, pour egg mixture
into the pan. Return to oven and bake for 25 to 30 minutes.

Serve hot. Put brown sugar, sour cream, and your favorite fruit
(strawberries and blueberries work exceptionally well) on top of
the puff and enjoy.

Yield: 4 to 6 puffs

Sallie's Puff Pastry Eggs Goldenrod

WHITE SAUCE
4 tablespoons butter
4 tablespoons flour
2 cups milk

Melt butter over low heat. Add flour and stir until well blended (approximately 4 minutes). Slowly add milk and continually stir until slightly set.

EGGS GOLDENROD
24 Pepperidge Farm puff pastry shells
12 hard boiled eggs, chopped
Salt and pepper
Bacon, cooked and crumbled
Fresh tarragon
Paprika

Prepare pastry shells as directed on package. Boil eggs the night before if desired. While pastry shells are baking, prepare white sauce and keep warm on stove. Wash fresh tarragon (dried can be used if necessary), dry, and set aside. When pastry shells are puffed and slightly brown, remove from oven. Place on plates and remove scored top from shells. Cover chopped eggs with plastic wrap and heat until warm (in microwave about 1 or 2 minutes). Spoon chopped eggs over and into pastry shells. Liberally drizzle white sauce over puff pastry shells. Sprinkle chopped bacon, a dash of paprika, salt, pepper, and tarragon over the shells. Push shell top upright and into lower shell to make a clamshell effect. Garnish plate with colorful fruit such as apple and orange slices or small grape bunches and serve.

Yield: 12 servings

Holden House
1102 West Pikes Peak Avenue
Colorado Springs, Colorado 80904
719-471-3980
www.HoldenHouse.com

THE SCENIC BEAUTY OF Colorado Springs and the Pikes Peak region offers something for everyone. "The Springs" is located just 60 miles south of Denver and has its own convenient regional airport. Sallie and Welling Clark meticulously restored the property in 1986. They continue to own and operate the inn and uphold the standards at Holden House. Savor the gourmet breakfasts, which might include freshly baked cinnamon streusel muffins, Sallie's famous Southwestern Eggs Fiesta, fresh fruit, freshly ground gourmet coffee, tea, and juice. Complimentary refreshments, an afternoon wine social, and a legendary bottomless cookie jar are just a few of the added touches you'll find here.

Captain's Inn at Moss Landing

8122 Moss Landing Road
Moss Landing, California 95039
831-633-5550
www.captainsinn.com

ENJOY WONDERFUL WATERFRONT views of birds and harbor seals from the Captain's Inn at Moss Landing. Walk quiet beaches, relax and enjoy plush beds, luxuriate with massage and deep soaking tubs, and eat a generous breakfast including warm oven-baked goodies. Guest can stay in the historic 1906 Pacific Coast Steamship Company building that has received a historic preservation award, or stay in our boathouse with guest rooms and, of course, boats! There is a coastal, nautical décor including antiques and original redwood molding. The Captain's Inn at Moss Landing features home-cooked breakfasts including traditional recipes from the owners' German grandmothers.

Messy Spinach Eggs

¼ small sweet yellow onion
1 cube butter
2 cups fresh spinach
3 large eggs
1 tablespoon cream
  Seasonings
¼ cup finely grated Monterey Jack cheese

Chop onion into small pieces and in a small pan sauté until clear and slightly browned; set aside. In small pan with melted butter, warm fresh spinach briefly, just enough to soften leaves; set aside. Mix eggs and cream with whisk. Melt butter in small skillet and pour in egg mixture on high temperature. Season eggs to taste, add onions, then add spinach over eggs. When eggs are partially cooked, stir so they will cook evenly. Continue to cook and stir, just as you would scrambled eggs. When done, add cheese. Dish is ready when cheese melts. Serve with German sausage or ham on the side.

Yield: 1 serving

Sweetheart Casserole

2 medium potatoes, peeled and chopped
8 eggs
½ cup cottage cheese
¼ cup sour cream
2 dashes Mrs. Dash seasoning
   Breakfast sausage, Canadian bacon, or chopped ham,
   cooked and drained (optional)
½ cup grated or shredded Cheddar or Swiss cheese

Preheat oven to 350°F.

Place potatoes and some water in baking dish with a lid.
Microwave for 5 minutes until tender. In mixing bowl, combine
eggs, cottage cheese, sour cream, and seasoning. Spray heart-
shaped baking dish with nonstick spray. Place sausage,
Canadian bacon, and/or ham in bottom of dish. (Any combination is good or meat may be arranged separately in a pattern.)
Blend the drained, cooked potatoes with the egg mixture and
pour on top of the meat. Bake for about 45 minutes or until
knife comes out clean when the middle is tested. Sprinkle
cheese on top.

Yield: 6 servings

Cameron's Crag

**Cameron's Crag
Bed and Breakfast**
P. O. Box 295
Branson, Missouri 65726
417-334-4720
1-800-933-8529
www.camerons-crag.com

CAMERON'S CRAG IS LOCATED JUST
three miles from Branson.
It is a special bed-and-
breakfast in a contemporary home
perched high on a bluff overlooking
Lake Taneycomo and the Branson
skyline. Each guest accommodation
features a entrance, hot tub, private
bath, king bed, and a spectacular view
of the lake and valley. Suites in the
detached guesthouse also offer full
kitchens and deluxe whirlpool tubs
for two.

Clefstone Manor
Bed & Breakfast

92 Eden Street
Bar Harbor, Maine 04609
207-288-8086
1-888-288-4951
www.clefstone.com

CLEFSTONE MANOR offers a relaxing refuge from everyday life in one of nature's magnificent meetings of land and sea, Mount Desert Island. The 1884 three-story Victorian mansion, perched on a hillside of terraced gardens, is one of only a few on "Millionaires Row" that survived the fire of 1947. Step back in time to a less harried, romantic era as you enter the inn. The common rooms are casually elegant with antique and period furnishings. Clefstone Manor offers fireside chats, a well-stocked library, games and puzzles, quiet reading on the piazza, and the peacefulness of country living. Explore the natural beauty of the island and Acadia National Park. The waterfront is within walking distance of the inn.

Three-Pepper Quiche

1	9-inch pastry crust
¼	each of a red, orange, and green bell pepper, seeds removed
1	cup grated Swiss cheese
4	eggs
2	cups light cream
¾	teaspoon salt
⅛	teaspoon ground black pepper
⅛	teaspoon cayenne pepper

Preheat oven to 400°F.

Place pastry crust in 9-inch quiche pan with removable bottom, crimping edges well to prevent crust shrinkage. Bake for 10 minutes; remove from oven. Raise oven temperature to 425°F.

Coarsely dice peppers and sauté in pan sprayed with nonstick spray until tender. Remove from heat; press between paper towels to remove excess moisture. Spread peppers in bottom of pastry crust. Spread cheese over peppers. Beat eggs lightly in bowl using wire whisk. Add cream, salt, black pepper, and cayenne pepper; beat lightly. Pour egg mixture over peppers and cheese. Do not overflow crust edges. Bake quiche for 15 minutes, then reduce oven temperature to 300°F and bake for an additional 30 minutes. Allow quiche to cool for 10 to 15 minutes before slicing.

Yield: 6 servings

Triple-Squash Frittata

1 acorn squash
1 butternut squash
3 zucchini squash
2 tablespoons garlic salt
½ cup brown sugar
⅓ cup butter
12 eggs
½ cup milk
1½ cups grated Fontina cheese
1½ cups grated Swiss cheese
1½ cups grated Cheddar cheese

Cut squash into bite-size pieces and put into sauté pan with butter, garlic salt, and brown sugar. Cook until squash is al dente and still colorful. Cool mixture. Spray a 9 x 13-inch pan with nonstick spray. Mix eggs and milk. Add cooled squash mixture and cheeses. Add more cheese if mixture appears soupy. Refrigerate overnight.

Preheat oven to 350°F. Bake for 45 minutes until top is browned and cheeses are melted.

Yield: 12 servings

Pine Ridge Inn
1200 Southwest Century Drive
Bend, Oregon 97701
541-389-6137
www.pineridgeinn.com

IN AN AREA KNOWN FOR its natural beauty, Pine Ridge Inn is distinguished by its spectacular location above the scenic Deschutes River Canyon. Cozy suites feature king-sized poster or library beds, vaulted ceilings, and living room areas. The inn's spa suites feature two-person Jacuzzi tubs in the bathing area and living rooms with decks overlooking Deschutes Canyon and the trendy Old Mill District. Combining the ambience of a small country inn and the amenities found only in a select number of luxury boutique hotels, Pine Ridge Inn offers unequaled comfort. Enjoy the afternoon manager's reception with wines, locally brewed beer, and seasonal snacks. The evening turndown and refreshment service includes ice, bottled waters, and a homemade pillow treat. Breakfast consists of a casual and friendly buffet of fruits, juices, homemade granola and hot porridge, bread goods, and a hot breakfast special of the day.

Camai Bed & Breakfast

3838 Westminster Way
Anchorage, Alaska 99508
907-333-2219
1-800-659-8763
www.camaibnb.com

ANCHORAGE'S PREMIER bed-and-breakfast offers three spacious, well-appointed suites (with private baths) and scrumptious full breakfasts. Camai Bed & Breakfast is located in a quiet residential neighborhood on Chester Creek's greenbelt. Moose frequently nibble flowers in the award-winning garden. Your hosts, Craig and Caroline Valentine, have lived in Alaska more than 30 years and look forward to sharing their knowledge of the state with their guests. Craig is a retired civil engineer; Caroline is a retired mathematics teacher who continues to teach but now at the university. Camai Bed & Breakfast is open year-round.

Easy Vegetable Quiche

2½	cups frozen mixed vegetables (broccoli, cauliflower, and carrots), thawed and drained
1¼	cups grated Cheddar cheese
4	eggs
¼	cup melted butter
½	cup Bisquick
1	cup whole milk
5 to 6	slices red bell pepper
1	fresh dill floweret

Preheat oven to 350°F. Lightly butter a 9-inch pie pan.

Spread vegetables in pan. Top with cheese. In a bowl, beat eggs. Mix in butter. Stir in Bisquick. Stir in milk. Pour mixture over vegetables. Arrange bell peppers slices on top as spokes on a wheel. Place dill floweret in the center. Bake for 30 to 35 minutes until golden brown.

Yield: 6 servings

Wild Rice Quiche

1 (10-inch) prepared pie shell
1 pound smoked turkey, diced
2 tablespoons bacon grease (or butter)
⅓ cup chopped fresh onion
¼ cup chopped fresh red bell pepper
1 cup cooked wild rice
2 cups shredded Swiss cheese
4 eggs
½ teaspoon salt
1 tablespoon Worcestershire sauce
1 cup half-and-half

Preheat oven to 425°F.

Place pie shell in a 10-inch glass quiche pan. In a skillet, sauté onion and pepper in oil or butter until transparent. Layer in pie shell turkey, onion mixture, cheese, and then rice. Mix eggs, salt, Worcestershire, and half-and-half on high speed in blender for 30 seconds. Immediately pour over mixture in pie shell. Bake for 15 minutes. Reduce heat to 325°F and continue baking for additional 30 minutes. Remove from oven and allow to rest for 15 minutes before cutting into wedges. Serve warm.

Yield: 6 servings

River House Bed and Breakfast Inn & Tepee
11052 Ventura Boulevard
Rockford, Illinois 61115
815-636-1884
www.riverhouse.ws

THE RIVER HOUSE BED AND Breakfast offers relaxing waterfront views, a taste-tempting gourmet breakfast, in-room fireplaces, and private screened porches overlooking a beautiful nature-filled backyard. Five wooded acres surround the inn, offering scenic views for the three deluxe accommodations. For those looking for an unusual lodging experience, the tepee is available.

B&B of Greensburg

119 Alwine Avenue
Greensburg, Pennsylvania 15601
866-888-0303
www.bbgreensburg.com

THE B&B OF GREENSBURG is an upscale bed-and-breakfast located in the heart of the Laurel Highlands. It is a great getaway for anyone looking for a romantic retreat with many pampered extras, such as a massage. The themed bedrooms: Wild Safari, Tropical Paradise, Victorian Room, and Celestial Room, all offer private baths, some with a Jacuzzi. All bedrooms are adorned in luxurious linens. There is a fireplace in the parlor and balconies overlooking the courtyard. An elegant full gourmet breakfast is served each morning at the large dining table, or guests can choose a cozy table for two in the private dining area.

Zucchini Breakfast Meal

4 cups unpeeled zucchini, thinly sliced
1 cup Bisquick
½ cup finely chopped onion
½ teaspoon oregano
4 eggs, slightly beaten
½ cup grated Romano cheese
2 teaspoons chopped parsley
½ teaspoon salt
⅓ cup vegetable oil
Dash of pepper

Preheat oven to 350°F. Grease a 13 x 9 x 2-inch pan.

In a large bowl, mix all ingredients together. Pour into prepared pan and bake for 25 minutes. Cut into 1 x 2-inch squares. Serve warm or at room temperature.

Yields 6 servings

APPETIZERS

PICTURE A THOUSAND secluded acres where family and friends gather regularly to enjoy the luxury of simple, natural pleasures: the sound of wind rustling through the trees; crickets, whippoorwill, and lonesome quail calling in the evening; enjoying the wraparound porches immersed in a good book; a family's collective laughter around a fire in the lodge; or an early morning fishing trip on a misty pond. This is the essence of White Oak Plantation. Two full plantation breakfasts are included in the cost of each room. Lunches are prepared daily, and cooks will be brought in to prepare evening meals for a minimum of seven adults. The meals are served in the antique-furnished dining hall and include a limitless buffet for lunch and an evening meal prepared in the Southern manner.

Artichoke Spread

1 (14-ounce) can artichoke hearts, drained, rinsed, and chopped
1 cup mayonnaise
1 cup grated Parmesan cheese
1/2 teaspoon garlic powder
Lemon juice to taste
Dash of Tabasco sauce
Paprika

Preheat oven to 350°F.

In a bowl, combine artichokes, mayonnaise, cheese, garlic powder, lemon juice, and Tabasco and mix well. Spoon into a lightly greased casserole dish. Sprinkle with paprika. Bake for 20 minutes. Serve hot with assorted crackers.

Yield: 8 servings

Almond Cheese Balls

 2 cups finely grated Cheddar cheese
 ¼ cup flour
 2 egg whites, beaten stiff
 1 cup coarsely ground blanched almonds
 1½ cups vegetable oil

In large bowl mix cheese and flour together. Add egg whites and gently fold in to form a dough. Spread almonds on sheet of waxed paper. Roll pieces of dough into about 20 individual balls. Roll each ball in the almonds to completely coat. Heat oil in medium-size skillet over medium heat. Add cheese balls and fry until lightly browned on all sides. Serve hot.

Yield: 20 cheese balls

Casa Europa Bed & Breakfast Inn & Gallery
840 Upper Ranchitos Road
Taos, New Mexico 87571
505-758-9798
1-888-758-9798
casa-europa@travelbase.com

IMMERSE YOURSELF IN THE magical world of the Southwest when you stay at Casa Europa. This spacious 18th-century Pueblo-style adobe rests under giant cottonwoods 1.6 miles from Taos Plaza, surrounded by open pastures and majestic mountain views. Pamper yourself while enclosed courtyards soothe you with a bubbling fountain set amid colorful flowers or a sauna and Jacuzzi set under a wooden portal. Each of the seven spacious guest rooms/suites features a sitting area with fireplace, private bath with shower or whirlpool tub, two with full-size hot tubs. A large kiva fireplace warms the elegant dining room where full gourmet breakfasts are served. Afternoon goodies are offered daily.

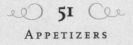

**Paradise Gateway
Bed and Breakfast
and Guest Cabins**
P.O. Box 84
Emigrant, Montana 59027
406-333-4063
www.paradisegateway.com

*P*ARADISE GATEWAY BED AND
Breakfast, nestled in the
majestic Absaroka
Mountains, is just minutes away from
scenic Yellowstone National Park. The
surrounding area boasts many activities, including hiking, horseback riding,
fishing, rafting, windsurfing, sightseeing, and much, much more. This
spacious country home sits on the
banks of the pristine Yellowstone River,
a noted blue-ribbon trout stream. Just
down the road, enjoy fine dining or
relax in the natural hot spring spas.
Paradise Gateway has two separate log
cabins, each nestled on its own very
private 20 acres. Guests can enjoy a
lazy afternoon on a deck overlooking
Emigrant Mountain or in a hammock
by the river.

Bacon and Tomato Spread

8   ounces cream cheese, softened
6   slices bacon, cooked crisp and crumbled
2   teaspoons prepared mustard
¹/₂   teaspoon celery seed
1   medium tomato, peeled, seeded, and finely chopped
¹/₂   cup green pepper, finely chopped

In a bowl, mix all ingredients together; chill. Perfect served with
veggie dippers. Great afternoon snack for guests upon arrival.

Yield: 2 cups

Bleu Cheese Mousse

6 egg yolks
6 tablespoons heavy cream
1½ tablespoons gelatin
4 tablespoons cold water
¾ pound Bleu cheese
1½ cups heavy cream, whipped
1 ounce poppy seeds
3 egg whites, stiffly beaten
Watercress
Caviar

In a saucepan, beat egg yolks with cream over low heat until mixture is creamy. In a separate saucepan, dissolve gelatin in cold water. Stir constantly over direct heat until no tiny granules or specks of gelatin are seen in the water. Add to the eggs and cream mixture. Force the cheese through a sieve. Add to gelatin mixture and cool. Fold in whipped cream, poppy seeds and egg whites. Pour mousse into an oiled mold and chill for at least 2 hours. Unmold onto a platter and garnish top with watercress and caviar. Serve with toast rounds.

Yield: 25 to 35 servings

Chalet Suzanne Country Inn
3800 Chalet Suzanne Lane
Lake Wales, Florida 33859
863-676-6011
www.chaletsuzanne.com

OWNED AND OPERATED BY THE Hinshaw family, Chalet Suzanne was born more than 60 years ago of Yankee ingenuity and Southern hospitality. The late Carl Hinshaw's mother, Bertha, was a gourmet cook, collector, and world traveler who had her own way of coping with the double disaster of her husband's death and loss of the family fortunes in the 1930s. To support her son and daughter, she turned her home into an inn and dining room, ignoring the gloomy predictions of friends. For 10 days, nothing happened. Then came her first guests, a family of five. A few days later, she was in business. The Chalet continued to grow and is now world famous for its soups and other delicacies. Its award-winning restaurant has been voted one of Florida's top 10 for many, many years and has been featured in every major food and travel magazine and guide.

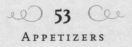

The 1842 Inn

353 College Street
Macon, Georgia 31201
1-877-452-6599
www.the1842inn.com

A S THE NAME IMPLIES, THE inn was built in 1842. It was the home of the former mayor of Macon. The 1842 Inn blends the amenities of a grand hotel and the ambience of a country inn. The guest rooms and public areas of the inn dwell within a Greek Revival antebellum house and an adjoining Victorian house that share a quaint courtyard and gardens. The 19 guest rooms, the parlors, and the library are tastefully designed with fine English antiques and paintings, Oriental carpets, tapestries, and elaborate draperies. The inn features a complimentary full breakfast served to guests, along with the morning newspaper, in their choice of three locations: their room, the parlor, or the courtyard.

Cheese-Straw Daisies

8	ounces sharp Cheddar cheese, grated
½	cup vegetable shortening
1	stick butter
³⁄₈	teaspoon cayenne pepper
1	teaspoon water
⅓	cup grated Parmesan cheese
2	cups all-purpose flour, sifted
1	teaspoon baking powder

Preheat oven to 350°F; convection oven to 300°F.

In a food processor, blend the Cheddar cheese. Add shortening and butter and blend again. Add cayenne pepper and water and blend again. Add Parmesan cheese, then add the flour and baking powder, one third at a time, blending for a few seconds between each addition.

Stuff a cookie press with the dough and using a star tip, push the dough out into daisies, 1 to 1½ tablespoons each, onto large baking sheets. Bake for 10 to 12 minutes. Let cool and serve.

Yield: 70 to 80 daisies

Chicken Liver Pâté

- 1   pound chicken livers
- 4   anchovies
- 1   cup cream
- ½   cup flour
- 3   tablespoons butter, softened
- 1   teaspoon salt
- ⅛   teaspoon celery salt
- 1   teaspoon pepper
- 1   egg
- ¼   teaspoon onion powder
-     Bacon (uncooked)

Preheat oven to 350°F.

Using a food processor or blender, process chicken livers and anchovies. Add cream. Blend together flour and butter to make a paste, then add to food processor. Add salt, celery salt, pepper, egg, and onion powder and mix well.

Line a 1-quart baking dish with bacon slices. Pour in the liver mixture. Fold bacon slices over the top. Place dish in a deep pan of hot water. Bake for 1¼ hours. Let cool and chill before unmolding. Serve with Melba toast or crackers.

Yield: 12 to 16 servings

Redfish Lake Lodge
P. O. Box 9
Stanley, Idaho 83278
208-774-3536
www.redfishlake.com

REDFISH LAKE LODGE is located at the headwaters of the main fork of the Salmon River in the heart of the Sawtooth National Forest and bordering the Sawtooth wilderness area. The dining room offers an excellent menu with a mountain atmosphere. The lodge was built for the sportsman, nature lover, photographer, horseback rider, and naturalist—in short, for the person who wants to turn his or her back upon the grinding roar of the civilized world and seek peace and quiet in untouched mountain country.

Whistling Swan Inn
110 Main Street
Stanhope, New Jersey 07874
973-347-6369
www.whistlingswaninn.com

TUCKED AWAY IN THE
Skylands of northwestern
New Jersey, you will find
the Whistling Swan Inn, a 10-bedroom
family home built circa 1900. All the
rooms have private baths, and a full
buffet-style breakfast is served in the
dining room. A stay at this delightful
inn is like a visit to your grandmother's
house. Nearby are wineries to tour,
ski slopes, antiquing, and a variety of
wonderful restaurants. Historic
Waterloo Village is minutes away.

Curry Vegetable Dip

5	(8-ounce) packages cream cheese, softened
5	cups mayonnaise
15	tablespoons lemon juice
15	tablespoons ketchup
15	tablespoons honey
50	drops Tabasco sauce
7$^{1}/_{2}$	teaspoons curry powder
15	tablespoons grated onion

Combine all ingredients. Serve with assorted raw vegetables.

Yield: 10 cups

Fried Green Tomatoes

2 large green tomatoes, cut into ¾-inch slices
1½ cups flour
2 eggs beaten with ½ cup water for egg wash
Salt and pepper
½ cup olive oil

Flour each side of the tomato slices. Dip into egg wash and flour again. Add salt and pepper to taste. In heavy skillet, heat olive oil and sauté tomatoes, turning once or twice until golden brown on both sides.

Yield: 8 servings

Vendue Inn
19 Vendue Range
Charleston, South Carolina 29401
843-577-79
1-800-845-7900
www.vendueinn.com

THE VENDUE INN SITS perfectly at the waterfront, in the heart of the Charleston Battery just steps from unique boutiques and art galleries, mouthwatering restaurants, and fascinating museums for which Charleston is known. The accommodations at the Vendue Inn reflect the history of Charleston, from indulgent suites with fireplaces and whirlpool tubs to charming historic quarters in the inn's original style. Stroll through the inn and discover something interesting around every corner and down every hallway—a family heirloom, an original artwork, a heritage quilt, or an antique replica. Your stay at the inn is your special time away. The Rooftop Bar & Restaurant offers perhaps the finest harbor view in the city, as well as dramatic rooftop views within the historic district. The intimate restaurant, The Library, exemplifies the inn's standards of excellence, offering progressive American cuisine prepared with a uniquely Charleston fair.

Redstone Inn
82 Redstone Boulevard
Redstone, Colorado 81623
970-963-2526
www.redstoneinn.com

WHEN YOU COME UPON Redstone, Colorado, a tiny mountain village hidden beneath massive red cliffs, you might not expect to find a first-class hotel and resort.

The Redstone Inn is the focal point of this 100-year-old Arts and Crafts town. All of it was created by mine owner John Osgood as a utopian community for his workers and their families. Open every day of the year, the Redstone Inn treats you to early 20th-century style at reasonable rates. After a day of hiking, tennis, horseback riding or fishing, there's nothing like a soak in the pool or hot tub. Whether you're planning a wedding, a special dinner to thank your employees, or a week-long conference, the creative Redstone Inn staff will do the work for you. You'll find everyday dining an event in itself at the Redstone Inn. People come from all over the state to enjoy the versatile cuisine. And the Redstone is easily accessible, even in winter. Colorado Highway 133 (designated as a scenic byway) is kept clear and safe year round. The Redstone is the perfect hub from which to explore the Colorado Rockies.

Ahi Nachos

2 pounds ahi tuna, fresh
1 cup light soy sauce
½ cup pure sesame oil
½ cup rice wine vinegar
½ teaspoon cayenne
2 tablespoons sesame seeds
2 tablespoons pickled ginger, cut julienne

Remove skin if present and dice ahi to ⅜ to ½-inch cubes. In a 2-quart bowl, combine soy sauce, sesame oil, vinegar, cayenne, sesame seeds, and ginger. Mix well with a whisk. Add ahi to bowl, mix well, and cover with plastic wrap or lid. Allow fish to marinate for 2 to 4 hours.

WASABI
½ cup wasabi
½ cup water

Add water to wasabi for a consistency that should resemble mustard. Mix well.

CHIPS
1 1-pound package egg roll or spring roll wrappers
Vegetable oil

Cut wrappers in stacks of 5 or 6 sheets to about 1½-inch squares. Separate the cut stacks into individual pieces. Deep-fry in vegetable oil. Remove from oil and drain on paper towels.

To assemble: About 10 to 15 minutes before serving time place chips on cookie sheet. Drain ahi in a colander, and place a serving (a little more than a teaspoon but a little less than a tablespoon) on each chip. Using a spoon or squeeze bottle, drizzle wasabi over nachos. Place on a serving tray or plate and serve at room temperature. Garnish with finely diced red bell peppers and/or green onion (cut julienne) or radish sprouts.

Yield: 20 servings

Green Garden Dip

1 cup cooked spinach, chopped
¼ cup mayonnaise
½ cup plain yogurt
1 cup low-fat sour cream
½ cup minced chives or green onion tops
½ cup minced fresh parsley
   Dill (optional)
   Lemon thyme (optional)
   Herb salt
   Fresh lemon juice
   Prepared horseradish (optional)

In a bowl, stir together all ingredients. For a smoother consistency, combine ingredients in blender or food processor and blend for a few minutes. Refrigerate. Garnish with fresh parsley and a calendula or nasturtium petal. Serve with sliced carrots, zucchini sticks, cherry tomatoes, cucumbers, or crackers.

Yield: 3 cups

Back of the Beyond
7233 Lower East Hill
Colden, New York 14033
716-652-0427

RELAX IN A CHARMING country mini-estate located in the Boston hills and ski area of western New York, situated 25 miles from Buffalo and 50 miles from Niagara Falls. Accommodations are in a separate chalet with three available bedrooms, 1½ baths, fully furnished kitchen, dining/living room, piano, pool table, and fireplace. Guests enjoy a full country breakfast. Organic herb, flower, and vegetable gardens are maintained for delightful strolling. A greenhouse is also part of the complex. There is a large pond for swimming and lovely woods for hiking.

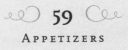

The Historic Taos Inn

125 Paseo del Pueblo Norte
Taos, New Mexico 87571
505-758-2233
www.taosinn.com

THIS HISTORIC ADOBE building is nestled in the heart of Taos's historic district. Thirty-three rooms and three suites are graced with Spanish colonial antiques, whimsical handmade furniture, and hand-woven Oaxacan bedspreads. The Adobe Bar and Doc Martin's Restaurant are award winners.

Guacamole

24	ripe avocados
6	jalapeños, (or to taste)
6	cloves garlic
1	yellow onion, cut into ¼-inch dice
1	cup lemon juice
	Salt to taste
2	tomatoes, diced
	Lemon or lime juice

Cut avocados in half, remove pits, and scoop meat out. Place jalapeños and garlic in food processor, pulse until coarsely chopped. Mix all ingredients thoroughly but do not mix too long. Squeeze lemon or lime juice over guacamole to prevent oxidation.

Yield: 20 to 24 servings

Hawaiian Pesto

½ cup chopped fresh ginger
½ cup chopped scallions
½ cup fresh coriander
1 teaspoon chopped garlic
½ cup macadamia nut oil or peanut oil
2 teaspoons sesame oil
Salt and freshly ground pepper
Juice of 1 lemon
2 teaspoons grated Parmesan cheese

In a small bowl, combine the ginger, scallions, coriander, and garlic. In a saucepan, heat the oils until they are hot; pour the oils over the ginger-scallion mixture. Add the salt and pepper, lemon juice, and Parmesan cheese and mix well. Refrigerate until ready to use.

Yield: 1½ cups

Hawaii's Hidden Hideaway
1369 Mokolea Drive
Kailua, Hawaii 96734
1-877-443-3299
808-262-6560
www.ahawaiibnb.com

A VISIT TO HAWAII'S Hidden Hideaway bed-and-breakfast is like a stay in paradise. For travelers tired of the crowded resort areas, the inn offers the stay they are looking for in a tropical paradise setting. Innkeeper Janice Nielsen has made her bed-and-breakfast just as beautiful and relaxing as its island surroundings. Each private unit overlooks lush greenery or the ocean. Nielsen offers a variety of sleeping arrangements and fantastic, one-of-a-kind hospitality that one rarely finds in this day and age. From the private lanai, guests can watch the sun rise over the turquoise ocean, making the sky a rainbow of red, orange, blue, and purple. Janice says that since many of her guests fly in from all over the world and arrive at various times, she makes it easy for them to enjoy breakfast at their convenience. She strives to bring joy and comfort to those who visit paradise, and guests are sure to become instant friends with this kind and cheerful woman who is filled with the aloha spirit.

Casa Sedona

55 Hozoni Drive
Sedona, Arizona 86336
1-800-525-3756
www.casasedona.com

CASA SEDONA IS A PEACEFUL, serene, award-winning inn where privacy and luxury abound. Conceived by a protégé of Frank Lloyd Wright, the inn was designed to maximize the surrounding views from every possible perspective. Sedona's highest and most spectacular red-rock peak dominates Casa Sedona's skyline. Be pampered; enjoy warm hospitality and great food. Breakfast and appetizers are served in the lush gardens with commanding red-rock views or in front of the fireplace. From your private balcony or large juniper-shaded patio, relax, listen to the sounds of the fountain, enjoy the majestic red-rock views and let your cares slip away.

Hot Fiesta Spinach Dip

- 1 cup chopped onion
- 1 cup salsa
- 1 (10-ounce) package chopped spinach, thawed and squeezed dry
- 2½ cups grated Jack cheese
- 8 ounces cream cheese, cut into cubes
- ½ cup sliced black olives
- 1 cup chopped pecans

Preheat oven to 400°F.

In a bowl, stir together onion, salsa, spinach, 2 cups of the Jack cheese, cream cheese, and olives. Transfer to serving dish and top with pecans. Bake for about 30 minutes until hot and bubbly. Top with remaining Jack cheese. Serve hot.

Yield: 18 to 20 servings

Hot Shrimp and Crab Dip

8 ounces cream cheese, softened
2 tablespoons chopped onion
1 tablespoon milk
3 ounces cooked crabmeat, flaked
3 ounces cooked shrimp, coarsely chopped
1/2 teaspoon minced garlic
1/2 teaspoon horseradish
    Salt and pepper
    Slivered almonds

Preheat oven to 350°F.

Combine cream cheese, onion, and milk in a medium bowl, mixing until slightly blended. Add crabmeat, shrimp, garlic, horseradish, and salt and pepper to taste. Stir until well blended. Spread the mixture evenly in a shallow 1-quart baking dish or 9-inch pie plate sprayed with nonstick cooking spray. Sprinkle almonds over the top. Bake for 15 to 20 minutes or until heated through. Serve hot with an assortment of crackers or herb toasts.

Yield: 12 servings

**The Inn at the
Round Barn Farm**
1661 East Warren Road
Waitsfield, Vermont 05673
802-496-2276
www.theroundbarn.com

At the Inn at the Round Barn Farm you will encounter a place that is elegant, luxurious, and charming. Many guests comment that this Vermont bed-and- breakfast feels like home the moment you step inside, with all of the comforts but none of the demands. The inn is located amidst 245 acres of majestic mountains, meadows, and ponds in the beautiful Mad River Valley. The talented and caring staff have crafted recipes that have worked their way into the Round Barn's cookbook, *Recipes and Reflections*.

Rosewood Country Inn

67 Pleasant View Road
Bradford, New Hampshire 03221
603-938-5253
www.rosewoodcountryinn.com

COUNTRY ELEGANCE AND AN atmosphere of warmth and relaxation surround this inn in the Sunapee region of New Hampshire. This 11-suite inn was built around 1850 in the early Victorian style. It offers fireplaces, whirlpool tubs, sunlit porches, and inviting common rooms. Nearby ponds, lakes, and streams offer swimming, fishing, and old-fashioned relaxation.

Mushroom Turnovers

1 (8-ounce) package cream cheese, softened
½ cup butter, softened
1½ cups plus 2 tablespoons flour
½ pound mushrooms, minced
1 small onion, minced
3 tablespoons butter
1 teaspoon salt
¼ teaspoon thyme
¼ cup sour cream
1 egg, beaten

Make ahead and freeze. Just pop out of the freezer and bake when needed.

In large bowl, cream together cheese and butter. Add 1½ cups flour and mix until soft dough forms. Wrap dough in wax paper and refrigerate at least 1 hour.

In medium skillet over medium heat, cook mushrooms and onion in butter until soft. Stir in salt, thyme, and remaining 2 tablespoons flour until blended. Stir in sour cream. Remove from heat and cool.

Preheat oven to 450°F. On floured board, thinly roll half the dough. Cut into circles with 3-inch cookie cutter. Save dough scraps and reroll into ball. Spoon 1 teaspoon of mushroom mixture on each circle. Brush edge with egg; fold over and seal. Prick with fork to let steam escape. Repeat with remaining dough and filling. Place turnovers on ungreased cookie sheets and brush turnovers with egg. Bake for 12 to 15 minutes until golden brown.

Yield: 50 turnovers

Roasted Tomato Tart
with Fresh Tomato Salsa

TART

- 4 tablespoons butter
- 1 tablespoon shortening
- 1 cup all-purpose flour
- 1 tablespoon coarsely chopped pine nuts, toasted
- 3 to 4 tablespoons water
- 2 tablespoons olive oil
- 1 teaspoon minced garlic
- ¼ teaspoon salt
- ¼ teaspoon ground black pepper
- 2 pounds (4 large) fully ripened tomatoes
- ½ cup Ricotta cheese
- 1 (5.2-ounce) package Boursin cheese
- 1 egg, separated
- 1 tablespoon minced basil
- 1¼ cups Fresh Tomato Salsa (recipe follows)
  Fresh basil leaves and extra toasted pine nuts

In a bowl, cut butter and shortening into flour, using 2 knives or a pastry blender, until mixture resembles large peas. Add pine nuts. Using a fork, stir in 1 tablespoon water at a time just until dough forms. Wrap in plastic wrap; chill up to 1 hour.

Preheat oven to 425°F.

In small bowl combine olive oil, garlic, salt, and pepper; set aside. Cut tomatoes into ½-inch-thick slices. Arrange slices on parchment-lined baking sheet; brush lightly with seasoned oil mixture. Roast until excess moisture has evaporated and tomatoes are slightly shriveled, about 20 minutes. Set aside.

Recipe continued on next page

Martine Inn
253 Oceanview Boulevard
Pacific Grove, California 93950
831-373-3388
www.martineinn.com

BUILT IN THE 1890S AS A private residence, today the Martine Inn is a beautifully renovated waterfront resort. Decorated with authentic Victoria-era antiques, many rooms feature fireplaces, claw-foot bathtubs, and ocean views. Guests who stay in this romantic getaway will wake up to a gourmet breakfast and relax each evening with hors d'oeuvres, antipasto, fruit, and wine.

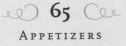

On lightly floured surface, roll pastry into an 11-inch circle. Fit into 9-inch tart pan. Trim edge; pierce pastry with fork tines. Bake until edges just start to brown, about 10 minutes. Remove from oven. Lower oven temperature to 350°F. In a bowl, blend together ricotta, Boursin, egg yolk, and basil. Beat egg white until frothy; gently stir into cheese mixture. Arrange tomato slices in prepared tart shell, overlapping as necessary. Pour cheese mixture over tomatoes; smooth top with knife. Bake until filling is set, about 35 minutes. Do not brown. Let cool.

To serve: Cut tart into wedges, top with fresh tomato salsa, and garnish with fresh basil leaves and toasted pine nuts, if desired.

FRESH TOMATO SALSA

- 1 **fully ripened tomato**
- 1 **tablespoon minced basil**
- ¼ **teaspoon salt**
- ¼ **teaspoon ground black pepper**

Seed tomato and coarsely chop. Toss with basil, salt, and pepper.

Yield: 8 servings

Shrimp and Black Bean Caviar

- 4½ cups water
- 1½ pounds medium-size fresh shrimp, unpeeled
- ⅔ cup chunky salsa
- ½ cup chopped purple onion
- ¼ cup finely chopped green bell pepper
- ¼ cup fresh lime juice
- 2 tablespoons chopped fresh cilantro
- 2 tablespoons canola oil
- 2 tablespoons honey
- ¼ teaspoon salt
- 1 (15-ounce) can black beans, drained

In a large saucepan, bring water to boil. Add shrimp and cook 3 to 5 minutes or until shrimp turns pink. Drain well and rinse with cold water. Cover and chill. Later, peel, devein, and finely chop shrimp.

In a bowl, combine shrimp and remaining ingredients. Cover and chill 2 to 4 hours, stirring occasionally. Serve with tortilla chips.

Yield: about 5 cups

Stone Hill Inn
89 Houston Farm Road
Stowe, Vermont 05672
802-253-6282
www.stonehillinn.com

NEW ENGLAND VACATIONS begin with Stone Hill Inn, a highly recommended Vermont bed-and-breakfast. Years of careful planning led to the 1998 construction of this romantic getaway in the mountains of Stowe, Vermont, a setting that is peaceful and quiet, yet near all the area has to offer. Stone Hill Inn offers an intimacy and a charm not found in most Vermont hotels and is exceptional among Vermont bed-and-breakfasts. Stowe is one of New England's most charming towns and has been welcoming visitors for two centuries. Stowe has long been known as the ski capital of the East. It's also a sophisticated little village with over 50 restaurants, unique owner-operated shops, and endless opportunities for outdoor adventure.

Night Swan Intracoastal Bed & Breakfast

512 South Riverside Drive
New Smyrna Beach, Florida 32168
386-423-4940
www.nightswan.com

IMAGINE—CRIMSON DAWNS, sipping coffee dockside, dancing dolphins and passing sailboats, warm evenings shared on the wraparound porch, and the gentle creak of rockers and porch swings. Night Swan is old Florida ambience. Located on the Intracoastal Waterway and nestled amid a canopy of live oaks, magnolia trees, and palms, the Night Swan is a destination all its own. Built in 1906, this early twentieth-century home features romantic, antique-filled interiors and sweeping sunny porches ideal for relaxing with a book or a tall drink. Innkeepers Martha and Chuck Nighswonger greet their guests with a choice of breakfast, complete with steaming hot coffee and freshly baked breads, served upon china and antique silver in the dining room.

Shrimp Nachos

1 pound shrimp, shelled and cooked
1 (4-ounce) can green chiles, drained
1 (2½-ounce) can sliced ripe olives, drained
8 ounces shredded Cheddar cheese, melted
1 cup chopped onions
½ cup mayonnaise
   Round tortilla chips

Preheat oven to 350°F.

Cut each shrimp into 2 to 3 pieces. In a bowl, combine shrimp with chilies, olives, cheese, onions, and mayonnaise. Place chips on a cookie sheet and top with ½ teaspoon of shrimp mixture on each chip. Bake for 8 minutes or microwave for 3 minutes.

Yield: 2 servings

Smoked Salmon Pizza
with Tempura Onion Rings

DOUGH

1   **cup warm water**
1   **teaspoon granulated sugar**
1   **teaspoon active dry yeast**
2   **cups all-purpose flour**
1   **tablespoon whole fennel seeds**
2   **tablespoons olive oil, divided**
2   **tablespoons yellow cornmeal**
½   **teaspoon salt**
½   **tablespoon grated Parmesan cheese**

Measure warm water into mixing bowl. Stir in sugar; sprinkle on yeast. Let puff for 7 or 8 minutes. With a dough hook, beat in flour to create a soft dough. Add fennel, 1 tablespoon olive oil, cornmeal, and salt; continue to mix 4 or 5 minutes. Cover with a damp kitchen towel; let rest for 1 hour.

Preheat oven to 400°F.

Roll dough out to fit a 12-inch pizza pan. Brush on remaining olive oil and sprinkle with Parmesan. Bake for 15 minutes or until golden brown.

TOPPINGS

4   **ounces cream cheese, softened**
8   **ounces smoked salmon, thinly sliced**
1   **ounce Columbia River caviar (optional)**
    Tempura Onion Rings (recipe follows)
1   **tablespoon minced chives**

Recipe continued on next page

Columbia Gorge Hotel
4000 Westcliff Drive
Hood River, Oregon 97301
1-800-345-1921
www.columbiagorgehotel.com

HE COLUMBIA GORGE Hotel has 40 rooms, each of them unique. All accommodations include a world-famous farm breakfast for two. Guests enjoy complimentary coffee service, a morning paper, an after-dinner champagne and caviar social, and nightly turn-down service featuring gourmet chocolates and a rose on the pillow. Nearby are the breathtaking views of the Columbia River, one of the premier windsurfing spots in the world.

Spread baked crust with softened cream cheese, arrange salmon on top, dot with caviar; heap on onion rings and sprinkle with chives.

TEMPURA ONION RINGS

- 1 **small onion, sliced into rings**
- ½ **cup buttermilk**
- ½ **cup all-purpose flour**
- ½ **teaspoon salt**
- ¼ **teaspoon freshly ground pepper**
  Oil as needed for deep frying

Place rings in shallow pan. Cover with buttermilk and let stand for 1 to 2 hours.

Preheat oil to 350°F. Combine flour, salt, and pepper. Remove onion rings from buttermilk with a fork, dip in seasoned flour, shaking off excess. Deep-fry until crisp and golden. Drain on paper towels.

Yield: 4 servings

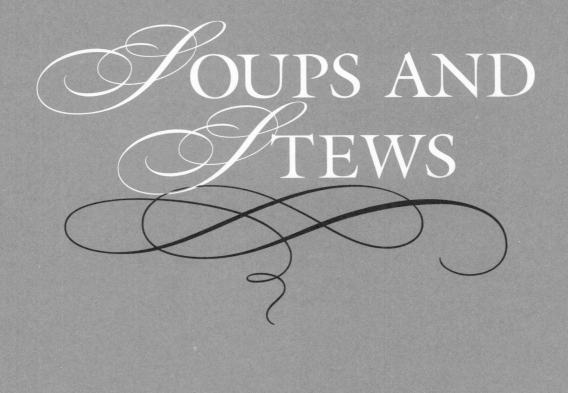

Soups and Stews

Snowvillage Inn
P. O. Box 68, Stewart Road
Snowville, New Hampshire 03832
603-447-2818
www.snowvillageinn.com

*S*NOWVILLAGE IS AN enchanting 18-room country inn situated on 10 acres of woodlands, sweeping lawns, and award-winning gardens. To the north are spectacular views of Mount Washington and the Presidential Range of the White Mountains. The Snowvillage Inn is quiet and secluded, yet only six miles from tax-free shopping in North Conway, New Hampshire, art galleries, skiing, hiking, canoeing, and all that the White Mountains have to offer.

Apple and Mushroom Bisque with Pistachio Cream

BISQUE

1 tablespoon olive oil
1 large onion, finely diced
1 large package domestic mushrooms, chopped
3 large apples (Granny Smiths are best), peeled and sliced
6 cups water or chicken stock
2 Yukon Gold potatoes
1 tablespoon tamari
1 cup heavy cream
   Kosher salt and pepper

Sauté onions in oil in a covered stockpot. When soft, add mushrooms and apples. Sauté briefly, then add stock. Bring to a boil; add potatoes. Reduce heat and simmer for 10 to 15 minutes or until potatoes are soft. Add tamari, and season with salt and pepper to taste. Process in food mill until smooth. Add cream and adjust flavor. Keep warm.

PISTACHIO CREAM

¼ cup pistachio nuts
¼ to ½ teaspoon salt (or to taste)
1 cup heavy cream

Process nuts until they are very finely ground. Scrape down and add salt and cream; process until smooth. Spoon dollops onto soup.

Yield: 6 to 8 servings

Avocado Soup with Shrimp and Grapefruit Salsa

Canyon Ranch
8600 E. Rockcliff Road
Tucson, Arizona 85750
520-749-9655
www.canyonranch.com

ANYON RANCH IS MORE THAN just a fabulous vacation. It's an experience that can influence the quality of your life, from the moment you arrive to long after you return home. Canyon Ranch is a place to relax, enjoy yourself, and explore your potential for a happier, healthier, more fulfilling life. Since 1979, Canyon Ranch has set the standard for health spas all over the world. You'll find everything you need, everything you want, at Canyon Ranch—where you're free to create a vacation that is uniquely yours. Change the way you live forever, come out and play, or simply unwind—every moment belongs to you.

SOUP

- 1 pound yellow tomatoes or enough to make
    1 cup tomato juice
- 1 pound yellow bell peppers or enough to make
    1 cup pepper juice
- ²/₃ cup tequila
- ²/₃ cup water
- 1 teaspoon salt
- 2 large avocados, peeled and seeded
- ¼ cup lime juice
- 3 tablespoons diced yellow onion
- 1 teaspoon minced jalapeño pepper

SALSA

- ½ cup rock shrimp, cooked
- ⅓ cup pink grapefruit segments
- ¼ cup minced yellow bell pepper
- 2 teaspoons chopped cilantro
    Pinch of salt

To make the soup: Using a juicer, juice yellow tomatoes and yellow bell pepper, separately. Make sure each measures 1 cup. In a small saucepan, bring tequila to a boil. Reduce by half. Combine all ingredients in a blender or food processor and purée until smooth.

To make the salsa: In a bowl, combine all salsa ingredients and mix well.

To serve: Ladle ¾ cup soup into each bowl and top with 2 tablespoons salsa.

Yield: 6 servings

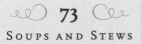

Izaak Walton Inn
290 Izaak Walton Inn Road
Essex, Montana 59916
406-888-5700
www.izaakwaltoninn.com

NUGGLED BETWEEN Glacier National Park and the Bob Marshall Wilderness, Izaak Walton Inn represents life at its best—quiet strolls, comfortable porch swings, skiing, hiking. A peaceful inn in a beautiful natural setting, it was built in 1939 to accommodate train crews who serviced the Great Northern Railway. Today the inn preserves its railroad heritage while offering country-style charm, excellent dining, a quiet, relaxing atmosphere, and incomparable warmth and hospitality—all in the majesty of the Montana Rockies. This is truly a place where time stands still and lets you catch up. The inn is listed on the National Register of Historic places.

Beef Barley Soup

1¼	pounds beef short ribs, cut in pieces
6	cups water
1	tablespoon margarine
1	cup chopped onion
½	cup diced celery
½	pound fresh mushrooms, sliced
1	teaspoon finely minced garlic
⅓	cup Burgundy wine
½	cup medium barley
1	tablespoon beef base
1	teaspoon salt
	Dash of black pepper
1	bay leaf
¼	cup chopped fresh parsley

In a stockpot, combine beef and water and bring to a boil. Boil until tender, about 2 hours. Skim and transfer meat to a plate to cool; reserve the broth. In a skillet, melt margarine; add onion, celery, mushrooms, and garlic. Cook until onion is golden, about 5 to 10 minutes. Remove meat from the bones and add to the broth, along with the wine, barley, and seasonings, and simmer, covered, until barley is cooked, about 30 minutes. Let cool, then refrigerate overnight.

Before serving, remove as much of the solidified fat as possible before heating the soup.

Yield: 6 servings

Black Bean Soup with Homemade Salsa

SALSA

- 2 medium vine-ripened tomatoes, coarsely chopped
- ½ bunch fresh cilantro, stems discarded, leaves coarsely chopped
- ¼ cup red onion, chopped
  Salt and pepper to taste
- 1 jalapeño, diced

SOUP

- 2 tablespoons olive oil
- 1 medium onion, diced
- 4 cloves garlic, sliced thin
- 1 medium carrot, diced
- 3 jalapeños, diced
- 1 pound dried black beans
- 2 tablespoons kosher salt
  Ground black pepper to taste

To make the salsa: Combine salsa ingredients in a bowl.

To make the soup: In a large soup pot, heat olive oil over medium heat. Add onion, garlic, carrot, celery, and jalapeños. Sauté until tender. Add black beans and cover them completely with cold water. Simmer until beans are tender. Add salt and season with pepper to taste. Let cool to room temperature. Transfer soup to food processor or blender and process until smooth. Refrigerate until ready to use or up to one week in an airtight container.

When ready to serve, warm soup in large soup pot over low heat until thoroughly hot. Ladle into bowls and top with fresh salsa.

Yield: 4 entrée servings; 6 appetizer servings

Swift House Inn
25 Stewart Lane
Middlebury, Vermont 05763
1-866-388-9925
802-388-9925
www.swifthouseinn.com

LIFE'S MOST MEMORABLE moments are spent with loved ones in exceptional places. The Swift House Inn is just such a place. Located in historic Middlebury, Vermont, this 21-room former governor's mansion offers the essence of New England warmth. Inside, candlelit dinners await you. Large, comfortable rooms offer modern amenities in period decor. Relax. Sip a glass of wine by the fire or ponder your favorite book in the library, while the kids explore the garden or sled on a nearby hill. Every window frames a picture of country tranquility, yet shops, museums, and Middlebury College are a short walk away.

Fryemont Inn

P. O. Box 459
Bryson City, North Carolina 28713
828-488-2159
1-800-845-4879
www.fryemontinn.com

A HISTORIC INN overlooking Great Smoky Mountains National Park, the Fryemont is famous for excellent food and lodging. Founded in 1923, it is a tradition in mountain hospitality and is listed in the National Register of Historic Places. Breakfast and dinner are served daily. In the Fryemont's spacious lobby you'll find a huge stone fireplace, large enough to burn 8-foot logs. This is an ideal setting for mingling with old and new friends or just relaxing after a day in the outdoors. Help yourself to a cup of coffee and take it through the French doors that lead to the rockingchair porch with its breathtaking view of the mountains.

BLT Soup

1/3 cup butter
1/3 cup flour
4 cups chicken broth
2 cups half-and-half
1 teaspoon ham base (see note)
8 slices bacon, cooked and crumbled
   Dash of nutmeg
1 large tomato, peeled and diced
1 cup chopped iceberg lettuce

Melt butter in a double boiler. Add flour and stir for 1 minute. Whisk in chicken broth. Place over direct heat and stir broth mixture constantly until thickened. Put back on double boiler and add half-and-half. Add ham base, bacon, and nutmeg. Cover and simmer for 30 minutes. Just before serving, reheat and add lettuce.

Yield: 4 to 6 servings

Note: Ham base can usually be found near the bouillon in the soup section of your grocery store.

Bouillabaisse

1/3 cup olive oil
1 1/4 cups sliced red onions
3/4 cup chopped celery
1/8 teaspoon minced garlic
2 cups fresh tomatoes, peeled, seeded, and diced
1 1/2 tablespoons tomato paste
1 1/2 tablespoons chopped fresh parsley
    Pinch of oregano
1/3 teaspoon salt
    Pinch of freshly ground pepper
1 cup dry white wine
1/3 cup fish stock or clam juice
    Pinch of saffron
8 mussels, washed and debearded
8 cherrystone clams, washed
4 petite lobster tails
1/2 pound medium shrimp, peeled and deveined
1/2 pound boneless sea bass fillet, cut into 1-inch squares
1/4 pound sea scallops
4 snow-crab claws, cooked
    Lemon slices
    Chopped fresh parsley

In a heavy pot, heat olive oil. Add onions, celery, and garlic; simmer for 2 minutes. Add tomatoes, tomato paste, parsley, oregano, salt, and pepper. Cook over low heat for 20 minutes. Add wine and cook an additional 10 minutes.

In a separate pot, bring fish stock and saffron to a boil. Add clams and mussels. Cover and simmer for 5 minutes. Remove clams and mussels. Discard any shells that have not opened.

Recipe continued on next page

Accomac Inn
6330 South River Road
P. O. Box 127
Wrightsville, Pennsylvania 17368
717-252-1521
www.accomacinn.com

ON AUGUST 27, 1739, A DEED was granted by John, Thomas, and Richard Penn, sons of William Penn, to James Anderson, for 35 acres of land—this was the birth of Anderson's Ferry and the Accomac Inn. Constructed in 1775, the inn at Anderson's Ferry began its long history of entertaining many distinguished guests. Indeed, the late 18th century saw the leaders of Colonial America—Samuel Adams, General Horatio Gates, Philip Livingston—pause at the inn on their way to and from meetings of the Continental Congress at York. In the many years that followed, the Accomac Inn flourished as a popular stopover for travelers and guests. Today, the inn remains true to the traditions of its historic past. Gourmet cuisine is served in the Lafayette Room, the Gold Room, and the Queen Anne Room.

Add lobster tails, shrimp, sea bass, and scallops, and cook slowly for 10 minutes. Add snow crab, clams, and mussels, and cook 5 minutes. Do not stir while seafood is cooking (to prevent breaking up the fish). Serve in ceramic or glass soup bowls or copper au gratins. Garnish with lemon slices and chopped parsley.

Yield: 4 servings

Broccoli/Pumpkin Soup

BROCCOLI SOUP

- 8 cups cooked broccoli, chopped
- 1 medium onion, finely chopped
- 4 cups vegetable or chicken broth
- 1½ to 2 cups half-and-half
- ⅔ cup white wine or brandy (optional)

In a stockpot, combine broccoli, onion, and broth. Heat to boiling. Stir in half-and-half. Pour soup into food processor or blender in batches and process until puréed. Reheat soup before serving.

PUMPKIN SOUP

- 6 cups fresh pumpkin or butternut squash (may use canned pumpkin if fresh not available)
- ¼ cup olive oil
- 2 large or 4 small leeks, thinly sliced
- 2 cloves garlic, minced
- 4 carrots, thinly sliced
- 6 cups vegetable or chicken stock
- 2 cups half-and-half
- 4 teaspoons curry powder
- 2 teaspoons cumin or to taste
  Fresh grated nutmeg to taste
  Sour cream
  Sprigs of greens such as cilantro or parsley

Preheat oven to 350°F. Using a knife, poke a few holes in pumpkin or squash and place on baking sheet. Bake for about 45 minutes or until tender when pierced with knife. Cool. Cut pumpkin in half, remove seeds and fiber, and scrape flesh from the skin.

Recipe continued on next page

**Ravenscroft Inn
Bed & Breakfast**
533 Quincy Street
Port Townsend, Washington 98368
1-800-782-2691
360-385-2784
www.ravenscroftinn.com

THE RAVENSCROFT INN, located in the heart of historic Port Townsend, offers a large, gracious great room where guests enjoy the fireplace, gather in the afternoon, and share the day's experiences with fellow travelers over coffee, tea, and refreshments. For a magical night's sleep select from eight well-appointed, spacious guest rooms, each with private bath, including two luxurious romantic suites. Many of the rooms offer soaking tubs, fireplaces, and French doors opening to the veranda, which offers views of a quaint seaport, Admiralty Inlet and the snow-clad Cascade Mountains, Mt. Rainier, and Mt. Baker.

Heat olive oil in a saucepan. Sauté leeks, garlic, and carrots, and sprinkle with curry powder and cumin for 3 to 4 minutes. Stir in broth and pumpkin. Simmer over low heat for about 15 to 20 minutes. Pour soup into food processor or blender in batches and process until puréed. Pour back into pan and stir in half-and-half. Reheat soup before serving.

To serve: Ladle pumpkin soup on one side of soup plate and broccoli soup on other side. Garnish with sour cream in a swirl design of hearts or Christmas trees and/or a sprig of greens.

Yield: 24 servings

Butternut Bisque

- 1 stick butter
- 1 medium Spanish onion, cut into medium dice
- 1 pound butternut squash, peeled, seeded, and cut into 10-plus pieces
- 1 can chicken broth
- 1 cup firmly packed brown sugar
- 2 tablespoons honey
- 1 tablespoon ground cinnamon
- ½ teaspoon ginger
- ½ teaspoon ground cloves
- ½ teaspoon nutmeg
- ½ cup half-and-half

Melt butter in 2-quart pot over medium heat, add onion, and cook until soft. Add squash, broth, brown sugar, honey, spice, and just enough water to cover squash. Increase heat to high and cook for about 30 minutes until squash is tender. Remove from heat and let cool for 30 minutes. Purée soup in food processor or blender until smooth, reserving some of the liquid, to adjust thickness if necessary. At this point soup base may be covered and refrigerated up to a week (or longer if frozen). When ready to serve, heat over medium heat and whisk in half-and-half.

Yield: 6 servings

The Village Inn
16 Church Street
Lenox, Massachusetts 01240
1-800-253-0917
www.villageinn-lenox.com

BUILT IN 1771, THIS AUTHENTIC New England inn has been catering to vacation and business travelers for more than 200 years. The comfortable rooms, fine cuisine, and friendly service have earned the Village Inn a reputation for exceptional hospitality. Located in the heart of the Berkshire Mountains, the inn has stenciled wallpapers and Oriental rugs in the public rooms to complement it's maple floors and unpretentious Federal architecture. Each of the 32 guest rooms is unique and individually furnished with country antiques and reproductions. Rumplestiltzkin's Restaurant, located at the Village Inn, serves hearty breakfasts and fabulous evening meals featuring Colonial-inspired dishes.

Murphin Ridge Inn

750 Murphin Ridge Road
West Union, Ohio 45693
1-877-687-7446
937-544-2263
www.murphinridgeinn.com

*S*ELECTED BY *National Geographic Traveler* as one of the top 54 inns in the United States, and achieving a spot on the prestigious National Geographic Geotourism MapGuide, this prize-winning inn welcomes you to 142 acres of four-season beauty. The inn offers spacious rooms, some with fireplaces or porches and two-person whirlpool baths. All are decorated with David T. Smith early American and Shaker reproduction furniture. The 1828 farmhouse features four dining rooms with original fireplaces, and gift shop. Enjoy award-winning regional cuisine, with ingredients gathered from the inn's gardens in season.

Carrot-Potato Soup à la Bobbie

1	pound unsalted butter
3	pounds white onions, sliced
6	pounds carrots, peeled and cut into chunks
5	pounds white potatoes, peeled and cut into chunks
4 to 5	quarts chicken or vegetable stock
3	tablespoons sugar
3	tablespoons dill
	Salt and pepper
1 to 2	cups heavy cream (as desired)

Sauté onions in butter until tender. Sprinkle sugar over onions and sauté 5 minutes more. Add carrots, potatoes, and stock; cook slowly until vegetables are tender. Purée in blender. Return soup to stockpot. Add dill and salt and pepper to taste. Finish with 1 to 2 cups heavy cream (as desired).

Yield: 20 servings

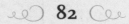

Carrot Vichyssoise

The Waterford Inne
258 Chadbourne Road
Waterford, Maine 04088
207-583-4037
www.waterfordinne.com

- 3 large russet potatoes, peeled and sliced
- 1 pound carrots, peeled and sliced
- 2 leeks, thinly sliced
- 3 cups chicken broth
- ½ teaspoon salt
- 2 tablespoons butter, melted
- 2 cups cream
- ¾ cup milk
  Chopped chives

Combine potatoes, carrots, leeks, broth, and salt in large, heavy saucepan. Cook, covered, until veggies are very tender, about 25 minutes. Purée in food processor. Beat in butter, cream and milk. Chill and serve cold or reheat over low heat, beating with wire whisk to blend well. Garnish with chopped chives.

Yield: 8 servings

THE WATERFORD INNE IS A 19th-century farmhouse situated on a country lane amidst 25 acres of fields and woods in Waterford, Maine. Outside, guests will find rolling terrain, a farm pond, and an old red barn. Inside are hand-hewn beams, wide pine floors, private rooms, and gourmet meals. The Waterford Inne is more than a bed-and-breakfast inn. It's distinctively different, a true country inn, lovingly restored and meticulously maintained. At your request, the innkeepers at the Waterford Inne offer you the opportunity to enjoy a gourmet meal, prepared to perfection and served in an intimate, cozy setting.

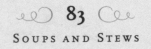

**The Patchwork Quilt
Country Inn**
11748 County Road 2
Middlebury, Indiana 46540
574-825-2417
www.patchworkquiltinn.com

THIS UNUSUAL AND DELIGHT-ful inn is located on a 340-acre working farm, where many of the foods served are grown. The inn began in 1962 as a vacation farm for city people. A few years later a new dining room, the Wood Shed, was added. In it there is a display of antique woodworking and logging tools and a collection of more than 75 plates from around the world. There is a homespun atmosphere at the Patchwork. The kitchen opens into the dining room, where grand, family-style meals are served in wonderful surroundings. Handmade quilts and patchwork tablecloths are available for purchase.

Chili Soup

2	pounds ground beef
1/2	cup chopped onion
1	tablespoon chili powder
1 1/2	tablespoons salt
1	cup flour
32	ounces ketchup
3	quarts water (or half water/half tomato juice)
1/2	cup brown sugar
1	can kidney beans

In a large skillet, combine ground beef, onion, chili powder, and salt. Add flour. In a kettle, mix ketchup, water, brown sugar, and kidney beans and cook 2 to 3 minutes, then add to ground beef mixture.

Yield: 8 to 10 servings

Chilled Cucumber Soup

2   cucumbers, peeled, seeded, and chopped
¼   cup fresh parsley, chopped
¼   cup celery leaves, chopped
2   tablespoons fresh dill, snipped
2   scallions, white part only, chopped
4   cups buttermilk
2   cups sour cream
2   tablespoons lemon juice
    Salt
    Thin cucumber slices

Combine cucumbers, parsley, celery leaves, dill, and scallions
with 2 cups of buttermilk in a food processor and purée.
Transfer to larger bowl and add remaining 2 cups buttermilk,
sour cream, lemon juice, and salt to taste. Cover and chill at least
6 hours before serving. Serve in chilled bowls. Garnish with
cucumber slices.

Yield: 4 to 6 servings

Horse and Hound Inn
205 Wells Road
Franconia, New Hampshire 03580
603-823-5501
www.horseandhoundnh.com

THIS LOVELY INN IS A QUIET
place on the valley slope
of Cannon Mountain. It
sits on the side of the Tucker Brook in a
quiet, secluded atmosphere. There are
lovely gardens in summer, a covered
garden for cocktails, and an extensive
collection of chamber music.

There is a small and interesting
library in the bar. There are fireplaces
and candles in both dining rooms,
where fine food is served. The larger
dining room was originally a
farmhouse, built in the early 19th
century. The rest of the inn was
constructed after World War II. It is a
unique inn in a beautiful section of
the nation.

The Inn at New Berlin
321 Market Street
New Berlin, Pennsylvania 17855
1-800-797-2350
570-966-0321
www.innatnewberlin.com

*T*HE *PHILADELPHIA INQUIRER* purports this inn to be, "A luxurious base for indulging in a clutch of quiet pleasures." A visit to central Pennsylvania wouldn't be complete without a stay at the Inn at New Berlin. In the heart of the pastoral Susquehanna Valley, this romantic getaway offers an abundance of life's gentle pursuits. Bike country roads and covered bridges less traveled; explore charming downtowns and mountain hiking trails; shop antique co-ops, Amish quilt shops, and artists' galleries. Meanwhile, back at the inn, innkeepers Nancy and John Showers invite guests to relax on the front porch, savor an exquisite meal and a glass of fine wine, and rediscover the nourishing aspects of simple joys and time together.

Union County Ham and Bean Soup with Rivels

SOUP
3 **tablespoons butter**
1 **cup diced carrots**
1 **cup diced onion**
1 **cup diced celery**
1 **pound diced smoked ham**
2 **cups dried great northern beans, soaked overnight**
3 **quarts ham stock**

RIVELS
1 **cup flour**
¼ **teaspoon salt**
¼ **teaspoon pepper**
1 **egg**

To make the soup: In heavy soup pot, melt butter over medium heat. Add carrots, onion, celery, and ham. Cook for 8 to 10 minutes, stirring. Add beans and stock, bring to a boil, and simmer for 20 minutes.

To make the rivels: Combine flour, salt, pepper, and egg in medium mixing bowl. Break mixture apart into small pieces, add rivels to simmering soup, and cook for an additional 15 minutes.

Yield: 6 to 8 servings

Crab and Brie Soup

- 1 stick butter
- 2 bunches green onions, chopped
- 4 cloves garlic, chopped
- 3 tablespoons flour
- 16 ounces chicken stock
- 8 ounces Brie
- 1 cup half-and-half
- 1 pound lump crabmeat
  Tony Chachere's Creole Seasoning or salt and pepper

Sauté green onions and garlic with butter in skillet. Add about 3 tablespoons of flour. Whisk together until thick. Add chicken stock. Remove outer crust from Brie, cube the cheese, and add to chicken stock until cheese melts. Stir in cream to your desired consistency. Add crabmeat and seasoning to taste, being careful not to break up lumps of crabmeat. Simmer until crabmeat is warm and serve.

Add fresh spinach and/or chopped red bell pepper, if desired.

Yield: 14 (4-ounce) servings

The Stockade
Bed & Breakfast
8860 Highland Road
Baton Rouge, Louisiana 70808
225-769-7358
1-888-900-5430
www.bbonline.com

THE STOCKADE BED & Breakfast is an elegant retreat within the heart of Louisiana's capital city. The Stockade is located near Louisiana State University and downtown Baton Rouge on historic Highland Road. Guests will experience the finest in Southern bed-and-breakfast lodging in this elegant, comfortable home filled with beautiful antiques, fine art, and luxury accommodations. The inn is a large, Spanish-style hacienda with five comfortable guest bedrooms. Once a Civil War stockade, there is still a reminder of the guarded entrance standing near the road. The property is listed on the National Register of Historic Places as an archeological site.

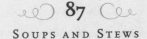

Barrow House Inn
524 Royal Street
P. O. Box 1461
St. Francisville, Louisiana 70775
225-635-4791
www.topteninn.com

*S*HADED BY A 200-YEAR-old live oak, Barrow House stands in the heart of the quaint town of St. Francisville. The original house was a saltbox structure built in 1809, and a Greek Revival wing added just before the Civil War. A large screened porch is the place to be for coffee in the morning and drinks in the evening. Rooms are furnished in antiques dating from 1840 to 1870. The inn's candlelight dinners, featuring New Orleans–style food, are well known in the area. Six plantations (open to the public) are close by.

Cream of Artichoke Soup

1 stick margarine
1 can artichoke hearts
2/3 cup onions, chopped
2 stalks celery, chopped
2 cloves garlic, minced
1 large baking potato, peeled and chopped
1 quart chicken stock
1/4 teaspoon white pepper
1 cup whipping cream
1 tablespoon brandy

Heat margarine in a saucepan. Add artichoke hearts, onions, celery, and garlic and sauté for 10 minutes. Add potato, chicken stock, and pepper. Cover and simmer for 20 to 30 minutes until potatoes are soft. Transfer to a food processor or blender in batches and purée. Return soup to the pan and stir in cream and brandy. Bring to a boil.

Yield: 6 to 8 servings

Curried Squash Soup

 2   sticks unsalted butter
 2   tablespoons curry powder
 2   onions, chopped
 2   large leeks, chopped
 2   bunches green onions, chopped (reserve a little of the
     greener parts for garnish)
 6   zucchini, unpeeled and grated
 6   summer squash, unpeeled and grated
     Salt and white pepper
12   cups chicken stock
 6   potatoes, peeled and sliced
 2   cups heavy cream

The Governor's Inn
86 Main Street
Ludlow, Vermont 05149
802-228-8830´
1-800-468-3766
www.thegovernorsinn.com

In a heavy pot, melt the butter. When butter foams and is quite fragrant, add curry powder and cook, while stirring, for 2 to 3 minutes. Add onions, leeks, and scallions; add zucchini and squash. Season with salt and pepper to taste. Sauté mixture briefly, then reduce heat, cover, and cook until squash is soft and juices have been extracted. Uncover and let juices reduce by half. When reduced add chicken stock and potatoes. Cook, uncovered, for 15 minutes or until potatoes are just cooked through.

To serve hot country style: Stir in cream and serve in warm soup bowls.

To serve chilled or hot as a puréed soup: Let the soup mixture cool, then purée in batches in blender or food processor. Strain the purée; stir in heavy cream. Garnish with reserved scallions.

Yield: 24 servings

HERE IS A HISTORIC village inn, originally built by Vermont governor William Wallace Stickney as his private dwelling. It stands as a classic example of the fine craftsmanship of the late Victorian period (circa 1890). Now it serves as a haven for enjoying life's pleasures and as a base for exploring Vermont.

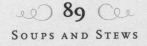

Glacier Bay Country Inn

P. O. Box 5
Gustavus, Alaska 99826
907-697-2288
www.glacierbayalaska.com

SITUATED NEAR THE CENTER of a 160-acre homestead, this inn offers the chance to experience Alaskan country living in a true wilderness setting. There are forests of towering spruce, hemlock, and pine; hay fields swaying in the breeze; meadows ablaze with wildflowers; bountiful gardens; meandering creeks; exceptional mountain views; and, deep in the woods, down a narrow winding road, this delightful, inviting inn. Marvelous food is one of its features.

Dan's Dy-No-Mite Vegetarian Chili

2 tablespoons olive oil
2 cups chopped onions
3/4 cup chopped celery
2 cloves minced garlic
2 cups tomato juice
2 cups chopped tomatoes
2 cups cooked kidney beans
2 cups sliced mushrooms
1 cup diced carrots
3/4 cup bulgur
1/4 cup red or white wine
3 tablespoons tomato paste
2 tablespoons green chilies
2 tablespoons mild chili powder
2 tablespoons lemon juice
1 tablespoon Worcestershire sauce
1 tablespoon ground cumin
2 teaspoons salt
3/4 teaspoon dried basil
3/4 teaspoon dried oregano
1/2 teaspoon Tabasco sauce
1/2 teaspoon pepper
1/4 teaspoon dried red pepper flakes

In large Dutch oven or kettle, sauté onions in olive oil. Add celery and garlic and cook until tender. Add remaining ingredients. Bring to boil and simmer for about an hour until the broth is thick and fragrant.

Yield: 4 to 6 servings

Gazpacho

1 clove garlic, pressed
3 tablespoons fresh lemon juice
3 cups fresh tomatoes, chopped
3 cups tomato juice
1 green bell pepper, cubed
½ cup fresh parsley, minced
2 cups cucumbers, peeled and chopped
2 tablespoons chives, minced
1 tablespoon salt
1 rounded teaspoon Lawry's Seasoned Salt
  Several dashes of Tabasco sauce to taste
⅓ cup good olive oil

Stir together all the ingredients. Refrigerate overnight.

Yield: 8 servings

The Newcastle Inn
60 River Road
Newcastle, Maine 04553
1-800-832-8669
207-563-5685
www.newcastleinn.com

A ROMANTIC COUNTRY INN located in Maine's mid-coast, famous for its beaches, lighthouses, and rocky shore. The inn's living rooms, sunporch, and deck are quiet, peaceful, and relaxing places from which to enjoy the wonders of coastal Maine. Overlooking the harbor, the inn's gardens abound in lupines and other perennials. Many of the inn's guest rooms feature canopy or four-poster beds, fireplaces, water views, Jacuzzis, soaking tubs, and air conditioning. Renowned for its dinner service, the inn's restaurant, Lupines, is open to the public and offers New England/ French cuisine with an emphasis on local, seasonal ingredients.

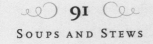

**1851 Historic
Maple Hill Manor**
2941 Perryville Road
Springfield, Kentucky 40069
859-336-3075
www.maplehillmanor.com

HE 1851 HISTORIC MAPLE Hill Manor is one of Kentucky's finest Bed and Breakfasts. The inn's colorful past includes stories of an antebellum plantation, use as a Confederate hospital, the childhood home of Phil Simms (former New York Giants quarterback), a popular dinner hall, and children's home. Today it is a nationally recognized bed-and-breakfast. This working farm is set on 14 tranquil acres in the heart of Kentucky's scenic Bluegrass region. The home is considered one of the best preserved antebellum homes in the Commonwealth. Guests awaken to the delightful strains of chamber music and the wafting aromas of freshly brewed coffee and hot-from-the-oven muffins. The day begins with a specially prepared breakfast served on fine china in the dining room.

Harvest Day Soup

- 1 pound sausage
- 1 large onion, finely chopped
- 2½ cups chicken broth
- 2 cups canned pumpkin
- 1 teaspoon lemon juice
- 2 cups hot milk
- ½ teaspoon nutmeg
- ¼ teaspoon cinnamon
  Salt and pepper to taste
  Chopped parsley

In large frying pan, brown and crumble the sausage. Remove sausage and sauté onions in drippings. In a large pot or crockpot, combine all the ingredients. Heat until hot. Serve sprinkled with parsley.

Yield: 8 to 10 servings

Maine Lobster Bisque

Tugboat Inn
80 Commercial Street
Boothbay Harbor, Maine 04538
207-633-4434
www.tugboatinn.com

4 cups salted water
2 (1-pound) Maine lobsters
3 sticks butter
½ cup flour
1 tablespoon paprika
32 ounces heavy cream
1 cup cream sherry
Dash of salt
Dash of cayenne pepper
Chopped fresh parsley

SAMPLE THE SIGHTS AND sounds of Boothbay Harbor's colorful waterfront. Savor the flavors of wonderfully fresh seafood, prime steaks, and perfect pasta. Relax and rejuvenate your spirit in the easy comfort of the Tugboat Inn. As renowned for its native cooking as for its panoramic views of Boothbay Harbor, the Tugboat Inn serves lobster bisque that is just the beginning of an unforgettable seafood experience.

In a 6-quart stockpot, bring salted water to a boil. Add lobsters and cook for 10 minutes. Remove lobsters and place in an ice bath to cool, saving water used to cook lobsters. When lobsters have cooled, pick out meat from the tails, knuckles, and claws and set aside. Save lobster bodies and shells. Combine lobster bodies and shells, 1 stick of the butter, and lobster water in stockpot and boil until liquid is reduced to 2 cups.

Using a thick-bottomed, 4-quart stockpot, melt 1 stick butter over low heat. Whisk in flour and paprika and slowly cook for 5 minutes making a roux, whisking continually. Add cream slowly and continue to cook on low heat, stirring often. Strain lobster liquid and add to cream mixture. Slowly bring to boil while stirring often. Turn off heat as soon as a boil is reached. Watch for scorching of cream mixture.

Cut lobster tail meat in half and remove intestinal vein. Remove any inedible parts from the claw meat. Dice lobster meat; combine with the cream sherry and the last stick butter, and sauté for 3 minutes. Add this to the cream mixture and stir until smooth and silky. Add salt and cayenne pepper, and simmer for 3 minutes. Serve in soup crocks. Garnish with chopped fresh parsley.

Yield: 8 servings

Note: Some prefer a bisque that is puréed and creamy. Although this recipe has bits of lobster meat and is creamy, the lobster meat can be puréed in a food processor after it has been cooked with the sherry and before being added to the cream mixture.

The Oxford House Inn
548 Main Street
Fryeburg, Maine 04037
207-935-3442
www.oxfordhouseinn.com

OHN AND PHYLLIS Morris are the innkeepers at this lovely Maine inn with charming and comfortable accommodations. The spacious turn-of-the-century yellow house boasts a large porch and big bay windows, creating an instant welcome to guests. The gourmet restaurant serves wonderful food with many creative and unusual dishes.

Maine Crab Chowder

½   pound salt pork or bacon
2   large onions
3   stalks celery
½   carrot
1   tablespoon dried tarragon
1   tablespoon lobster, crab, or shrimp paste
3   pounds potatoes, peeled and diced
2   pounds fresh Maine crabmeat
1   pint heavy cream
    Tabasco sauce
    Salt and freshly ground pepper

With the fine blade of a meat grinder, grind pork, onions, celery, and carrot into a stockpot. Add tarragon and lobster paste. Simmer over medium heat until tender but not brown. In another pan, cover potatoes with cold water and slowly boil until they are slightly underdone. Add potatoes and their water to vegetable mixture. Bring to a slow boil. Add the crabmeat and bring to a boil, then remove from the heat. Just before serving, bring to the boiling point and add the cream. Add Tabasco, salt, and pepper to taste.

Yield: 8 to 10 servings

New Mexican
Green Chile Stew

5 pounds lean pork roast, cut into bite-size cubes
1¼ cups flour
Salt and pepper
5 teaspoons Accent
5 (32-ounce) cans stewed tomatoes or 10 (16-ounce) cans
15 large russet potatoes, peeled and cut into
bite-size pieces
5 large yellow onions
5 fresh garlic cloves
5 teaspoons dried oregano
15 small cans chopped green chilies or 30 fresh green
chile peppers, chopped
15 to 20 cups water

Brown meat in large stew pan until cooked. Sift in flour, salt and pepper to taste, and Accent. Add tomatoes, potatoes, onions, garlic, oregano, and green chilies. Simmer until potatoes are tender. Cooking time is approximately 1 hour.

Yield: 20 servings

Elaine's,
A Bed and Breakfast
72 Snowline Estates
P. O. Box 444
Cedar Crest, New Mexico 87008
1-800-821-3092
www.elainesbnb.com

ELAINE'S OFFERS CHARM, ELEGANCE, and gracious hospitality in a beautiful three-story log house, nestled in the evergreen forests of the Sandia Peaks. The breathtaking alpine views make this a storybook getaway. Located on the historic Turquoise Trail, it's perfect for the vacationer or the business traveler. Here's an invitation to slow down, take your shoes off, enjoy a cup of coffee in front of a huge country fireplace, read a book, and (if you must) catch up on any work there wasn't time for during the day. Located on 4 acres of mountain property adjoining the Cibola National Forest, this spacious hideaway can accommodate 20 people in boardroom style.

The Irma Hotel

1992 Sheridan Avenue
Cody, Wyoming 82414
307-587-4221
www.irmahotel.com

THE IRMA HOTEL WAS BUILT by Colonel William F. "Buffalo Bill" Cody in 1902 and named for his daughter, Irma. The hotel is the grand old lady of downtown Cody, reflecting Buffalo Bill's style and the essence of Western hospitality. The hotel's restaurant serves the tourists traveling to nearby Yellowstone Park, as well as locals, and offers a menu to fill the needs of both.

Outback Curried Lamb Stew

8	tablespoons olive oil
2	pounds lamb cut into 1-inch chunks
1/2	cup flour
4	medium carrots, cut into 1-inch chunks
2	medium onions, cut into 1-inch chunks
4	stalks celery, cut into 1-inch chunks
2	large potatoes, cut into 1-inch chunks
2	turnips, cut into 1-inch chunks
1/8	teaspoon cayenne pepper
2	cloves garlic
1 1/2	teaspoon salt
2	teaspoons curry powder
2	teaspoons paprika
1	teaspoon nutmeg
2 1/4	cups water

Heat olive oil in a large frying pan. Add lamb and cook until brown. Slowly add flour, stirring constantly to make a gravy of sorts. Add all the vegetables to mixture, then all the seasonings. Cook and stir for 4 to 5 minutes. Now add the water and simmer until vegetables are tender, but firm.

Yield: 8 servings

Potato, Leek, and Sweet Pea Soup

- 1 **stick butter**
- 1 **pound leeks**
- 2 **pounds Yukon Gold potatoes, cut into ½-inch dice**
- ¼ **pound fresh or frozen peas, blanched**
- ½ **quart cream**
  Salt and pepper to taste

Heat butter in large pot. Sauté cleaned leeks until caramelized. Add potatoes and sauté for 10 minutes. Cover with water and simmer until cooked. Remove from heat. Stir in peas (adding them cold helps to cool the soup for blanching and gives it a softer green color). Transfer mixture to blender or food processor (in batches if needed) and purée, adding cream to thin as needed. When finished adjust seasoning with salt and pepper.

Yield: 1 gallon

The Red Lion Inn
30 Main Street
Stockbridge, Massachusetts 01262
413-298-5545
www.redlioninn.com

WHEN YOU STEP INSIDE THE red lion inn, you enter a world of friendly courtesy and hospitality. This lovely Berkshire Hills town was once an Indian village. The inn was built in 1773 as a small tavern and stagecoach stop for vehicles traveling the Boston, Hartford, and Albany runs. During its life, the inn has sheltered five United States presidents. There is the charm of Staffordshire china, colonial pewter, and 18th-century furniture. The fare is traditional New England with many Continental specialties.

Nassau Inn
Palmer Square
Princeton, New Jersey 08544
609-921-7500
www.nassauinn.com

L OCATED IN THE HEART OF Princeton, this great inn enjoys a long and illustrious legacy as the university town's social hub. Originally built in 1756, the expanded inn now features 218 guest rooms (each appointed with handsome period furnishings), three restaurants, and abundant meeting and conference space. Innkeeper Lori Rabon subscribes to a unique spirit of management that combines old-fashioned country charm with all the appointments of today's finest hotels. Dining opportunities at the inn include Palmer's, where award-winning cuisine is featured at dinnertime under the direction of executive chef Don Woods; the Greenhouse, overlooking famous Palmer Square, where meals are served in a more casual atmosphere; and the Tap Room, whose menu offers hearty American fare.

Irish Potato, Leek, and Cheddar Soup

1	stick plus 2 tablespoons butter
1½	pounds leeks, thinly sliced
8	ounces yellow onions, diced into small pieces
¾	cup all-purpose flour
2	quarts prepared vegetable stock, strained
1	pint heavy cream
8 to 10	ounces shredded Cheddar cheese
	Salt and pepper
1	pound potatoes, steamed with skin on and diced

Melt butter in large stockpot over medium heat. Add leeks and onions and sauté until onions become translucent. Add flour and mix until all of flour is absorbed into the butter. Cook for approximately 3 to 5 minutes over low heat. Add strained vegetable stock and bring to boil, stirring constantly. Add heavy cream and return to a boil. Stir in the cheese until it is all incorporated into the soup. Season to taste with salt and pepper. Finally, add the potatoes and bring to a simmer, being careful potatoes do not stick to bottom of pot.

Yield: 14 cups

Pot Au Fe Fruits De Mer/ Seafood Stew

- 1 stick butter
- 4 (8-ounce) lobster tails, split in half, then shelled
- 8 (U-8) diver sea scallops, muscle removed
- 2 tablespoons herbes de Provence
- 1 shallot, finely diced
    Coarse cracked pepper to taste
- 8 (U-8) shrimp, peeled and deveined
- 4 ounces cognac or brandy
- 1 (5.2-ounce) box Boursin cheese with herbs
- 1 cup heavy (40%) whipping cream
- 12 New Zealand Greentip mussels, cleaned and shucked

Heat a large skillet or sauté pan. Add butter, then add lobster tails and scallops; season with herbs, shallots, and pepper. Lightly brown on both sides. Add shrimp and brown. Pull pan off heat and flambé with cognac. When flame burns out, add cheese and cream. Simmer, add mussels, and continue to simmer. This sauce can be thin or thick. Serve in a bowl or crock, with your favorite vegetables, rice, or potatoes.

Yield: 4 servings

The French Manor
Huckleberry Road
P. O. Box 39
South Sterling, Pennsylvania 18460
1-800-523-8200
570-676-3244
www.thefrenchmanor.com

HERE IS AN ELEGANT French chateau and mountain inn. Modeling it after his chateau in the south of France, Joseph Hirshhorn created a private retreat where he could enjoy the solitude of the mountains and the serenity of Mother Nature. Having breakfast or tea on the veranda with a view to the surrounding hilltops gives guests this same feeling. The accommodations and authentic French cuisine are unmatched in the area. At the French Manor, old-world charm and furnishings are seamlessly joined with all the modern conveniences. Enjoy miles of trails for hiking, mountain biking, picnicking, snowshoeing, and cross-country skiing. The innkeepers are Ron and Mary Kay Logan.

Richmond Hill Inn
87 Richmond Hill Drive
Asheville, North Carolina 28806
1-888-742-4550
828-252-7313
www.richmondhillinn.com

*R*OMANCE IS ENCOUR-
aged every moment.
The 1889 mansion
known as Richmond Hill was built as
the private residence of ambassador
and congressman Richmond Pearson.
Designed by James G. Hill, it was one
of the most elegant and innovative
structures of its time. Despite being a
half hour's carriage ride from Asheville,
the estate was a center of social and
political activity for many years. The
Queen Anne–style mansion—with its
grand entrance hall and spacious
rooms—could accommodate large
gatherings, and Richmond's beautiful
and vivacious wife, Gabrielle, was a
gracious hostess. The inn is perched
on a hillside, and each room is
uniquely decorated and furnished with
antiques.

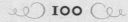
Smoked Salmon Chowder

 4 strips bacon
 5 cups finely chopped onion
 ½ cup all-purpose flour
 8 large white potatoes (about 1½ pounds), peeled and
    cut into ½-inch cubes
 4 cups fish stock
 2 pounds smoked salmon, cut into ¼ x ⅛-inch strips
 4 quarts heavy cream (or milk)
 1 stick butter
    Salt and pepper

In a skillet, cook the bacon, stirring frequently, for about 5
minutes. Add onions and cook another 5 minutes. Add flour,
stirring briskly to blend. Add potatoes and fish stock. Simmer
for 30 minutes. Add salmon, cream, butter, and salt and pepper
to taste. Bring chowder just to a boil. Remove from heat and
serve.

Yield: 24 servings

Southwestern Lentil Soup

    2 cups chicken stock
    1 cup lentils
    ½ onion, finely diced
    3 carrots, finely diced
    3 stalks celery, finely diced
    2 cans diced tomatoes
    1 teaspoon ground cumin
    1 teaspoon chili powder
    ½ teaspoon cayenne pepper
       Salt and pepper

In a stockpot, cook lentils in chicken stock. In a frying pan, sauté vegetables until soft in a small amount of butter or oil. Add tomatoes, cumin, chili powder, and cayenne to vegetable mixture. When lentils are soft, add vegetable mixture to lentils and simmer for about 20 minutes. Adjust seasonings and add salt and pepper to taste.

Yield: 8 to 10 servings

The Geneva Inn
N 2009 South Lake Shore Drive
Lake Geneva, Wisconsin 53147
262-248-5680
www.genevainn.com

EXPERIENCE DISTINCTIVE European charm and exceptional luxury at the Geneva Inn, located directly on the shores of Geneva Lake, a premier recreation area in Wisconsin. Discover a truly relaxed, unrestrained style of comfort, intimate accommodations, breathtaking lake views, and uncommon architectural craftsman-ship. Enjoy the private marina, the exercise facility, and the spectacular cuisine at the renowned Grandview Restaurant. Guests will find seclusion and comfort in the peaceful atmosphere of this traditional inn that is tastefully decorated in English-country style. Common areas of the inn include a three-story atrium with raised-hearth fireplace, piano lounge, landscaped terrace, and patio. Boat owners can tie up at the inn's private marina.

L'Auberge Provençale

P. O. Box 190
White Post, Virginia 22663
540-837-1375
www.laubergeprovencale.com

IF YOU WANT TO EXPERIENCE the ambience of southern France without the expense of going there, a visit to L'Auberge Provençale may be your answer. Settled in rolling farm country near the Blue Ridge Mountains, with a flower-lined walkway and sweeping front porch, it is a charming retreat. Owner/chef Alain Borel and his wife Celeste are a perfect team. Chef Borel explains, "Cooking is like breathing in my family. It was always a part of our lives, and I never gave any thought to another line of work." He calls his cooking "cuisine moderne." "Classic French cooking is very rich and heavy and nouvelle cuisine is extremely light with small portions," he explains. The Borels develop the menu together. It changes seasonally to feature the freshest ingredients. Guests can dine in one of two intimate dining rooms or a solarium with windows providing a lovely view of the countryside.

Spring Stew with Lamb and Young Vegetables

16	baby turnips
1	cup shelled young green peas (1½ pounds unshelled)
1½	pounds baby lima beans
20	young asparagus spears, ends snipped off
12	young leeks
6	tablespoons unsalted butter
2½	pounds lamb sirloin or other lean, tender cut, trimmed of fat, cut into cubes
2	tablespoons all-purpose flour
¾	teaspoon salt
1	teaspoon freshly ground black pepper
1	cup dry white wine
2½	cups chicken or vegetable broth
24 to 28	small new potatoes, unpeeled
28 to 30	small, young carrots, peeled
4	cloves garlic, crushed
3	tablespoons fresh chives, minced
2	tablespoons fresh flat-leaf parsley, minced

Trim turnips leaving about ½ inch of greens attached. Place turnips in a steamer rack over boiling water. Cover and steam until tender enough to be pierced with the tip of a knife, about 8 to 10 minutes. Set aside. Steam peas, lima beans, and asparagus over boiling water until tender to the bite (6 to 7 minutes for peas, less for the asparagus). Set aside. Carefully rinse the leeks; cut the whites and tender greens into 2-inch lengths. You should have about 12 pieces. Mince enough of the remaining tender green tops to fill ¼ cup. Set leeks and leek greens aside.

In a large, heavy-bottomed saucepan, melt butter over medium heat. When butter is foamy, add lamb and sauté, turning as needed, until meat is lightly browned on all sides (5 to 6 minutes). Sprinkle the flour, salt, and pepper over lamb and continue to cook, stirring often, until flour has turned quite brown (3 to 4 minutes). Raise heat to high, pour in wine, and use a wooden spoon to deglaze pan by scraping up any browned bits stuck to the bottom of pan. Add about half the broth and continue to stir until all the bits are scraped up and incorporated into the liquid. Add remaining broth and potatoes. Cover with a tight-fitting lid; reduce heat to medium-low and simmer for 10 minutes.

Stir in carrots, leeks, garlic, and the ½ cup of leek greens; cover and cook until carrots and potatoes are tender when pierced with the tip of a knife (another 8 to 10 minutes). Then add turnips, peas, limas, and asparagus, turning them gently into the simmering stew. Cover and cook for 2 or 3 minutes longer, just long enough for the flavors to incorporate.

If you like a thicker stew, scoop out 1 or 2 potatoes plus a little broth and purée them together in a blender or food processor, or mash with a fork or potato masher, and stir them back into the stew. Taste for salt, then stir in all but about 1 teaspoon of chives and parsley. Serve the stew, sprinkling with remaining herbs.

Yield: 20 servings

Hotel Carter

301 L Street
Eureka, California 95501
707-445-1390
www.carterhouse.com

THIS SPECTACULAR VICTORIAN inn has received so many accolades, it's impossible to list them all. It is located in the small, culturally rich seaport town of Eureka in the heart of the Redwood Empire. Hotel Carter style and hospitality, and its insistence on quality, creativity, friendliness, and taste, have impressed travelers, authors, and chefs from coast to coast and around the world.

Stew of Potatoes, Cèpes, and Squash

½ cup finely minced dry cèpes (porcini mushrooms)
½ cup very hot, but not boiling, water
2 tablespoons extra-virgin olive oil
1 tablespoon finely minced shallots
½ teaspoon finely minced garlic
½ tablespoon finely minced fresh thyme
1 cup finely diced yellow Finn potatoes
1 cup finely diced acorn or other fleshy squash
1 cup homemade vegetable stock
½ cup heavy cream
  Salt and freshly ground black pepper

Soak dried mushrooms in hot water until tender, but not mushy, about 3 to 4 minutes. Remove mushrooms from soaking liquid and gently squeeze out excess moisture. Discard any hard stems; dice mushrooms. Heat olive oil in a heavy sauté pan until very hot but not smoking. Add shallots, garlic, and thyme; sauté for 1 minute. Add squash, potatoes, and rehydrated mushrooms to pan and sauté until the starches start to "rope," adhering lightly to the bottom and sides of the pan. Add stock and cream and simmer until potatoes are just tender, about 20 to 25 minutes. Season with salt and pepper to taste.

Yield: 6 servings

Summary Squash Soup

1 cup chopped onion
1 teaspoon minced garlic
3 pounds zucchini and/or yellow squash, quartered
   lengthwise, then cut into ¼-inch slices
4 tablespoons butter
1 cup chicken or vegetable stock
2 cups half-and-half
   Salt and pepper
1 cup whipping cream
   Sour cream
   Chives

Sauté onion 3 minutes, then add garlic and sauté 3 more minutes. Add squash and sauté about 10 minutes. Do not let onion or garlic brown. Add stock and simmer until squash is soft. Add half-and-half and simmer another minute or two. Purée in blender or food processor in batches. Check thickness and taste. Add cream and salt and pepper to taste. Garnish with sour cream and chopped chives.

Yield: 8 servings

**High Meadows
Vineyard Inn & Restaurant**
55 High Meadows Lane
Scottsville, Virginia 24590
434-286-2218
www.highmeadows.com

THIS FAMOUS INN IS CONSID-ered Virginia's vineyard inn, just minutes south of Charlottesville and just north of historic Scottsville. The inn occupies a grand house, where guests stay in beautifully appointed rooms, each furnished with individually collected period antiques, original botanicals, and steel engravings. Twenty-two acres of gardens, footpaths, forests, and ponds guarantee privacy and quiet. High Meadows is on the National Register of Historic Places.

Wildflower Bed & Breakfast

P. O. Box 575
Angel Fire, New Mexico 87710
505-377-6869
www.angelfirenm.com/wildflower

WILDFLOWER BED &
Breakfast is located
deep in the southern
Rocky Mountains of northern New
Mexico, approximately 40 miles south
of the Colorado border. Hosts Joan and
Dean Douglass make every effort to
ensure that their guests have a pleasurable stay. After enjoying outdoor
activities, guests find a host of cozy
corners in which to read or relax.
During the summer, spring, or fall,
you are invited to enjoy refreshments
on the spacious front porch or sunny
back deck. In the winter, relax before
a blazing fire in the two-story great
room.

Swedish Fruit Soup

½ cup pitted prunes
½ cup raisins
½ cup dried apricots
3½ cups water
1 whole cinnamon stick
2 apples, peeled and sliced
2 pears, peeled and sliced
2 cups canned sour pitted cherries, with juice
1 small package cherry gelatin

In a saucepan, combine prunes, raisins, apricots, water,
cinnamon stick, apples, and pears. Bring to a boil and simmer
for 15 minutes, until fruit is tender. Add cherries and bring to a
boil. Add gelatin and stir gently until it is dissolved. Let soup
cool, then refrigerate. Dish will be soft.

Yield: 8 servings

*Note: This makes a good brunch dish with yogurt or for dessert with
whipped cream and a dash of nutmeg.*

Sweet Potato
and Coconut Soup

    4 tablespoons unsalted butter
    4 large shallots, minced
    3 cups sweet potatoes, peeled and diced
  ½ bunch of cilantro, stems and leaves minced separately
3¾ cups stock
1¾ cups coconut milk
       Salt and pepper
       Toasted coconut

In a stockpot, melt butter, add shallots and cook for 2 to 3 minutes. Stir in sweet potatoes. Cover with buttered parchment paper; sweat for 10 minutes over low heat. Stir in cilantro stems; cook for 1 to 2 minutes. Add stock and coconut milk and bring to simmer. Cook for 20 to 30 minutes, until potatoes are tender. Add cilantro leaves. Purée, using a hand blender or food processor. Garnish with toasted coconut.

Yield: About 2 gallons

The Checkerberry Inn
62644 County Road 37
Goshen, Indiana 46528
574-642-0198
www.checkerberryinn.com

AT THE CHECKERBERRY Inn, the visitor will find a unique atmosphere, unlike anywhere else in the Midwest. The individually decorated rooms and suites will please even the most discerning guests. Every room has a breathtaking view of the unspoiled rolling countryside. A top-rated restaurant serves only the freshest foods, using herbs and other ingredients from the local countryside.

Inn at Ellis River

P. O. Box 656
Jackson, New Hampshire 03846
1-800-233-8309
603-383-9339
www.innatellisriver.com

THE 20 ROOMS AND THE separate cottage, all named after local waterfalls, are beautifully appointed with period antiques and a wide variety of traditional and modern amenities. The inn is located in the quaint village of Jackson, which lies at the edge of the 750,000-acre White Mountain National Forest, surrounded by spectacular natural beauty. It nestles in a landscape of covered bridges, white steepled churches, rolling farmland, mountain grandeur, and cascading waterfalls. Bring back the romance of life, and let the serenity of the inn, the river, and the mountains create cherished memories. Come and rejuvenate at the Inn at Ellis River.

Three-Onion Soup

6   green onions
3   tablespoons butter
1   large yellow onion, cut in half crosswise and thinly sliced
1   medium red onion, cut in half crosswise and thinly sliced
3   tablespoons whole-wheat flour
4   cups water
1   14½-ounce can vegetable broth
1   tablespoon Madeira wine
8   slices white bread, crusts trimmed
½   cup grated Gruyère cheese
2   teaspoons honey
½   teaspoon ground black pepper

With a sharp knife, cut white part of green onions crosswise into slices. Cut green tops crosswise into 3-inch lengths, then lengthwise into strips; keep strips separate from slices. In a 4-quart saucepan, heat butter over medium heat, add yellow onions, red onions, and white part of green onions; sauté 12 to 15 minutes or until onions are translucent and very soft. Sprinkle onions with flour and mix well. Add water, vegetable broth, and Madeira. Bring to a boil over high heat. Reduce heat to low, partially cover pan, and cook for 20 minutes.

Meanwhile prepare cheese toasts. Heat broiler. Cut bread in half diagonally to form triangles. Place bread triangles on baking sheet and toast until brown. Turn triangles over and toast other sides. Evenly sprinkle with cheese and broil 20 seconds or just until cheese melts.

Stir green onion strips, honey, and pepper into soup. Divide soup among 8 serving bowls. Place 2 cheese toasts in center of each bowl and serve.

Yield: 8 (1-cup) servings

Chilled Gold Tomato Soup (Gazpacho)

   6 pints yellow tomatoes, core removed, quartered
   2 cups cucumber, peeled and seeded
 ½ cup scallion bulb, white only
   2 cups roasted yellow bell pepper
 ¼ cup jalapeños, seeded
   1 tablespoon fresh chopped garlic
 ¼ cup garlic oil (available at most supermarkets)
   2 cups fennel bulb, sliced
1½ cups toasted panko, golden tan
 ½ cup rice vinegar
   2 cups extra-virgin olive oil
     Salt and pepper
 ½ cup fresh lemon juice
     Zest from 2 lemons, grated
   2 cups vegetable stock

Purée all ingredients very fine. Pass through fine china cap. Adjust seasoning.

Yield: ½ gallon or 5 servings

Ojai Valley Inn and Spa
905 Country Club Drive
Ojai, California 93023
805-646-5511
www.ojairesort.com

HE PEACEFUL AND VERDANT Ojai Valley is 90 minutes northwest of Los Angeles, east of Santa Barbara. The inn reflects the genteel Southern California lifestyle of the early 1900s. The beauty of the surroundings and the artistry of the inn's staff assures one's visit will become a special memory. The same can be said of dining at the Ojai Valley Inn, one of the very finest inns in the world.

Washington House Inn

Corner of Washington
and Center Streets
W 62, N 573 Washington Avenue
Cedarburg, Wisconsin 53012
262-375-3550

WASHINGTON HOUSE INN is an experience in romance, elegance, and comfort. A lovely collection of antique Victorian furniture, a marble-trimmed fireplace, and freshly cut flowers offer a warm reception. Listed on the National Register of Historic Places and located in the heart of Cedarburg's historic district, the inn offers elegant lodging within walking distance of festivals, unique shops, galleries, and a local winery.

Winterfest Fruit Soup

1	(8-ounce) package dried mixed fruit
1	cup dried apricots
½	cup raisins
5½	cups water
3	cinnamon sticks
¼	cup quick-cooking tapioca
1	orange, sliced thin
¾	cup sugar
⅓	cup currant jelly

In a 3-quart pan, combine mixed fruit, apricots, raisins, 3 cups of water, and cinnamon sticks. Cover and simmer until fruit is plump. Stir in tapioca, cover, and cook until the sauce is thickened and the fruit is tender. Add remaining 2½ cups water, orange slices, sugar, and jelly. Cook until well blended and tapioca is tender. Remove the cinnamon sticks. Serve warm.

Yield: 6 to 8 servings

Note: This soup is especially appropriate for a brunch menu.

Wisconsin Cream of Cheddar Soup with Country Bacon

- 2/3 cup butter or margarine
- 1 cup finely chopped celery
- 1/3 cup all-purpose flour
- 1/4 teaspoon salt
- 1/4 teaspoon pepper
- 1 1/2 cups chicken stock or broth
- 2 cups light cream
- 2 cups milk
- 2 cups (8 ounces) finely shredded sharp Cheddar cheese
- 8 slices bacon, cooked crisp and crumbled
- 1/2 cup finely chopped green onion

In a large saucepan, melt butter over medium heat. Stir in celery. Cook and stir 8 to 10 minutes or until celery is just tender. Stir in flour, salt, and pepper. Add chicken broth. Cook and stir until mixture is thick and bubbly. Cook and stir 1 to 2 minutes more. Add cream and milk alternately to broth mixture. Heat through. Stir in cheese. Cook and stir until cheese is melted. Just before serving, sprinkle with bacon and green onions. Serve immediately.

Yield: 8 to 10 servings

The Victorian Villa
601 North Broadway Street
Union City, Michigan 49094
517-741-7383
www.avictorianvilla.com

THE VICTORIAN VILLA IS situated in a quaint and charming 19th-century river village, on an acre of peacefully landscaped Victorian gardens and grounds, where you can relax and sip the gentler side of life. It's a place where you can enjoy an afternoon tea in the gingerbread gazebo, share a bottle of wine and stretch out on the jewel-green lawn, unwind by the goldfish pond, and pass the day listening to a century-old fountain play its familiar bubbling refrain. And in the evening, enjoy a relaxing and elegant seven-course champagne dinner for two in the villa's gourmet restaurant, Victoria's.

The Orchard Inn

Highway 176
P. O. Box 128
Saluda, North Carolina 28773
1-800-381-3800
828-749-5471
www.orchardinn.com

NO MATTER WHERE YOU start, the Orchard Inn is a perfect destination. Situated on a 12-acre mountaintop with stunning views, this national historic structure has long been a favorite retreat. It has wraparound porches and large, inviting living room with stone fireplace. Guest quarters are furnished with period pieces and antiques. Cottages feature fireplaces, whirlpools, and private decks. Enjoy award-winning cuisine while overlooking the gardens, vineyard, and mountains.

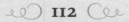
Zucchini Velvet Soup

8 cups water
3 tablespoons chicken base
8 zucchini, chopped
2 Vidalia onions, chopped
½ teaspoon curry powder
1 cup cream cheese
2 cups heavy cream

Bring water and chicken base to a boil. Add zucchini, onion, and curry. Simmer until tender. Turn off heat and stir in cream cheese. Purée mixture thoroughly in blender or food processor. Add heavy cream. Return to heat or served chilled.

Yield: About 12 servings

Salads

Black Point Inn
519 Black Point Road
Prout's Neck, Maine 04074
207-883-2500
www.blackpointinn.com

WITH ITS WOODWORK OF water-stained pine and very old decorative murals of England the dining room of this great hotel on the New England coast is charming and beautiful. Picture windows overlook the gardens and the sea. The food is as appealing as the view—sumptuous buffets at poolside, delectable seafood, and New England dishes. First settled about 1630, Prout's Neck was deserted by the colonists 60 years later after trouble with the French and Indians. In 1702, colonists started a new trading post and permanently settled the area. The Black Point Inn was built in 1878 and has been a beloved destination for many generations.

Asian Slaw with Soy-Sesame Dipping Sauce

SLAW

¼ cup carrot, cut into thin strips 1 to 2 inches long
¼ cup Daikon radish (Japanese radish), peeled and cut into thin strips 1 to 2 inches long
¼ cup red bell pepper, cut into thin strips 1 to 2 inches long
¼ cup yellow bell pepper, cut into thin strips 1 to 2 inches long
¼ cup bok choy or other cabbage, cut into thin strips 1 to 2 inches long
¼ cup scallions or green onion, cut at an acute angle

In a bowl, combine all slaw ingredients and mix well.

DIPPING SAUCE

½ cup soy sauce
1 tablespoon sesame oil
1 tablespoon rice wine vinegar
1 tablespoon honey
1 stalk of scallion or green onion, cut at an acute angle
1 teaspoon garlic, minced
1 teaspoon fresh ginger, minced
1 teaspoon Daikon radish (Japanese radish), finely grated
Dash of pepper

In a bowl, combine soy sauce, sesame oil, vinegar, and honey. Mix well. Add garlic, ginger, scallions, and radish to soy mix. Add pepper and adjust amount of honey to taste.

To serve: Serve slaw in center of plate with sushi rice and a drizzle of dipping sauce. For a round, compact shape, use a ring mold or similar tool to form the rice and slaw.

Yield: 2 to 3 servings; makes 2 cups dipping sauce

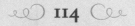

Black Bean Salad

 1 can black beans
½ cup diced red bell pepper
¼ cup diced red onion
¼ cup cilantro, torn into small pieces
½ cup roasted corn cut from cob (or frozen, if fresh
     is unavailable)
¼ cup olive oil
    Juice of 1 lime
    Salt and pepper to taste

Gently toss all ingredients in medium-size bowl. Let sit at room temperature for ½ hour to allow flavors to combine.

Yield: 6 servings

Southmoreland on the Plaza Bed and Breakfast
116 East 46th Street
Kansas City, Missouri 64112
816-531-7979
www.southmoreland.com

SOUTHMORELAND ON the Plaza Bed and Breakfast sets a new standard for bed-and-breakfast hospitality and comfort. Located just two blocks off Kansas City's famous Country Club Plaza, the inn blends classic New England bed-and-breakfast ambience with small hotel amenities. Twelve guest rooms in the main inn and a luxury suite in the carriage house offer private baths, telephones, and parking. Each room has a special feature, such as a treetop deck, fireplace, or Jacuzzi. A stay at Southmoreland on the Plaza includes a gourmet breakfast in the morning, complimentary wine and hors d'oeuvres in the late afternoon, and hot beverage service and sweets in the evening.

The Duke Mansion

400 Hermitage Road
Charlotte, North Carolina 28207

704-714-4400
1-888-202-1009
www.dukemansion.org

THE DUKE MANSION, BUILT in 1915 and listed on the National Register of Historic Places, offers 20 unique guest rooms in true Southern splendor and with a full breakfast. The rooms are residential in their decor and appointed with beautiful artwork and furnishings, giving you a breathtaking image of what it was like to be a member of the prestigious Duke family, who made the mansion their home. All rooms have queen- or king-sized beds, private baths, exquisite linens, luxurious robes, and a gourmet good-night treat. The Duke Mansion is an integral part of Charlotte's most prestigious and beautiful neighborhood, and is situated on 4½ acres of beautiful grounds. Its professional culinary staff and beautiful public rooms can accommodate family or business celebrations of 10 to 300 guests.

The Great Country Inns of America Cookbook

Black-Eyed Pea Salad with Honey Mustard Glazed Fried Chicken

1	pound dry black-eyed peas
½	cup finely diced celery
¾	cup finely diced carrot
½	cup finely diced red onion
¼	cup finely diced red bell, green bell, and yellow bell pepper

DRESSING

3	cups mayonnaise
¾	teaspoon celery seed
½	teaspoon dry mustard
½	tablespoon sugar
¾	teaspoon granulated garlic
1	teaspoon salt
¾	teaspoon pepper
½	teaspoon Tabasco sauce
½	tablespoon Worcestershire sauce
1	teaspoon apple cider vinegar

CHICKEN

1	cup self-rising flour
	Salt, pepper, and cayenne pepper to taste
2	cups vegetable oil
2	boneless skinless chicken breasts, diced into ½-inch cubes
2	tablespoons honey
1	tablespoon Grey Poupon mustard

Soak the peas overnight in water.

Combine celery, carrots, onion, and bell peppers in mixing bowl. In a large bowl, stir together dressing ingredients. Add the dressing to the vegetable mixture and stir to combine. Cover and refrigerate overnight.

Drain peas, rinse with cold water, and transfer to a saucepan. Cover peas with warm water and cook until they are al dente. Drain and rinse with cold water again. Let stand until completely cooled. Add peas to the dressing and vegetable mixture and chill for 1 hour.

Take the chicken and toss with some seasoned self-rising flour. Fry in vegetable oil until golden brown and floating. Take the honey and mustard and combine in a bowl. Toss fried chicken in the honey-mustard mixture while chicken is still hot.

In a serving dish, place the warm fried chicken on top of the black-eyed pea salad for a wonderful combination of two Southern favorites.

Yield: 10 servings

The Queen Anne
Inn & Resort

70 Queen Anne Road
Chatham, Cape Cod,
Massachusetts 02633
508-945-0394
www.queenanneinn.com

NAMED AFTER QUEEN Anne of England, the Pilgrims' major benefactor and financial supporter, the Queen Anne Inn is located on Queen Anne Road in Chatham on outer Cape Cod. "Discovered" in the 1980s by the widow of an American president, who used the Queen Anne for her private parties at the beginning and end of her summer vacations on Cape Cod, the inn became very popular without ever losing its understated and simple elegance, which gives the thoughtful and sophisticated traveler a true sense of place.

*The Great Country Inns
of America Cookbook*

Bloody Mary Salad

VINAIGRETTE

2 beefsteak tomatoes, cored and roughly chopped
1 stalk celery, cleaned and roughly chopped
3/4 root fresh horseradish, ground and mixed with
    1 tablespoon white balsamic vinegar
1 teaspoon Tabasco sauce
1 teaspoon Worcestershire sauce
1/4 ounce white balsamic vinegar
1/4 cup Rain Organic Vodka
2 teaspoons kosher salt
1 teaspoon cracked black pepper
1/4 cup cane syrup
1/4 cup grapeseed oil

SALAD

1/2 pint red currant tomatoes, cut in half
1/2 pint yellow currant tomatoes, cut in half
1/2 pound petite celery greens
1/4 root fresh horseradish, peeled and shaved thinly
    on a mandoline

To make the vinaigrette: Combine beefsteak tomatoes, celery, ground horseradish, Tabasco, Worcestershire, 2 tablespoons of white balsamic vinegar, vodka, salt and cracked black pepper in a blender and purée until liquefied. Place some cheesecloth in a strainer and pour the puréed liquid onto the cheesecloth. Leave in refrigerator to drain overnight.

Place reserved liquid into a saucepan with cane syrup and remaining 2 tablespoons white balsamic vinegar. Reduce until slightly syrupy. Cool liquid and combine with the grapeseed oil.

To make the salad: In a mixing bowl, combine red and yellow currant tomatoes with vinaigrette and salt and pepper to taste.

To assemble: Place a round ring mold in the center of a plate and pack the tomato mixture to a ¼-inch thick layer. Remove the ring mold, then repeat with the remaining tomato mixture on three more plates.

In another mixing bowl, combine the celery greens with vinaigrette and salt and pepper to taste. Stack ¼ of celery greens vertically in center of each tomato ring. Top with a few shavings of fresh horseradish and drizzle some of the remaining vinaigrette around the plate.

Yield: 4 servings

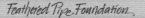
Feathered Pipe Ranch
P.O. Box 1682
Helena, Montana 59624
406-442-8196
www.featheredpipe.com

LOCATED IN THE HEART OF the Montana Rockies, the Feathered Pipe Ranch is one of the country's premier retreat centers. Surrounded by miles of forested mountains, the ranch is blessed with a sparkling lake, pristine water, clean air, and abundant wildlife. The Feathered Pipe Ranch offers yoga and wellness workshops that focus on remembering the interconnectedness of all life. Tepees, tents, yurts and natural log and stone buildings offer a variety of lodging options. In the kitchen, gourmet natural food is the ranch's specialty, featuring organic ingredients prepared with a commitment to health and well-being.

A Caesar Salad

4 cloves garlic, rubbed into wooden bowl then minced
1 cup olive oil
1 egg, coddled in boiling water for 1 minute
Juice of 1 large lemon
1½ teaspoons Worcestershire sauce
½ teaspoon prepared mustard (Dijon is nice)
½ teaspoon horseradish
1 teaspoon freshly ground black pepper
½ cup freshly grated Parmesan cheese
Lettuce—enough for 15 people
Croutons

In wooden bowl, whisk together garlic, olive oil, and egg. Whisk in lemon juice, Worcestershire, mustard, horseradish, and pepper. Just before serving, dribble dressing over lettuce, sprinkle on Parmesan and toss.

Serve with croutons, which can be made by cubing old bread and sautéing it in butter with garlic powder, basil, dill, paprika, and oregano. Or melt butter with spices, pour over cubed old bread in a bowl, and stir until coated. Spread onto a baking sheet and bake at 375 degrees until golden and crunchy.

Yield: 15 servings

Cauliflower Salad

DRESSING

1 **cup sour cream**
1 **cup mayonnaise**
1 **package Good Seasons Cheese & Garlic**
  Salad Dressing Mix

SALAD

1 **head cauliflower, broken into small flowerets**
1 **package radishes, cut into thin slices**
1 **bunch green onions, sliced thin (less if desired)**
3 **tablespoons sesame seeds or poppy seeds**

In a bowl, whisk together the dressing ingredients. Add the cauliflower, radishes, and onions and stir to combine. Stir in sesame seeds.

Yield: 8 servings

Blue Spruce Inn
677 South 3rd Street
Lander, Wyoming 82520
1-888-503-3311
bluespruce@rmisp.com

SURROUNDED BY GIANT blue spruce trees, enjoy warm Western hospitality in the relaxed luxury of an early 20th-century inn from the Arts and Crafts period. Three queen guest rooms and one twin (convertible to king) all have private baths. The Blue Spruce Inn is decorated with objects gathered during the travels of your retired air-force hosts. This is a perfect place to stay while you explore the Wind River Mountains and the charming town of Lander.

The Inn at Cavalier
9417 Highway 18
Cavalier, North Dakota 58220
701-265-8739
www.bbonline.com/nd/cavalier/

*H*ERE IS AN EARLY 1900S inn located in downtown Cavalier, 21 miles from Minnesota and 15 miles from Canada. The inn has three bedchambers with climate control, all-season porches, Victorian tearoom, claw-foot tubs, handmade gifts, collectibles, and a home-cooked breakfast. The inn is open Memorial Day to Labor Day. There are facilities for meetings and receptions. The innkeeper is Geraldine Geiger.

Mock Chicken Salad

1 can Chicken and Rice Soup
1 package lemon Jell-O
1 can tuna (or chicken)
1 cup diced celery
1 cup whipped cream
1/2 cup chopped walnuts (optional)
1/2 cup salad dressing
2 teaspoons grated onion

Heat soup. Add Jell-O. Cool and whip. Add tuna or chicken, celery, whipped cream, walnuts if used, salad dressing, and grated onion. Set in an 8 x 8-inch pan.

Yield: 9 servings

Scarlett O'Hara Gelatin Salad

1¼ cups cranberry juice

1 (3-ounce) package cherry gelatin

½ cup Southern Comfort

3 tablespoons lime or lemon juice

¼ cup sugar

1 cup halved seedless grapes

½ cup finely chopped celery

1 cup pitted Bing cherries

½ cup chopped pecans or walnuts

Heat cranberry juice and in it dissolve the cherry gelatin. Remove from heat and add Southern Comfort, lime juice, and sugar; chill until gel begins. Fold in grapes, celery, cherries, and nuts. Finish chilling and serve on bed of fresh lettuce dotted with pecans.

Yield: 4 to 6 servings

Gone with the Wind Bed and Breakfast

14905 West Lake Road
Branchport, New York 14418
607-868-4603
www.gonewiththewind
onkeukalake.com

THIS STATELY STONE MANSION on a rolling hillside a hundred feet above the clear water of Keuka Lake was opened in April of 1989. Since that time Linda and Robert Lewis have been guiding and serving thousands of guests. Most guests walk the many trails on the 14 acres, swim the waters of the private cove, or just enjoy the tranquilizing effect of gazebo-gazing as the sounds and ripples bring relaxation. Everyone enjoys chatting around the breakfast tables while they relish breakfasts of fruit, home-baked Rhett's rhubarb coffee cake, one of Aunt Pittypat's many flavors of pancakes, or Ashley's stuffed French toast.

The Patchwork Quilt
Country Inn
11748 County Road 2
Middlebury, Indiana 46540
574-825-2417
www.patchworkquiltinn.com

HIS UNUSUAL AND DELIGHT-ful inn is located on a 340-acre working farm, where many of the foods served are grown. The inn began in 1962 as a vacation farm for city people. A few years later a new dining room, the Wood Shed, was added. In it there is a display of antique woodworking and logging tools and a collection of more than 75 plates from around the world. There is a homespun atmosphere at the Patchwork. The kitchen opens into the dining room; here grand, family-style meals are served in wonderful surroundings. Handmade quilts and patchwork tablecloths are available for purchase.

German Slaw

1	medium head cabbage, finely shredded
1	green bell pepper, seeded and finely chopped
1	medium onion, finely chopped
1	carrot, grated
¾	cup vinegar
¾	cup vegetable oil
1½	cups sugar
1	teaspoon salt
1	teaspoon celery seed

In a bowl, mix cabbage, bell pepper, onion, and carrot.

In a saucepan, combine vinegar, vegetable oil, sugar, salt, and celery seed. Bring to boil. Remove from heat and immediately pour over cabbage mixture. Cover tightly; allow to cool, then refrigerate.

Yield: 1 to 1½ quarts

Hot Spinach Salad
with Hot Bacon Dressing

2	pounds fresh spinach
6	pounds uncooked sliced bacon, cut in ¼-inch pieces
4½	cups chopped sweet onions
3	cups cider vinegar
1½	cups sugar
3	cups water
3	bay leaves
3	sprigs fresh thyme
3	tablespoons arrowroot or cornstarch
¾	cup cold water
	Salt and pepper to taste
1½	pounds fresh sliced mushrooms
12	hard-cooked eggs, coarsely chopped

Remove stems from spinach and wash in two or more changes of cold water. Drain well and dry thoroughly. Chill. Fry bacon in a heavy skillet until lightly browned and all fat is cooked out. With slotted spoon, transfer bacon to a bowl. Pour off all but a thin coating of fat. Add onions and sauté over medium heat until soft and transparent.

Add vinegar, sugar, water, bay leaves, and thyme and bring to a simmer, stirring until sugar is dissolved. Mix arrowroot with cold water and whisk into simmering mixture. Return bacon to pan and simmer mixture for 10 minutes. Adjust seasoning with salt and pepper to taste. Remove bay leaves and thyme. Refrigerate if not using immediately. Place spinach, right side up, in 24 salad bowls. Place mound of chopped eggs in center. Just before serving, heat bacon dressing and ladle over salads.

Yield: 24 servings

**Walden
Country Inn & Stables**
1119 Aurora Hudson Road
Aurora, Ohio 44202
330-562-5508
www.waldenco.com

WITH JUST 25 LUXURIOUS suites, Walden Country Inn & Stables is the perfect hideaway for relaxing getaways, timeless weddings, and executive retreats. The elegantly proportioned buildings surround a 175-year-old barn and silo located on 32 acres, and horses roaming in the pasture provide the drama of strength, color, and majesty. Dramatic glass walls bring in natural light and contrast with the traditional farmhouse feel of the buildings. Guests enjoy a host of recreational activities, world-class dining, unobtrusive service, and a wealth of meeting space.

**Savannah's
Country Cottage Hideaway**
Route 1, Box 201
Catoosa, Oklahoma 74015
918-266-7121

*H*ERE IS A RESTFUL HIDE-
away overlooking a
glistening lake, a 20-
acre forest of majestic trees, and 10
acres bordering a bubbly creek. Glass
doors open onto wide balconies for
breathtaking views.

Savannah's Lake Salad

1   head Romaine lettuce
2   oranges, segmented
1   large red onion, thinly sliced
1   bottle of French or French-bacon salad dressing
¼   cup almonds, toasted in skillet

Scatter lettuce on a plate. Add onion and arrange several orange
segments on top. Drizzle with some dressing. Sprinkle with
toasted almonds.

Yield: 4 servings

Layered Lettuce Salad

- 1 head lettuce, broken into small pieces
- 1 cup celery, diced
- 4 hard-cooked eggs, sliced
- 1 (10-ounce) package frozen green peas, thawed
- ½ cup green pepper, diced
- 1 medium onion, diced
- 8 slices bacon, cooked and crumbled
- 2 cups mayonnaise
- 1 to 2 tablespoons sugar
- 4 ounces Cheddar cheese, shredded
  Parsley

Layer first 7 ingredients in order given in a 12 x 9-inch glass dish. Combine mayonnaise and sugar, spread evenly over top of salad. Sprinkle with cheese. Cover and refrigerate 8 to 12 hours. Garnish with parsley before serving.

Yields: About 12 servings

Magnolia Manor
418 North Main Street
Bolivar, Tennesee 38008
731-658-6700
www. magnoliamanorbolivartn.com

MAGNOLIA MANOR IS an elegant antebellum home and an excellent example of Georgian architecture. Records show that General Ulysses S. Grant chose the house to serve as his headquarters. The current owners, Mr. and Mrs. James Cox, have worked toward restoring the home with its original color scheme and furnishings.

The Greyfield Inn
Cumberland Island, Georgia 32035
904-261-6408
www.greyfieldinn.com

THE GREYFIELD INN ON Cumberland Island is a luxurious, romantic oceanfront mansion, built in 1900 and furnished today as it was then. In true Southern fashion, the Greyfield takes great pride in dining. Each morning, guests awaken to a full and satisfying breakfast that includes one of the chef's specialties. The day's island explorations are accompanied by a satisfying picnic lunch. During the cocktail hour each evening, hors d'oeuvres are served in the oceanfront bar. Dinner is a casually elegant affair, served in the glow of candlelight. It features fresh and creative cuisine, accompanied by selections from the inn's wine cellar.

Marinated Mushroom and Artichoke Salad

DRESSING
- 4 cups extra-virgin olive oil
- 1 cup fresh lemon juice
- 3 ounces minced garlic
- 1 tablespoon salt
- 1 tablespoon ground black pepper
- 1 cup minced fresh parsley
- 1/2 cup chives

SALAD
- 3 pounds large button mushrooms, stemmed and sliced
- 1 large red onion, 1/2-inch sliced
- 6 to 8 cups 1-inch snap beans
- 1 cup rough chopped kalamata olives, patted dry
- 6 cans artichoke hearts, halved and patted dry
- 2 cups feta cheese
- 4 large handfuls spinach, quickly chopped

Mix dressing ingredients together thoroughly.

In a salad bowl, combine mushrooms, onions, artichoke hearts, beans, and olives. Add dressing and toss to combine. Cover and refrigerate overnight. Strain vegetables in morning and toss with spinach and feta. Save dressing for further use. Goes well with warm pita chips and hummus.

Yield: 30 to 40 servings as lunch side salad

Old-Fashioned Cabbage Slaw

6 cabbages
½ tablespoon salt
1 teaspoon pepper
1 tablespoon celery seed
½ cup sugar
1 green bell pepper, chopped
¼ cup pimiento, chopped
½ tablespoon onion, grated
½ cup vegetable oil
1 cup white vinegar

Finely chop cabbage in food processor; transfer to large bowl. Add remaining ingredients; mix thoroughly, cover, and chill before serving.

Yield: 25 servings

BonnyNook Inn
414 West Main
Waxahachie, Texas 75165
972-938-7207
1-800-486-5936
www.bonnynook.com

"OLD-WORLD ELEGANCE WITH 21st-century comfort" is the motto of this delightful inn. There is a Victorian parlor with a game table, a piano, and comfortable seating areas. A seven-course dinner for two is served in the private candlelit dining room. A full breakfast is served on your schedule in the dining room. Dishes include homemade coffee cakes, fruit dishes, and specially prepared entrées.

Hickory Bridge Farm
96 Hickory Bridge Road
Orrtanna, Pennsylvnnia 17353
1-800-642-1766
717-642-5261
www.hickorybridgefarm.com

ICKORY BRIDGE FARM, located 9 miles west of Gettysburg, was the first to offer bed-and-breakfast accommodations to guests in Adams County. At Hickory Bridge Farm, your hosts take pride in cleanliness and well-kept grounds. You will experience privacy and very comfortable accommodations. All meals are farm fresh and bountiful. A full country breakfast is offered every day except Sunday, when guests will receive a basket breakfast at their doorstep with the Sunday news.

Old-Fashioned Potato Salad

8	cups coarsely chopped cooked potatoes
4	chopped hard-cooked eggs
1/2	cup finely chopped onion
1/3	cup sweet pickle relish
1/2	cup chopped celery
3/4	cup mayonnaise or salad dressing
1/3	cup sugar
1/3	cup evaporated milk (more as needed)
1/3	cup cider vinegar
2	teaspoons prepared mustard
1	teaspoon salt

Combine potatoes, eggs, onion, relish, and celery in a very large mixing bowl. In separate bowl, stir together mayonnaise, sugar, evaporated milk, cider vinegar, mustard, and salt. Add dressing to potato mixture and stir gently. Cover and chill for 4 to 24 hours. Stir in a little additional evaporated milk to moisten the salad after chilling, if necessary.

Yield: 9 servings

Overnight Layer Salad

1 head shredded iceberg lettuce
1 cup sliced celery
1 cup chopped green bell pepper
½ cup sliced green onions
1 package frozen peas, thawed under hot water
1 can sliced water chestnuts
1½ cups mayonnaise
3 tablespoons sugar
1 cup grated cheese
1 pound cooked and crumbled bacon

Layer vegetables in large salad bowl in order given above. Spread top with mayonnaise. Sprinkle sugar over top of mayonnaise. Sprinkle cheese over everything. Cover tightly and refrigerate overnight. Before serving, toss with bacon.

Yield: 20 servings

Trail's End, A Country Inn
5 Trail's End Lane
Wilmington, Vermont 05363
802-464-2727
www.trailsendvt.com

NESTLED AMONG THE pines along a quiet country road, Trail's End offers traditional New England hospitality in a secluded setting on 10 acres of beautifully kept grounds. The inn provides a wide variety of facilities for your comfort and enjoyment, including a heated outdoor swimming pool, a clay tennis court, a stocked trout pond, lovely flower gardens, and a game room with 8-foot Olhausen pool table. The decor can be described as sophisticated country, while being warm, comfortable, and inviting. There are 15 picture-perfect rooms, all with private baths, including four fireplace rooms and two fireplace suites with canopy beds and whirlpool tubs. Each is furnished with family heirlooms and antiques. The inn is conveniently located in the heart of southern Vermont, just five minutes from the Mount Snow and Haystack ski areas.

The Brentwood
Bed & Breakfast

6304 Murray Lane
Brentwood, Tennessee 37027
1-800-332-4640
www.brentwoodbandb.com

HIS 5-ACRE COUNTRY ESTATE is minutes from fine dining and the historic attractions of Nashville. Private decks overlook the rolling hillside, and fireplaces warm the cool evenings. The drive over the stream, through the trees, and up to the white columns welcomes you to the classic hospitality of the Brentwood. The casual elegance of the interior and eclectic combination of traditional furnishings, family and European antiques, and objets d'art create an atmosphere of quiet relaxation. A stay at the Brentwood includes a full, hot, gourmet breakfast.

Poppy Seed Dressing Salad

½ cup sugar
1 teaspoon salt
1 teaspoon prepared mustard
1 tablespoon poppy seeds
¼ cup vinegar
⅔ cup vegetable oil
¼ cup grated onion
   Lettuce (enough for 4 servings)
1 can Mandarin oranges, drained
   Slivered almonds

In tightly covered jar (or in blender), shake sugar, salt, mustard, poppy seeds, vinegar, oil, and onion. Tear up lettuce. Add oranges and almonds. Mix well and add dressing (shake well before using).

Yield: 4 servings

Ribbon Salad

FIRST LAYER

- 1 (3-ounce) package lime Jell-O
- 1 cup hot water
- 1 (8-ounce) can crushed pineapple with juice

Dissolve Jell-O in hot water. Add pineapple. Pour into a loaf pan or other mold and let set in the refridgerator until fairly firm.

SECOND LAYER

- 1 (3-ounce) package lemon Jell-O
- 1 cup hot water
- 1 (3-ounce) package cream cheese
- ½ cup chopped nuts

Dissolve Jell-O into hot water. Combine cream cheese and nuts and gradually add liquid mixture until well blended. Pour over first layer and let set until firm.

THIRD LAYER

- 1 (3-ounce) package red Jell-O (strawberry or cherry)
- 1 cup hot water
- ½ can whole cranberry sauce

Dissolve Jell-O in hot water. Stir in cranberry sauce. Pour over the other layers and let set overnight. Cut and serve on a lettuce leaf.

Yield: 12 to 15 servings

**The Queen Anne Inn
Bed and Breakfast**
420 West Washington Avenue
South Bend, Indiana 46601
1-800-582-2379
www.queenanneinn.net

RELAX AND RELIVE THE past in this 1893 Victorian mansion. Crystal chandeliers placed throughout the home add warmth to the Victorian decor. The inn offers six spacious air-conditioned bedrooms with private baths. Guests may relax and chat in the common rooms or on the wide porches surrounding this historic home. Staying at the Queen Anne Inn may bring back many memories of the past or dreams of what you may wish you had experienced as a child.

The Governor's Inn

86 Main Street
Ludlow, Vermont 05149
802-228-8830
1-800-468-3766
www.thegovernorsinn.com

THIS HISTORIC VILLAGE INN originally built by Vermont governor William Wallace Stickney as his private dwelling, it stands as a classic example of the fine craftsmanship of the late Victorian period (circa 1890). Now it serves as a haven for enjoying life's pleasures and as a base for exploring Vermont.

Rice Salad for a Crowd

SALAD

6	cups raw long-grain white rice
1½	cups unsalted butter
	Salt and pepper
1½	cups sliced almonds, toasted
3	(6-ounce) jars marinated artichoke hearts, drained and cut lengthwise into quarters
1½	cups frozen green peas, cooked
¾	cup chopped pimiento
3	bunches thinly sliced green onions
1½	pounds sliced marinated mushrooms
1½	cups sliced black olives
1½	pounds diced salami
1½	cups chopped fresh parsley
	Watercress
	Cherry tomatoes

VINAIGRETTE

4½	teaspoons dried basil
4½	teaspoons dried tarragon
3	teaspoons Dijon-style mustard
¾	cup red wine vinegar
¾	cup salad oil
	Salt and pepper to taste

To make the salad: Add rice and salt to a large pot of boiling water. Cook on low heat for 18 minutes. Drain the rice and rinse with warm water. Add butter and salt and pepper to taste and dry in a 250°F oven for 30 minutes, stirring occasionally with a fork. Transfer to a large bowl and add the remaining salad ingredients.

To make the vinaigrette: Combine all vinaigrette ingredients in a bowl and mix well.

To assemble: Add vinaigrette to salad and mix well. Pack tightly into oiled ring molds or Bundt pans. Refrigerate overnight. Remove from mold and garnish with watercress and cherry tomatoes.

Yield: 36 servings

Hartstone Inn

41 Elm Street

Camden, Maine 04843

207-236-4259

www.hartstoneinn.com

UILT IN 1835, THIS ARCHITEC-turally splendid historic inn is an enchanting, mansard-style Victorian bed-and-breakfast in the heart of Camden. The inn is perfectly situated for those who prefer staying in the center of Camden village, close to good shopping and with easy access to Camden Harbor. Beyond the inn's pillared entranceway is a quiet world of peace, charm, and elegance, sprinkled with period antiques and exotic orchids. Each en suite guest room is a unique experience in pampered luxury. Many rooms offer lace canopy beds with fluffy feather duvets, Jacuzzi tubs, and fireplaces. Elegant china, fine crystal, and internationally award-winning cuisine make Chef Michael's breakfast and dinner truly memorable and romantic experiences. Creative menus feature local Maine ingredients, and five-course dinners change to reflect the seasons.

Avocado and Papaya Salad

- ¼ cup white wine vinegar
- 2 tablespoons fresh lime juice
- 1 teaspoon Dijon-style mustard
- ¼ cup olive oil
- 4 ripe avocados
- 4 ripe papayas
- 2 sprigs cilantro, chopped
  Salt and pepper
  Lime wedges
  Cilantro sprigs

In a bowl, whisk together vinegar, lime juice, and mustard. While whisking vigorously, drizzle in the olive oil. Cut the avocados and papayas in half. Remove and discard the avocado pit and papaya seeds and scoop out the flesh using a melon baller. Mix the papaya and avocado together in a bowl. Add dressing and chopped cilantro and toss. Season with salt and pepper to taste. Garnish with lime wedges and cilantro sprigs.

Yield: 6 to 8 servings

Shaved Oriental Vegetable Salad with Orange-Ginger Vinaigrette

SALAD

3 medium carrots, peeled
2 small yellow squash
1 large zucchini
½ head Napa cabbage, washed
1 medium red pepper
6 stalks celery

Cut vegetables ¹/₃₂-inch thick with knife, mandoline, or food processor fitted with small slicing disc. Use only flesh of zucchini and squash. Refrigerate until ready to serve.

VINAIGRETTE

¼ cup soy sauce
   Zest and juice of 2 oranges
1 cup rice vinegar
1 tablespoon finely chopped fresh garlic
2 tablespoons grated fresh ginger
1 tablespoon black sesame seeds, toasted
1 tablespoon sesame seeds, toasted
¼ cup honey
   Salt and pepper
2 cups salad oil
¼ cup sesame seed oil

Mix all ingredients except salad oil and sesame seed oil. Blend oils together and slowly whisk into remaining ingredients.

To serve: Toss all vegetables with vinaigrette to coat. Arrange on serving platter. Garnish platter as desired.

Yield: 12 servings

The Swag
2300 Swag Road
Waynesville, North Carolina 28785
1-800-789-7672
www.theswag.com

THERE ARE CERTAIN EXPERIENCES in life that cannot be duplicated: sitting before a breath taking view on a porch above a garden in full bloom; walking along moss-lined trails underneath 20-foot blooming rhododendron that span overhead like a cathedral ceiling.;wrapping yourself in a hand-woven coverlet, listening to spring showers as you warm your toes and read by firelight. The Swag is a place for rest, rejuvenation, discovery, and creation. The Swag is built out of century-old hand-hewn logs and located atop a 5,000 foot mountain. The Great Smoky Mountains National Park is just a step beyond the backyard. With wonderful panoramic views, the Swag is located just outside of Waynesville, North Carolina (about 50 minutes west of Asheville).

Glacier Bay Country Inn

P. O. Box 5
Gustavus, Alaska 99826
907-697-2288
www.glacierbayalaska.com

SITUATED NEAR THE CENTER of a 160-acre home-stead, this inn offers the chance to experience Alaskan country living in a true wilderness setting. There are forests of towering spruce, hemlock, and pine; hayfields swaying in the breeze; meadows ablaze with wildflowers; bountiful gardens; meandering creeks; exceptional mountain views; and, deep in the woods, down a narrow winding road, this delightful, inviting inn. Marvelous food is one of its features.

Shrimp Salad

12	ounces seashell macaroni, cooked and cooled
½	pound small shrimp, cooked
½	cup onion, chopped
1	cup celery, diced
2	tomatoes, seeded and diced
½	green bell pepper, seeded and diced
2	dozen snow peas, cut in 1-inch pieces
2	cups mayonnaise
2	tablespoons fennel, chopped
2	tablespoons dill, chopped
½	teaspoon white pepper
½	teaspoon salt

Combine macaroni, shrimp, and vegetables in a large bowl. In another bowl, blend mayonnaise, herbs, and seasonings together. Stir dressing into macaroni mixture. Chill well before serving.

Yield: 12 servings

Southwestern Ensalada de Pan

12 tablespoons hot pepper vinegar
24 chopped garlic cloves
4½ cups extra-virgin olive oil
24 cups slightly stale bread cubes (¾-inch)
3 pounds vine-ripened red tomatoes, cut into
    ½-inch wedges
3 cups chopped avocado
1½ cups chopped fresh cilantro
3 teaspoons kosher salt (or to taste)
3 teaspoons white pepper
   Grated Monterey Jack cheese

In a medium bowl, whisk together vinegar, garlic, and pepper. Whisk in olive oil. Add remaining ingredients and salt. Toss to combine well. Let salad stand for 15 minutes at room temperature before serving. Just before serving, sprinkle cheese on top of salad.

Yield: 24 to 30 servings

**Rancho de la Osa
Guest Ranch**
P. O. Box 1
Tucson, Arizona 85633
1-800-872-624
www.ranchodelaosa.com

RANCHO DE LA OSA, OR Ranch of the "She Bear," is one of the last great Spanish haciendas still standing in America. During the Mexican Revolution, Pancho Villa was said to have fired shots at the hacienda. When you stay at Rancho de la Osa you can hold a Mexican cannonball that was found in the stucco walls of the hacienda dining room. Typically, the sun shines more than 300 days a year. This elegant building welcomes each guest with a warm and inviting ambience. Furnished with Mexican antiques, the hacienda is a gentle reminder of the fascinating history of this magnificent old Spanish land grant.

Oakwood Inn

Oakwood Retreat
& Conference Center
702 East Lake View Road
Syracuse, Indiana 46567
574-457-5600
www.oakwoodpark.org

YOU ARE ALWAYS WELCOME at Oakwood. Leave the world behind as you enter the beautiful, 42-acre facility. Walking paths, tall oaks, friendly people, and a panoramic view of Lake Wawasee, Indiana's largest natural lake, greet you as you enter this century-old Christian retreat center. The staff looks forward to being your hosts. On the premises is the Wawasee Room Restaurant, which offers a prime-rib and crab-leg buffet every Friday and Saturday night. As would be expected, lodging accommodations are first class.

Spinach and Bermuda Onion Salad with Orange-Basil Vinaigrette

VINAIGRETTE

- ½ cup orange juice concentrate
- 4 cloves garlic, peeled, crushed, and finely chopped
- 1 cup fresh basil, chopped
- ¼ cup red wine vinegar
- 1 teaspoon salt
- 1 teaspoon white pepper
- ¼ cup extra-virgin olive oil
- 2 cups canola oil

SALAD

- 1 Bermuda onion, peeled and julienned (can substitute Vidalia or Roasted Spanish)
- 2 navel oranges, peeled and segmented
  Spinach

To make the vinaigrette: Using a food processor or in a small container with a hand blender, combine the vinaigrette ingredients except for the oils and process. While mixture is still being processed, add oil slowly and emulsify the vinaigrette. (It's ok if it breaks; it just needs to be shaken well before pouring on the salad.) Transfer to a jar and refrigerate until needed.

To make the salad: Slice the onion thinly and combine with spinach and orange segments. Add dressing and toss lightly.

Yield: 4 servings

Spring Pea Pod and Asparagus Salad on Bibb Lettuce with Bourbon Dressing

Inn at Woodhaven
401 South Hubbards Lane
Louisville, Kentucky 40207
502-895-1011; 1-888-895-1011
www.innatwoodhaven.com

SALAD

- 1 **pound pea pods**
- 1 **cup sliced cherry tomatoes**
- 1 **pound asparagus**
- 6 **heads Kentucky Bibb lettuce**

Steam pea pods and asparagus until just tender but still crisp. Put on ice bath. Gently clean lettuce. Place a bed of lettuce on each plate, then arrange pea pods and asparagus and tomatoes on top.

DRESSING

- ¾ **cup vegetable oil**
- ¼ **cup red wine vinegar**
- ¾ **cup mayonnaise**
- 8 **ounces sour cream**
- 8 **ounces cottage cheese**
- 1 **teaspoon chopped chives**
- 2 **cloves garlic, minced**
  Splash of bourbon

Combine dressing ingredients in a bowl and whisk until well blended. Can be stored in refrigerator for one day in a glass jar.

Pour salad dressing over or serve on the side in small pitcher.

Yield: 8 servings

THE INN AT WOODHAVEN offers lovely lodging accommodations close to Louisville attractions, restaurants, and shopping. Spacious accommodations and hearty breakfasts are staples at this historical bed-and-breakfast inn. Featuring elaborately carved woodwork, winding staircases, and spacious rooms tastefully decorated with antiques, the inn offers romance and relaxation. Rest, relax, read, and enjoy the many porches and gardens. Take a stroll around the grounds or the Brown Park and Beargrass Nature Preserve, both only a block away. Make yourself at home in the common areas, where you will find books, magazines and after-dinner liqueurs.

Thomas Shepherd Inn

300 West German Street
P. O. Box 3634
Shepherdstown, West Virginia 25443
304-876-3715
www.thomasshepherdinn.com

NESTLED IN THE BEAUTIFUL lower Shenandoah Valley along the Potomac, the Thomas Shepherd Inn bed-and-breakfast is a place where life slows down long enough for you to enjoy it. Walk to wonderful restaurants and unique shops from the convenient location in downtown Shepherdstown, in the Eastern Panhandle of West Virginia. The inn is only minutes away from Civil War landmarks such as Antietam Battlefield and Harpers Ferry, and outdoor activities like hiking on the Appalachian Trail, biking on the C&O Canal Path, or water fun on the Potomac River. At the Thomas Shepherd Inn, guests are treated to a full hearty breakfast with true West Virginia hospitality. The inn was built circa 1868 and is part of historically preserved Sheperdstown, a community listed in the National Register of Historic Places, and the state's oldest settlement.

Tarragon Chicken Salad

- 1 whole chicken or 2 chicken breasts, poached
- 2 tablespoons minced fresh tarragon
- 1½ tablespoons balsamic vinegar
- 2 tablespoons oil
- 2 tablespoons mayonnaise
- ¼ cup crème fraiche (see below)
  Salt and white pepper to taste
  Boston lettuce

Poach chicken in stock if possible with carrots, celery, onion, peppercorns, and bouquet garni. Tear chicken into pieces while still warm. Combine with remaining ingredients, adjusting to taste.

Serve on Boston lettuce; garnish with fresh tarragon sprig and/or edible flowers such as nasturtium, pansy, daylily, or honeysuckle.

CRÈME FRAICHE

Add ¼ cup buttermilk to heavy cream; let set at room temperature for about 12 hours and then refrigerate until ready to use.

Yield: 4 servings

Texas Jicama Salad

2 large jicama, peeled and cut into pieces the size
    of french fries
4 green onions, cut into ¼-inch pieces
3 jalapeno peppers, seeded and cut into thin strips
¼ cup red bell pepper
¼ cup green bell pepper
1 tablespoon finely minced fresh cilantro
¾ cup dry-roasted peanuts

DRESSING
⅓ cup rice wine vinegar
¼ cup white sugar
1½ teaspoons curry powder
5 tablespoons olive oil

Cut red and green peppers in ¼-inch pieces, removing all seeds.
Whisk the dressing ingredients together. Toss with vegetables.
Chill overnight until ready to serve.

Yield: 6 to 8 generous servings

The Baldpate Inn
4900 South Hwy 7
Estes Park, Colorado 80517
970-586-6151
www.baldpateinn.com

THE BALDPATE INN, LOCATED seven miles south of Estes Park, Colorado, and next to Rocky Mountain National Park, is a classic mountain getaway offering bed-and-breakfast lodging, a specialty restaurant, and spectacular views. Built in 1917, the inn has been attracting guests for 85 years to its main lodge and cabins. The Baldpate boasts comfortable accommodations, award-winning dining, and the world's largest key collection at its perch on Twin Sisters Mountain at an elevation of 9,000 feet. From this historic inn you can enjoy hiking, fishing, wildlife watching, or mountain climbing.

Chico Hot Springs Resort
Highway 89 South
P. O. Box 134
Pray, Montana 59065
406-333-4933
www.chicohotsprings.com

OCATED IN SOUTH-CENTRAL Montana's Paradise Valley, Chico Hot Springs Resort is high country at its best. The Absaroka mountain range defines the eastern skyline, the Gallatin range lies to the west, and the famous Yellowstone River runs between the two. Chico's history centers on its hot pools, whose "restorative" powers have been put to use for over a century. The water in the pools is between 100° and 104°F and includes no chlorine or other chemicals. The food at the resort is absolutely wonderful.

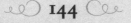

Thai Duck Salad

The succulent duck adds a touch of elegance and richness to this simple salad. It is ideal as a light meal or as a dinner salad. Prepare the vinaigrette a day before serving it on this salad.

THAI VINAIGRETTE
Juice of 1 lime
1 **tablespoon minced garlic**
1 **tablespoon brown sugar**
2 **cups rice wine vinegar**
3/4 **cup extra-virgin olive oil**
2 **teaspoons sesame oil**
1 **tablespoon honey**
1 **tablespoon Tabasco sauce**

In a bowl, whisk all vinaigrette ingredients together and let stand overnight.

SALAD
1 **roasted Muscovy duck**
1 **pound mixed greens**
1 **red bell pepper, sliced**
5 **scallions, chopped**
1/4 **cup canned Mandarin orange segments, drained**

Remove skin from cooled duck and shred meat by hand; place in a large bowl. In a separate bowl, combine greens, pepper, and scallions; add duck meat. Just before serving, add oranges and toss salad with vinaigrette, coating thoroughly.

Yield: 4 to 6 servings

Wilted Spinach Salad

- 3 ounces brown sugar
- 1 teaspoon Worcestershire sauce
- 2 ounces dry mustard
- 6 ounces red wine vinegar
- 1½ cups oil
- 2 ounces bacon, cooked and diced
- 3 ounces smoked duck, julienned
- 5 ounces fresh spinach

Mix all ingredients except spinach in a saucepan; heat until steaming. Pour over spinach and toss. Flambé tableside.

Yield: 1 or 2 servings

Columbia Gorge Hotel
4000 Westcliff Drive
Hood River, Oregon 97301
1-800-345-1921
www.columbiagorgehotel.com

HE COLUMBIA GORGE Hotel has 40 rooms, each of them unique. All accommodations include a world-famous farm breakfast for two. Guests enjoy complimentary coffee service, a morning paper, a champagne and caviar social, and nightly turn-down service featuring gourmet chocolates and a rose on your pillow. Nearby are the breathtaking views of the Columbia River, one of the premier windsurfing spots in the world.

BREADS

Hedrick's Country Inn
7910 North Roy L. Smith Road
Nickerson, Kansas 67561
1-888-489-8039
www.hedricks.com

TRUE TO THE WESTERN heritage of Kansas, the inn reflects the image of Main Street in the Old West, complete with an outdoor balcony that is accessible from each room. The viewing atrium, kid's corner, and sitting room are open to guests. The inn offers a relaxing, quiet, country atmosphere, with the fun of safari-type rooms. Each guest room is decorated in honor of an animal here on the farm and highlighted with original wall murals by local artists. Exotic touches include mosquito netting, zebra sheets, Peruvian rugs, hand-painted ostrich eggs, llama-wool footwarmers, and much more. Included in the price of your room is a country breakfast, after which guests are treated to tours of the farm. You will feed giraffes, cuddle kangaroos, and be kissed by camels.

Almond–Poppy Seed Bread

BREAD

3	cups flour
2½	cups sugar
1	teaspoon baking soda
3	eggs
1¼	cups oil
1½	cups buttermilk
1½	teaspoons vanilla extract
1½	teaspoons almond extract
1½	teaspoons butter extract
1	tablespoon poppy seeds

Preheat oven to 350°F. In a large mixing bowl, stir flour, sugar, and baking soda together with a fork. In a medium mixing bowl, beat eggs, then add oil, buttermilk, and extracts. Mix until blended. Fold in poppy seeds. Pour into two greased and floured loaf pans. Bake for 50 to 60 minutes or until toothpick inserted in center comes out clean. Let bread cool completely before removing from pans.

GLAZE

½	teaspoon vanilla extract
½	teaspoon almond extract
½	teaspoon butter extract
¼	cup orange juice
1	cup sugar

Heat all glaze ingredients in a small saucepan over low flame until sugar dissolves and mixture is smooth. Turn up heat until mixture is at a gentle boil for about 1 minute. Remove from heat and pour over warm bread while still in loaf pans.

Yield: 2 loaves

Banana–Chocolate Chip Muffins

¾ cup soy flour
¾ cup brown rice flour
1 cup sugar
1 teaspoon baking soda
½ cup unsweetened applesauce
1 teaspoon vanilla extract
4 egg whites
3 large bananas, mashed
1 cup chocolate chips

Preheat oven to 375°F. Spray mini muffin pans with nonstick spray.

Sift flours, sugar, and baking soda together in a large bowl. Add remaining ingredients and mix. Fill muffin cups with batter (a 1-inch scoop is perfect) and bake for 16 minutes. As soon as possible, transfer muffins from pans to wire rack to cool.

Yield: 3 dozen mini muffins

**Gillum House
Bed & Breakfast**
35 Walnut Street
Shinnston, West Virginia 26431
304-592-0177; 1-888-592-0177
www.gillumhouse.com

THE GILLUM HOUSE HAS A great front porch with a comfortable glider and lots of books to choose from. Awaken to the aroma of baking each morning of your stay, as Kathleen Panek makes muffins, adapted to be very low fat or fat-free (sugar-free muffins also available) for a healthy, delicious breakfast. Enjoy a different mouth-watering entrée each morning. The full breakfast is served at the time you specify in the morning (between the hours of 3 AM and noon). The Gillum House has a tea for every tea drinker—choose from 70 teas currently available or freshly ground coffee. (Several homemade custom-flavored coffees are also available.)

**Andrews Inn
and Garden Cottages**
Zero Whalton Lane
Key West, Florida 33040
1-888-263-7393
www.andrewsinn.com

O REACH THIS CHARMING
Key West bed-and-
breakfast, you wander
down a shaded lane just a few steps off
Duval Street. Andrews Inn immediately
offers peace and tranquility as you
enter through a garden gate. A
shimmering pool is nestled in a lush
tropical garden of coconut palms,
Spanish lime, hibiscus, and jasmine.
All of the guest rooms surround the
shimmering pool and are beautifully
appointed with white wicker furniture,
tropical décor, and a unique collection
of artwork. Enjoy a champagne
continental breakfast and full cocktail
hour daily while relaxing in this tropical
oasis.

Banana-Walnut Bread

2 cups pre-sifted flour
1 teaspoon baking soda
1 teaspoon baking powder
1 cup sugar
½ teaspoon salt (optional)
2 eggs
½ cup vegetable oil
¼ cup sour milk (add 1 teaspoon vinegar to milk)
3 large or 4 small mashed bananas
¾ cup walnuts

Preheat oven to 350°F. Coat a 9 x 5 x 2-inch loaf pan with vegetable oil or cooking spray. You may also use a muffin tin to make muffins.

In a medium-size bowl, mix flour, baking soda, baking powder, sugar, and salt. In a larger bowl, mix eggs, oil, sour milk, and bananas. Fold dry ingredients into wet ingredients by hand (about 20 strokes) until well mixed. Fold in walnuts. Pour batter into loaf pan. Place large pieces of nuts on top by gently pushing them into batter. Bake for about 50 minutes (25 minutes for muffins). Place on rack to cool for 10 minutes before removing from pan.

Yield: 1 loaf

Beer Bread

6 ounces Alaskan Amber beer (let it get flat)
5⅓ cups bread flour, divided
1¾ cups water, at 110°F
¼ cup stone-ground mustard
1 tablespoon salt
1 package instant yeast

In a saucepan, bring beer to a boil. Stir boiled beer into 1⅓ cups of the flour. Let cool in mixer bowl, then add 4 remaining cups flour, water, mustard, salt, and yeast. Preheat oven to 350°F. Mix dough on medium speed for 10 minutes. Let rise until doubled; punch down. Divide dough into 2 ovals, slit top ½-inch deep. Let rise second time. Bake for 25 minutes or until golden.

Yield: 2 loaves

The Historic Silverbow Inn
120 Second Street
Juneau, Alaska 99801
1-800-586-4146
www.silverbowinn.com

JILL RAMIEL AND KEN Alper look forward to seeing you at the Silverbow Inn bed-and-breakfast during your next visit to Juneau, Alaska's capital city. Housed in a newly remodeled 1914 building, the Silverbow is a boutique hotel, which blends the comforts and convenience of a bed-and-breakfast with the character and charm of a European-style urban pension. The lobby contains an eclectic collection of antiques and personal memorabilia. There is a large breakfast table, easy chairs, a library, games, and puzzles. Each room is individually decorated and equipped with a full bath, cable television, and a private phone line. After a good night's sleep in the lodging accommodations you will wake up to the wonderful breakfast buffet of hot bagels, breads, and pastries from the bakery. Breakfast also includes gourmet sausages, yogurt, cheese, fresh fruit, eggs, homemade granola, fresh-brewed coffee, tea, and juice. Your hosts, who live in the building, are available to share their extensive knowledge of Juneau and Alaska. They want your stay to be as special as possible.

The Heartstone Inn

35 Kings Highway
Eureka Springs, Arkansas 72632
479-253-8916
www.heartstoneinn.com

THE HEARTSTONE INN IS decorated with a mix of interesting antiques and cozy country accents, including an abundance of grapevine wreaths, old lace, painted furniture, and handcrafted accessories. It has 10 lovely guest rooms, all with private baths. Porches both upstairs and down are popular gathering places on summer nights. A large, comfortable parlor invites guests to meet and share their Eureka Springs discoveries.

Best Zucchini Bread

3	eggs
1	cup oil
2	cups sugar
2	teaspoons vanilla extract
2	cups shredded zucchini
1	(8-ounce) can crushed pineapple, drained
3	cups flour
2	teaspoons baking soda
1½	teaspoons cinnamon
1	teaspoon salt
¾	teaspoon nutmeg
¼	teaspoon baking powder
1	cup chopped dates
1	cup chopped pecans

Preheat oven to 350°F. Grease two 9 x 5-inch loaf pans.

In a large bowl, beat together eggs, oil, sugar, and vanilla until thick. Stir in remaining ingredients. Pour into prepared pans and bake for 1 hour or until tester comes out clean.

Yield: 2 loaves

Blueberry-Corn Muffins

1 cup yellow cornmeal
1¼ cups low-fat buttermilk
1¼ cups flour
1½ teaspoons baking powder
1½ teaspoons baking soda
⅓ cup sugar
1 egg, slightly beaten
¼ cup dark molasses
⅓ cup melted butter or margarine
1 cup fresh or frozen blueberries

Preheat oven to 400°F. Grease a muffin tin with nonstick spray coating.

In a bowl, mix together cornmeal and buttermilk; set aside for about 20 minutes. In another bowl, mix together flour, baking powder, baking soda, and sugar. Whisk in egg, molasses, butter, and cornmeal/buttermilk mixture until thoroughly moistened. Add blueberries with a spoon. Fill muffin cups evenly with batter. Bake for 25 to 30 minutes or until slightly brown and done. Remove from oven and allow to rest a minute or so before removing from tins.

Yield: 12 muffins

Holden House
1102 West Pikes Peak Avenue
Colorado Springs, Colorado 80904
719-471-3980
www.HoldenHouse.com

THE SCENIC BEAUTY OF Colorado Springs and the Pikes Peak region offers something for everyone. "The Springs" is located just 60 miles south of Denver and has its own convenient regional airport. Sallie and Welling Clark meticulously restored the property in 1986. They continue to own and operate the inn and uphold the standards at Holden House. Savor the gourmet breakfasts, which might include freshly baked cinnamon streusel muffins, Sallie's famous Southwestern Eggs Fiesta, fresh fruit, freshly ground gourmet coffee, tea, and juice. Complimentary refreshments, an afternoon wine social, and the legendary bottomless cookie jar are just a few of the added touches guests will find here. Distinctive hospitality and personalized service are hallmarks of Holden House.

Christmas Farm Inn
Route 16 B
P. O. Box CC
Jackson, New Hampshire 03846
603-383-4313
www.christmasfarminn.com

THE ORIGINAL BUILDING OF this great, old inn was constructed as a basic Cape Cod cottage in 1777. Other structures took shape a few years later. The inn began taking in boarders as far back as 1899. Here is pure comfort away from the crowds, no noisy telephones, no traffic jams—just delightful surroundings, great food, great everything in the tranquil setting of the White Mountains. This is a paradise for the countless travelers who beat pathways to its doorstep.

Blueberry-Molasses Muffins

12	cups white sugar
12	eggs
6	cups oil
2	cups molasses
1½	gallons flour
2	tablespoons ground ginger
2	teaspoons ground nutmeg
4	tablespoons ground cinnamon
4	tablespoons baking soda
3	quarts buttermilk
3	quarts blueberries

Preheat oven to 350°F (325°F for convection oven).

In a large bowl, mix together the sugar, eggs, oil, and molasses. In another bowl, mix together the flour, ginger, nutmeg, cinnamon, and soda. Alternately add buttermilk and dry mixture to wet mixture. Gently add blueberries. Pour batter into muffin cups or greased muffin pans. Bake for 25 minutes conventional oven (20 minutes in convection oven).

Yield: 4 dozen muffins

Cinnamon Rolls

2½ cups warm water
2 packages yeast
1 box white cake mix
4½ cups flour
   Butter
   Cinnamon and sugar

In a large bowl, combine warm water, yeast, cake mix, and flour. Turn dough onto floured board and knead for 8 to 10 minutes. Let rise until doubled.

Preheat oven to 350°F. Divide dough in half. Roll out each half. Spread with butter. Sprinkle with cinnamon and sugar. Roll up and cut into slices. Let rise. Bake for 20 minutes. Frost if desired.

Yield: 3 dozen rolls

Antique City Inn
400 Antique City Drive
Walnut, Iowa 51577
1-866-541-7378
www.antiquecityinn.com

S A GUEST AT THE Antique City Inn bed-and-breakfast, you will have your choice of five rooms in the house or a cozy private cottage on the back lawn. You can enjoy the large wraparound front porch with the porch swing and wicker chairs. Or relax on the lawn furniture in the afternoon and toast some marshmallows on the open pit in the evening. The parlor and living room are always available for guests. The dining room is where you will enjoy a full breakfast, lots of hot coffee or tea, and good old-fashioned Walnut hospitality.

Six Sisters Bed & Breakfast
149 Union Ave
Saratoga Springs, New York 12866
518-583-1173
www.sixsistersbandb.com

HE SIX SISTERS BED AND Breakfast is a uniquely styled 1880s Victorian-style inn, located just a 10-minute walk from downtown. The front entrance entices you with an outstanding display of original tiger oak and multicolored stained glass. Inside, the rich golden oak floors and Italian verde marble are adorned with classical Orientals, antiques, and Victorian touches of yesterday and today. The Six Sisters' ideal location presents the opportunity to stroll to a variety of shops, restaurants, antique stores, and boutiques. Each guest room has its own private bath. Some rooms have private porches. A full breakfast is served each morning.

Corn Bread Olé

1½	sticks butter
¾	cup sugar
4	eggs
1	(4-ounce) can chopped green chiles
1	(16-ounce) can cream-style corn
½	cup grated Jack and Cheddar cheese
1	cup flour
1	cup cornmeal
4	teaspoons baking powder
½	teaspoon salt

Preheat oven to 350°F.

In a bowl, cream together butter, sugar, and eggs. Add chilies, corn, and cheese and mix. Add flour, cornmeal, baking powder, and salt. Pour batter into an 8 x 12 x 2-inch baking dish. Reduce oven temperature to 300°F and bake for approximately 70 minutes.

Yield: 10 servings

*The Great Country Inns
of America Cookbook*

Cranberry Bread

- 1 cup brown sugar
- 1 teaspoon butter, softened
- 1 egg
- 2 cups unbleached flour
- 1½ teaspoons baking powder
- ½ teaspoon baking soda
  Juice and zest of 1 orange
  Water or cranberry juice
- 1 cup raw cranberries, halved
- 1 cup walnuts meats, chopped

Preheat oven to 325°F. Butter a loaf pan well.

In a bowl, combine butter sugar and egg and mix well. Sift in flour, baking powder, and baking soda. Combine orange juice and enough water or cranberry juice to make ¾ cup liquid. Add liquid to batter. Add orange zest, cranberries, and nuts. Pour batter into pan and bake for 60 to 65 minutes. The bread slices better the day after it's baked. It can also be frozen.

Yield: 1 large loaf

Note: You can double the recipe and make 3 smaller loaves.

Back of the Beyond
7233 Lower East Hill
Colden, New York 14033
716-652-0427

RELAX IN A CHARMING country mini-estate located in the Boston hills and ski area of western New York, situated 25 miles from Buffalo and 50 miles from Niagara Falls. Accommodations are in a separate chalet with three available bedrooms, 1½ baths, fully furnished kitchen, dining/living room, piano, pool table, and fireplace. Guests enjoy a full country breakfast. Organic herb, flower, and vegetable gardens are maintained for delightful strolling. A greenhouse is also part of the complex. There is a large pond for swimming and lovely woods for hiking.

Captain Whidbey Inn
2070 Captain Whidbey Inn Road
Coupeville, Washington 98239
1-800-366-4097
360-678-4097
www.captainwhidbey.com

*L*OCATED ON THE SHORE of Whidbey Island's Penn Cove is the Captain Whidbey Inn. Island hospitality awaits guests, and a variety of accommodations are available. The quaint rooms of the historic main inn, the rustic cabins, and the cozy secluded cottages, feature featherbeds, down comforters, artwork, antiques, and books. The history of the inn goes back to 1907, before there were bridges and cars on the island. Guests were brought in by paddlewheel steamer, and the Whid Isle Inn, as it was originally called, was quite the resort.

Gingerbread-Raisin Scones

8	cups all-purpose flour
1¼	cups packed brown sugar
4	tablespoons baking powder
1	tablespoon ground cinnamon
2	teaspoons ground ginger
½	teaspoon ground cloves
6	ounces chilled butter, cut into pieces
1	cup milk
4	eggs
¾	cup molasses
4	teaspoons vanilla extract
2	cups raisins

Preheat oven to 400°F.

Using electric mixer fitted with pastry cutter blade, mix together flour, brown sugar, baking powder, cinnnmaon, ginger, and cloves in a mixing bowl. Cut in butter until mixture resembles coarse meal. In a separate bowl, mix milk, eggs, molasses, and vanilla. Add to flour mixture along with raisins. Stir until dough forms a ball. Divide dough into 4 equal balls. On a floured surface, roll out each ball 1-inch thick, then cut into eighths. Place on sheet pans lined with parchment paper and bake for 12 to 18 minutes or until lightly brown around the edges. Uncooked scones can be frozen and baked later; baking times will be longer.

Yield: About 32 scones

Golden Raisin Buns
with Lemon Frosting

**Custer Mansion
Bed and Breakfast**
35 Centennial Drive
Custer, South Dakota 57730
605-673-3333l
1-877-519-4948
www.custermansionbb.com

BUNS

1 **cup water**
½ **cup butter**
¼ **teaspoon salt**
1 **teaspoon sugar**
1 **cup flour**
4 **eggs**
½ **cup golden raisins plumped (see note)**

Preheat oven to 375°F. Combine water, butter, sugar, and salt in a saucepan and bring to boil. Add flour all at once. Over low heat, beat with wooden spoon about 1 minute or until mixture pulls away from sides of pan and forms a smooth, thick dough. Remove from heat. Continue beating about 2 minutes more to cool slightly. Add eggs, one at a time, beating after each until mixture has satiny sheen. Stir in raisins. Drop heaping tablespoonfuls about 2 inches apart on greased baking sheets. Bake for 30 to 35 minutes until doubled in size, golden, and firm. Transfer buns to wire rack to cool slightly.

FROSTING

1 **tablespoon butter**
1½ **tablespoons heavy cream**
1 **cup confectioners' sugar**
½ **teaspoon lemon extract**
½ **teaspoon vanilla extract**

In a saucepan, melt butter, then stir in heavy cream. Remove from heat. Stir in confectioners' sugar until smooth. Stir in extracts. (Add more cream if necessary to make a spreading consistency.) While buns are still warm, gently spread frosting over top and sides. *Note: To plump raisins, cover with hot water. Let stand 5 minutes. Drain well.*

Yield: 20 buns

Custer Mansion is a Victorian Gothic structure built in 1891 by Newton Tubbs, who came to the Black Hills after gold was discovered in 1876. Restored and listed on the National Register of Historic Homes, it is once again a favorite gathering place for guests and friends, who can count on a hearty, home-cooked breakfast during their visit. In the spacious dining room, guests will be served a variety of cooked fruits, such as broiled grapefruit, poached pears, and candied oranges, complemented by favorites such as John Wayne Casserole, Overnight French Toast, and piping-hot cinnamon rolls. Freshly brewed coffee, tea, and an assortment of fruit juices are conveniently located in the adjacent butler's pantry. Custer Mansion offers five lovely guest rooms, all with private baths. Each room is named after a song and decorated accordingly.

Inn at Hickory Grove
State Route 80
Cooperstown, New York 13326
607-547-1313
www.hickorygroveinn.com

I N THE EARLY 1800S, Hickory Grove was a popular stagecoach stop for travelers bound from Cooperstown to the Cherry Valley turnpike. The early steamboats, which ferried freight and passengers to the lakeside dwellings, also stopped at the inn to provide for the passengers' refreshment. The area was purchased from local Indians in 1769. The inn was built shortly after 1800 by the Van Ben Schoten family, and for the past century and a half has been noted for good food and relaxation. Marie Curpier is the owner/innkeeper.

Grandma's Brown Bread

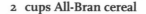

    2 cups All-Bran cereal
 1½ cups milk
  ½ cup sugar
  ½ cup molasses
    2 eggs
    2 cups white flour
    1 teaspoon baking soda
    1 teaspoon baking powder

Preheat oven to 350°F. Spray 5 mini or 2 large loaf pans with cooking spray, then flour pans.

In a bowl, stir together All Bran and milk. Add sugar and eggs. Then add dry ingredients; mix thoroughly. Bake for 25 to 30 minutes.

Yield: 5 mini loaves or 2 large loaves

The Great Country Inns of America Cookbook

Hawaiian Banana Bread

3 cups all-purpose flour

2 cups sugar

1 teaspoon baking soda

½ teaspoon salt

1 teaspoon ground cinnamon

1 cup nuts (optional)

3 eggs

1½ cups oil

2 mashed bananas

1 (8-ounce) cans crushed pineapple, well drained

2 teaspoons vanilla extract

Preheat oven to 350°F. Grease 5 mini loaf pans.

In a large bowl, combine flour, sugar, baking soda, salt, cinnamon, and nuts. In a separate bowl combine eggs, oil, bananas, pineapple, and vanilla. Add the wet mixture to the dry ingredients and mix just until blended. Divide batter among loaf pans. Bake for 45 to 50 minutes or until a toothpick inserted in the center comes out clean. Cool on a rack and loosen sides of loaves to remove from pans. Freezes well.

Yield: 5 mini loaves or 40 servings

The Inn at Harbor Hill Marina
60 Grand Street
Niantic, Connecticut 06357
860-739-0331
www.innharborhill.com

ARISE EACH MORNING TO panoramic views of the picturesque marina in the Niantic River harbor. Tucked away from the hustle and bustle of everyday life and in pure New England style, this traditional, early 1900s, waterside inn provides an amazing experience for the senses. Your hosts are Dave and Sue Labrie, who say: "As our guests, we promise you our own gracious hospitality and indulgent pampering." Sail the Seven Seas at this seaside bed and breakfast and experience classic water views to entertain you, comfortable rooms to relax you, candlelit breakfasts to pleasure you, charming gardens to entice you, culinary treats to tempt you, and cozy porches to enfold you, all while you collect memories to take with you.

The Millsaps Buie House
628 North State Street
Jackson, Mississippi 39202
601-352-0221
www.millsapsbuiehouse.com

A SPLENDID SOUTHERN welcome awaits you at this stately Queen Anne mansion, a Victorian landmark that has remained in the same Mississippi family for four generations. At the Millsaps Buie House, the 19th-century grandeur of spacious high ceilings, elegant millwork, and glowing stained glass meets the 21st century amenities of a small luxury hotel—all just steps away from Jackson's historic state capitol. With 11 distinctively appointed guest rooms, and a sumptuous hot breakfast, the Millsaps Buie House hosts loyal business travelers and romantic weekend visitors. Both return again and again, and they're always welcomed back like treasured friends of the family.

Hearty Bran Muffins

2   cups boiling water
2   cups 100% bran flakes
3   cups sugar
1   cup plus 2 tablespoons shortening
4   eggs, beaten
1   quart buttermilk
5   cups all-purpose flour
5   teaspoons baking soda
1   teaspoon salt
4   cups All-Bran cereal

Preheat oven to 375°F.

In a large bowl, pour boiling water over bran flakes and mix in remaining ingredients in the order given. Store in refrigerator; use batter as needed. Will keep for 2 weeks. Bake in greased muffin tins at for 15 to 20 minutes.

Yield: 24 to 36 muffins

Honey-Corn Muffins

2 boxes Jiffy cornbread/muffin mix (or any
   cornbread/muffin mix)
1 can cream style corn

HONEY BUTTER
½ cup butter
½ cup honey

Follow directions on box for preparing cornbread. Stir corn into batter. Bake according to directions on box. In a small saucepan, melt the butter and stir honey in. When muffins are done, remove from oven and while still hot, brush on lots of honey butter.

Yield: 12 to 15 muffins

St. Francis Inn
279 St. George Street
St. Augustine, Florida 32084
904-824-6068
www.stfrancisinn.com

OCATED IN ST. AUGUSTINE Antiqua, the restored historic district of the nation's oldest city, this St. Augustine bed-and-breakfast inn is rich in old world charm and modern comforts. The inn has a swimming pool and provides complimentary bicycles for touring historic downtown St. Augustine. (A walk through St. Augustine's historic district is not to be missed.) Individually decorated rooms and suites, many with antiques, fireplaces, and Jacuzzis, are nestled in a walled courtyard. A swimming pool, private balconies, full gourmet breakfasts, and evening socials add to the ambience.

Sylvan Lake Resort

24572 South Dakota Highway 87
Custer, South Dakota 57730
605-574-2561
www.custerresorts.com

*L*OCATED IN THE NORTHERN tip of Custer State Park, this resort inn overlooks the scenic Black Elk Wilderness Area and is bordered by the spired granite rock formations that highlight the Needles Highway. The original lodge burned down from unknown causes, and in 1936 the present lodge was constructed. The fresh pine-scented air, the crystal-clear waters of Sylvan Lake, and the magnificent view of Harney Peak from the rock patio are amenities unique to Sylvan Lake Resort. There is gourmet dining in the lodge's dining room under the supervision of executive chef Charles Etzrodt.

Indian Fry Bread

5	cups all-purpose flour
10	teaspoons baking powder
4	tablespoons sugar
1/2	teaspoon salt
2	tablespoons olive oil
2	eggs, beaten
2	cups water

Sift together flour, salt, sugar, and baking powder. In a separate bowl mix oil, eggs, and water. Add dry ingredients to wet ingredients and mix well. Knead dough for 3 minutes. Turn out on floured surface and roll to 3/4-inch thickness. Cut into large triangular pieces. Cover tightly in plastic wrap with parchment paper in between and refrigerate until needed. Fry the bread in hot oil until brown.

Yield: 8 servings

Irish Soda Bread

〰〰〰〰〰〰〰〰

5 cups flour
1 cup sugar
1 tablespoon baking powder
1 teaspoon baking soda
1½ teaspoons salt
1 stick unsalted butter, at room temperature, cut into squares
3 cups raisins
3 to 4 tablespoons caraway seeds
2½ cups buttermilk
1 large egg
2 tablespoons butter, melted

Preheat oven to 350°F. Cut parchment paper to fit in ovenproof skillet that is about 12 inches in diameter with 2- to 3-inch sides. Place parchment in skillet and butter it.

In a large bowl, whisk together flour, sugar, baking powder, baking soda, and salt. Use your hands to add butter and rub together with dry ingredients until the mixture resembles coarse crumbs. Stir in caraway seeds and raisins.

In a separate bowl, whisk together buttermilk and egg. Add to the dough in the big bowl and stir with a wooden spoon until well incorporated. Transfer the sticky dough to prepared skillet. Smooth out the top so the dough forms a slight mound in the center.

Put a slit in the top of the dough to air while baking. Drizzle melted butter on top and bake for about an hour or so. The bread is cooked when a tester or fork comes out clean after gently piercing the center. Let cool in the skillet for about 15 minutes, and then carefully remove bread from the skillet and let cool completely on a rack.

Yield: 12 servings

Inn at Sunrise Point
P. O. Box 1344
Camden, Maine 04843
207-236-7716
www.srinns.com/sunrisepoint

A PAMPERING SEASIDE haven, this bed-and-breakfast inn offers spectacular ocean views and all the luxuries you should expect. The Inn at Sunrise Point is set within a secluded, 4½-acre oceanfront hideaway and just minutes from picturesque Camden. Sleep soundly in the wonderful sea air, comforted by the gentle murmur of waves outside your window. Awaken to the breathtaking sight of the sunrise across Penobscot Bay before enjoying a complimentary gourmet breakfast in the inn's bright conservatory or ocean room. Later, browse in the cherry-paneled library with a glass of fine wine and select a good book.

Los Poblanos Inn

4803 Rio Grande Boulevard NW
Albuquerque, New Mexico 87107
505-344-9297
www.lospoblanos.com

S ET AMONG 25 ACRES OF lavender fields and lush formal gardens, Los Poblanos Inn is one of the most prestigious historic properties in the Southwest. The inn was designed by the region's foremost architect, John Gaw Meem, "the Father of Santa Fe Style," and is listed on both the New Mexico and national registers of historic places. Guest rooms are in a classic New Mexican style with kiva fireplaces, carved ceiling beams, hardwood floors, and antique New Mexican furnishings. Guests can relax around the Spanish hacienda–style courtyard or spend hours exploring the property's extensive gardens and organic farm. Detailed tours highlight the property's cultural, political, agricultural, and architectural history.

Lavender-Lemon-Blueberry Muffins

MUFFINS
1 **cup sugar**
1 **stick butter**
2 **large eggs**
1 **teaspoon vanilla**
2 **teaspoons lemon zest**
2 **cups flour**
2 **teaspoons baking powder**
1/4 **teaspoon salt**
1/2 **cup milk**
1 **teaspoon Provence lavender blossoms, dried and crushed**
2 **cups blueberries**

GLAZE
Juice of 1 lemon
1/2 **cup sugar**

Preheat oven to 350°F.

In large mixer bowl, mix together sugar and butter. Add eggs, one at a time. Add vanilla and lemon zest. Sift together flour, baking powder, and salt in a separate bowl. Add the dry ingredients to the wet mixture a little at a time (by hand) alternating with milk, until just moistened. Fold in lavender blossoms and blueberries. Do not overmix. Spoon batter into greased muffin cups until 3/4 full. Bake for 25 to 30 minutes until golden brown.

In a small bowl, whisk lemon juice and sugar together to form a glaze. Pour over muffins while warm. Let cool. Remove from tin.

Yield: 12 muffins

Lemon Bread

¾ cup shortening
1½ cups sugar
3 eggs
2¼ cups flour
¼ teaspoon baking soda
¼ teaspoon salt
¾ cup buttermilk
Grated zest of 1 lemon
¾ cup chopped nuts

GLAZE
¾ cup sugar
Juice of 1 lemon

Preheat oven to 350°F. Grease 3 regular-sized loaf pans.

In a large bowl, cream shortening and sugar. Beat in eggs. In another bowl, combine the flour, baking soda, and salt. Add to the egg-sugar mixture. Stir in buttermilk, then add lemon zest and nuts. Divide batter among the loaf pans. Bake for 30 to 35 minutes.

In a small bowl, stir together the sugar and lemon juice to make a glaze. While bread is still warm, drizzle over the loaves.

Yield: 3 loaves

Historic Anderson House
333 Main Street West
Wabasha, Minnesota 55981
651-565-2500
www.historicandersonhouse.com

The Historic Anderson House is a true step back into yesterday. Most of the furniture dates back to the inn's opening in 1856. This is the oldest operating country inn west of the Mississippi. The present innkeepers, Teresa and Mike Smith, are keeping Grandma Anderson's personality and plans in place, though it has been years since she purchased and ran the hotel. Her remarkable knowledge of food is still the cornerstone of the inn's success. The ever-filled cookie jar is still present at the front desk. Grandma's famous chicken noodle soup, Dutch cinnamon rolls, and chicken and dumplings still lend great interest and excitement to the daily menus. As in Grandma's day, shoes left outside the door are meticulously shined. Cold feet will produce a hot brick for your bed, carefully presented in a quilted envelope.

Historic American River Inn

Main and Orleans Streets
Georgetown, California 95643
1-800-245-6566
www.americanriverinn.com

S TEP BACK IN TIME AT THIS historic Queen Anne– style bed-and-breakfast inn, complete with old-fashioned hospitality and early 1900s antique furnishings. The Historic American River Inn, with its elegant country-Victorian guest rooms and suites, creates a sense of nostalgia and serenity for its guests. Each morning of your stay, after a comfortable night's rest on an antique feather bed with down comforter you will be treated to a gormet breakfast by the gracious innkeepers. The Historic American River Inn stands in all its splendor amidst the towering pines and fresh mountain air of the Sierra Nevada, ever basking in its Gold Rush glory, always beckoning and delighting guests.

Lemon-Date-Pecan Muffins

½ cup brown sugar
6 tablespoons unsalted butter
5 tablespoons lemon juice
¼ cup honey
½ cup sour cream
1 egg
1 tablespoon grated lemon zest
1¼ cups flour
1½ teaspoons baking powder
½ teaspoon baking soda
¼ teaspoon salt
1 cup chopped dates
1 cup chopped pecans
¼ cup hot water

Preheat oven to 400°F.

Combine brown sugar, butter, lemon juice, and honey in a saucepan until hot. Whisk sour cream, egg, and lemon zest together in a bowl. Whisk in brown sugar mixture. Combine flour, baking powder, baking soda, and salt in another bowl and stir into wet ingredients. Add dates, pecans, and hot water and stir until blended. Bake for 20 minutes in 14 buttered muffin cups.

Yield: 14 muffins

Mango Bread

4 eggs
1 cup shortening
2 cups sugar
2 teaspoons baking soda
2 cups mango pulp
4 cups flour
1 cup macadamia nuts or walnuts, chopped (optional)

Preheat oven to 350°F. Spray two large loaf pans with nonstick spray.

In a bowl, mix together all ingredients. Pour half of batter into each pan. Bake for 50 minutes to 1 hour. The juicier the mango pulp, the longer it may take to bake. Insert a toothpick deep into the middle to see if there is still unbaked batter in the center. Serve hot or cold.

Yield: 2 large loaves

Penny's Place Inn Paradise Bed and Breakfast
1440 Front Street
Lahaina, Maui, Hawaii 96761
808-661-1068
www.pennysplace.net

Penny's Place Inn Paradise Bed and Breakfast is located on the island of Maui on world-famous Front Street in historic Old Lahaina Town. Set just 150 feet from the water's edge, the inn offers ocean views of Lana'i, Moloka'i, and the leeward beaches of Lahaina, and of the Kaanapali Resort and golf-course area. Guests can relax and talk on the large balcony or in the Victorian turret. As each new day begins and as the sun rises over the pineapple fields, you can enjoy a complimentary breakfast served in the first-level of the turret. The "ono grinds," as the locals would say, include a selection of fresh island fruits (some from our own trees), Kona coffee, teas, juices, pastries, breads, island jams, and cereals and is served every day except Sunday.

Hickory Bridge Farm
96 Hickory Bridge Road
Orrtanna, Pennsylvania 17353
1-800-642-1766; 717-642-5261
www.hickorybridgefarm.com

A QUAINT COUNTRY retreat offering farmhouse-style accommodations, Hickory Bridge Farm offers five bedrooms (some with whirlpool baths) and four private cottages with fireplaces. Dinner is served in a beautiful restored Pennsylvania barn decorated with hundreds of antiques. All meals are farm fresh and bountiful. A full, hot country breakfast is served every day except on Sunday when an extended continental breakfast is taken to guests' rooms. The farm is located 9 miles west of Gettysburg, Pennsylvania, on 75 beautiful acres along a mountain stream—a wonderful place to relax while visiting Gettysburg or antiquing in the area.

Old-Fashioned Potato Bread

1	medium-size potato, cut into pieces
2	packages dry yeast
2	tablespoons butter or margarine
2	tablespoons sugar
2	teaspoons salt
1	cup milk, slightly warm
5½ to 6	cups flour

Cook potato in a saucepan in small amount of water until tender; drain and reserve liquid. Mash potato and measure ¾ cup; set aside. Add enough water to reserved liquid to make 1 cup; cool to 105 to 115°F. In a large mixing bowl, dissolve yeast in potato liquid. Add butter and stir well. Stir in sugar, salt, milk, mashed potatoes, and 1 cup flour. Gradually stir in enough flour to make a stiff dough. Turn dough out onto a floured surface and knead until smooth and elastic, about 8 minutes. Place in a well-greased bowl, turning to grease the top. Cover and let rise in a warm place free from drafts for 1 hour or until doubled.

Punch down dough, divide it in half, and shape each piece into a loaf. Place in 2 well-greased 8 x 4 x 3-inch loaf pans. Cover and let rise until doubled, about 30 minutes. Preheat oven to 375°F. Bake for 25 minutes or until loaves sound hollow when tapped.

Yield: 2 loaves

Orange-Blossom Muffins

2 eggs, slightly beaten
1/2 cup sugar
1/4 cup oil
1/2 cup orange juice concentrate, undiluted
1/2 cup water
2 packages biscuit mix (We use Biskits)
1/4 cup Smucker's Orange Marmalade
1/2 cup chopped pecans

TOPPING

2 cups granulated sugar
1 cup brown sugar
1 cup white flour
3/4 cup butter
1/2 cup crushed pecans

Preheat oven to 425°F. Grease muffin pans.

Combine first 5 ingredients. Add sifted biscuit mix. Stir in marmalade and pecans; fill muffin cups 2/3 full. Mix topping ingredients together and sprinkle generously on top of muffin batter. Bake for 10 minutes or until brown. Be sure to use small muffin tins.

Yield: 12 muffins

Excelsior House
211 West Austin Street
Jefferson, Texas 75657
903-665-2513
www.theexcelsiorhouse.com

THIS SPLENDID INN HAS BEEN in continuous operation since the 1850s. It was restored in 1961 by the Jessie Allen Wise Garden Club. The brick-and-timber structure was built by Captain William Perry. It has 14 rooms, each furnished in period furniture and featuring museum-quality antiques. The Presidential Suite features a pair of lavishly appointed rooms, each named for former guests, presidents Ulysses S. Grant and Rutherford B. Hayes. The huge ballroom and magnificent dining room are crowned by two large French Sevres chandeliers. Delicious food is served in the dining room.

The Inn at Stockbridge
Route 7, Box 618
Stockbridge, Massachusetts 01262
413-298-3337
www.stockbridgeinn.com

HE INN AT STOCKBRIDGE has been welcoming friends, both old and new, with warmth and hospitality since 1906. Stockbridge is the heart of the Berkshires, a lovely town described by Norman Rockwell as "the best of America, best of New England." Secluded on 12 peaceful acres among stately oaks and towering pines, the inn is truly an oasis from the hectic, outside world, where one can contemplate the stillness of the country yet enjoy celebrated shops, restaurants, and galleries. Antiques, collectibles, and luxury are very much at home in this 1906 Georgian-style mansion. Awaken to the aroma of freshly brewed coffee and enjoy a homemade, breakfast in the formal dining room.

Orange-Blueberry Bread

1½ cups all-purpose flour
2 teaspoons baking powder
½ teaspoon salt
1 stick butter, at room temperature
¾ cup sugar
2 large eggs
    Grated zest of 1 large orange
½ cup fresh orange juice
1 tablespoon vanilla extract
1 cup blueberries

GLAZE
⅓ cup orange juice
⅓ cup sugar

Preheat oven to 350°F. Coat 9 x 5 x 3-inch loaf pan with vegetable spray.

Thoroughly mix flour, baking powder, and salt in medium bowl. Cream butter and sugar in large bowl of an electric mixer for 3 minutes or until light and fluffy. Beat in eggs, one at a time, then orange zest, orange juice, and vanilla. On low speed, blend in dry ingredients for only a few seconds or until not quite combined. Fold in blueberries with rubber spatula just until combined. DO NOT OVERMIX. Spoon batter into prepared pan, smoothing it on top. Bake for 1 hour or until tester comes out clean.

Meanwhile, for the glaze stir orange juice and sugar together until sugar is dissolved. When bread is removed from oven, pierce top in several places with toothpick. Stir glaze and slowly drizzle over bread. Allow it to cool in pan for 20 minutes. Turn out onto rack and serve warm or at room temperature.

Yields: 1 loaf

Pineapple Nut Bread

4 eggs
2/3 cup sugar
2/3 cup melted shortening
4 cups flour
6 teaspoons baking powder
2 teaspoons salt
1½ cups chopped pecans
2 cups crushed pineapple, undrained

Preheat oven to 350°F.

In a large bowl, beat eggs and sugar together. Stir in shortening. Add flour, baking powder, and salt; blend. Add nuts and pineapple, stirring just enough to combine. Pour batter equally into two loaf pans. Bake for 1 hour.

Yield: 2 loaves

My Blue Heaven
1041 Fifth Street
Pawnee City, Nebraska 68420
402-852-3131

LEGEND HAS IT THAT THE town of Pawnee City is on the exact spot where the largest village of the Pawnee Indians was located. The name "Pawnee" was supposedly derived from the word "pony," and the Pawnee were known as "the tribe of many ponies." Visitors flock to My Blue Heaven for small-town hospitality and all the comforts of home, including bountiful breakfasts.

Hope-Merrill House

P. O. Box 42
Geyserville, California 95441
707-857-3356
www.hope-inns.com

THE HOPE-MERRILL HOUSE, a vintage Victorian inn welcomes travelers in grand style to the California wine country. The inn is a striking example of the Eastlake stick-style Victorian architecture popular between 1870 and 1885. It is noted for its major architectural, cultural, and historical significance and is now listed in Sonoma County Landmarks Register. Built entirely of redwood, it has the original quarter-sawn oak graining on all doors and woodwork. The stunning silk-screened wallpapers lighten the house, and a variety of bold, striking motifs accent each room. The dining room is where guests gather for a five-course country breakfast.

Popovers

4	tablespoons Crisco
4	eggs
2	cups whole milk or half-and-half
2	cups unbleached all-purpose flour, sifted
2	teaspoons sugar
¼	teaspoon salt
2	tablespoons butter, melted

Preheat oven to 450°F. Prepare a popover pan or 8 custard cups. Place ½ tablespoon of Crisco into each cup and place in oven while preparing batter.

In a mixing bowl or blender combine the eggs, milk, flour, sugar, and salt, and whisk or blend just until well combined. Stir in the melted butter. Remove popover pans from the oven and fill cups about three-quarters full. Bake until golden brown and firm to the touch, about 35 minutes. If you prefer drier interiors, remove the popovers from the pans or cups and replace them at an angle. Pierce each with a skewer, turn off the heat, and let them stand in the oven, with the door ajar, for about 8 minutes. When done, serve immediately.

Yield: 8 large popovers

Note: The secret to successful popovers is very hot popover pans and not skimping on Crisco or butter. For maximum puffiness, avoid overbeating the batter or opening the oven door until the popovers are almost done. Serve piping hot with plenty of butter and jam or honey.

Pumpkin Bread or Muffins

Seaward Inn
44 Marmion Way
Rockport, Massachusetts 01966
978-546-3471
www.seawardinn.com

²/₃ cup margarine

2²/₃ cups sugar

4 eggs

1 (15-ounce) can pumpkin puree

²/₃ cup water

3¹/₃ cups sifted flour

¹/₂ teaspoon baking powder

2 teaspoons baking soda

1¹/₂ teaspoons salt

1 teaspoon ground cinnamon

1 teaspoon ground cloves

¹/₄ teaspoon ground ginger

¹/₄ teaspoon nutmeg

²/₃ cup chopped nuts, raisins, or dates (optional)

For bread, preheat oven to 350°F grease and flour two 9 x 5-inch loaf pans. For muffins, preheat oven to 400°F and grease muffin tins.

In a bowl, cream margarine and sugar. Add eggs one at a time, beating well after each addition. Add pumpkin purée and water. Sift together flour, baking powder, baking soda, salt, cinnamon, cloves, ginger, and nutmeg. Stir into pumpkin mixture. Stir in nuts or fruit. Pour equal amounts of batter into each loaf pan. Bake for 1 hour. For muffins, fill muffin tins two-thirds full and bake for 25 minutes.

Yield: 2 loaves or 40 to 45 muffins

SEAWARD INN IS BEAUTI-fully situated on one of Cape Ann's peninsulas, with the ocean just off its doorstep. New England's famous rocky coast, with the rise and fall of the tide, presents an ever-changing panorama of sea, clouds, and light. Guests enjoy this outlook from lawn chairs at the edge of the shore. Across the front of the inn is a large, glass-enclosed garden terrace. Spacious grounds, including lawns interspaced with rock gardens, flower gardens, and shrubs and trees provide a relaxing atmosphere. Interesting and varied meals are carefully prepared and served.

Sea Witch Manor Inn

71 Lake Avenue
Rehoboth Beach, Delaware 19971
302-226-9482
www.bewitchedbandb.com

A CLASSIC VICTORIAN, THIS adults-only bed-and-breakfast strives to offer everything the discriminating traveler has come to expect: elegance, quiet, charm, hospitality, comfort, and attention to details. The Sea Witch Manor sits on a beautiful, quiet, tree-lined street that meets the sea in historic downtown Rehoboth Beach. It's a romantic year-round getaway with delicious food, exquisite accommodations, and an ambience that marries character and comfort. Delightfully decorated with antiques and period furnishings, the Sea Witch Manor Inn is a feast for all senses.

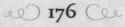
Pumpkin-Ginger Scones

- ½ cup sugar, divided
- 2 cups all-purpose flour
- 2 teaspoons baking powder
- 1 teaspoon ground cinnamon
- ½ teaspoon baking soda
- ½ teaspoon salt
- 5 tablespoons butter
- 1 egg
- ½ cup solid pack pumpkin, packed
- ¼ cup sour cream
- ¼ cup finely chopped crystallized ginger

Preheat oven to 425°F.

Set aside 1 tablespoon of sugar. Combine remaining sugar, flour, baking powder, cinnamon, baking soda, and salt in large bowl. Cut in 4 tablespoons of the butter with pastry blender or 2 knives until mixture resembles coarse crumbs. Beat egg in small bowl; add pumpkin, sour cream, and ginger. Beat until well blended. Add pumpkin mixture to flour mixture and stir until soft dough forms. Turn out dough onto well-floured surface; knead 10 times. Roll out dough into 9 x 6-inch rectangle with a lightly floured rolling pin. Cut dough into six 3-inch squares with a lightly floured knife. Cut each square diagonally in half, making 12 triangles. Place triangles 2 inches apart on ungreased baking sheet.

Melt remaining 1 tablespoon butter. Brush triangles with butter, sprinkle with reserved sugar, and bake 10 to 12 minutes or until golden brown and a wooden pick inserted in center comes out clean. Cool on wire rack 10 minutes. Serve warm or completely cooled.

Yield: 12 scones

Refrigerator Angel Biscuits

1 package dry yeast
½ cup warm water
5 cups flour
3 tablespoons sugar
1 tablespoon baking powder
1 teaspoon baking soda
1 teaspoon salt
2 cups buttermilk
¾ cup plus 2 tablespoons shortening

Preheat oven to 375°F.

Dissolve yeast in the warm water and let stand 10 minutes. Sift flour, sugar, baking powder, baking soda, and salt into a large bowl. Cut in the shortening. Stir in buttermilk and dissolved yeast. Work only until well moistened. Do not overmix. Put in a large covered plastic container and refrigerate until ready to use (it will keep for a week). Take out only as much as needed. Carefully roll ½- to ¾-inch thick on a well-floured surface. Cut with 2½-inch biscuit cutter. Bake for 12 minutes.

Yield: 4 dozen biscuits

Arch Cape House (formerly St. Bernards)
3 East Ocean Lane
Cannon Beach, Oregon 97102
503-436-2800

THE ARCH CAPE HOUSE IS located between a forest and the sea, and most of the rooms have an ocean view. Formal floral gardens add to the natural beauty of the inn. The interior provides the elegance of a castle decorated with European antiques. Two great state parks are nearby, as well as a long white-sand beach. Kayaking and horseback riding are available.

Sachem Bed & Breakfast
508 West Main Street
Baldwyn, Mississippi 38824
662-365-9586
sachem@bellsouth.net

ACHEM BED & BREAKFAST is located just minutes away from many Mississippi Civil War attractions and close to Tupelo's many other attractions. Sachem is a large Southern home, and large oak trees provide welcome shade on those warm summer evenings. A large, spacious front porch lets one relax and enjoy the unceasing song of the katydids in the wild and magic nighttime. Guests will find a warm greeting and each morning wake to a great home-cooked breakfast, including bacon, eggs, waffles with special syrup, and always sweet bread—sometimes international style.

Aunt Tess's Butterhorns, and Rolls

5½ cups flour
1 cup margarine
½ cup sugar (for sweet bread, see below)
1 teaspoon salt
1½ cups warm water
2 packages dry yeast
3 eggs, beaten
    Grated rind of 1 lemon
    Butter and cinnamon (for butterhorns)

Combine all ingredients. For sweet bread mix well and refrigerate overnight. If making rolls, use only 1 tablespoon of the sugar. Cover with a wet towel overnight to keep dough moist and refrigerate overnight.

Preheat oven to 350°F.

Divide dough into 8 portions and roll out. Cut dough into triangles to make curves for butterhorns. For butterhorns, add butter and cinnamon to rolled out dough. After rolling out dough, let rise to double in size. Bake until golden (about 20 minutes).

Yield: 3 dozen

The Great Country Inns of America Cookbook

Spoon Bread in a Mug
with Glazed Apple Slices

SPOON BREAD

¾ cup stone-ground cornmeal (preferably white)
1 cup cold water
⅓ pound regular sausage
¼ pound hot sausage
2 tablespoons minced scallions
2 cups buttermilk
3 eggs, beaten
⅓ cup freshly grated Parmesan cheese
¾ teaspoon salt
1 tablespoon sugar

GLAZED APPLES

¼ cup sugar
2 Golden Delicious apples, each cut into 8 wedges

Preheat oven to 375°F. Grease 4 ovenproof mugs.

To make the spoon bread: In a small bowl, stir together cornmeal and water. Set aside. Brown and break up sausage. While sausage is browning, beat together the scallions, buttermilk, eggs, cheese, salt, and sugar. In a saucepan, bring an additional 1 cup water to boil. Quickly add the cornmeal mixture, whisking continuously. Cook until very thick, 2 to 4 minutes. Remove from stove and add sausage and buttermilk mixture. Blend well. Spoon batter into mugs, filling them three-quarters full. Sprinkle with additional Parmesan. Bake for 30 to 35 minutes until lightly browned and puffy.

Recipe continued on next page

The Loghouse & Homestead
P.O. Box 130
Vergas, Minnesota 56587
218-342-2318
www.loghousebb.com

THE LOGHOUSE & Homestead is one of Minnesota's 10 favorite bed-and-breakfasts. Luxury, pampering, and privacy are its hallmarks. Three miles of hiking trails wind through the hills, fields, and maple woods of the Homestead's 115-acre property—all adjacent to nearly a mile of private wooded lakeshore. Canoes, rowboats, lawn games, and snowshoes offer guests the best of Minnesota's seasonal activities. Skiers with their own equipment can break trail on lake or land. This bed-and-breakfast boasts a multitude of amenities, including in-room fireplaces, whirlpools for two, luxury linens, and private breakfasts. All five guest rooms have balconies or porches with lake views. Elegant and romantic, it is a perfect place for honeymoons and weddings.

To prepare apples: While mugs are baking melt sugar in a nonstick pan over moderately high heat. Add apples. Stir quickly with 2 forks until apples are coated and are browned. Don't overcook.

To serve, garnish mugs with a sprig of parsley. Loop a small napkin through the handle for easy handling and place on a plate with 4 apple wedges.

Yield: 4 servings

Strawberry-Nut Bread

6 eggs, beaten

2 cups salad oil

3 cups sugar

2 teaspoons vanilla extract

4 cups frozen strawberries, thawed and mashed, not drained

6 cups flour

2 teaspoons baking soda

½ teaspoon baking powder

2 teaspoons salt

1 cup chopped walnuts or pecans

Preheat oven to 325°F. Grease 4 loaf pans.

In a large bowl, combine eggs, oil, sugar, and vanilla. Beat well. Add strawberries. Combine dry ingredients and gradually add to strawberry mixture. Stir in nuts. Pour into loaf pans and bake for 1 hour or until pick inserted in center comes out clean.

Yield: 4 loaves

The Queen Victoria
102 Ocean Street
Cape May, New Jersey 08204
609-884-8702
www.queenvictoria.com

THE QUEEN VICTORIA IS A renowned bed-and-breakfast in the center of historic Cape May, New Jersey, one block from the beautiful Cape May beaches, antique shopping, gourmet dining, and historic Cape May tours. Twenty-one inviting and romantic rooms and suites with private baths are decorated with period antiques in the Victorian style and the tradition of a historic Cape May bed-and-breakfast. Inn stays include a full breakfast and a delicious afternoon tea with sweets and savories in the British fashion.

Publick House

227 Main Street
Sturbridge, Massachusetts 01566
508-347-3313
www.publickhouse.com

WHEN COLONEL EBENEZER Crafts founded this famous inn in 1771, America was an English colony. The original building was a tavern and a pub. Not much has changed since the inn's beginnings, which is extremely pleasing to the owners and the thousands who visit. A strong feeling of history permeates the structure. The most famous of the famous have walked through the front door for more than 200 years. Always present is the magnificent aroma of delicious food being prepared. The inn is located on the common of the colorful town of Sturbridge.

Sweet Rolls

- 2 **cups milk, scalded**
- 3 **tablespoons sugar**
- 1/2 **stick butter**
- 1 **teaspoon salt**
- 1 **envelope or cake of yeast**
- 1/3 **cup lukewarm water**
- 2 **eggs, beaten**
- 5 **cups all-purpose flour**
- 2 **cups chopped pecans**

SWEET ROLL BUTTER
- 8 **ounces brown sugar**
- 2 **ounces butter, softened**
- 2 **ounces margarine, softened**
- 2 **ounces corn syrup**
- 3/4 **ounce honey**

In a large bowl, combine milk, sugar, butter, and salt and stir; let cool. Soften yeast in lukewarm water and add to milk mixture. Beat in eggs and add flour gradually. Turn out on a lightly floured surface and knead until smooth and not sticky. Place dough in a buttered bowl, brush with melted butter and cover with a towel. Let rise in a warm place 2 hours or until doubled in bulk.

While the dough is rising, prepare the sweet roll butter by combining all the ingredients in a bowl.

Punch dough and roll out with a rolling pin into a long narrow strip about 3 to 4 inches wide. Sprinkle top of dough with a mixture of sugar and cinnamon (9 parts sugar to 1 part cinnamon). Roll up tightly as you would a jelly roll and cut into slices about 1½ inches thick. Place a sliced roll into a greased muffin tin that has been filled with 1 tablespoon of sweet roll butter and pecans. Let rolls rise until almost double in size.

Preheat oven to 350°F. Bake rolls for 20 to 25 minutes. Remove from oven and let sit for 5 minutes. Carefully invert onto a tray large enough to hold all the rolls.

Yield: 1½ to 2 dozen rolls

MEATS

The Fearrington House
Country Inn & Restaurant

2000 Fearrington Village
Pittsboro, North Carolina 27312
919-542-2121
www.fearringtonhouse.com

*R*ETREAT TO THE
Fearrington House
Country Inn and
one of its luxuriously decorated
rooms and suites. Each of the 33 guest
rooms has been created with its own
distinct character and is surrounded
by stunning vistas of trellised gardens,
water sculptures, and manicured
English gardens. Once settled into
their intimate accommodations, inn
guests are encouraged to experience
afternoon tea, which includes a
selection of fine teas, finger
sandwiches, delicate pastries, and
fresh-baked scones with clotted cream
and strawberry jam. A gourmet
breakfast is also included, and guests
select from hearty choices such as
shrimp and grits, full English breakfast,
homemade granola, and eggs
Benedict. Southern fine dining is
available in the restaurant. An escape
to Fearrington restores and relaxes
guests. Days are spent strolling the
expansive grounds, browsing the
boutique village shops, experiencing a
soothing massage, or just relaxing on a
front-porch rocker watching a pasture
full of curious belted Galloway cows.

Braised Beef

1 (3-pound) short rib of beef
1 onion, chopped
1 carrot, chopped
1 leek, chopped
1 clove garlic, chopped
1 gallon warm beef stock

Sweat off the vegetables until brown, then place in a roasting pan. Then seal off the ribs until brown on all sides. Cover with warm stock and braise for about 2½ hours at 325°F. Check to see if they may are tender; depending on the size, whether they may need more or less time.

Yield: 6 servings

Succulent Pork Tacos

The Inn at El Canelo Ranch
P. O. Box 487
Raymondville, Texas 78580
956-689-5042
www.elcaneloranch.com

1 pound pork loin or pork tenderloin
Salt and seasoned pepper to taste
4 tablespoons olive oil, divided
¼ cup onion, cut into thin slices
1 clove garlic, mashed and minced
¼ cup green bell pepper, julienned
¼ cup red bell pepper, julienned
½ cup zucchini, julienned
½ cup yellow squash, julienned
½ cup fresh cabbage, thinly shredded
Corn tortillas

Freeze pork for about an hour to make slicing easier. Very thinly slice or shave pork. Spread on a baking sheet and sprinkle with seasoned pepper and other seasoning as desired. In a large frying pan, heat 2 tablespoons of the olive oil over medium-high heat. Add pork and stir-fry just until meat is no longer pink. Remove pork from pan, leaving excess oil in pan; keep pan hot. Add remaining 2 tablespoons olive oil to pan and heat to sizzling. Add onion and sauté for 1 minute. Add garlic and sauté for 1 minute. Add remaining vegetables and stir-fry for 2 to 3 minutes. Return pork to frying pan and stir-fry until heated through. Transfer to serving platter and serve immediately, accompanied by plenty of fresh corn tortillas, preferably homemade. Can also be served with flour tortillas, if preferred.

Yield: 6 to 8 servings

EXPERIENCE THE BEST OF BOTH worlds—savor the relaxed pace of a secluded South Texas mesquite-country ranch while enjoying luxurious accommodations and gourmet meals. Located just south of the famous King Ranch, El Canelo Ranch offers services to satisfy a variety of interests. Abundant wildlife provides opportunities for ardent sportsmen, while native and migratory birds enthrall other outdoor enthusiasts, such as bird watchers and photographers. This historic working cattle ranch has been in continuous family ownership and operation for 150 years. While still raising Texas Longhorns and registered Charolais cattle, the family offers others the opportunity to enjoy this unique ranch experience.

**Soldier Meadows
Ranch and Lodge**
16912 Mt. Rose Highway
Reno, Nevada 89511
775-849-2219
www.soldiermeadows.com

DATING BACK TO 1865, WHEN IT was known as Camp McGarry, Soldier Meadows Ranch and Lodge lies in the Black Rock Desert about three hours north of Reno. Soldier Meadows is a family owned working cattle ranch, offering lodging for family vacations, peaceful getaways, and hunting. In addition to the lodge and ranch headquarters, there are over 500,000 acres of public and private land to enjoy. You should be prepared to enjoy a few days of living history, leaving the cares of the world behind and entering another era. You don't have to ride to enjoy this ranch. Soldier Meadows makes a wonderful base camp for explorations. You may choose to go chukar or mule deer hunting, fishing, hiking, mountain biking, or 4-wheeling. The open, expansive beauty and natural hot springs are enough to rest any weary soul.

Open Barbecue–Style Tri-Tip

3	pounds beef tri-tip
2	teaspoons garlic powder
3	tablespoons Dijon-style mustard
2/3	cup bottled steak sauce
1/4	cup prepared horseradish, undrained
1 1/2	teaspoons sugar

Sprinkle garlic powder over tri-tip and then brush both sides with the mustard. Cook tri-tip over open hickory and coal fire for 7 minutes on each side twice (28 minutes total). Combine steak sauce, horseradish, and sugar. Baste tri-tip with sauce. Transfer to platter and slice with grain.

Yield: 8 servings

Edwardo's Southwestern Oven-Barbequed Spare Ribs

4 pounds country-style pork ribs
Liquid smoke
Salt and pepper
Paprika
Sauce (see below)

Preheat oven to 400°F.

Brush ribs with liquid smoke. Sprinkle salt, pepper, and paprika on both sides. Brown ribs in oven for 15 minutes on each side. Drain and add the sauce. Bake at 325°F for 1½ to 2 hours or until tender.

SAUCE

2 tablespoons vinegar (we use Cana Winery)
¼ cup lemon juice
5 tablespoons brown sugar
⅛ teaspoon cayenne pepper
1 cup Heinz ketchup
3 tablespoons Worcestershire sauce
2 tablespoons prepared mustard
1 cup water

Reduce oven to 325°F.

In a large bowl, combine all the sauce ingredients. Pour over ribs and bake for 1½ to 2 hours until tender.

Yields enough sauce for 6 to 8 country-style spareribs

Gone with the Wind Bed and Breakfast
14905 West Lake Road
Branchport, New York 14418
607-868-4603
www.gonewiththewind
onkeukalake.com

THIS STATELY STONE MANSION on a rolling hillside a hundred feet above the clear water of Keuka Lake was opened in April of 1989. Since that time Linda and Robert Lewis, innkeepers/owners, have been guiding and serving thousands of guests. Most guests walk the many trails on the 14 acres, swim the waters of the private cove, or just enjoy the tranquilizing effect of gazebo gazing as the sounds and ripples bring relaxation. Everyone enjoys chatting around the breakfast tables while they relish breakfasts of fruit, home-baked Rhett's rhubarb coffee cake, one of Aunt Pittypat's many flavors of pancakes, or Ashley's stuffed French toast.

Old Rittenhouse Inn

301 Rittenhouse Avenue
P. O. Box 584
Bayfield, Wisconsin 54814
715-779-5111
www.rittenhouseinn.com

FOUR YEARS AFTER THEIR honeymoon in Bayfield, Wisconsin, Mary and Jerry Phillips fell in love all over again. The object of their affection: a gracious Queen Anne–style mansion atop a grassy green knoll in the village of Bayfield on Lake Superior's south shore. Built in 1890, the inn features elegant Victorian dining and lodging at its very best.

Beef Stroganoff

- 3 pounds top sirloin, cubed or cut into thin strips
- 8 tablespoons butter (1 stick) or olive oil
- 2 large sweet onions, thinly sliced (about 3 cups)
- ½ cup sour cream
- 2 tablespoons tomato paste
- 1 cup slivered mushrooms
  Salt and fresh grated pepper

In a large skillet, heat butter or oil on medium-high heat. Add beef and sauté for 1 minute, turning frequently. Reduce heat to medium, add onion and sauté for 1 minute, stirring continually. Reduce heat to medium, add onion, sauté 1 minute, stirring continually. Remove from heat, transfer beef to warm bowl and keep warm. Stirring continually, combine sour cream and tomato paste in skillet until smooth. Return skillet to low heat, adding mushrooms and beef. Season to taste with salt and pepper. Heat until warm. Serve over rice or noodles.

Yield: 8 servings

Note: This is a very simple dish, requiring quickness of preparation and the freshest and best of ingredients. If you can, use wild mushrooms like morels. You may also add ¼ cup sherry or cognac.

*The Great Country Inns
of America Cookbook*

Beef Wellington
with Port Wine Sauce

Winchester
Inn and Restaurant
35 South Second Street
Ashland, Oregon 97520
541-488-1113
www.winchesterinn.com

1 (3-pound) beef tenderloin
8 (2 x 2-inch) frozen puff pastry squares, thawed

TENG DAH MARINADE
1 cup water
1 cup soy sauce
2 pinches anise, crushed
1 tablespoon horseradish
1/2 teaspoon nutmeg
1 tablespoon minced garlic
1/4 cup sugar
1/3 cup lemon juice
1/2 teaspoon cinnamon

ONCE USED AS A HOSPITAL, today this same structure is the well-known Winchester Inn, a Victorian country inn, offering lodging and full-service dining to the public. Completely renovated by the Gibbs family in 1983, the structure is on the National Register of Historic Places. It honors the past yet adapts itself to the present, an exquisite blend of comfort and tradition. The elegant dining room overlooks tiered gardens and patio seating and offers a unique, eclectic menu.

Mix all ingredients. Marinate beef in the marinade at least 8 hours or overnight.

SPINACH PINE NUT PESTO
1/2 cup olive oil, divided
2 teaspoons minced garlic
1/4 cup pine nuts
2 cups fresh spinach, washed
   Salt and pepper

Sauté garlic and pine nuts in 1 tablespoon olive oil, add spinach and sauté until limp. Purée in blender, slowly adding remaining olive oil. Salt and pepper to taste.

Recipe continued on next page

1 **cup Ruby port wine**
½ **cup heavy cream**
1 **stick butter, cut up into small pieces**

Bring port to a boil. Add heavy cream and return to a boil. Continue boiling until sauce reduces and thickens. Remove from heat, whisk in butter a small piece at a time.

Preheat oven to 400°F

To prepare the beef tenderloin: After marinating, cut the beef into 2-ounce pieces. Cut the puff pastry into 2½-inch squares. Put 1 heaping teaspoon of spinach pesto in the middle of the square. Set a 2-ounce piece of tenderloin on the spinach pesto. Wrap the tenderloin in the puff pastry, folding the edges to seal the bundle. Brush with an egg wash. Bake for 15 minutes or until gold brown.

To serve: Pour a pool of port wine sauce on a serving plate and set 3 mini Beef Wellingtons on the wine sauce.

Yeild: 8 servings of 3 pieces each

Low-Fat Cajun Turkey Meatloaf

4½ pounds ground turkey
  3 large onions, chopped
1½ cups fresh bread crumbs
1½ cups fresh parsley, chopped
  9 large cloves garlic, chopped
  3 tablespoons plus 6 teaspoons Cajun seasoning
       (your favorite)
  3 lightly beaten egg whites
  3 teaspoons ground cumin
     Salt and pepper to taste
     Spicy mustard to taste

Preheat oven to 350°F.

In a large bowl, combine all ingredients except the mustard. Divide mixture among three 9 x 5-inch loaf pans. Cover with foil and bake for 20 minutes. Remove foil, spread top of loaves with spicy mustard and bake uncovered for another 35 minutes. Let meatloaf stand in pans 10 minutes, then remove from pans and cut into slices.

Yield: 25 servings

**The Seal Beach
Inn and Gardens**
212 5th Street
Seal Beach, California 90740
1-800-HIDEAWAY
www.sealbeachinn.com

THE FINELY APPOINTED SEAL Beach Inn and Gardens in Seal Beach is one of Southern California's finest country inns. This historic, exquisitely renovated bed-and-breakfast brings romance and quiet mystique to your lodging experience. Offering an elegant spirit of place, the inn envelops a peaceful brick courtyard that features lush garden niches, European fountains, colorful and fragrant flowers, ornate ironwork, and handsome furnishings. Suites and rooms are beautiful, comfortable, and individually unique. The inn is just 300 yards from the beach and three blocks from restaurants and shops.

TLC Bed & Breakfast

9330 Wilson Road
Pilot Point, Texas 76258
972-814-1125
1-877-391-1642
www.tlcbandb.com

T O QUOTE OWNER/ innkeeper Chad Giesting: "Welcome to TLC Bed & Breakfast. You have finally found the best scrapbooking retreat for your group in northeast Texas. This enchanting two-story ranch is set up perfectly for scrapbooking or other group retreats. Our five charming bedrooms and memory-making room are catered to make your retreats as comfortable as possible. Only one hour from most anywhere in the Dallas or Fort Worth areas and two hours from Oklahoma City, TLC is very accessible. Yet it is tucked far enough away to allow you to thoroughly relax for a one-of-a-kind weekend away to create your memories."

Cavatini

1½ pounds ground beef
1 (32-ounce) jar of your favorite spaghetti sauce (we prefer Ragu Thick & Hearty)
1½ cups uncooked pasta (we use three different kinds, the smaller the pasta, the better)
1 package Hormel sliced pepperoni
12 ounces shredded Mozzarella cheese

Preheat oven to 350°F.

In a large frying pan, brown beef and drain off fat. Add sauce and season to taste. Cook pasta according to package direction and drain. Combine pasta and sauce mixture in a 13 x 9-inch baking dish. Smooth mixture out, top with pepperoni, and then cheese. Bake for 45 minutes or until cheese is completely melted. You can cover and refrigerate before baking if needed.

Yield: 6 to 8 servings

Delicious Ham Hash

12 pounds new red potatoes, cut into ¼-inch pieces
3 sticks butter
6 cups diced onion
3 pounds ham steak, cut into ¼-inch pieces
1½ cups chopped fresh parsley

Put potatoes in a pan of water and bring to a boil. Boil for 2 minutes, then drain. Melt butter in a skillet. Add onion and sauté. Then add ham pieces and potatoes. Simmer gently 5 minutes. Toss with parsley before serving.

Yield: 25 servings

The Inn at Cedar Falls
21190 State Route 374
Logan, Ohio 43138
1-800-653-2557; 740-385-7489
www.innatcedarfalls.com

ARTISTICALLY PREPARED dinners are served daily in the restaurant's 1840 log cabins. Antique-appointed guest rooms in a barn-like structure have rockers and writing desks and offer sweeping views of meadows, woods, and wildlife. There are quaint cottages ideal for two, or secluded, fully equipped 19th-century log cabins accommodating up to four. The rugged and beautiful Hocking Hills State Park, with glorious caves and waterfalls, flanks the inn's 75 acres on three sides. A variety of cooking classes, wine tastings, and patio parties are scheduled year round.

English Rose Inn

195 Vermont Route 242
Montgomery Center, Vermont 05471
802-326-3232
1-888-303-3232
www.englishroseinnvermont.com

THE ENGLISH ROSE INN IS nestled within the gorgeous Green Mountains of Vermont, a location providing a beautiful backdrop for any occasion. The inn offers warm, luxurious accommodations, fine dining at Paddington's Restaurant, and spectacular mountain views. You will enjoy a pleasurable, romantic, Victorian getaway in the 25-room 1850s farmhouse, which features 14 beautifully decorated guest rooms and suites. Lace curtains, hardwood floors, and crocheted and homemade heirloom quilts adorn the antique-filled rooms.

English Shepherd's Pie

5 large potatoes
2 tablespoons butter
¼ cup milk or whipping cream
   Salt and pepper
1 pound lean ground beef
1 large tomato, chopped
6 mushrooms, sliced
2 tablespoons parsley, chopped
   Dash of Worcestershire sauce
1 cup brown gravy
1 package frozen peas

Preheat oven to 400°F.

Cook potatoes in salted water; drain, cool, and peel. Mash in a large bowl with butter and milk and season to taste with salt and pepper. Set aside. Sauté beef until browned, stirring to keep meat crumbly. Season to taste with salt and pepper. Add tomatoes, mushrooms, parsley, tomato paste, Worcestershire sauce, and gravy. Stir to mix. Add peas and cook about 5 minutes. Turn mixture into casserole dish, spread potatoes evenly over meat, and bake for about 40 minutes until top is crispy brown.

Yield: 6 to 8 servings

Farm-Style Sausage Bake

Kaltenbach's
Bed and Breakfast
743 Stony Fork Road (Kelsey St)
RD #6, Box 106A
Wellsboro, Pennsylvania 16901
570-724-4954
www.pafarmstay.com/kaltenbachs

6 medium potatoes (about 2 pounds), peeled and cubed
3 or 4 green onions, sliced
2 cloves garlic, minced
2 tablespoons butter or margarine
¾ cup milk
2 egg yolks
Dash of pepper
Dash of ground nutmeg
2 tablespoons dried parsley flakes
1 pound smoked sausage, sliced
½ cup shredded Mozzarella cheese
2 tablespoons grated Parmesan cheese
1 teaspoon dried thyme or sage

Preheat oven to 400°F.

Cook potatoes in boiling, salted water until tender. Drain and transfer to a mixing bowl; mash potatoes. Add onions, garlic, butter, milk, egg yolks, pepper, and nutmeg; beat until light and fluffy. Stir in parsley, sausage, and cheeses. Spoon into a greased 2-quart baking dish. Sprinkle with thyme. Bake for 30 minutes or until lightly browned and heated through.

Yield: 6 servings

LEE KALTENBACH INVITES you to share life on this 72-acre Tioga County farm, an ideal vacation for the whole family. Nestled among the rolling hills surrounding Wellsboro in north-central Pennsylvania is a sprawling country home that provides comfortable lodging, home-style breakfast, and warm hospitality. Charming handmade quilts, heirlooms of the Kaltenbach family, are displayed throughout the inn, adding a refreshing, country atmosphere. Take a walk through meadows, pastures, and forest, which bloom with wildflowers in spring and summer and are touched by God's palette in fall.

The Manor Farm Inn

26069 Big Valley Road NE
Poulsbo, Washington 98370
360-779-4628
www.manorfarminn.com

Y OU ARE ALWAYS WELCOME at the Manor Farm Inn. The gracious innkeeper, Janet Plemmons, hopes you enjoy your picturesque tour of this delightful inn. Here, amid 25 pastoral acres tucked within gentle green hills, you will be welcomed with the warmth of a treasured friend. The century-old, weathered white farmhouse, its porches and veranda posts framed by delicate climbing rose vines, beckons you to leave behind the stressful demands of modern life and enter a simpler, slower, and softer world. Inside, you'll discover country French pine antiques rich with patina, baskets overflowing with flowers, cozy fire-lit nooks, and unpretentious charm. Accommodations are not so much rooms as private retreats. Everywhere you turn, there is beauty and serenity to renew your spirit.

Florentine Pork and Cheese

6   pork chops
    Salt and pepper
    Flour
    Oil
3   packages chopped spinach
1   cup Swiss cheese

Season pork chops to taste with salt and pepper, dredge in flour, and brown in oil until golden brown. Turn down heat and simmer 30 minutes or until tender. Cook spinach and set aside.

SAUCE

1   (10-ounce) can chicken broth
1/2 bay leaf
1   carrot, sliced
1   onion, sliced

Place ingredients in pan and bring to boil. Turn down heat and simmer 10 to 15 minutes. Set aside.

ROUX

6   tablespoons butter
6   tablespoons flour
1 3/4 cups milk

Melt butter and add flour. Cook 2 minutes, stirring constantly. Add milk and stir until thickened. Add sauce and cook until smooth.

Preheat oven to 375°F. Grease a shallow pan with butter. Put spinach in bottom of pan and lay chops on top of spinach. Cover chops with sauce and top with cheese. Cook for 15 minutes to melt and brown cheese.

Yield: 6 servings

Greek-Style Lamb Chops

4 whole lamb shanks (13 to 14 ounces each)
3 large cloves garlic, cut into slivers
   Salt and cracked pepper
2 medium onions, sliced
¾ cup virgin olive oil
¼ teaspoon dried oregano
   Pinch of cinnamon
1 pound plum tomatoes, peeled, seeded, and
   coarsely chopped
1 cup dry white wine
2 cups chicken stock
1 cup orzo
½ cup grated Kefalotori or Parmesan cheese

Preheat oven to 400°F.

With a paring knife, remove as much of the fat and sinew (tendon) from the lamb shanks as possible. Pierce the lamb shanks and insert garlic slivers into meat (3 or 4 to each shank). Salt and pepper generously. Place shanks in roasting pan just large enough to hold them. Cover with onion slices and drizzle with oil. Roast for 25 minutes.

Sprinkle meat with oregano and cinnamon. Spoon tomatoes onto each shank; pour in wine. Return to oven and roast for 45 minutes more.

Remove lamb from pan and set aside. Add chicken stock to pan and stir in orzo. Place lamb on top and return to oven. Cook until orzo is tender and has absorbed the liquid. Remove pan from oven and cover tightly with foil. Let stand 10 minutes. Serve hot with grated cheese.

Yield: 4 servings

Dockside Guest Quarters
Harris Island Road
P.O. Box 205
York, Maine 03909
207-363-2868
www.docksidegq.com

THE LUSTY FAMILY continues to celebrate many years as owners and operators of Dockside. The guest quarters have accommodations to satisfy everyone. Beginning in the "Maine House," built in the 1880s, there are beautifully restored colonial bedrooms overlooking York Harbor. Dockside is situated on its own peninsula, which provides a panorama of both the ocean and harbor activity. The Dockside dining room is adjacent to the guest quarters and has a complete and varied menu.

**High Meadows Vineyard
Inn & Restaurant**
55 High Meadows Lane
Scottsville, Virginia 24590
434-286-2218
www.highmeadows.com

THIS FAMOUS INN IS CONSID-
ered Virginia's vineyard
inn, just minutes south
of Charlottesville and just north of
historic Scottsville. The inn occupies a
grand house, where guests stay in
beautifully appointed rooms, each
furnished with individually collected
period antiques, original botanicals,
and steel engravings. Twenty-two acres
of gardens, footpaths, forests, and
ponds guarantee privacy and quiet.
High Meadows is on the National
Register of Historic Places.

Grilled Chipotle Pork Loin in Peach Chutney

2 tablespoons chipotle powder
1 tablespoon cumin
1 teaspoon pepper
8 pork loin chops, bone in or boneless
1 lime

In a small bowl, stir together chipotle powder, cumin, and pepper. Sprinkle ½ teaspoon on each side of each chop. Put chops in a pan and squeeze some fresh lime juice over chops. Cover and refrigerate until 30 minutes before grilling.

Grill chops until just done (still a little pink). Transfer to plates and cover with ¼ cup of hot chutney.

CHUTNEY
½ cup finely chopped red onion
½ cup chopped red bell pepper (¼-inch dice)
2 cups fresh or frozen peaches, peeled and pitted
1 tablespoon peeled and minced fresh ginger
1 cup sugar
2 tablespoons red wine vinegar

In a saucepan, sauté onions and peppers in a little butter until soft. Add peaches, ginger, and sugar, then vinegar. Bring to a boil and simmer until it just starts to thicken.

Yield: 8 servings

Grilled Pork Tenderloin

Pork tenderloin

MARINADE
Juice of 1 lemon
3 **cloves garlic, minced**
1 **medium onion, diced**
1 **tablespoon curry powder**
1 **tablespoon chili powder**
¾ **cup light soy sauce**
½ **cup canola oil or light olive oil**

In a bowl, combine all marinade ingredients. Put pork tenderloins in a sealable plastic bag (large zip locks work well) and pour marinade over them. Marinate, refrigerated, at least 8 hours or up to 24. The longer it marinates, the better it is. Allow 20 minutes for meat to reach room temperature before grilling.

Preheat grill 10 minutes. Remove meat from marinade and grill, turning to sear all sides at the beginning. Reduce heat or move meat to cooler part of grill to finish cooking. Do not overcook, or pork will become dry. It should still be pink in the center. Let meat rest, lightly covered with foil for 10 minutes before slicing into ½-inch thick pieces to serve. Corn pudding, green beans almandine, and fresh sliced tomatoes are excellent accompaniments.

Yields according to number of tenderloins

Fox Creek Inn
49 Chittenden Dam Road
Chittenden, Vermont 05737
1-800-707-0017
www.foxcreekinn.com

THE FOX CREEK INN, formerly the Tulip Tree Inn, offers excellent amenities and a high standard of service. When you come to Fox Creek, you will get a chance to relax and enjoy life as it should be enjoyed, at a slow pace. Here you'll have time to sit in front of your own fireplace or languish in your own private Jacuzzi. You'll find time to rekindle your relationship with life.

Greenock House Inn
249 Caroline Street
Orange, Virginia 22960
540-672-3625
1-800-841-1253
www.greenockhouse.com

GREENOCK HOUSE INN IS A beautiful Victorian farmhouse dating from 1880. The house currently sits on over 5 gorgeous acres, which secludes it from the town. Specimen trees planted near the end of the 1800s regally overlook the house—black walnut, cypress, maple, oak, and white ash (one ash is said to be over 200 years old). Sit on the wraparound porches and enjoy your evening hors d'oeuvres and wine. Hors d'oeuvres run the gamut from English tea to international cheese platters to Spanish tapas served with tea, wine, or beer. Often, the buffet will feature items from many different parts of the world, providing a variety of tastes. The specialty at the inn is the cuisine. After years of owning restaurants, the hosts, Lill and Rich Shearer, decided to slow down the pace and move to a country inn. But there is no doubt they still love food and cooking.

Ham and Pea Pasta

2	tablespoons butter
1	teaspoon crushed red pepper
8	slices Danish ham (sandwich style), cut into ½-inch squares
1	cup heavy cream
¼ to ½	cup grated Asiago cheese
1	cup frozen peas
4	cups cooked rotini or other pasta

Brown butter in a large skillet. Add pepper and ham. Toss to coat and to separate ham pieces. Add cream and simmer until cream sauce has thickened enough to coat the back of a spoon. Add cheese and peas. Leave the pan on the heat just long enough to cook the peas. Just before serving, add the pasta. Toss to coat. Serve with garlic bread.

Yield: 2 servings

Spicy Honey-Glazed
Bacon or Ham

Thickly sliced bacon or ham
1 **cup firmly packed light-brown sugar**
1 **cup honey**
½ **cup dry white wine**
¼ **cup Dijon-style mustard**
1 **tablespoon toasted and ground cumin seeds**
2 **teaspoons toasted and ground coriander seeds**
½ **teaspoon red pepper flakes**

Preheat oven to 350°F.

Arrange bacon in a jellyroll pan and bake in oven until almost crisp, about 18 minutes. Process remaining ingredients in a food processor until smooth, about 10 seconds. Drain fat from bacon pan and then brush one side of bacon with the glaze and return to oven for 10 minutes. Turn bacon over, brush other side with glaze and bake 10 minutes more.

Yield according to amount of bacon or ham

The Shelburne Inn
4415 Pacific Way
P. O. Box 250
Seaview, Washington 98644
360-642-2442
www.theshelburneinn.com

AN UNSPOILED 28-MILE stretch of wild Pacific seacoast is just a short walk through rolling sand dunes from this inviting country inn. It was originally built in 1896 as a retreat for visitors from Portland, Oregon, and has operated continuously since that time. Art Nouveau stained glass windows and period antique furniture highlight the inn. Guests delight in all of the dining experiences offered at the Shelburne Inn. The innkeepers' gourmet breakfast is complimentary with a room. The nationally acclaimed Shoalwater Restaurant, with its award-winning wine cellar, and the well-stocked, more casual Heron & Beaver Pub/Cafe are right on the premises. At the Shelburne, travelers have found warm hospitality, wonderful food, and comfortable shelter for over a century.

Los Pinos Ranch

P. O. Box 24
Glorieta, New Mexico 87535
(October–May)
Route 3, Box 8
Terrero, New Mexico 87573
(June–September)

1-505-757-6213
www.lospinosranch.com

*L*OS PINOS RANCH IS where the road ends and the trail begins. This small, private, historic guest ranch is nestled in the heart of the Sangre de Cristo Range of the southern Rockies. Situated at an elevation of 8,500 feet and surrounded by lofty peaks, the ranch is perched above the wild and scenic Pecos River. A profusion of wildflowers and many species of birds and animals abound in the sub alpine setting. Los Pinos recaptures the serenity and ambiance of an earlier, simpler time. Originally built as a summer residence, the main lodge shares its origins with New Mexico statehood. Since the early 1920s, Los Pinos has been a relaxing haven for guests.

Italian Beef Roast

2   (5-pound) beef rump roasts with fat trimmed off
3   teaspoons garlic salt or 2 teaspoons granulated garlic
1   tablespoon dried oregano
2   teaspoons fennel seed
2½ teaspoons chili powder
1   teaspoon anise seed
1½ teaspoons paprika
1   tablespoon plus 1 teaspoon Italian seasoning
8   ounces tomato paste
    Salt to taste
2½ quarts water

Mix seasonings in water in adequate size roasting pan (or pans) or ovenproof casserole (or casseroles) so that beef will be mostly covered by the liquid. Braise beef roasts if desired before adding to liquid. Roast in 350°F oven for 1 hour, then reduce heat to 300°F and cook for another 2 to 3 hours. Check with meat thermometer if necessary. Allow beef to cool a bit before slicing. Thicken sauce with a little flour and return sliced beef to sauce for reheating. Serve over noodles or gnocchi pasta with Italian-style green beans as a side vegetable.

Yield: 20 servings

Rack of Lamb
with French Lentil Ragout

Jacksonville Inn
175 East California
Jacksonville, Oregon 97530
1-800-321-9344
541-899-1900
www.jacksonvilleinn.com

RAGOUT

 2 ounces applewood-smoked bacon, diced
 1 onion, diced
 1 carrot, diced
 3 ribs of celery, diced
10 shiitake mushroom caps, diced
 1 pound French green lentils
 1 quart rich lamb or beef stock
 1 teaspoon minced garlic
 1 teaspoon fresh thyme
 1 bay leaf

Cook bacon in heavy skillet to render its fat. Add onion, carrot, celery, and mushrooms. Cook until onions are translucent. Add lentils, stock, and herbs and bring to a simmer. Cook for 20 to 30 minutes or until lentils are soft but not mushy. Season to taste and keep warm.

LAMB

 3 racks of lamb
   Dijon-style mustard
   Seasoned bread crumbs

Preheat oven to 350°F.

Sear lamb racks in a skillet over high heat until browned all over. Let them cool. Spread them with a thin layer of mustard, then press breadcrumbs into the mustard. Bake for 25 to 30 minutes for medium-rare meat. To serve, slice racks into double chops and arrange on the plate over the lentil ragout.

Yield: 6 servings

HOUSED IN ONE OF GOLD-Rush Jacksonville's early permanent structures, the inn perpetuates the nostalgic romances of that era. Built in 1861, the walls of the dining area and lounge were built of locally quarried sandstone, and specks of gold are still visible in the mortar. The inn extends to its visitors the ambience of early western America, an epicurean experience associated with superb dining, and luxurious hotel accommodations.

Wayside Inn Since 1797
7783 Main St.
Middleton, Virginia 22645
1-877-869-1797
www.alongthewayside.com

THE WAYSIDE INN SINCE 1797 has been serving the public for over 200 years. Nestled in the Shenandoah Valley, at the foot of the Massanutten Mountains, this distinctive inn gracefully blends its 18th-century ambience with 21st-century comfort. Lodging at the inn includes 24 guest rooms and suites, each decorated with its own unique period theme. Dining at the inn is available year round and features fresh regional American cuisine. Meals are served in seven delightful dining rooms by servers in authentic colonial costumes.

Maple-Bourbon Pork Loin

PORK

- 1 **pork loin**
- 1 **tablespoon coarse salt**
- 1 **tablespoon coarse black pepper**
- 1 **cup Maple-Bourbon Glaze (recipe follows)**
- 2 **cups Marinated Dried Fruits (recipe follows)**

Salt and pepper the pork loin and place on a rack in a roasting pan. Brush on maple-bourbon glaze before cooking. Cook pork until desired doneness, basting occasionally while in the oven. Serve slices of pork loin over dried fruits.

This recipe can be used with any cut of pork for roasting. We use a center-cut loin with 8 ribs, which are "frenched" similar to a crown roast.

MAPLE-BOURBON GLAZE

- 2 **cups water**
- 2 **cups sugar**
- 1 **tablespoon cornstarch, dissolved in cold water**
- 1 **tablespoon Vermont maple syrup**
- 1 **teaspoon maple extract**
- ¼ **cup bourbon**

Mix water and sugar and bring to a boil. Add cornstarch to thicken and allow it to cook a few minutes. Stir in maple syrup, maple extract, and bourbon.

DRIED FRUITS

- 1 cup raisins
- 3 cups dried apricots
- 1/4 cup gold raisins
- 1/4 cup dried papaya, diced
- 1/4 cup dried pineapple
- 1/4 cup currants
- 1 tablespoon fresh chopped parsley
- 1/4 cup bourbon
- 1/8 teaspoon cayenne pepper
- 3/4 cup apple cider
- 3/4 cup brown sugar
- Dusting of salt and pepper

Combine all ingredients and let soak overnight. Drain and roast for 30 minutes at 350°F before serving. Serve warm.

Yield: 6 servings

The Rose Farm Inn

Roslyn Road
Block Island, Rhode Island 02807
401-466-2034
www.rosefarminn.com

THE FARMHOUSE HAS BEEN in the Rose family for five generations. It was built in 1897 by James Rose. In 1980 Robert Rose reconstructed the farm house as an inn, preserving its great beach-stone porch and early 1900s architecture. The most elegant rooms have king-size canopy beds and ocean views. Bordered by stone walls and flower gardens, the inn has a shady front porch and comfortable sundeck where guests may relax and enjoy quiet moments. The inn is known for its natural setting, romantic rooms, and informal hospitality. A working farm until 1963, the twenty acres of farmland are now home to marsh hawks, ring-necked pheasant, and white-tailed deer.

*The Great Country Inns
of America Cookbook*

Meatloaf Florentine

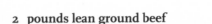

 2 pounds lean ground beef
 1 (10-ounce) box frozen spinach, thawed, water squeezed out
 1 pound (4 cups) Mozzarella cheese, shredded
 1 egg
 1 medium onion, chopped
 ½ teaspoon basil
 ½ teaspoon oregano
 ½ teaspoon salt
 ½ teaspoon garlic, chopped

Preheat oven to 350°F. Lightly oil 2 loaf pans.

Mix all ingredients together in a large bowl. Place in loaf pans and bake for 45 to 60 minutes.

Yield: 6 servings

Meatballs and Dressing

1 cup sweetened condensed milk
2 pounds ground beef
2 (10¾-ounce) cans condensed golden mushroom soup
¼ cup Worcestershire sauce
2 tablespoons ketchup

Preheat oven to 350°F.

In a bowl, mix condensed milk and ground beef and roll out into 12 balls. Make an indentation in the center of each meatball so the dressing can go in the hollow. Prepare your favorite chicken dressing. Place meatballs in large, shallow, ovenproof casserole dish. Fill the cavity of each meatball with the dressing. Mix together the soup, Worcestershire, and ketchp and pour over stuffed meatballs. Bake for 1 hour

Yield: 12 servings

My Blue Heaven
1041 Fifth Street
Pawnee City, Nebraska 68420
402-852-3131

LEGEND HAS IT THAT THE town of Pawnee City is on the exact spot where the largest village of the Pawnee Indians was located. The name "Pawnee" was supposedly derived from the word "pony," and the Pawnee were known as "the tribe of many ponies." Visitors flock to My Blue Heaven for small-town hospitality and all the comforts of home, including bountiful breakfasts.

*J*UST UP THE HILL FROM Nowata's historic downtown lies Rabbit Run. Built in 1926 by oilman Hubbard Reed, Rabbit Run is a stately red-brick home with white shutters and ivy-covered walls outside, casual elegance and comfort inside. Centrally located in Oklahoma's Green Country, Rabbit Run makes an ideal place to rest and recharge in between exploration and discovery of the area's many historical and cultural attractions, events, and festivals. There are over 50 antique and collectible shops within 30 minutes of the inn. And if you're looking for that special place for an anniversary, honeymoon, or romantic getaway, Rabbit Run can provide what you need. From the spacious rooms and gourmet breakfast to fine cuisine by Rabbit Run's certified chef, you'll be pleasantly surprised by the attention to detail.

Pan-Seared Medallions of Beef with Jack Daniel's and Artichoke Cream

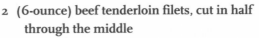

2 (6-ounce) beef tenderloin filets, cut in half through the middle
2 tablespoons butter
6 artichoke hearts, cut in half
2 tablespoons finely chopped shallots
1 tablespoon coarse Dijon-style mustard
2 tablespoons Jack Daniel's whiskey
1/2 cup heavy cream
Salt and pepper to taste

Preheat a nonstick skillet over medium-high heat add medallions and sear 2 to 3 minutes on each side. Remove meat from pan and keep warm. Add butter to hot pan, then shallots and artichokes and sauté for 1 minute. Add mustard and Jack Daniel's. Reduce by half. (The whiskey can be flamed to burn off the alcohol but this should only be done by someone experienced with the process.) *Caution:* The vapors from the whiskey could ignite, so hold pan away from your body; if the whiskey ignites it will burn out in a few seconds. Add cream, salt, and pepper and reduce by half.

Return meat to pan along with any accumulated juices and turn several times to coat meat with sauce. Transfer medallions to plates, top with artichokes, and drizzle both heavily with sauce.

Yield: 2 servings

Pork Scaloppini with Peaches

½ cup assorted dried fruits, primarily light colored
½ cup brandy
2 eggs
3 (3-ounce) portions of free-range, hammered
  pork tenderloin
½ cup flour
1 fresh local, organic peach, peeled and cut
  into small slices
¼ cup sliced almonds, lightly toasted
¼ cup white port
¼ cup demi-glace

In a small bowl, soak dried fruits in brandy. In another bowl whisk the eggs with a splash of milk to make an egg wash.

Coat the pork slices with the flour and then dip in the egg wash. Heat a little butter and a splash of extra-virgin olive oil in a sauté pan. Add pork and cook until golden on the face-down side. Flip the pork and pour out excess pan oil. Then deglaze the pan with the white port and simmer for 1 minute until alcohol cooks off. Add soaked fruits, half the peaches, and half the almonds to the sauté pan with the pork and toss until ingredients are coated. Add the demi-glace and swirl until well incorporated.

In a separate pan, warm the remaining peaches and almonds. Place the pork on 3 plates first, then spoon remaining ingredients over top. At the very end, garnish with the reserved warmed peaches and almonds.

Yield: 3 servings

Note: This dish is accented well with simple mashed potatoes, sweet mashed potatoes, and sautéed fresh vegetables.

Inn on Church Street
201 Third Avenue West
Hendersonville,
North Carolina 28739
828-693-3258
www.innspiredinns.com

INN ON CHURCH STREET is a beautiful mountain inn of distinction, located in the heart of historic downtown Hendersonville and just moments away from mountain adventures. It is listed on the National Register of Historic Places. This 1921, three-story brick inn has guest rooms graciously decorated in a European boutique style. Enjoy the innkeepers' gooey chocolate chip cookies upon arrival, while you relax in the rocking chairs on the wraparound porch. Then celebrate the next morning with the chef's all-natural country breakfast. The perfect getaway for vacationers and business travelers alike.

Applewood Inn

13555 Highway 116
Guerneville, California 95446
1-800-555-8509
www.applewoodinn.com

THE APPLEWOOD INN, WITH
its acclaimed wine-
country restaurant, is a
popular Sonoma area destination for
food and wine enthusiasts. This
historic inn is an ideal starting point
for excursions into every corner of
Sonoma's wine country as well as
neighboring Napa Valley. Each guest
room boasts fine Italian linens and
European down comforters, as well as
soothing garden or forest views. A stay
at the Applewood includes a full
country breakfast.

Rosemary-Marinated Pork Loin

MARINADE

1   **cup picked rosemary**
1   **cup peppercorns**
12 **cloves garlic**
12 **shallots**
½   **cup kosher salt**
1   **cup brown sugar**
1   **cup olive oil**

PORK

1   **pork loin, cleaned and tied**

To make the marinade: In a food processor, pulse together rosemary, peppercorns, garlic, and shallots. Pulse the machine enough to break up the spices. Add salt and brown sugar. Let machine run and begin to add the oil in a steady stream until all the oil is incorporated and ingredients have made a paste.

Put pork in pan big enough to hold it and the marinade. Coat the loin with the marinade, refrigerate, and let it rest for 4 hours or overnight.

Preheat oven to 375°F.

When ready to cook the loin, wipe off excess marinade and sear in a hot pan with oil. Transfer loin to a baking sheet and cook for about 1 hour or until internal temperature is 140 degrees. Remove from oven and let rest for 10 minutes before slicing.

Yield: 6 servings

Sausage and Wild Rice Casserole

1 (6-ounce) package long-grain and wild rice mix
   (such as Uncle Ben's)
1 pound ground hot pork sausage
1 pound ground beef
1 large onion, chopped
8 ounces fresh mushrooms, sliced
1 (8-ounce) can sliced water chestnuts, drained
1/3 cup chopped fresh parsley
3 tablespoons soy sauce
1/2 cup sliced natural almonds

Cook rice mix according to package directions. Cook sausage and ground beef in a large skillet, stirring until it crumbles and is no longer pink. Drain and pat dry with paper towels. Cook onion and mushrooms in same skillet over medium heat for 7 minutes or until tender, stirring occasionally. Combine rice, sausage and beef, onion and mushrooms, water chestnuts, parsley, and soy sauce; stir well. Spoon mixture into an ungreased 13 x 9-inch baking dish. Cover and chill casserole overnight.

Remove from refrigerator and let stand at room temperature 30 minutes. Preheat oven to 350°F. Sprinkle casserole with almonds. Bake for 40 minutes or until thoroughly heated.

Yield: 8 to 10 servings

Totten Trail Historic Inn
P. O. Box 224
Fort Totten, North Dakota 58335
701-766-4874
www.tottentrailinn.com

STAYING HERE IS A UNIQUE chance to experience the frontier past. Totten Trail Historic Inn, located at the Fort Totten North Dakota State Historic Site, now has bed-and-breakfast accommodations furnished in period style (1870–1910). The building was constructed by the United States government in 1869 to serve as quarters for four officers and their families who were stationed at Fort Totten Military Post. In the inn today, some rooms have a private bath and others share a baths with one other room. Phones and wireless internet are in every room. Catered dinners and parties in the parlor can be arranged for10 to30 people. The Fort Totten North Dakota State Historic Site is located on the southern shore of Devils Lake in north-central North Dakota.

Two Meeting Street Inn
2 Meeting Street
Charleston, South Carolina 29401
843-723-7322
www.twomeetingstreet.com

Two Meeting Street Inn is Charleston's oldest inn, welcoming guests for over half a century. Located in the heart of the historic district, the Queen Anne mansion was given as a wedding gift by a bride's loving father in 1890. The elegant inn features a carved English oak stairwell and Tiffany windows, as well as owners Pete and Jean Spell's collection of antiques and silver. The softly curved, two-tiered verandas overlook the manicured, landscaped garden and Charleston's harbor. Guests enjoy a Southern continental breakfast and gracious afternoon tea in the dining room or on the piazza. To quote a guest, "Never have we stayed in a place so beautiful or so lovingly cared for, nor have we ever felt as pampered. Thank you for making our stay both comfortable and memorable."

Sausage Wellingtons

2 to 3	pounds sage-flavored sausage
3	tablespoons dehydrated onion
¼	teaspoon cayenne pepper
2	(8-ounce) packages cream cheese
1	(10-ounce) package Cheddar cheese
3	packages Pepperidge Farms puff pastry sheets
4	egg whites

In a large skillet, brown together the sausage, dehydrated onion, and cayenne pepper. When brown, drain on paper towel–lined cookie sheet for 10 minutes. Return to skillet on low heat and add cream cheese and Cheddar cheese. Simmer until cheeses are melted, and mix well. Let cool completely.

Preheat oven to 375°F.

When pastry sheets are almost thawed but still stiff and cold, unfold and flatten. Cut opposite the folds in thirds, then cut those strips in halves—this will make perfect squares. Each sheet makes 4 squares. Spoon about 2 to 3 tablespoons of sausage-cheese mixture into center of pastry squares, fold diagonally, and press edges of pastry together to seal. Place on ungreased cookie sheet about 2 to 3 inches apart. Extra filling may be refrigerated for 3 or 4 days. Beat 4 egg whites until frothy; brush tops of pastries. Bake for 20 to 25 minutes until puffy and golden brown. For convection oven, bake 15 to 20 minutes. These can be made a day ahead and tightly covered and refrigerated.

Yield: 24 servings

Serving suggestion: Drizzle Wellingtons with warm hollandaise sauce, then top with a couple of Roma tomato slices and a sprig of fresh parsley or rosemary.

Grilled Sirloin Steak with Gorgonzola, Spiced Walnuts, and Blueberry-Balsamic Vinaigrette

~~~~~~~

Prepare the topping ahead of time so that you can put this dish together easily when the steaks come off the grill.

BLUEBERRY-BALSAMIC VINAIGRETTE

- ½ cup blueberries
- ½ cup good balsamic vinegar
- 1 teaspoon honey
- 1 clove garlic
- ½ teaspoon Dijon-style mustard or whole-grain mustard
- 1 cup vegetable oil
- Pinch of salt

Combine the blueberries, vinegar, honey, and garlic in a small saucepan and bring to a low boil. Turn off the heat and allow the mixture to cool a little. Once the mixture has reached room temperature, pour it into a blender and add the mustard. Purée on high and slowly add the vegetable oil. Salt to taste. The vinaigrette will easily last up to two weeks in the refrigerator. Putting it in a clean plastic ketchup bottle allows you to easily serve it. Yields enough for 10 steaks.

To prepare spiced walnuts: Toss some chopped walnuts with a little vegetable oil, a pinch of sugar, and a dash of cinnamon.

To assemble: Crumble Gorgonzola (substitute Blue cheese if necessary) over grilled steaks, sprinkle with walnuts, and drizzle with the balsamic vinaigrette.

Inn at Woodstock Hill
94 Plaine Hill Road
Woodstock, Connecticut 06281
860-928-0528
innwood@snet.net

THE INN'S MAIN HOUSE, originally constructed in 1816 by John Truesdell for William Bowen, has undergone a number of reconstructions, renovations, and additions over the years. As it appears today, the massive clapboard house has a steeply pitched hip roof and dormers on all faces. The property remained in the Bowen family until after the death of Gardner Richardson's widow, Dorothea, who bequeathed the farm to the University of Connecticut in 1981 as a memorial to Richardson's son, Lt. Peter Bowen. The farm was returned to the family in 1985. The main house and barn were converted to use as an inn and restaurant, known as the Inn at Woodstock Hill. Most of the farmland remains in the Bowen family as it has for three centuries.

POULTRY

The Mainstay Inn
635 Columbia Avenue
Cape May, New Jersey 08204
609-884-8690
www.mainstayinn.com

A PAIR OF WEALTHY gamblers pooled their resources in 1872 and built an elegant, exclusive clubhouse for their friends. They spared no expense and hired a famous architect to design a grand villa. This beautiful building is now the Mainstay Inn in the heart of historic Cape May. It looks much as it did when the gamblers were there. The six spacious guest rooms are furnished with splendid antiques, much as they were in the 19th century.

Aunt Betty's Chicken Pie

FILLING
3 cups cooked chicken, diced
½ cup milk
½ cup sour cream
2 (10¾-ounce) cans cream of chicken soup

Preheat oven to 375°F.

In a saucepan, heat all filling ingredients. Transfer to a 9 x 12-inch pan or 2-quart casserole.

TOPPING
½ teaspoon salt
1 egg, beaten
¾ cup milk
½ cup cornmeal
1 cup buttermilk pancake mix
2 cups shredded Cheddar cheese

In a bowl, combine all topping ingredients except cheese. Fold in cheese. Spoon topping over hot chicken mixture. Bake for 20 to 30 minutes.

Yield: 8 servings

Chicken-Artichoke Casserole

SAUCE

2 **cups water**
2 **chicken bouillon cubes**
1 **cup margarine**
½ **cup flour**
½ **teaspoon cayenne pepper**
1 **tablespoon granulated garlic**
4 **ounces shredded Cheddar cheese**
2 **ounces shredded Swiss cheese**

FILLING

6 **boneless, skinless chicken breasts, cooked and**
   cut into cubes
2 **(16-ounce) cans artichoke hearts**
1 **pound fresh mushrooms, sliced**

Preheat oven to 350°F.

To make the sauce: Bring wter to a boil in a saucepan. Add bouillon cubes and stir to dissolve. Add margarine. Remove from heat and add remaining sauce ingredients. Stir well.

To make the filling: Combine filling ingredients and transfer to a 9 x 13-inch ovenproof glass baking dish.

Pour sauce over filling. Bake for 30 minutes.

Yield: 12 servings

BonnyNook Inn
414 West Main
Waxahachie, Texas 75165
972-938-7207
1-800-486-5936
www.bonnynook.com

OLD WORLD ELEGANCE WITH 21st-century comfort is the motto of this delightful inn. There is a Victorian parlor with a game table, a piano, and comfortable seating areas. Downstairs and upstairs porches overlook gardens and historic homes. Each bedroom is furnished with period antique suites, including comfy seating nooks and private baths, some with Jacuzzis. A full breakfast is served on your schedule in the dining room. Dishes include homemade coffee cakes, fruit dishes, and specially prepared entrées. A seven-course dinner for two is served in the private candlelit dining room.

Excelsior House

211 West Austin Street
Jefferson, Texas 75657
903-665-2513
www.theexcelsiorhouse.com

THIS SPLENDID INN HAS BEEN in continuous operation since the 1850s. It was restored in 1961 by the Jessie Allen Wise Garden Club. The brick and timber structure was built by Captain William Perry. It has 14 rooms, each furnished in period furniture and featuring museum-quality antiques. The presidential Suite features a pair of lavishly appointed rooms, each named for former guests Presidents Ulysses S. Grant and Rutherford B. Hayes. The huge ballroom and magnificent dining room are crowned by two large French Sevres chandeliers. Delicious food is served in the dining room.

Chicken Excelsior House

6   chicken breasts
    Garlic salt
1   teaspoon paprika
3   tablespoons lemon juice
1   can mushroom soup
1   carton sour cream
¼   cup sherry
1   medium-size can mushrooms and stems
    Generous dash cayenne pepper

Preheat oven to 375°F.

Sprinkle chicken with garlic salt. Melt margarine or butter, add paprika and lemon juice. Roll chicken in margarine mixture and place on baking sheet. Bake for 1 hour or until tender. Make sauce of sour cream, sherry, and mushrooms and pour over chicken. Bake for 15 minutes.

Yield: 6 servings

Chicken Skewers with Orange-Chipotle-Mustard Sauce

Four Kachinas Inn

512 Webber Street
Santa Fe, New Mexico 87505
505-982-2550
1-800-397-2564
www.fourkachinas.com

SAUCE

1	(6-ounce) can frozen orange juice
3	tablespoons chipotle chilies
2	tablespoons honey
2	tablespoons Dijon-style mustard
1	teaspoon minced garlic
1/3	cup chopped fresh cilantro, packed
3	tablespoons fresh lime juice
1/2	teaspoon salt
2	tablespoons vegetable oil
2	pounds boneless chicken breast cut into thin, 1-inch wide strips
1 1/2	cups Orange-Chipotle-Mustard Sauce

To make the sauce: Place all sauce ingredients in food processor or blender and puree until smooth; set aside.

To assemble: Thread chicken strips onto skewers in a long ribbon fashion. Grill or broil chicken skewers until meat is fully cooked. Place cooked skewers into large glass baking pan. Pour the sauce over skewers and toss until coated. Serve warm.

Yield: 6 servings

Note: Lamb, shrimp, scallops, or pork can be substituted for chicken.

WELCOME TO FOUR Kachinas Inn. Located on a quiet residential street in the Don Gaspar historic district, Four Kachinas Inn bed-and-breakfast is a short walk down Old Santa Fe Trail to the historic plaza, a travelers' destination for more than 350 years. The inn offers five spacious rooms, all with private bathrooms. Rooms are furnished with quality Southwestern art and locally made crafts. Collector-quality Navajo rugs, kachina dolls, Spanish colonial art, regional landscape paintings, and handcrafted furniture complete the comfortable Southwestern theme.

The Mansion of Golconda

222 South Columbus Street
Golconda, Illinois 62938
618-683-4400
www.mansionofgolconda.com

BUILT AS A PRIVATE HOME by a former mayor of Golconda, this gabled mansion on the Ohio River has been a licensed hotel since 1928. Many travelers and boarders have enjoyed the hospitality of various owners since that time. A costly renovation in 1981 has restored the joy and light to the delicately curved pressed glass windows. The restaurant seats 60 in beautifully decorated formal dining rooms. It draws diners from a 100-mile radius, with cuisine best described as ethnic American. From deep-fried chicken to elegant French-inspired entrées, there is a dish for every palate. Golconda is a typical sleepy river town with early 1900s facades reflecting a simpler time.

County Lime Chicken

SAUCE
- 1 cup honey
- ½ cup Rose's lime juice
- ½ cup chicken stock
- 2 tablespoons minced green onions
- Grated zest of 1 lime
- ⅛ teaspoon tarragon
- ¼ teaspoon thyme
- 2 ounces butter

CHICKEN
- 4 chicken breasts, cut in half
- Flour
- 1 tablespoon vegetable oil
- 1 tablespoon butter
- Chopped parsley
- Finely chopped pistachios

To make the sauce: In a saucepan, simmer honey, lime juice, stock, and green onions until well blended. Add zest and herbs. Whisk in butter.

To make chicken: Dredge chicken breasts in seasoned flour. Heat vegetable oil and butter in skillet. Add chicken and sauté until cooked through. Nap with sauce. Spoon sauce over chicken and garnish with parsley and pistachios.

Yield: 8 servings

Fried Chicken

2   cups buttermilk
2   tablespoons onion powder
1   tablespoon plus 2 teaspoons kosher salt
2   tablespoons Old Bay seasoning
1   tablespoon plus 1 teaspoon cayenne pepper
2½ teaspoons fresh cracked black pepper
5   boneless skinless chicken breasts
3   cups self-rising flour
1   tablespoon granulated garlic
2   quarts peanut oil

In a 1-gallon Ziploc freezer bag, combine buttermilk, 1 tablespoon of the onion powder, 1 teaspoon of the salt, 1 teaspoon of the cayenne, and 1 teaspoon of the cracked pepper. Add chicken breasts to the bag and remove all air. Coat chicken evenly. Refrigerate for 48 hours, tossing the chicken occasionally.

Combine flour, garlic, and remaining ingredients in a large dish. With the chicken still coated heavily (do not remove excess), toss the chicken in the flour mixture. Let chicken stand in flour mixture for 1 hour, recoating often.

Pour oil into a 1-gallon pot. Attach a deep-fry thermometer. Heat oil at medium-high to 350°F. Add two pieces of chicken at a time to prevent oil from overflowing. Reduce heat to medium-low and fry for 15 minutes, turning chicken over occasionally. Maintain oil temperature at around 300°F. Chicken should be golden brown. With a pair of tongs transfer chicken to a cooling rack (or a paper towel). Internal temperature of chicken should be 165°F for 15 seconds. Serve with your favorite country side dishes.

Yield: 5 servings

The Duke Mansion
400 Hermitage Road
Charlotte, North Carolina 28207
704-714-4400
1-888-202-1009
www.dukemansion.org

THE DUKE MANSION, BUILT in 1915 and listed on the National Register of Historic Places, offers 20 unique guest rooms in true Southern splendor and with a full breakfast. The rooms are residential in their decor and appointed with beautiful artwork and furnishings, giving you a breathtaking image of what it was like to be a member of the prestigious Duke family who made this mansion their home. The Duke Mansion is an integral part of Charlotte's most prestigious and beautiful neighborhood, and is situated on 4½ acres of beautiful grounds.

Kirschke House
Bed and Breakfast

1124 West Third Street
Grand Island, Nebraska 68801
308-381-6851
www.iloveinns.com/bed_and_break
fasts/nebraska/kirschkehouse.htm

*E*ARLY 20TH-CENTURY SHOWPLACE, the Kirschke House, was built in 1902 by the prominent contractor, Otto Kirschke, as his family home. The vine-covered two-story brick home features architectural highlights, including a windowed cupola, turret, and stained glass windows over the open oak staircase. The guest rooms reflect the ambience of the exterior and are accented with Victorian lace, period furnishings, and antique accessories. Your host's love for cooking and entertaining is reflected in both her gourmet and down-home country cooking, served elegantly in the dining room or in your room.

Hawaiian Chicken

SAUCE
2¼ cups brown sugar
1½ cups vinegar
 1 tablespoon plus 1½ teaspoons salt or to taste
 1 tablespoon soy sauce
2¼ cups ketchup
 3 cans chunk pineapple with juice

CHICKEN
 3 large fryer chickens, cut into pieces
   Garlic powder to taste
   Beaten eggs
   Flour
   Butter

Combine sauce ingredients in a saucepan and cook for ½ an hour.

Preheat oven to 350°F.

Sprinkle chicken with garlic powder; let stand for 5 minutes. Dip chicken in beaten egg and roll in flour. Brown in skillet with butter. Put chicken in an ovenproof casserole and cover with sauce. Bake for 45 minutes.

Yield: 12 servings

Jamaican Chicken

MARINADE
½ cup vegetable oil
2 tablespoons cider vinegar
2 tablespoons fresh lime juice
1 teaspoon ground allspice
1 teaspoon garlic, minced
1 teaspoon ginger root, minced

SAUCE
3 tablespoons marinade
¼ cup green onions, chopped
3 tablespoons all-purpose flour
1 cup chicken stock
¼ cup dry white wine
¼ cup heavy cream

1½ pounds skinless, boneless chicken breasts,
cut in ½-inch wide strips
Rice or pasta (such as fettuccine), cooked

To make the marinade: In a saucepan, combine marinade ingredients and simmer for 5 minutes. Set aside 3 tablespoons to be used in sauce. Let cool, then combine with chicken. Marinate at least 4 to 6 hours in refrigerator.

To make the sauce: In a saucepan, combine reserved marinade and green onion and sauté for 3 minutes. Add flour and stir for another 3 minutes. Add stock, wine, and cream. Bring to simmer and cook 15 minutes. Keep sauce warm.

To make the chicken: Drain chicken. Sauté chicken in reserved 3 tablespoons of the marinade in a pan for 4 to 5 minutes until cooked but still tender. Serve chicken over cooked rice or pasta with sauce on top.

Yield: 6 servings

Barrow House Inn
524 Royal Street
St. Francisville, Louisiana 70775
225-635-4791
www.topteninn.com

SHADED BY A 200-YEAR-old live oak, Barrow House stands in the heart of the quaint town of St. Francisville. The original house was a saltbox structure built in 1809, and a Greek Revival wing added just before the Civil War. A large screened porch is the place to be for coffee in the morning and drinks in the evening. Rooms are furnished in antiques dating from 1840 to 1870. The inn's candlelight dinners, featuring New Orleans–style food, are well known in the area. Six plantations (open to the public) are close by.

English Rose Inn
195 Vermont Route 242
Montgomery Center, Vermont 05471
802-326-3232
www.englishroseinnvermont.com

THE ENGLISH ROSE INN is nestled within the gorgeous Green Mountains of Vermont, a location providing a beautiful backdrop for any occasion. The inn offers warm, luxurious accommodations, fine dining at Paddington's Restaurant, and spectacular mountain views. You will enjoy a pleasurable, romantic, Victorian getaway in the 25-room 1850s farmhouse, which features 14 beautifully decorated guest rooms and suites. Lace curtains, hardwood floors, and crocheted and homemade heirloom quilts adorn the antique-filled rooms. At Paddington's, you will experience world-class cuisine at its best, exquisitely prepared and presented by, the inn's own award-winning chefs who take great pride in using the highest quality products available.

Lady Chatterley's Chicken

4	(6-ounce) boneless, skinless chicken breasts
	Salt and pepper
1½	cups plain bread crumbs
¼	teaspoon dried thyme (1 tablespoon fresh)
¼	cup slivered almonds
½	cup flour
2	eggs, beaten
2	tablespoons butter
2	tablespoons olive oil

Lightly pound chicken breasts to make them uniform in size. Season each breast with salt and pepper. Mix thyme and almonds in bread crumbs. Coat chicken with the flour, shaking off excess. Dip chicken in beaten egg and coat with bread-crumb mixture. On medium heat melt butter and olive oil in a sauté pan and add chicken breasts. Cook on each side until golden brown or until cooked through, about 8 minutes on each side. Serve with your favorite potatoes or mixed green salad.

Yield: 4 servings

Lemon Chicken

MARINADE

1 teaspoon sherry
1 teaspoon soy sauce
¼ teaspoon salt
1 tablespoon cornstarch
1 egg, beaten
  Pinch of white pepper

2 boneless chicken breasts
  Flour
½ cup oil
1 tablespoon rice wine
½ teaspoon minced garlic
1 teaspoon instant custard powder
1 tablespoon sherry
1½ tablespoons sugar
¼ teaspoon salt
1 tablespoon vinegar
½ cup water
½ tablespoon sesame oil
½ teaspoon hot pepper oil
  Juice and rind of 1 lemon
2 slices fresh ginger
2 teaspoons cornstarch mixed with 2 tablespoons water

Mix marinade ingredients together in a bowl. Marinate chicken for 20 minutes.

Coat chicken with flour. Heat oil in wok or heavy skillet and fry chicken on both sides until golden brown. Add rice wine and cover briefly to steam in flavors. Remove chicken from pan and

Recipe continued on next page

Dockside Guest Quarters
Harris Island Road
P.O. Box 205
York, Maine 03909
207-363-2868
www.docksidegq.com

HE LUSTY FAMILY CONTINUES to celebrate many years as owners and operators of Dockside. The guest quarters have accommodations to satisfy everyone. Beginning in the "Maine House," built in the 1880s, there are beautifully restored colonial bedrooms overlooking York Harbor. Dockside is situated on its own peninsula, which provides a panorama of both the ocean and harbor activity. The Dockside dining room is adjacent to the guest quarters and has a complete and varied menu, featuring Maine lobster and other treats from the sea.

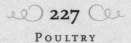

chop into bite-sized pieces. Reheat pan, add garlic, and simmer a few seconds. Combine rice wine, garlic, custard powder, sherry, sugar, salt, vinegar, water, sesame oil, hot pepper oil, and lemon juice (not lemon rind) to form a sauce and add to pan. Add lemon rind and ginger slices. When mixture boils, thicken with cornstarch and water. Remove ginger and lemon rind. Pour over chicken and serve.

Yield: 4 servings

Olive-Chicken Mozzarella

¼ cup flour
¼ teaspoon salt
4 whole boneless, skinless chicken breasts, cut into bite-size pieces
¼ cup olive oil

Combine flour and salt in plastic bag and coat chicken. Brown chicken in olive oil. Arrange chicken in a shallow 2-quart baking dish.

1 clove garlic, crushed
1 medium onion, chopped fine
1 (8-ounce) can sliced mushrooms, drained
1 (14-ounce) jar spaghetti sauce
½ teaspoon oregano
½ cup sliced pimiento-stuffed olives
1 (6-ounce) package sliced Mozzarella cheese

Preheat oven to 350°F.

Sauté garlic and onion in chicken drippings until onion is tender. Stir in mushrooms, spaghetti sauce, oregano, and olives. Pour sauce over chicken. Cut cheese slices into strips and place on top of chicken. Bake until chicken is tender, about 30 minutes.

Yield: 6 to 8 servings

Blue Spruce Inn
677 South 3rd Street
Lander, Wyoming 82520
1-888-503-3311
bluespruce@rmisp.com

SURROUNDED BY GIANT blue spruce trees, enjoy warm Western hospitality in the relaxed luxury of an early 20th-century inn from the Arts and Crafts period. Three queen guest rooms and one twin (convertible to king) all have private baths. The Blue Spruce Inn is decorated with objects gathered during the travels of your retired air-force hosts. This is a perfect place to stay while you explore the Wind River Mountains and the charming town of Lander.

The Wolfeboro Inn
90 North Main Street
Wolfeboro, New Hampshire 03894
603-569-3016
www.wolfeboroinn.com

THIS BEAUTIFUL INN IS located on Lake Winnipesaukee, one of the nation's most beautiful lakes. Wolfeboro is America's oldest summer resort. The charming building is located in the heart of town. Built in 1812, its rugged exterior has withstood the elements for nearly two centuries. The dining room offers delectable fare after your jaunt into the White Mountains or a day on the lake.

Pecan-Crusted Chicken with Frangelico Cream Sauce

CHICKEN

- **4 boneless chicken breasts**
- **Salt and pepper**
- **3 eggs**
- **½ cup milk**
- **2 cups crushed pecans**
- **1 cup coarse bread crumbs**
- **1 cup flour**
- **Canola oil**

Rinse and trim the fat off chicken. Lightly salt and pepper one side of each breast and set aside. In a bowl, mix eggs and milk. In a separate bowl, mix pecans and bread crumbs. In a third bowl, have the flour ready. Coat the chicken breasts in the flour, then dip in the egg mixture, then into the pecan mixture, pressing down to coat well. Set chicken aside.

SAUCE

- **1 cup Frangelico liqueur**
- **3 cups light cream**
- **½ cup sugar**
- **Pinch of salt**
- **Roux (1 tablespoon flour and 1 tablespoon melted butter)**

In a saucepan, reduce Frangelico to half. Add cream, sugar, and salt. Bring to light boil (careful not to burn), then add roux to thicken. While sauce is cooking, heat a deep skillet with about ½ an inch of canola oil. Once fully heated, place coated chicken breasts in oil and cook for 4 minutes on each side. Serve chicken with sauce drizzled on top.

Yield: 4 servings

Pechuga de Pollo Borracho

Flour
2 (8-ounce) skinless and boneless chicken breasts
1 teaspoon olive oil
¼ teaspoon chopped shallots
¼ teaspoon chopped garlic
Pinch of sage
Pinch of cumin
1 teaspoon capers
1 teaspoon sun-dried tomatoes
1 tablespoon diced prosciutto ham strips
2 tablespoons tequila
½ cup chicken stock
2 tablespoons heavy cream
Salt and pepper
Cilantro leaves, for garnish

Dredge chicken breasts in flour and sauté in olive oil until browned. Add shallots, garlic, sage, cumin, capers, tomatoes, and prosciutto. Sauté until tender. Add tequila, chicken stock, and cream; cook until liquid reduces to a thick sauce. Transfer chicken to plates and pour sauce over it. Garnish with cilantro leaves.

Yield: 2 servings

102 Brownstone
Boutique Hotel
102 West 118th Street
New York, New York 10026
212-662-4223
www.102brownstone.com

*I*F YOU SEEK AN EXHILARATing New York experience, stay at the 102 Brownstone. In a beautiful private apartment or elegant private suite you can enjoy the city with all the comfort, convenience, and privacy of home. The accommodations are designed for the senses, and the warm ambience contributes to the sense of retreat. The 102 Brownstone offers the convenience of a hotel with the warmth and comfort of home. Guests keep their own schedules and enjoy the privacy they deserve while on vacation. Full apartments offer the option of home-cooked meals or early morning coffee.

Poulet Pignant

1½	pounds boneless chicken breast
	Salt and pepper
2	tablespoons olive oil
3	medium cloves garlic, chopped
4	anchovies
	Crushed red pepper to taste
½	cup cooking wine
1	cup vegetable broth
1	tablespoon capers
	Dried red peppers, thinly chopped
2	scallions, diced

Cut chicken breast into strips and season with salt and pepper. Heat olive oil in sauté pan. Add garlic and anchovies and sauté for 1 minute. Be careful not to burn the garlic. Add crushed red pepper. Add chicken strips and fry for 2 minutes. Add wine and vegetable broth. Cook for 5 minutes over low heat. Add capers and dried red peppers. Cook for 3 minutes. Add scallions and cook for 1 minute. Serve and enjoy with a white wine.

Yield: 4 servings

Quick Quiche—Chicken

1 (9-inch) prepared piecrust
½ cup mayonnaise
2 tablespoons flour
2 eggs, beaten
½ cup milk
   Large can chicken, drained
8 ounces Swiss cheese
½ cup rehydrated dried minced onion

Mix mayonnaise, flour, eggs, and milk until blended. Stir in chicken, cheese, and onion. Pour into piecrust. Bake at 350°F for 40 to 45 minutes.

Yield: 6 servings

Rosevine Inn Bed and Breakfast
415 South Vine
Tyler, Texas 75702
903-592-2221
www.rosevine.com

EXPERIENCE THE OLD-FASHIONED concept of "guest housing" at the Rosevine Inn Bed and Breakfast, an excellent alternative to the ordinary hotel routine. Located in "the rose capital of the world," Tyler's first bed-and-breakfast is situated on one of Tyler's quaint brick streets near the Azalea District. Return to your carefree days when your biggest worry was when can we go out to play? When do we go to bed, and what's for breakfast? You're a guest at the Rosevine Inn. There are six guest rooms including one suite. Guest accommodations are cheerfully decorated with antiques and wallpaper, and each room has a private bath. A short distance from the inn are numerous antique and craft shops.

Snowvillage Inn
Stuart Road
Snowville, New Hampshire 03832
603-447-2818
www.snowvillageinn.com

THIS EARLY 1900S SUMMER retreat for writer Frank Simonds was later converted into an inn by a Swiss couple. Today, the inn's decor and cuisine reflect this harmonious blend of New England and European-Alpine traditions. The comfortably furnished guest rooms are all named after writers. Here is a European-style country inn, where every room offers a breathtaking view of the White Mountains and Mount Washington. Not only is Snowvillage Lodge high above the ordinary in elevation, but also in everything about it. The dining room brings you memorable cuisine carefully prepared and served with elegance.

Roast Duckling with Cabernet-Poached Pear Sauce

3 ducklings
Salt and pepper to taste

Preheat oven to 400°F.

Rinse ducklings under cold water and pat dry. Season with salt and pepper and truss legs. Set on a rack in a roasting pan and roast in oven for 30 minutes. Reduce heat to 350°F and roast for 2 more hours turning, the duck pans in oven every half hour. While ducks roast, prepare sauce.

SAUCE
1¼ cups granulated sugar
 1 cinnamon stick
10 whole peppercorns
 2 whole cloves
 4 cups Cabernet
 4 Bartlett pears, peeled and halved

Bring all ingredients to a simmer and cook until pears are just soft. Remove pears and set aside to cool. Strain wine. Return to heat and reduce until slightly thickened. When pears are cool enough to handle, return them to the wine and heat through.

Allow ducks to cool enough to handle and carve and debone. Serve with the sauce.

Yield: 12 servings

Roasted Game Hens with Espresso Sauce

~~~~~~~~~~~~~~~~~~~~~~

SAUCE

- ½ cup espresso or strong coffee
- 2 tablespoons fresh lemon juice
- ¼ teaspoon paprika
- 2 tablespoons brandy
- ½ cup Dijon-style mustard
- 3 tablespoons unsalted butter

GAME HENS

- 4 Cornish game hens, about 1 pound each
- 1 teaspoon salt
- ½ teaspoon pepper
- 2 slices lemon, cut in half

Place oven rack in lower third of oven and preheat to 375°F.

Combine sauce ingredients in a small saucepan. Heat to boiling, lower to simmer, and cook for 1 minute. Set aside.

Rinse hens with cold water; dry well. Season cavities with salt and pepper; place a half slice of lemon in each and divide 1 tablespoon sauce equally between each cavity. Tie or skewer hens and roast breast side up in a shallow baking pan. Brush with a little of the sauce and cover loosely with a foil tent. Roast for 30 minutes, remove foil, and brush with sauce. Roast for 30 to 45 minutes longer, until juices run clear when pricked. Cover with tent again if necessary to prevent overbrowning. Transfer to a heated platter and keep warm.

Remove excess fat from roasting pan, pour in remaining sauce, and bring to a boil. Lower heat and simmer until sauce becomes a syrup (about 2 or 3 minutes). Spoon sauce over hens and serve.

Yield: 4 servings

Red Castle Inn
109 Prospect Street
Nevada City, Caifornia 95959
530-265-5135
www.redcastleinn.com

AS THE FIRST NEVADA CITY bed-and-breakfast and one of the first in California, the incomparable Red Castle Inn has been acclaimed for its singular sense of time and place for more than four decades. On a quiet, tree-lined street in an uncommon wooded setting with unsurpassed views of the enchanting historic Gold Rush town, this Nevada City inn offers travelers a glimpse of what life was like more than 100 years ago. Cross the threshold of the spectacular 1860 Gothic Revival mansion (which in 1960 became the premier Nevada City bed-and-breakfast) into another time . . . another century . . . an atmosphere of vintage refinement at once tranquil, romantic, and genteel. Discover what was called "the tasteful interlude" in true 19th-century style.

Applewood Inn
13555 Highway 116
Guerneville, California 95446
1-800-555-8509
www.applewoodinn.com

THE APPLEWOOD INN, WITH its acclaimed wine-country restaurant, is a popular Sonoma County destination for food and wine enthusiasts. This historic inn is an ideal starting point for excursions into every corner of Sonoma County's wine country as well as neighboring Napa Valley. Each guest room boasts fine Italian linens and European down comforters, as well as soothing garden or forest views. A stay at the Applewood includes a full country breakfast.

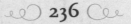
236

Roasted Chicken with Apple, Quince, and Black Pepper Stuffing

STUFFING

1¼	cups unsalted butter
2½	cups chopped celery
2½	cups chopped onion
2½	cups chopped quince
1¼	teaspoons salt
5	teaspoons freshly cracked black pepper or to taste
1¼	teaspoons lemon thyme
20	cups cubed dry French bread
5	cups peeled, cored, and chopped Golden Delicious apples
1¼ to 2½	cups good-quality chicken broth

Melt butter in a large skillet. Add celery, onion, and quince and cook until tender but not brown. Stir in salt, pepper, and lemon thyme. In a large bowl, combine the bread cubes and apples. Add cooked vegetable mixture and lightly toss with just enough of chicken broth to moisten. Stuffing may be baked in the birds or separately in a foil-covered baking dish. Uncover for the last 10 to 15 minutes.

5	whole roasting chickens (3½ to 4 pounds each)
	Salt and pepper

Preheat oven to 400°F.

Season outside of birds with salt and pepper. Sear on all sides over heat. Place in a large roasting pan (or pans) and roast for approximately 30 to 45 minutes.

Yield: 20 servings

Spring Chicken
with Roasted Red Pepper Sauce

8 ounces cream cheese
1 tablespoon fresh tarragon or 1 teaspoon dried
  Pinch of salt and pepper
4 chicken breasts
  Oil
  Red Pepper Sauce (recipe follows)

Preheat oven to 350°F.

Combine cream cheese, tarragon, and salt and pepper in a food processor and mix well. Pound chicken breasts to ¼-inch thickness. Spoon ¼ cup cream cheese mixture into center of each breast and wrap. Use a toothpick to close if necessary. Season outside with salt, pepper, and oil. Bake for 15 to 20 minutes or until center reaches 160°F.

RED PEPPER SAUCE

1 jar roasted red peppers
1 clove garlic
1 large shallot
½ cup white wine
2 cups chicken broth

In a food processor, purée red peppers, garlic, and shallots. Put white wine in a saucepan and reduce by half. Add red pepper mixture and bring to simmer. Add chicken broth and bring to a boil. Reduce heat and simmer for 5 minutes. Thicken with slurry if necessary.

Yield: 4 servings

Brightwood Inn
2407 North Illinois Route 178
Oglesby, Illinois 61348
815-667-4600
www.brightwoodinn.com

BUILT IN 1996 AND NESTLED on 14 acres of meadow within the confines of Matthieseen State Park, the Brightwood Inn was designed to resemble a vintage farmhouse, complete with veranda and rocking chairs. The Brightwood Inn has eight beautiful guest rooms, each with its own unique personality and style. In the morning, the dining room serves a full breakfast to inn guests. The evening meal is open to both guests and the general public. The inn serves a five-course traditional country-inn menu.

Madewood Plantation House

4250 Highway 308
Napoleonville, Louisiana 70390
1-800-374-7151
www.madewood.com

THE MADEWOOD PLANTATION House is a circa 1846 National Historic Landmark mansion that was once part of a sugarcane plantation. A stay at the Madewood begins with a wine and cheese reception in the library, followed by a set-menu dinner served in candlelit elegance. There are five bedrooms in the main house and three more in the informal Charlet House, an early 19th-century riverboat captain's house that is connected to the main mansion by an oak-tree-shaded patio. A full plantation breakfast is served each morning.

Artichoke-Stuffed Chicken Breast

6 boneless chicken breasts
6 well-drained artichoke hearts, cut in half
6 slices bacon (turkey bacon can be substituted)
2 tablespoons unsalted butter
2 tablespoons flour
1 cup white wine (optional)
3 cups scalded milk (or 4 cups if omitting wine)
1/2 medium onion, finely chopped
1 pint sliced mushrooms
  Salt and pepper

Place two halves of artichoke on each chicken breast and fold breast in half. Wrap one slice of bacon around chicken and hold in place with toothpick. Set chicken aside. In a saucepan, melt butter. Add flour and whisk until light brown. Gradually stir in the scalded milk, then add the onion and mushrooms. Season with salt and pepper to taste. Cook sauce for about about 15 minutes.

Preheat oven to 350°F.

Layer chicken breast in a large baking dish. Pour sauce over chicken, cover, and bake for 1 to 1½ hours.

Yield: 6 servings

Superb Fried Chicken, Southern-Style

- 2 packages Good Seasons Italian or Mild Italian salad dressing mix
- 3 tablespoons plus 2 teaspoons flour
- 2 teaspoons salt
- ¼ cup lemon juice or vinegar
- 2 tablespoons margarine or vegetable oil
- 1 (3-pound) broiler chicken, cut up
- 3 cups vegetable oil
- 2 cups milk or club soda
  Pancake mix

Combine salad-dressing mix, flour, salt, lemon juice, and margarine to form a paste. Spread paste evenly over chicken pieces, being sure coating is even (or seasonings will be too potent). Place pieces in large baking dish, cover, and refrigerate at least 2 hours or overnight.

About 1 hour before serving, heat oil in heavy saucepan or electric frying pan, keeping oil at depth of 3 inches. Put milk or soda in a deep, narrow bowl and dip chicken pieces in it. Let excess drip off, then dust lightly but evenly in pancake mix. Dry pieces a few minutes without letting them touch each other. Fry chicken for 5 to 6 minutes, or until browned. Transfer to cookie sheet, still not letting pieces touch.

Preheat oven to 350°F. Bake for about 40 minutes.

Yield: 4 servings

Historic Anderson House
333 Main Street West
Wabasha, Minnesota 55981
651-565-2500
www.historicandersonhouse.com

The Historic Anderson House is a true step back into yesterday. Most of the furniture dates back to the inn's opening in 1856. This is the oldest operating country inn west of the Mississippi. The present innkeepers, Teresa and Mike Smith, are keeping Grandma Anderson's personality and plans in place, though it has been years since she purchased and ran the hotel. Her remarkable knowledge of foods is still the cornerstone of the inn's success. The ever-filled cookie jar is still present at the front desk. Grandma's famous chicken noodle soup, Dutch cinnamon rolls, and chicken and dumplings still lend great interest and excitement to the daily menus. As in Grandma's day, shoes left outside the door are meticulously shined. Cold feet will produce a hot brick for your bed, carefully presented in a quilted envelope.

Old Drovers Inn
196 East Duncan Hill Road
Dover Plains, New York 12522
845-832-9311
www.olddroversinn.com

OLD DROVERS INN OFFERS A fascinating dining experience with a wide-ranging menu in a setting more than 200 years old. Great care is taken to provide only the finest cuisine, and much personal attention is given to the many who constantly beat a pathway to the doorstep. Most people visit Old Drovers savor its luncheons and dinners. The romantic dining room has red leather benches, low wood ceilings, rough beams, and stone walls. The luxury hotel has lodgings upstairs.

Turkey Hash with Mustard Sauce

HASH

 1 cup potatoes, boiled but slightly underdone, finely diced
 1½ cups diced, cooked white turkey meat
 2½ cups diced, cooked dark turkey meat
 ¼ cup finely chopped onion, sautéed lightly (optional)
 Clarified butter
 MSG (optional)
 Chopped fresh parsley

Mix hash ingredients together in bowl. Heat a 7-inch seasoned or Teflon-lined frying pan with clarified butter almost to smoking point. Add hash mixture, sprinkle a few crystals of MSG over the top (if desired). Cover, reduce heat to medium, and cook until edges of hash appear brown. Turn out into a heated shallow casserole dish. Crisp, brown side should face up in casserole. Garnish with pinch of diced fresh parsley. Serve with sauce on the side.

SAUCE

 3 cups chicken stock
 ½ cup beef broth or consommé
 ½ cup prepared mustard, regular or Dijon-style
 2 tablespoons Coleman dry mustard (must use Coleman; some other brands leave bitter aftertaste)
 Salt to taste
 Roux to thicken (melted butter mixed with flour)

In a saucepan, combine all sauce ingredients except the roux and bring to a boil. When boiling, add roux slowly to thicken sauce. When thickened, remove from heat. Serve sauce as aside dish with hash.

Yield: 4 servings hash, 1 quart sauce

Tuscan Turkey Torta Rustica

THE
BLENNERHASSETT

Blennerhassett Hotel
320 Market Street
Parkersburg, West Virginia 26101
304-422-3131
www.blennerhassetthotel.com

4	pounds brioche dough
2	pounds sliced Provolone
1½	pounds peppered turkey breast, cubed
1½	pounds artichoke hearts, quartered
2	pounds ricotta
2	ounces fresh garlic, chopped
1	tablespoon dried basil
1	tablespoon dried oregano
1	teaspoon salt
1	teaspoon freshly grated nutmeg
1	pound spinach leaves, sautéed and drained well
2	ounces toasted pine nuts
1	pound red bell peppers, grilled, seeded, and halved
	Egg wash, as needed

Spray a 12-inch springform pan with nonstick pan coating. On a floured surface, roll out 3 pounds of dough to ¼- to ½-inch thickness. Line the pan with dough, allowing 1 inch of dough to hang over sides. Trim away excess dough. Layer one-quarter of provolone on top of dough. Distribute turkey and artichokes evenly over cheese.

In a separate bowl, combine ricotta, garlic, basil, oregano, salt, and nutmeg. Cover turkey and artichokes with ricotta mixture. Layer with another ½ pound Provolone and press down firmly to remove air pockets. Spread spinach over Provolone. Sprinkle spinach with pine nuts. Cover with another quarter of provolone. Place pepper halves over Provolone and cover peppers with remaining sliced Provolone.

THIS HISTORIC HOTEL BOASTS well over 100 years of hospitality, luxurious accommodations, exceptional service, and understated elegance. Its restaurant is world class, featuring European cuisine and impeccable service. Parkersburg enjoys the wonderful ambience of the Ohio Valley, and the Blennerhassett offers country-inn amenities in an in-town location.

Recipe continued on next page

Preheat oven to 375°F.

Roll out remaining dough to ¼ to ½-inch thickness and cover torta. Trim away excess dough; pinch and roll top dough with overhanging bottom dough to seal the torta. Brush top of torta with egg wash and bake for 15 minutes.

Remove from oven, cover with aluminum foil, and put back in oven for 50 to 60 minutes. Chill for at least two hours before slicing. Serve with a side salad, fresh sliced fruit, or your favorite soup.

Yield: 12 to 16 servings

Yogurt Chicken

1 cup bread crumbs
¼ cup grated Parmesan cheese
2 tablespoons dried minced onion
1 teaspoon garlic powder
1 teaspoon Mrs. Dash seasoning (or regular seasoned salt)
¼ teaspoon dried oregano
¼ teaspoon dried thyme
   Dash of coarse-ground pepper
4 whole chicken breasts, skinned and halved
1 cup plain yogurt
¼ cup melted butter
2 teaspoons sesame seed

Preheat oven to 375°F.

Place crumbs, Parmesan cheese, onion, garlic powder, Mrs. Dash seasoning, oregano, thyme, and pepper in a shallow pan and stir to combine. Rinse chicken and pat dry. Coat chicken with yogurt then roll in crumb mixture. Place chicken meaty side up in a lightly greased baking pan. Drizzle butter over chicken. Sprinkle with sesame seeds. Bake for 45 to 50 minutes or until chicken is tender.

Yield: 8 servings

Audrie's B&B
23029 Thunderhead Falls Road
Rapid City, South Dakota 57702
605-342-7788
www.audriesbb.com

THE ULTIMATE IN CHARM AND Old World hospitality, Audrie's B&B offers spacious suites and cottages that are furnished with comfortable European antiques. All lodgings feature a private entrance, private bath, patio, hot tub, and Black Hills–style breakfast. Each provides you with a setting that quiets your heart and says, "Breathe deep, you have all the time in the world." This country home and 7-acre estate is surrounded by thousands of acres of national forest in a secluded Black Hills setting. This is the area's first and finest bed-and-breakfast establishment.

SEAFOOD

Elkhorn Inn & Theatre

U.S. Route 52, Landgraft
P. O. Box 100
Eckman, West Virginia 24829
304-862-2031
www.elkhorninnwv.com

THE ELKHORN INN, IN Landgraff, West Virginia, between Eckman and Kimball, is just 30 minutes from Bluefield, West Virginia, and Virginia. The newly restored, historic "Coal Heritage Trail" inn with train-view guest rooms, balcony, and patio, is on trout-filled Elkhorn Creek and near some of the best ATV trails in the eastern United States. The inn provides bed-and-breakfast accommodations in 13 air-conditioned guest rooms, meals, and elegant dining room. The inn features a patio cafe, antique claw-foot bathtubs, bathrobes, signature toiletries, 1930s furnishings, art and antiques, and a cozy fireplace lounge. The gift shop has vintage American quilts, original jewelry, artwork, and handcrafted West Virginia coal statuettes. There is an art studio for use by artists staying at the inn.

Dan's Almond-Crusted, Pan-Fried Trout

1 cup almonds, ground
1 cup dried, seasoned bread crumbs or stuffing mix
  Salt and crushed pepper to taste
½ tablespoon oregano
¼ teaspoon paprika
¼ teaspoon cumin
⅓ cup all-purpose flour
½ cup mayonnaise
4 rainbow or brook trout, boned and filleted,
  or 4 catfish fillets
  Vegetable oil

In a bowl, mix bread crumbs, almonds, and spices. Place flour in a second bowl. Roll fish fillets in flour to dry. With a spatula, cover each fillet with mayonnaise, and roll in bread crumb mixture to coat. Heat about 1 inch of vegetable oil in a large skillet over medium heat. Cook fillets, turning once, until both sides are brown and fish flakes, about 5 minutes per side. Suggested side dishes are new potatoes and fresh green beans.

Yield: 4 servings

Baked Bluefish

- 1 (8- to 10-pound) fresh bluefish, scaled and gutted
- 1 teaspoon salt
- 1 teaspoon pepper
- 2 large carrots, coarsely chopped
- 1 large onion, coarsely chopped
- 5 stalks celery, coarsely chopped
- ½ bunch dill, coarsely chopped
- ½ bunch basil, coarsely chopped
- ½ bunch parsley, coarsely chopped
- 1 cup dry white wine
- ¼ cup butter, melted

Preheat oven to 350°F.

Season bluefish inside and out with salt and pepper. Stuff with vegetables and herbs. Lay fish on a large baking pan. Place excess vegetables around fish. Pour the wine and melted butter over fish. Bake at for 45 minutes or until fish flakes easily.

Yield: 10 to 12 servings

The 1661
Inn and Hotel Manisses
P. O. Box 1
Block Island, Rhode Island 02807
401-466-2421
www.blockislandresorts.com

THE 1661 INN IS LOCATED IN Old Harbor's historic district and overlooks the Atlantic Ocean. The ocean-view dining room features a canopied outdoor deck, so that guests enjoy great food either indoors or out. The inn's partner, Hotel Manisses, was built in 1870 and completely restored in 1972. The 18 guest rooms are furnished with early 1900s furniture. The lovely dining room's menu offers unusual selections, from freshly shucked seafood to masterfully prepared entrées.

SEAFOOD

**The Plantation Inn
Bed and Breakfast**
174 Lahainaluna Road
Lahaina, Maui, Hawaii 96761
1-800-433-6815
www.theplantationinn.com

THE PLANTATION INN IS Maui's premier bed-and-breakfast. Early 20th century architectural style combined with modern amenities such as air conditioning, sound proofing, tiled baths, pool, and Jacuzzis offer guests a tranquil oasis in the heart of Maui's historic Lahaina Town. Less than two blocks from the waterfront, the inn has 19 rooms and suites, each with its own custom interior design. Antiques, stained glass, hardwood floors, brass and poster beds, extensive wood trim, and sprawling verandas re-create the charm of old Hawaii. The Plantation Inn is home to Gerard's Restaurant, one of the finest French restaurants in North America. Romantic and inviting, Chef Gerard Reversade's contemporary island-French cuisine consistently earns some of the highest ratings in Hawaii.

Calamari with Lime and Ginger

3 tablespoons sesame oil
3 tablespoons peanut oil
  Salt and pepper
3 pounds calamari, cleaned, gutted, and sliced ¼-inch thick
1 scallion, sliced ¼-inch thick
2 ounces fresh ginger, peeled and diced small
3 limes, peeled and sectioned (save juice that comes out during peeling and sectioning)

Heat two heavy sauté pans and add both oils. Season the calamari with salt and pepper. Sauté on high heat to retain tenderness and crispiness. Cook only a few seconds. Turn off heat. Add scallions, ginger, and lime juice. Transfer to a heated serving plate. Decorate with the lime sections and serve immediately.

Yield: 6 servings

Cod with Winter Citrus

4   thick cod fillets
¼   pound dried chickpeas (or 1 can cooked)
2   cloves garlic
2   shallot bulbs
½   carrot, peeled
½   onion, peeled but root end left intact
2   dried bay leaves
    Salt
½   cup Yuzu juice, found in high-end Asian food stores (can substitute ¼ cup grapefruit juice and ¼ cup lemon juice if unavailable)
2   tablespoons candied Yuzu or lemon rind (optional)
2   blood oranges
2   navel oranges
2   Meyer lemons (can omit if unavailable)
2   Palestine limes (can omit if unavailable)
1   fennel bulb, julienned
2   Belgian endives, quartered
2   cups fresh baby spinach (not bagged if possible; can substitute frozen)

To prepare the chickpeas: If using dried chickpeas, soak them overnight. The next day, drain and rinse peas and place in a large pot. Cover with about 2 inches cold water and bring to a boil. Skim and scum, then add 1 clove garlic, 1 shallot bulb, the carrot, onion, and bay leaf. Cook at a simmer until the peas are tender. Towards the end of cooking, season with salt and cook 10 minutes longer. Drain and cool chickpeas.

Chop the remaining garlic clove and shallot bulb, sauté in olive oil until translucent, add the chickpeas, and sauté over medium heat. Deglaze pan with the Yuzu juice and add the candied Yuzu. Reduce mixture until almost dry.

Recipe continued on next page

Home Hill French Inn & Restaurant
703 River Road
Plainfield, New Hampshire 03781
603-675-6165
www.homehillinn.com

WELCOME TO HOME HILL Inn, a romantic, French-inspired retreat set on 25 secluded acres in Plainfield, New Hampshire. Experience the luxury of beautifully appointed rooms, an award-winning French restaurant, pampering body-massage treatments, and a boutique featuring fine linens, bath products, and pottery from Provence. Our seasonal packages include access to nearby golf courses and ski resorts. Breathtaking views, fine dining, and attentive services make Home Hill Inn the ideal location for special functions and corporate retreats.

Place the chickpeas in a food processor and process, adding more olive oil or Yuzu juice to taste. Also season with salt, white pepper, and a little sugar to taste. Set aside.

To prepare the citrus: Remove the segments from 1 of each of the citrus fruits and juice the rest, mixing all the juices.

To prepare the fish: Sauté or poach the cod.

To serve: Place a dollop of the chickpea purée in the center of each plate and reserve in a warming oven. Sauté the fennel and endive in olive oil with the remaining chickpeas. Once warm, remove to the plates, dividing evenly and keep warm. Deglaze the pan with the citrus juice, reduce by half, and check the seasoning. Add some olive oil if necessary to round out the flavor.

Pour the sauce around each of 4 plates, reserving about 2 tablespoons in the pan. Return the pan to the heat and add some more olive oil and the spinach. Cook until spinach is just wilted and divide among the 4 plates. Place the cod in the center on top of puréed chickpeas and spread citrus sections around the outside. Serve immediately.

Yield: 4 servings

Creamy Lobster Succotash on Cheese Biscuits

CHEESE BISCUITS

- 2 cups all-purpose flour
- 1 tablespoon salt
- 1 tablespoon baking powder
- ½ cup cheddar cheese, shredded and packed tight
- 1 teaspoon dill
- 8 tablespoons butter
- ¼ cup buttermilk

In medium bowl, sift dry ingredients and add cheese and dill. Cut in butter. Add buttermilk and mix until combined. Roll out the dough and cut into biscuits. Bake at 425°F for 15 minutes.

LOBSTER SUCCOTASH

- 1 tablespoon butter
- ½ cup red onion, diced
- ½ cup country ham, diced
- 1 teaspoon garlic, minced
- 1 sprig fresh thyme
- ¾ cup corn, cut from cob or frozen whole kernels
- 1 pound lobster meat, uncooked
- ¼ cup white wine
- 2 cups heavy cream
- ¾ cup lima beans, cooked
  Salt and pepper, to taste

In a large skillet melt butter on medium heat and cook red onion and country ham until onion is soft. Add garlic, corn, and lobster and cook until lobster is nearly cooked through. Deglaze the pan with wine and add heavy cream. When cream reduces by a third, add cooked lima beans. Cook until beans are warm. Add salt and pepper. Spoon mixture over biscuits.

Yield: 4 servings

Camberley's Martha Washington Inn
150 West Main Street
Abingdon, Virginia 24210
540-628-3161
www.marthawashingtoninn.com

THE BUILDINGS that now constitute Camberley's Martha Washington Inn have long been the most outstanding historic buildings of this section of the country. The center building, erected in 1830 by General Francis Preston as a residence, has been associated with the social life, the culture, and the educational progress of the area since that time. In 1937, the property was converted into a 100-room inn. The main dining room seats 300. It is especially famous for its superb southern dishes, including Old Virginia country ham, fried chicken, spoon bread and hot biscuits.

Crab Maidstone

The Inn at Mitchell House
8796 Maryland Parkway
Chestertown, Maryland 21620
410-778-6500
www.innatmitchellhouse.com

½ cup butter
4 egg yolks
½ cup whipping cream
3 tablespoons lemon juice
½ teaspoon dry mustard
   Old Bay seasoning to taste (available in most
     supermarkets)
3 tablespoons chopped fresh parsley
1 pound lump crabmeat

In a large microwavable ovenproof bowl, melt butter. In a separate bowl, beat yolks, whipping cream, lemon juice, mustard, and Old Bay. Stir this mixture into butter. Microwave uncovered on high for about 3 minutes (stir a few times). Cook until thick, whisking until smooth. Fold in parsley and crabmeat. Divide mixture among 4 scallop dishes and broil until brown. Asparagus and crusty bread are great side dishes.

Yield: 4 servings

NESTLED ON 10 ROLLING acres, surrounded by woods and overlooking Stoneybrook Pond, this historic manor house, built in 1743, greets you with warmth and affords a touch of tranquility. Innkeepers Jim and Tracy Stone offer gracious hospitality typically found in days past. Their six-bedroom inn, with parlors and numerous fireplaces, provides a casual and friendly atmosphere. Depending upon the season, you may be awakened in the morning by birdsong or migrating geese. At sunset, white-tailed deer, a red fox, or a rare soaring eagle add to the scene. It is truly a nature-lover's paradise. The inn is a pleasant 10-mile drive from Chestertown, a charming colonial town steeped in history and filled with quaint shops. If traveling by boat, the Tolchester Marina is a mere half mile away.

Grilled Ahi
with Thai Onion Sauté

ONION SAUTÉ

1   large leek, cleaned and julienned
1   large red onion, julienned
¾   cup Thai Vinaigrette (see page 144)

Sauté leek and onion until soft; add vinaigrette and cook until all liquid is almost absorbed.

TUNA

4   (8-ounce) yellowfin tuna fillets (also excellent
    with mahi mahi)
    Salt and pepper

Preheat grill. Season tuna with salt and pepper to taste. Grill for 2 to 3 minutes on each side to serve rare.

To serve: Spoon onion sauté on top of tuna. This dish is nice served on a bed of cooked Asian noodles, such as rice stick or soba.

Yield: 4 servings

Chico Hot Springs Resort
Highway 89 South
P. O. Box 134
Pray, Montana 59065
406-333-4933
www.chicohotsprings.com

THE CHICO HOT SPRINGS resort is high country at its best—it is located in south-central Montana's Paradise Valley. The Absaroka mountain range defines the eastern skyline, the Gallatin range the west, and the famous Yellowstone River runs between the two. Chico's history centers on its hot pools, whose "restorative" powers have been put to use for over a century. The water in the pools is between 100 and 104°F add includes no chlorine or other chemicals. The food is absolutely wonderful.

The Inn
at Meander Plantation

2333 North James Madison Highway
Locust Dale, Virginia 22948
540-672-4912
www.inn@meander.net

THE INN AT MEADER PLANTA-
tion is a beautiful 1776
country inn. Centrally
located an hour from Washington DC,
Fredericksburg, and Charlottesville, it
offers fine dining and luxurious
accommodations surrounded by 80
acres of rolling landscape in the
foothills of the Blue Ridge Mountains
of Virginia. Guests come to the inn to
rest and enjoy the pleasures of a
simpler life in true Virginia country-inn
style. Stroll through formal boxwood
gardens or wander woods and fields
where wildlife abounds. At this stately
colonial mansion you will find plenty of
private areas for reading, writing, or
quiet contemplation. Or join other
guests for pleasant conversation in the
parlor where Thomas Jefferson and
General Lafayette were frequent
visitors. A baby grand piano is ready
for impromptu concerts.

Grilled Marinated Tuna

MARINADE
½ cup soy sauce
½ cup orange juice
¼ cup olive oil
¼ cup tomato paste
2 tablespoons fresh parsley, minced
3 cloves garlic, minced
2 teaspoons lemon juice
1 teaspoon dried oregano
1 teaspoon ground black pepper

6 tuna steaks (can also use swordfish, kingfish,
   or mahi mahi)
Orange slices
Parsley

In a bowl, whisk together marinade ingredients. Place fish steaks in a single layer in a shallow dish. Pour marinade over, cover with plastic wrap, and refrigerate for 1 hour.

Prepare a broiler or a fire for grilling. Remove fish from marinade and grill about 5 inches from the heat for 4 to 5 minutes on each side, or just until the fish is firm. Garnish with orange slices and parsley.

Yield: 6 servings

Halibut Chowder

 2 cups diced onions
 4 cups diced celery
 ¼ cup oil
 8 cups chopped potatoes
 2 teaspoons salt
 2 teaspoons white pepper
 16 cups water
 4 cups chicken stock
 4 cups cream
 8 cups diced fresh halibut
   Chopped fresh parsley

In a stockpot, sauté onions and celery in oil. Add potatoes, salt, and pepper; cover with the water and boil until tender. Add chicken stock and bring to boil. Reduce to a simmer and stir in the cream. Add halibut and bring back just to a simmer (don't overcook or the chowder will taste fishy). Ladle into bowls and garnish with parsley.

Yield: 24 to 32 servings

Glacier Bay Country Inn
P. O. Box 5
Gustavus, Alaska 99826
907-697-2288
www.glacierbayalaska.com

SITUATED NEAR THE CENTER of a 160-acre homestead, this inn offers the chance to experience Alaskan country living in a true wilderness setting. There are forests of towering spruce, hemlock, and pine; hayfields swaying in the breeze; meadows ablaze with wildflowers; bountiful gardens; meandering creeks; exceptional mountain views; and, deep in the woods, down a narrow winding road, this delightful, inviting inn. Marvelous food is one of its features.

The Bucksville House
4501 Durham Road
Kintnersville, Pennsylvania 18930
610-847-8948
www.bucksvillehouse.com

The Bucksville House bed-and-breakfast, a registered Bucks County historical landmark, provides the visitor not only with country charm, but also with over 200 years of Pennsylvania history. Built in 1795, the Bucksville House has had several lifetimes and expansions as an 1830s holtel, a tavern, and as a speakeasy during the Prohibition period. Innkeepers Barbara and Joe Szollosi purchased the Bucksville House bed-and-breakfast as an "ultimate handyman's special" in 1984 and began welcoming guests a year later. The house's décor reflects its 1790s to 1840s origin. Period reproductions include four-poster beds, a country kitchen table and cabinet, desk, bureau, and backgammon set. Restored 19th-century pieces, antique collectibles, original art, and nearly 100 quilts (the earliest homespun quilt dates to the 1800s) decorate the bed-and-breakfast throughout.

King Crab and Artichoke Casserole

¼ cup melted butter
2 tablespoons chopped onion
½ teaspoon salt
¼ teaspoon curry powder
2 tablespoons flour
1 cup milk
1 tablespoon lemon juice
1 (6-ounce) package frozen crabmeat, thawed
1 package artichoke hearts, thawed
1 cup grated sharp Cheddar cheese
½ cup bread crumbs

Melt butter in a saucepan. Add onions and sauté. Add salt, curry, flour, and milk, and cook until thick. Stir in lemon and crabmeat.

Preheat oven to 350°F.

Put artichokes in bottom of a casserole dish. Sprinkle cheese over, cover with sauce, and sprinkle with bread crumbs. Bake for 30 minutes.

Yield: 3 servings

Fergie's Lime Crusted Haddock

1 lime
¼ cup white wine
1½ cups fresh bread crumbs
¼ cup melted butter
4 (8-ounce) skinless haddock fillets
Salt and pepper

Preheat oven to 400°F.

Grate zest from lime. Cut lime in half and squeeze juice into another bowl. Combine bread crumbs, lime zest, half the butter, and half the lime juice. Place haddock fillets in a shallow baking dish. Season fillets with salt and pepper to taste. Combine remaining lime juice and butter and drizzle over and around fillets. Coat each fillet evenly with bread-crumb mixture. Bake for 10 to 12 minutes or until bread crumbs are golden brown.

Yield: 4 servings

English Rose Inn
195 Vermont Route 242
Montgomery Center, Vermont 05471
802-326-3232
www.englishroseinnvermont.com

THE ENGLISH ROSE INN IS located in the picturesque northeast kingdom of Vermont, offering warm luxurious accommodations, fine dining at the inn's Paddington's Restaurant, and spectacular mountain views. You will enjoy a pleasurable, romantic, Victorian getaway in the 25-room 1850s farmhouse, which features 14 beautifully decorated guest rooms and suites. Lace curtains, hardwood floors, and crocheted and homemade heirloom quilts adorn the antique-filled rooms. A stay includes a deluxe gourmet breakfast, world-class cuisine, and much, much more. Mary Jane and Gary Bouchard-Pike are the gracious innkeepers.

The Red Lion Inn

30 Main Street
Stockbridge, Massachusetts 01262
413-298-5545
www.redlioninn.com

W HEN YOU STEP INSIDE THE Red Lion Inn, you enter a world of friendly courtesy and hospitality. This lovely Berkshire Hills townwas once an Indian village. The inn was built in 1773 as a small tavern and stagecoach stop for vehicles traveling the Boston, Hartford, and Albany runs. During its life, the inn has sheltered five United States presidents. There is the charm of Staffordshire china, colonial pewter, and 18th-century furniture. The fare is traditional New England with many Continental specialties.

Lobster Casserole

- 2 cups water
- 4 lobsters (about 1½ pounds each)
- 2 teaspoons salt
- 1 tablespoon plus 1 teaspoon chopped parsley stems
- ¼ cup Old Bay seasoning
- ½ cup dry sherry
- ¾ cup butter
- 1 cup dried bread crumbs
- ⅓ cup chopped parsley
- ½ teaspoon dried thyme
- 1 tablespoon plus 1 teaspoon ketchup
- 8 slices white bread
- ¾ cup (1½ sticks) butter
- 1 tablespoon plus 1 teaspoon paprika
- 1 lemon, cut into wedges

Preheat oven to 350°F. Butter a 4-quart ovenproof casserole dish or 4 individual ramekins.

Place water in a large steamer and bring to a boil. Reduce heat to bring water to a simmer. Place lobsters, salt, parsley stems, and Old Bay seasoning in the steamer and cook for 12 to 15 minutes or until lobster shells turn red and meat is cooked. Clean and cut up the lobsters, removing tail, claw, and leg meat. Split tail meat in half, then cut each half into 6 pieces. Leave claw meat whole, but remove the cartilage. There should be approximately 1 cup of meat from each lobster.

Place the lobster meat in prepared casserole dish or ramekins, and drizzle ¼ cup of the sherry over top. Melt the butter. In a small bowl, combine the remaining ¼ cup sherry, ¼ cup melted butter, bread crumbs, ¼ cup of the chopped parsley, thyme, and ketchup. Mix well and sprinkle this mixture over the lobster (do not pat it down). Cut remaining ¼ cup butter into small pieces and place over bread crumb mixture. Bake for 12 to 15 minutes, until bubbly hot.

Meanwhile, cut crusts off the bread and toast the slices. Cut toast in half to form triangles, and butter them with the remaining ¼ cup melted butter. Dip tips in paprika. Dip tips of lemon wedges in remaining 4 teaspoons chopped parsley. Serve the casserole, accompanied by the toast and lemon wedges. Coleslaw and roasted potatoes are excellent accompaniments to this dish.

Yield: 4 servings

Steamboat Inn
42705 North Umpqua Highway
Steamboat, Oregon 97447-9703
1-800-840-8825
541-498-2230
www.thesteamboatinn.com

THE STEAMBOAT INN IS located 38 scenic miles east of Roseburg, Oregon, on Highway 138. It commands a breathtaking view of the North Umpqua River. Nestled among the towering firs of the Umpqua National Forest, the inn is a perfect lodging base for the numerous nearby attractions, such as Crater Lake National Park, Diamond Lake, excellent wineries, and a wildlife safari park. Fishing at its most challenging, trails for hikers, and swimming are all within minutes of the inn. The inn's cafe offers a menu featuring homemade soups, pies, breads, and other delicious treats available for breakfast and lunch. The inn is small enough to allow groups the exclusive use of the entire facility during the winter months.

Red Snapper with Jalapeño-Lime Marinade

MARINADE

- 2 fresh jalapeño peppers, seeded and chopped (see note)
- 1/3 cup chopped yellow onion
- 1 heaping tablespoon minced fresh ginger root
- 1 teaspoon minced fresh rosemary
- 1 teaspoon salt
- 1/4 cup lime juice
- 1/4 cup water

- 1 1/2 pounds fresh red snapper fillets, bones removed, trimmed of any fat
- 1/2 cup Seasoned Flour (recipe follows)
- 2 teaspoons butter
- 2 teaspoons olive oil
  Lime wedges

Purée marinade ingredients to make a thick marinade.

Place the fish in a noncorrosive baking pan, cover with the purée and marinate 1 to 2 hours in refrigerator, turning occasionally. Remove fillets from marinade and lightly dredge in seasoned flour, shaking off any excess. Melt butter and olive oil in a skillet over medium heat. Sauté fillets for 3 to 4 minutes per side, until the fish flakes easily with a fork. Arrange on serving platter and garnish with lime wedges if desired.

^{1}/$_2$ cup flour
1^1/$_4$ teaspoons dried rosemary
1^1/$_4$ teaspoons dried marjoram
^{1}/$_4$ teaspoon salt
^{1}/$_8$ teaspoon pepper
^{1}/$_8$ teaspoon cayenne pepper

Combine all of the above ingredients, mixing well. This flour is easy to keep on hand, as it holds well under refrigeration.

For a quick entrée, add ^{1}/$_3$ cup freshly grated Parmesan to the above and coat either boned chicken breasts or fresh fish fillets. Sauté in butter or olive oil until done. The whole process should take 10 to 15 minutes.

Yield: 4 servings

Note: When working with hot peppers, be sure to wear plastic gloves and keep your hands away from your eyes and face.

Gaston's White River Resort

1777 River Road
Lakeview, Arkansas 72642
870-431-5202
www.gastons.com

GASTON'S WHITE RIVER RESORT began in 1958 when Al Gaston, Jim Gaston's father, purchased 20 acres of White River frontage with six small cottages and six boats. Now the resort covers over 400 acres with 2 miles of river frontage and has 79 cottages, ranging in size from two double beds and a bathroom to a two-story cottage with 10 private bedrooms. As the premier trout-fishing resort in America, Gaston's has caught and cooked a lot of trout. Over the years, it has developed what may be the world's largest collection of recipes—brought together from many sources, including the Gaston family and the finest restaurants. You will never find a more magnificent view than the one from our restaurant. Almost rivaling the tranquil beauty of the river view is the cozy atmosphere created by the collection of old tools, antiques, and historic photography.

*The Great Country Inns
of America Cookbook*

Salmon Croquettes

1½ cups flour
¾ teaspoon baking soda
3 large cans red salmon
  Salt and pepper
6 eggs, beaten
1½ cups buttermilk
  Lemon juice and/or chopped green onions (optional)

Mix flour and baking soda together in a bowl. Add remaining ingredients and mix well. Form mixture into 24 patties. Refrigerate. When chilled, fry until golden brown. Drain on absorbent paper.

Yield: 24 servings

Scalloped Oysters

- ½ cup dry bread crumbs
- ½ cup coarse cracker crumbs
- 5 tablespoons butter, melted
- 1 pint oysters
- ½ teaspoon salt
- ⅛ teaspoon pepper
- ⅛ teaspoon nutmeg
- 2 tablespoons fresh parsley, chopped
- 1 (10-ounce) can mushroom soup

Preheat oven to 350°F.

Combine bread crumbs, cracker crumbs, and butter. Place half of mixture in a greased casserole dish. Arrange oysters in layers, sprinkling each layer with salt, pepper, nutmeg, and parsley. Pour soup over oysters. Top with remaining crumbs. Bake for 1 hour.

Yield: 4 servings

Robert Morris Inn
314 North Morris Street
Oxford, Maryland 21654
410-226-5111
www.robertmorrisinn.com

THE ROBERT MORRIS INN was built prior to 1710 by ship's carpenters and was used as a residence by Robert Morris. His son, Robert Morris, Jr., helped finance the Revolutionary War and was a signer of the Declaration of Independence, the Articles of the Confederation, and the United States Constitution. This is truly a historic place to raise a glass of beer and enjoy seafood along the Chesapeake Bay.

Litchfield Plantation

P.O. Box 290
Pawley's Island,
South Carolina 29585
1-800-869-1410
www.litchfieldplantation.com

AS YOU ENTER THE Litchfield Plantation through the wrought-iron gates, and ride down the quarter-mile Avenue of Live Oaks shrouded in Spanish moss, you feel transported in time, your heartbeat slows, and your cares slip away. Litchfield Plantation, an extraordinary bed-and-breakfast retreat, is located on the principal 600 acres of a 1750s coastal rice plantation. It has been meticulously transformed into a country inn with some of the most exceptional accommodations you will ever encounter. Gourmet dining is available in the Carriage House Club.

Grilled Scallops with Corn Salsa and Shellfish Cream

SALSA

 3 ears corn, roasted in husk
 ½ red pepper, cut into small dice
 ½ yellow pepper, cut into small dice
 ¼ red onion, cut into small dice
 2 tablespoons fresh cilantro, chopped
 1 tablespoon olive oil
   Juice of 1 lime
 ¼ jalapeño pepper, minced
   Salt and pepper

Remove the husk from the corn and cut the kernels from the cob. Place in bowl and add the remaining ingredients. Mix and season with salt and pepper. Refrigerate until ready to serve.

SHELLFISH CREAM

 1 tablespoon paprika
 1 (8-ounce) can shellfish stock
 ½ tablespoon lobster base
 1 cup heavy cream
   Cornstarch slurry
   Salt and pepper

Combine paprika, stock, lobster base, and cream in a saucepan and bring to a boil, stirring occasionally. Thicken with cornstarch slurry and add salt and pepper to taste. Keep warm.

12 large sea scallops
1 tablespoon blackening spice
1 cup corn salsa (recipe above)
1½ cups shellfish cream (recipe above)
4 crispy beet curls
4 cilantro sprigs

Prepare a fire or preheat a gas grill. Season scallops with blackening spice. Grill scallops 4 to 5 minutes on each side.

To assemble: Place ¼ cup of salsa in the center of each of 4 plates. Arrange 3 scallops around the salsa. Place a spot of shellfish cream in each of the three spaces between the scallops (2 ounces total per plate). Top with beet garnish and cilantro sprig.

Yield: 4 servings

The Hermosa Inn

5532 North Palo Cristi
Paradise Valley, Arizona 85253
1-800-241-1210
www.hermosainn.com

The Hermosa Inn was hand built by cowboy artist Lon Megargee as his home and studio. Its 35 hotel accommodations and acclaimed on-site restaurant, Lon's at the Hermosa, have been restored with careful attention to modern-day comforts, while preserving original charm and authentic touches. Enjoy the serenity of the hotel courtyard fountains and fireplaces with friends and business associates. Pathways ramble through The 6½-acre grounds, marked by gracious olive and mesquite trees, towering palms, fragrant citrus and brilliant flowers. The restaurant is known for award-winning artful American cuisine, wood-grilled steaks, and fresh seafood.

Georges Bank Sea Scallops with Black Truffle Spaetzle, Lemon-Butter Sauce, and Organic Spinach

SPAETZLE

2½ cups flour
5 eggs
½ cup whole milk
1 tablespoon truffle oil
2 large black truffles, finely chopped
   Salt and pepper
   Olive oil
   Butter

In a bowl, mix flour into eggs. Add milk, truffle oil, truffles, and a touch of salt. Push dough through a large perforated pan or colander into boiling water. Shock spaetzle in ice water. Lightly oil with olive oil to prevent it from sticking together. Reheat spaetzle in whole butter. Finish with salt and pepper.

SAUCE

1 tablespoon butter plus ½ pound unsalted butter,
   cut in small cubes
1 shallot, chopped
   Zest and juice of 1 lemon
½ cup white wine
2 tablespoons heavy cream

Melt the 1 tablespoon butter in a small saucepan on low heat. Add shallot and lemon zest and cook until translucent. Add wine and reduce down until dry. Add cream and lemon juice, then slowly whisk in cubed butter over low heat; do not add too quickly or the sauce will become too cold and separate.

10 sea scallops (10/20 count)
Sea salt
White pepper
Clarified butter

Season scallops with sea salt and white pepper to taste. Melt clarified butter in a frying pan on very high heat. Add scallops and sauté for about 5 minutes; scallops should brown slightly and lose their translucency.

SPINACH

¼ pound fresh spinach, washed well
Olive oil
Salt and pepper

In a hot sauté pan, quickly sauté spinach in a little olive oil. Season with salt and pepper.

To assemble: Place a small pile of spinach in the middle of 2 large dinner plates. Place a small pile of spaetzle over the spinach. Place 5 scallops around the spaetzle and drizzle the sauce around the outside. Serve immediately. Garnish with a little micro amaranth (spinach family) and serve.

Yield: 2 servings

Captain Whidbey Inn

2070 Captain Whidbey Inn Road
Coupeville, Washington 98239
1-800-366-4097
360-678-4097
www.captainwhidbey.com

LOCATED ON THE SHORE of Whidbey Island's Penn Cove is the Captain Whidbey Inn. Island hospitality awaits guests, and a variety of accommodations are available. The quaint rooms of the historic main inn, the rustic cabins, and the cozy secluded cottages, feature featherbeds, down comforters, artwork, antiques, and books. The history of the inn goes back to 1907, before there were bridges and cars on the island. Guests were brought in by paddlewheel steamer, and the Whid Isle Inn, as it was originally called, was quite the resort.

Sesame Seed–Crusted Halibut with Lemon-Sage Butter

LEMON-SAGE BUTTER

- 4 pounds softened butter
- 8 tablespoons chopped fresh sage leaves
- 8 tablespoons minced garlic
  Juice and grated zest of 4 lemons

Place all ingredients in large bowl of electric mixer and whip until fluffy. Shape into four 12- to 14-inch logs; wrap each log in waxed paper. Chill until butter is firm. Recipe makes extra that can be frozen for later use.

FISH

- 4 cups sesame seeds
- 2 cups all-purpose flour
  Salt and white pepper
  Milk, (for dipping)
- ½ to ¾ cup olive oil
- 20 (6-ounce) halibut fillets
  Alder wood planks (see note)

Preheat oven to 425°F.

In a shallow pan, mix sesame seeds, flour, and salt and pepper to taste. Place milk in a shallow bowl or pan. Dip fish in milk then dredge in sesame seed–flour mixture to give fillets a light coating. Heat oil over high heat in a nonstick sauté pan (or pans) until oil is smoking. Add fillets and brown each side—about 30 seconds per side. Transfer browned fish to a wood plank and bake for about 10 to 15 minutes or until fish feels firm to the touch.

Place each fillet on a serving plate and top with a tablespoon of lemon-sage butter.

Yield: 20 servings

Note: Native Americans used wood to barbecue fish on open fire pits. The planks give the halibut a hint of charred wood and helps to keep the fish tender. Alder wood planks for baking fish can be found in some home-improvement stores. (Untreated hickory, cherry, or cedar planks work well too.)

102 Brownstone
Boutique Hotel
102 West 118th Street
New York, New York 10026
212-662-4223
www.102brownstone.com

*I*F YOU SEEK AN EXHILARAT-ing New York experi-ence, stay at the 102 Brownstone. In a beautiful private apartment or elegant private suite you can enjoy the city with all the comfort, convenience, and privacy of home. The accommodations are designed for the senses, and the warm ambience contributes to the sense of retreat. The 102 Brownstone offers the conven-ience of a hotel with the warmth and comfort of home. Guests keep their own schedules and enjoy the privacy they deserve while on vacation. Full apartments offer the option of home-cooked meals or early morning coffee.

Shredded Cod

1½	pounds dried boneless cod
3	tablespoons olive oil
3	large cloves garlic, crushed
	Juice of 1 lime
1	small white onion, sliced
	Fresh parsley, chopped
	Crushed red hot pepper (optional)

Place fish pieces in a pot full of water, bring to a boil, and cook for 2 minutes. Remove pot from heat and drain. Add cold water to the pieces of cod and shred. Place the shredded cod in the same pot, bring to a boil, and cook for 5 minutes. Remove from heat and drain.

Heat olive oil in a sauté pan. Add garlic and sauté. Add shredded cod. Reduce heat to low. Add lime juice and cook for 3 minutes. Add ½ cup of water and cook for 3 more minutes. Add the onion, parsley, and red hot pepper. Cook for 1 more minute. Serve with your favorite white wine.

Yield: 4 servings

Spicy Shrimp and Green Tomatoes

John Rutledge House Inn
116 Broad Street
Charleston, South Carolina 29401
1-800-476-9741
www.charminginns.com

BUILT IN 1763 BY JOHN Rutledge, a signer of the U. S. Constitution, this antebellum home is now an elegant bed-and-breakfast inn. Located in the heart of the historic district, the inn is a reminder of a more gracious time. Guests enjoy afternoon tea, wine, and sherry in the ballroom where patriots, statesmen, and presidents have met. There is evening turn-down service with chocolates at bedside, and pastries are delivered to guest rooms each morning.

- 1 small shallot, peeled
- 2 cloves garlic, peeled
- 2 tablespoons red hot sauce
- ¾ cup canola oil
- 1 teaspoon salt
- 1 pinch white pepper
- Shrimp
- Oil, for frying
- ½ cup corn flour
- ½ cup all-purpose flour
- 2 tablespoons Old Bay seasoning
- 1 cup buttermilk
- 1 green tomato, sliced about ½-inch thick

Place shallot, garlic, and hot sauce in a blender and blend until smooth. Slowly add oil to the mixture while it is still blending. Season shrimp with salt and pepper. Pour the marinade over shrimp and refrigerate for about a half hour.

Heat fryer oil to 350°F. Preheat grill.

Mix the two flours and Old Bay seasoning together in a shallow dish. Place buttermilk in another shallow dish. Dredge tomato slices in flour mixture to completely coat, then dip in buttermilk and back into flour mixture. Place tomatoes in fryer and cook until golden brown.

Remove shrimp from marinade and grill until pink (about 2 minutes per side). Place them on top of the fried green tomatoes and place over a fresh tomato sauce. Serve immediately.

Yield: 1 or 2 servings

The Checkerberry Inn
62644 County Road 37
Goshen, Indiana 46528
574-642-0198
www.checkerberryinn.com

A T THE CHECKERBERRY Inn, the visitor will find a unique atmosphere, unlike anywhere else in the Midwest. The individually decorated rooms and suites will please even the most discerning guests. Every room has a breathtaking view of the unspoiled rolling countryside. A top-rated restaurant serves only the freshest foods, using herbs and other ingredients from the local countryside.

Shrimp Napoleon

NAPOLEON

- 1 small eggplant
- 1 zucchini
- 1 yellow squash
- 1 roasted red bell pepper
- 1 large portabella mushroom

24 shrimp, deveined and cleaned

VEGETABLE MARINADE

- ½ cup extra-virgin olive oil
- ¼ cup minced garlic
- ¼ cup minced shallots

SHRIMP MARINADE

- 1 teaspoon balsamic vinegar
- 1 tablespoon olive oil
- 1 tablespoon lime juice
  Pinch of salt and pepper

SAUCE

- 1 cup olive oil
- 1 cup balsamic-fig vinegar (available at health-food or specialty-food store)
- 1 tablespoon salt and pepper mixture

GARNISH

  Lemon wedges
- ¼ cup chopped parsley

Slice all vegetables lengthwise (as evenly as possible). Stir vegetable marinade ingredients together. Add vegetables and marinate for 30 minutes.

Whisk together sauce ingredients and set aside.

Preheat grill. Grill vegetables 5 to 7 minutes per side. Remove from grill and cover with foil. Grill shrimp only 2 to 3 minutes per side.

To assemble: Layer vegetables and shrimp. Drizzle with sauce and garnish with lemon wedges and parsley. Serve immediately.

Yield: 5 servings

Chalet Suzanne Country Inn

3800 Chalet Suzanne Lane
Lake Wales, Florida 33859
863-676-6011
www.chaletsuzanne.com

OWNED AND OPERATED BY THE Hinshaw family, Chalet Suzanne was born more than 60 years ago of Yankee ingenuity and Southern hospitality. The late Carl Hinshaw's mother, Bertha, was a gourmet cook, collector, and world traveler who had her own way of coping with the double disaster of her husband's death and loss of the family fortunes in the 1930s. To support her son and daughter, she turned her home into an inn and dining room, ignoring the gloomy predictions of friends. For 10 days, nothing happened, and then came her first guests, a family of five. A few days later, she was in business. The Chalet continued to grow and is now world famous for its soups and other delicacies. Its award-winning restaurant has been voted one of Florida's top 10 for many, many years and has been featured in every major food and travel magazine and guide.

Shrimp Suzanne with Dill

SAUCE

1/2	cup sour cream
1/2	cup mayonnaise
1/2	cup grated, peeled, and seeded cucumber
1/3	cup minced onion
1 1/2	tablespoons chopped fresh dill
1 1/2	teaspoons fresh lemon juice
	Garlic to taste
	Salt and freshly ground pepper to taste
8	drops Tabasco sauce
1/4	teaspoon caraway seeds

1	pound shrimp (25 to 30 count), cooked, peeled, and cleaned
	Bibb lettuce

Combine all sauce ingredients in a large bowl. Stir in the shrimp, mix well, and refrigerate. Serve on a bed of Bibb lettuce, either as individual servings or in a lettuce-lined bowl.

Yield: 4 to 6 servings

Shrimp Waterloo

8 to 10   large shrimp
      Lemon juice
      Salt and pepper
   2   teaspoons oil plus 1 to 2 teaspoons butter
  1/2   stick plus 1 teaspoon butter
  1/4   cup dry vermouth
1 or 2   cloves garlic, crushed
      Fresh parsley, minced
      Minced dill or thyme (optional)
  1/2   cup white wine

Sprinkle shrimp with lemon juice and salt and pepper to taste. Heat a saucepan on medium-high heat and add oil and 1 or 2 teaspoons butter. Add shrimp and sauté on both sides until pink. Add vermouth and ignite it. Flambé shrimp. Remove shrimp immediately after flame has died and keep warm.

Add 1 teaspoon butter to pan. Sauté garlic, parsley, and dill or thyme. Add wine and dash of lemon juice and reduce sauce to half. Stir remaining butter into sauce; add salt and pepper to taste. Add shrimp and heat, but do not boil sauce. To serve, place sauce on plates and arrange shrimp. Serve with rice and asparagus.

Yield: 2 servings

Waterloo Country Inn
28822 Mt. Vernon Road
Princess Anne, Maryland 21853
410-651-0883
www.waterloocountryinn.com

STEP BACK IN TIME AND share the elegance and beauty of this fully restored, historic, 1750s hidden jewel. The luxurious pre–Revolutionary War waterfront estate was built by a prominent Somerset County landowner, Henry Waggaman, in the 18th century. Restoration to the mansion began in 1995, and since 1996 the Waterloo has been an elegant country inn. The estate is listed in the National Register of Historic Places. The Waterloo Country Inn is situated on a tidal pond, a paradise for nature lovers where history is ever present and every sunset is a celebration. An outdoor pool, canoes, and bicycles give you the opportunity to enjoy the serene, peaceful atmosphere. Stroll through the beautiful gardens and the majestic forest, which has a wide variety of trees and shrubs, some unique to the area.

**Munro House
Bed & Breakfast**
202 Maumee Street
Jonesville, Michigan 49250
517-849-9292
1-800-320-3792
www.munrohouse.com

HE MOST COMFORTABLE Lodging in South Central Michigan" is at the Munro House bed-and-breakfast in downtown Jonesville. Getaway packages include chef night, murder-mystery dinner, romance, massage, and spa services. This historic Greek Revival mansion was once a station on the Underground Railroad. Munro House may be the oldest bed-and-breakfast in southern Michigan that was originally built as a private residence (1834). Your hosts, Lori and Mike Venturini, serve as ambassadors to the world, as guests from 50 states and 43 countries on 6 continents have enjoyed small-town American hospitality in this unlikely crossroads.

Marinated Shrimp
with Avocado Sauce

1½	pounds large shrimp, shelled and deveined
½	teaspoon ground cumin
½	teaspoon chili powder
½	teaspoon paprika
2	tablespoons orange juice
	Zest of 1 orange
	Olive oil
1	tablespoon chopped fresh cilantro
	Salt and pepper

Combine shrimp with cumin, chili powder, paprika, orange juice, orange zest, olive oil, and cilantro. Add salt and pepper to taste. Thread shrimp onto skewers that have been soaked in cold water for 30 minutes. Place shrimp on a pan and broil for a few minutes on each side. Serve with avocado dipping sauce.

AVOCADO SAUCE

2	tablespoons extra-virgin olive oil
1	tablespoon chopped fresh cilantro
1	ripe avocado
½	onion, finely chopped
	Juice of ½ lime
	Salt and pepper

Dice avocado and immediately combine with cilantro, onion, and lime juice. Season to taste with salt and pepper.

Yield: 4 to 6 servings

Slow-Roasted
Salmon à la Point

1 fennel bulb, sliced
1 onion, sliced
2 ribs celery, sliced
1 bunch fresh thyme, chopped
   Olive oil as needed
6 (7-ounce) salmon fillets
   Kosher salt and freshly ground white pepper

Preheat oven to 400°F.

Toss vegetables with olive oil and spread evenly on a sheet pan.
Roast for 3 minutes. Allow to cool to close to room temperature.
Reduce oven temperature to 225°F. Place rack over vegetables
and spray well with olive oil (make sure there is no oxidation on
the rack). Season salmon fillets with salt and pepper to taste and
place on rack ½ inch apart (they cannot be touching). Cover with
another sheet pan and roast for 20 to 30 minutes (start to check
at 18 minutes). Cook until salmon is *à la pointe* or just done.
Serve immediately.

Yield: 6 servings

The Old Tavern at Grafton
Townshend Road
P. O. Box 9
Grafton, Vermont 05146
802-843-2231
www.old-tavern.com

ANY CALL THIS NEW England's most elegant little inn. And rightfully so. The inn has a heritage that goes back almost as far as the country's; it first opened only 12 years after America's independence and has been impeccably restored. The rich lineage and unspoiled colonial beauty of the Old Tavern are evident everywhere in Grafton. It was a favorite stop on Boston-Montreal stagecoach runs. The dining room features traditional New England fare prepared with master culinary skill.

The Coit House Bed & Breakfast

502 North Fourth Avenue
Sandpoint, Idaho 83864
208-265-4035
www.coithouse.com

ANDPOINT HAS SO MANY things to offer, and the Coit House is centrally located to enjoy them all—just blocks from all the shopping and restaurants and "City Beach." Whether it's with a hot cocoa after an exciting day of skiing at Schweitzer, or lemonade after a busy day at the beach, sit back and relax at this beautifully restored 1907 Victorian manor, offering a unique bed-and-breakfast style. Each of the rooms is equipped with a private bath, queen pillow-top bed, telephone, and cable television. There is a family suite that sleeps four and has a kitchenette. The Coit House is also the ideal choice for family reunions, wedding parties, holiday celebrations, business meetings, and reunions. Your gracious hosts are Laura and Gary Peitz.

Smoked Salmon and Eggs

1	large red onion, coarsely chopped
1	cup sour cream
1	pint half-and-half
1	teaspoon garlic powder
	Butter
12	eggs
8	ounces cream cheese
1 to 2	ounces smoked salmon, crumbled
	Finely chopped chives

Steam onion until slightly firm. Set aside. Stir together sour cream and half-and-half. Stir in garlic powder. Refrigerate.

Beat eggs. Pour into hot buttered pan. Add red onion to taste. Add 7 pea-sized dollops of cream cheese to eggs while cooking. Stir so eggs do not brown. While eggs are still moist, fold in salmon. After eggs are firm, transfer to a platter and top with sour cream mixture. Sprinkle entire platter with chives and serve.

Yield: 6 servings

Snapper Tropical

- ¼ cup vegetable oil
- ¼ cup flour
- 4 (8-ounce) snapper fillets
- ½ cup fish stock (or unsalted chicken broth)
- ½ cup dark rum
- 4 fresh basil leaves, chopped
- ½ cup orange juice
- 1 tablespoon butter
- 2 cups diced fresh fruit, such as banana, orange, strawberry (see note)
  Salt and pepper

Preheat oven to 350°F.

Heat vegetable oil in a pan while lightly dredging snapper in flour and shaking off all excess. Add snapper to pan and sauté both sides until lightly browned, then discard oil.

Deglaze pan with fish stock and rum and reduce for 2 to 3 minutes. Add basil, orange juice, and butter to thicken sauce. Add fruit and salt and pepper to taste. Place in oven for a final 4 to 5 minutes of cooking. Transfer fish to plates and top with fruit sauce.

Yield: 4 servings

Note: For variety, you can use such seasonal fruit combinations as kiwi, mango, papaya, pear, apple, grape, or peach.

BEAL HOUSE
Inn & Restaurant
FINE DINING & LODGING

Beal House Inn
247 Main Street
Littleton, New Hampsire 03561
603-444-2661
www.bealhouseinn.com

THE BEAL HOUSE INN IS A Main Street landmark in Littleton. The Federal Renaissance building was constructed in 1833 and has been used as an inn for 54 years. It is tastefully decorated with antiques and collectibles. Wonderful food is served by candlelight and fireside, including in hot popovers served with preserves and pure maple syrup.

Silver Thatch Inn

3001 Hollymead Drive
Charlottesville, Virginia 22911
434-978-4686
www.silverthatch.com

THIS HISTORIC INN BEGAN ITS life as a barracks built in 1780 by Hessian soldiers captured during the Revolutionary War. As wings were added in 1812 and 1937, it served as a boys' school, a tobacco plantation, and a melon farm. It has been providing elegant candlelit dining and gracious lodging in antique-filled guest rooms and since the 1970s. Relax and unwind in the intimate English pub. The inn offers a special dining experience in its three intimate dining rooms. Contemporary cuisine is offered, featuring grilled meat and fish with healthy and eclectic sauces. Whenever possible, the innkeepers work with local farmers to ensure that the finest, freshest produce will reach their dining guests. All breads, muffins, cookies, and fabulous desserts are homemade. An extensive selection of wines will complement your dining experience. Jim and Terri Petrovits are the efficient and hospitable innkeepers.

Spicy Thai Steamed Mussels

- 2½ pounds whole mussels
- ⅓ cup fresh lime juice
- 13½ ounces unsweetened coconut milk
- ⅓ cup dry white wine
- 1½ tablespoons Thai red curry paste (available in Asian food markets)
- 1½ tablespoons minced garlic
- 1 tablespoon fish sauce (available in Asian food markets)
- 1 tablespoon palm sugar (or half brown and half granulated)
- 2 cups chopped cilantro sprigs
  Lime wedges

Scrub mussels well and remove beards. In an 8-quart kettle, combine lime juice, coconut milk, wine, curry paste, garlic, fish sauce, and sugar over high heat. Bring to a boil and boil for 2 minutes, stirring constantly. Add mussels, tossing to combine. Cook, covered, stirring occasionally, until opened, 5 to 8 minutes. (Discard any unopened mussels.) Toss cilantro with mussels. Serve with lime wedges and croutons toasted with sesame oil.

Yield: 6 servings

SIDE DISHES

Cincinnati's Weller Haus Bed and Breakfast Inn

319 Poplar Street
Newport, Kentucky 41073
859-431-6829
www.wellerhaus.com

Cincinnati's Weller Haus Bed and Breakfast is two side-by-side historic homes that rival any downtown Cincinnati hotel. This Preservation Award–Winning bed-and-breakfast, located in northern Kentucky and within walking distance of downtown Cincinnati, is listed on the National Register of Historic Places. Amenities and personal service make this an ideal accommodation for your Cincinnati lodging. Enjoy the small-town atmosphere only a historic district can provide, with all of the conveniences of downtown Cincinnati only a short walk across the Ohio River. Antique-appointed guest rooms with private baths have all the modern amenities you could want, while they take you back in time.

Overnight Asparagus Casserole/Strata

- 1 pound fresh asparagus, trimmed and cut into 1-inch pieces
- 4 English muffins, split and toasted
- 2 cups (8 ounces) shredded cheese (Swiss, Cheddar, or Colby)
- 1 cup diced cooked ham
- 1/2 cup chopped sweet red pepper
- 1/2 cup chopped red onion
- 8 eggs
- 2 cups whole milk
- 1 teaspoon salt
- 1 tablespoon Mrs. Dash seasoning
- 1 teaspoon ground mustard
- 1/4 teaspoon pepper

Bring water to boil and cook asparagus for 3 minutes. Drain and immediately place in ice water. Drain and pat dry. Arrange 6 English muffin halves, cut side up, in a greased 13 x 9 x 2-inch baking dish. Fill in spaces with remaining muffin halves. Sprinkle with 1 cup of the cheese, asparagus, ham, red pepper, and onion. In a bowl, whisk eggs, milk, salt, Mrs. Dash, mustard, and pepper. Pour into baking dish. Cover and refrigerate overnight.

Remove casserole from refrigerator 30 minutes before baking. Sprinkle remaining cheese on top.

Preheat oven to 375°F. Bake for 40 to 45 minutes, or until a knife inserted in center comes out clean. Let stand 5 minutes before cutting.

Yield: 6 to 8 servings

Asparagus Bundles
with Hollandaise

6   slices cooked ham
6   thin slices Swiss cheese
1   (10-ounce) can asparagus spears, drained
    Half of a 17-ounce package frozen puff pastry, thawed
1   tablespoon butter, melted
    Hollandaise sauce (recipe follows)

Preheat oven to 425°F.

Place 1 slice Swiss cheese atop 1 ham slice. Top with 1 asparagus spear. Roll up. Trim asparagus if necessary. Repeat to make 6 bundles. Cut puff pastry into 6 equal rectangles. Brush lightly with melted butter. Wrap each pastry sheet around 1 asparagus bundle, sealing seams and ends well. Place seam-side down in shallow baking pan so sides do not touch. Brush with remaining butter. Bake for 18 to 20 minutes or until golden. Serve with hollandaise sauce.

HOLLANDAISE SAUCE

1   stick butter
3   egg yolks
2   tablespoons lemon juice

Melt butter in microwave. Place egg yolks and lemon juice in blender and blend for 30 seconds. Pour in hot butter slowly while blending; blend until slightly thickened.

Yield: 6 servings

The Empress of Little Rock
2120 South Louisiana Street
Quapaw Quarter Historic District
Little Rock, Arkansas 72206
501-374-7966
www.theempress.com

*I*MAGINE AN EVENING IN the family parlor at the Biltmore estate—you are surrounded by luxurious antiques, and the warmth of the fire draining away the tension of a busy corporate day. You are stretched out in your smoking jacket or Victorian dressing gown, and that you have special book you've been postponing for the "tright time." The Hornibrook Mansion, now known as The Empress of Little Rock, was completed in 1888 at the exorbitant cost of $20,000 and using exclusively Arkansas materials. Designed by Max Orlopp and Casper Kusener, it has been described in the National Register of Historic Places as the best example of ornate Victorian architecture in Arkansas and the most important existing example of Gothic Queen Anne style in the region.

The Greyfield Inn
Cumberland Island, Georgia 32035
904-261-6408
www.greyfieldinn.com

THE GREYFIELD INN ON Cumberland Island is a luxurious, romantic oceanfront mansion, built in 1900 and furnished today as it was then. In true Southern fashion, the Greyfield takes great pride in dining. Each morning, guests awaken to a full and satisfying breakfast that includes one of the chef's specialties. The day's island explorations are accompanied by a satisfying picnic lunch. During the cocktail hour each evening, hors d'oeuvres are served in the oceanfront bar. Dinner is a casually elegant affair, served in the glow of candlelight. It features fresh and creative cuisine, accompanied by selections from the inn's wine cellar.

Black-Eyed Peas

6 cups dried black-eyed peas
2 medium red bell peppers, finely diced
2 medium yellow bell peppers, finely diced
2 medium green bell peppers, finely diced
2 red onions, finely diced
3 tablespoons minced garlic
4 jalapeño peppers, finely diced (optional)
3 tablespoons ground cumin
2 tablespoons ground coriander powder
4 ounces extra-virgin olive oil
 Zest and juice of 4 limes
1 bunch cilantro, roughly chopped
10 stalks scallion greens, sliced
2 ounces apple cider vinegar (or red wine vinegar)
 Salt and pepper

Soak peas in 20 cups of water for 1 hour. While peas are soaking, finely diced bell peppers, onion, garlic, and jalapeños. Transfer vegetables to a bowl and add lime juice and zest along with cumin and coriander. Set aside. Combine cilantro and scallions in a small bowl.

After peas have soaked, stir them around and strain out all the loose husks. Strain water and add 20 cups fresh water or enough to cover peas by 6 inches. Bring to boil and simmer until done (about 1 hour). Strain and cool on a sheet tray.

When peas have cooled, transfer 4 cups to a food processor and purée. Add vinegar, a pinch of salt and pepper, and the vegetable mixture; mix and stir well. Heat in a round or large pan. If needed, add water—maybe ½ to ¾ cup—to moisten and prevent from sticking to bottom. When heated through, add cilantro and scallions and season with salt and pepper. Serve with grilled mahi or cobia, mixed greens, grapefruit segments, and avocado and lime vinaigrette.

Yield: 25 to 30 servings

Blennerhassett Morel Risotto

- 1 box Arborio rice
- 3 tablespoons olive oil
- 2 cups fresh morels, sliced
- 3 shallots, minced
- 1 teaspoon saffron
- 2 quarts vegetable stock
- 1 cup Marsala wine
- 1 cup Asiago cheese, shredded
- 1 pound whole butter
- 1 teaspoon black pepper
- 1 teaspoon sea salt

Sauté morels and shallots in olive oil. Add rice and stir to coat rice well. Gradually add 1 quart of the vegetable stock and stir frequently as stock becomes absorbed into rice. Add the wine and stir. Add remaining stock until rice is almost saturated. Add saffron, cheese, and whole butter and stir constantly until cheese and butter have blended into rice mixture. Add salt and pepper to taste.

Yield: 8 to 12 servings

THE
BLENNERHASSETT

Blennerhassett Hotel
320 Market Street
Parkersburg, West Virginia 26101
304-422-3131
www.blennerhassetthotel.com

THIS HISTORIC HOTEL BOASTS well over 100 years of hospitality, luxurious accommodations, exceptional service, and understated elegance. Its restaurant is world class, featuring European cuisine and impeccable service. Parkersburg enjoys the wonderful ambience of the Ohio Valley, and the Blennerhassett offers country-inn amenities in an in-town location.

White Oak Plantation Resort

5215 County Road 10
Tuskegee, Alabama 36083
334-727-9258
www.whiteoakplantation.com

*P*ICTURE A THOUSAND secluded acres where family and friends gather regularly to enjoy the luxury of simple, natural pleasures: the sound of wind rustling through the trees; crickets, whippoorwill, and lonesome quail calling in the evening; enjoying the wraparound porches immersed in a good book; a family's collective laughter around a fire in the lodge; or an early morning fishing trip on a misty pond. This is the essence of White Oak Plantation. Two full plantation breakfasts are included in the cost of each room. Lunches are prepared daily, and cooks will be brought in to prepare evening meals for a minimum of seven adults. The meals are served each day in the antique-furnished dining hall and include a limitless buffet for lunch and an evening meal prepared in the Southern manner.

Cabbage Au Gratin

5   heads cabbage, shredded
5   cups cream sauce (recipe follows)
2   cups grated Cheddar cheese

Boil cabbage and drain.

Preheat oven to 400°F.

Layer the cabbage, cream sauce, and cheese (in that order) in a large ovenproof casserole (or casseroles) until all are used (ending with cheese on top). Bake until bubbly, about 15 minutes.

CREAM SAUCE

10   tablespoons butter
10   tablespoons flour
2½   teaspoons salt
½   teaspoon pepper
5   cups light cream or milk

Make a roux by melting butter in frying pan, adding flour and stirring constantly until thoroughly mixed and thickened. Add salt and pepper, then light cream or milk. Continue stirring until thickened.

Yield: 20 servings

Custer's Cavalry Pinto Beans

    1   pound pinto beans
    1/2 cup diced celery
    1/2 cup diced onions
    1/2 cup diced carrots
    2   tablespoons minced fresh garlic
        Salt and pepper

Soak beans overnight in 2 gallons of water. Drain and rinse
beans. Replace 2 gallons of water in pot. Add vegetables and salt
and pepper to taste and bring to a rumbling boil; reduce heat
and let simmer for 2 hours or until beans are soft.

Yield: 6 servings

Sylvan Lake Resort
24572 South Dakota Highway 87
Custer, South Dakota 57730
605-574-2561
www.custerresorts.com

*L*OCATED IN THE NORTHERN
tip of Custer State
Park, this resort inn
overlooks scenic Black Elk Wilderness
Area and is bordered by the spired
granite rock formations that highlight
the Needles Highway. The original
lodge burned down from unknown
causes, and in 1936 the present lodge
was constructed. The fresh pine-
scented air, the crystal-clear waters of
Sylvan Lake, and the magnificent view
of Harney Peak from the rock patio
are amenities unique to Sylvan Lake
Resort. There is gourmet dining in the
lodge's dining room under the supervision of executive chef Charles Etzrodt.

The Millsaps Buie House

628 North State Street
Jackson, Mississippi 39202
601-352-0221
www.millsapsbuiehouse.com

A SPLENDID SOUTHERN welcome awaits you at this stately Queen Anne mansion, a Victorian landmark that has remained in the same Mississippi family for four generations. At the Millsaps Buie House, the 19th-century grandeur of spacious high ceilings, elegant millwork, and glowing stained glass meets the 21st-century amenities of a small luxury hotel—all just steps away from Jackson's historic state capitol. With 11 distinctively appointed guest rooms, and a sumptuous hot breakfast, the Millsaps Buie House hosts loyal business travelers and romantic weekend visitors. Both return again and again, and where they're always welcomed back like treasured friends of the family.

Creamy Cheese Grits

   3 cups water
  ½ stick butter
   1 cup 5-minute grits (we recommend 5-minute grits
       instead of instant grits for a better consistency)
   8 ounces Velveeta, cubed
       Pinch of salt
       Dash of garlic powder (optional)

Bring water to a boil in a saucepan. Add butter. When melted, add grits. Cook, stirring constantly, on low heat until grits are done. Add cheese, salt, and garlic powder. Continue stirring until all cheese is melted and grits are smooth. Add a little more hot water if grits are too thick.

Yield: 6 to 8 servings

Confetti-Herb Squash

8 cups yellow squash, cooked, drained, and mashed
8 eggs, well beaten
2 cups evaporated milk
2 sticks margarine, melted
4 tablespoons sugar
4 tablespoons flour
3 cups grated Swiss cheese
  Salt and pepper
8 tablespoons chopped fresh tarragon
4 tablespoons chopped fresh basil
2 cups chopped onion
1 cup chopped red bell peppers
1 cup chopped green bell peppers
  Dry bread crumbs

Preheat oven to 350°F.

Combine ingredients in order given (except bread crumbs); mix well. Pour into one or more greased glass casseroles. Top with bread crumbs. Bake for about an hour or until center is set.

Yield: 24 servings

Note: This dish can be made ahead and baked the following day. Or it can be baked and frozen, then later defrosted and reheated covered with foil.

**Highlawn Inn
Bed and Breakfast**
171 Market Street
Berkeley Springs, West Virginia
25411
304-258-5700
www.highlawninn.com

HIGHLAWN INN BED AND Breakfast is a small, intimate retreat ideal for a sentimental journey or a quiet group meeting. Beautifully appointed rooms and a convenient location make this bed-and-breakfast a perfect place to spend the night. Meticulous restoration and authentic furnishings are blended in a bouquet of unique rooms. Individual porches, sitting areas for tea, varied bed styles, and claw-foot tubs—all immersed in an atmosphere of thoughtful privacy—promise cherished memories for couples bent on escape.

**The Blue Belle Inn
Bed & Breakfast**
513 West 4th Street
St. Ansgar, Iowa 50472
877-713-3113
www.bluebelleinn.com

*L*OCATED IN ST. ANSGAR, Iowa, "the best little hometown in Iowa," the Blue Belle Inn Bed & Breakfast awaits you! Rediscover the romance of the 1890s while enjoying the comfort and convenience of the new millennium in one of six distinctively decorated guest rooms. The interior of this Queen Anne Victorian is highlighted by fireplaces, wood floors, tin ceilings with ornate moldings, and eight-foot maple pocket doors. A gleaming maple banister winds to the second floor and opens onto a balcony overlooking sprawling maple trees, flowers, and a fish pond. Candlelight, lace-covered tables, heirloom china, and festive foodstuffs featuring German, English, French, Italian, Scandinavian, or American country cuisines provide an unforgettable dining experience.

*The Great Country Inns
of America Cookbook*

Old-Fashioned Scalloped Corn Pie

CRUST

1¼ cups (1 sleeve) fine cracker crumbs
½ cup butter, melted

Combine cracker crumbs and butter. Set aside half for topping and press other half into a 9-inch pie tin.

FILLING

2 tablespoons melted butter
2 cups creamed corn, fresh or frozen
½ teaspoon salt
  Pepper
1¼ cups milk, divided
2 tablespoons flour
½ teaspoon onion powder
2 eggs, beaten

Preheat oven to 400°F.

In a saucepan, combine butter, corn, salt, pepper to taste, and 1 cup of the milk. Cook for 3 minutes over medium heat, stirring. Mix together flour and remaining ¼ cup milk until smooth. Add to corn mixture and stir until thick. Add onion powder and eggs to corn mixture slowly, stirring. Pour mixture into pie tin. Cover with remaining crumbs. Bake for 20 minutes.

Yield: 1 pie

Corn Pudding

6 cups sweet corn, cut from cob (16 to 18 ears); or use
  thawed and drained frozen corn

2 cups light cream

6 egg yolks

½ stick butter, melted

2 tablespoons flour

2 tablespoons sugar

2 teaspoons salt (reduce salt if using canned corn)

3 to 4 dashes of cayenne pepper

2 teaspoons baking powder

¼ teaspoon freshly ground black pepper

6 egg whites

Whiz half the corn, the cream, egg yolks, and melted butter in
blender for a few seconds. In a large bowl, mix together remaining corn kernels, flour, sugar, salt, cayenne, baking powder, and
pepper. Stir in mixture from the blender. (This may all be done a
day ahead if more convenient. Just allow time to bring
everything back to room temperature before proceeding.)

Preheat oven to 375°F. Butter two 1½ quart casseroles or one 3-
quart casserole.

When ready to bake, beat egg whites stiff, stir in about a cupful
of corn batter, then fold in the rest. Divide batter between the
casseroles. Bake until firm, about 30 minutes. If one large
casserole is used, allow 15 to 20 minutes longer to bake.

Yield: 8 to 10 servings

Fox Creek Inn
49 Chittenden Dam Road
Chittenden, Vermont 05737
1-800-707-0017
www.foxcreekinn.com

THE FOX CREEK INN,
formerly the Tulip Tree
Inn, offers excellent
amenities and a high standard of
service. When you come to Fox Creek,
you will get a chance to relax and enjoy
life as it should be enjoyed, at a slow
pace. Here you'll have time to sit in
front of your own fireplace or languish
in your private Jacuzzi. You'll find time
to rekindle your relationship with life.

**Soldier Meadows
Ranch and Lodge**
16912 Mt. Rose Highway
Reno, Nevada 89511
775-849-2219
www.soldiermeadows.com

ATING BACK TO 1865, when it was known as Camp McGarry, Soldier Meadows Ranch and Lodge lies in the Black Rock Desert about three hours north of Reno, Nevada, and 60 miles beyond Bruno's Country Club in Gerlach, Nevada. Soldier Meadows is a family owned Nevada lodge and working cattle ranch offering lodging for family vacations, peaceful getaways, and hunting. Besides the lodge and ranch headquarters, there are over 500,000 acres of public and private land to enjoy. The ranch headquarters includes the main lodge, refurbished stone house (the original cavalry officers' quarters, now the ranch foreman's home), rock stables, and willow corrals. The park-like lawns and natural hot springs are truly an oasis in the Black Rock Desert. The open, expansive beauty and natural hot springs are enough to rest any weary soul.

Desert Sour Cream Potatoes

    8 medium potatoes
    1 stick butter or margarine, melted
    2 cups grated cheese (assorted Jack, Cheddar,
         and American)
  1/3 cup grated onion
    1 pint sour cream
    1 (7-ounce) can chopped green chilies (optional)

Parboil potatoes until done. Let cool. Grate potatoes and add remaining ingredients. Mix well. Transfer mixture to a casserole. Preheat oven to 350°F. Bake until completely hot, 45 minutes to 1 hour, depending on dish size.

Yield: 6 to 8 servings

Healthy Eggplant Parmesan

- 1 cup bulgur wheat
- 1 large eggplant, cut into ½-inch thick slices
- 4 egg whites
  Kosher salt
  Vegetable oil
- ½ pound of buffalo mozzarella, cut into thin slices
- ¼ cup reduced-fat Kraft Parmesan cheese
- 1 (20-ounce) can crushed tomatoes

Preheat oven to 400°F.

Soak bulgur wheat in hot water and set aside (for approximately twenty minutes). Drain the water from the bulgur wheat and lay the bulgur wheat out on a flat plate. Mix in one large pinch of kosher salt. Dip eggplant slices into the egg whites. Pat both sides of the eggplant with the bulgur wheat so that it sticks to both sides. Fry eggplant slices in vegetable oil for about a minute on each side. Transfer eggplant to a plate lined with paper towels.

Pour half the crushed tomatoes on the bottom of a large, flat baking dish. Place eggplant on top. Place mozzarella slices on top of the eggplant and sprinkle Parmesan cheese on top. Pour the remaining tomatoes on top. Bake for 30 to 40 minutes.

Yield: 4 servings

1871 House

East 60s off Park Avenue
New York, New York 10021
212-756-8823
www.1871house.com

THE 1871 HOUSE IS NEW York City's "country inn," offering apartment-style accommodations with a bed-and-breakfast atmosphere. The apartments are located in a landmarked, circa 1871 five-story townhouse built in the architectural style of the much-loved New York City row house, or brownstone. The low-profile 1871 House is small, quiet, private, and residential with an old-world ambience. It feels like a secret hideaway from the moment you enter its intimate lobby. 1871 House offers relatively affordable accommodations in a shopping- and museum-convenient area of the Upper East Side called the Upper East Side Historic District.

Trail's End Guest House

180 Gay Drive
Kerrville, Texas 78028
830-377-1725
www.fredericksburg-
lodging.com/trails-end/

COME GET AWAY TO A PRIVATE and tranquil location perched on one of Kerr County's highest elevations. Trail's End Guest House is a unique bed-and-breakfast located just 10 minutes from downtown Kerrville and an hour from San Antonio. Yet, while relaxing by the pool, sitting on your deck, or walking the property, you feel as though you are isolated from the world. The owners, David and Desiree Farrar, after being kicked off the corporate merry-go-round, decided that it was time to live their dream of having a simpler life in the beautiful Texas hill country. That is what brought them to Trail's End. The Farrars bought their house in November, 2002 and immediately began working on creating a private guesthouse setting. The house is located at the dead-end of a dead-end road on 23 beautiful acres.

Garlic Potatoes

20	small red potatoes
1	cup cold water
1	teaspoon salt
8	cloves garlic, finely chopped
	Olive oil
1/2	cup parsley, finely chopped
2	sticks salted butter
1/2	teaspoon fresh ground white pepper

Wash and dry potatoes and leave them to air in a cool, dry place for 7 days.

In a large pot, combine water and salt over high heat. Begin cutting potatoes in irregular chunks into the pot as water heats. Add garlic to pot, stir, and lower to medium heat. Cover with tight-fitting lid. Check every few minutes and stir to keep from sticking. As water steams off, add enough olive oil to coat potatoes. Keep stirring. When potatoes are almost cooked through add parsley. (Different types of parsley will make the taste different, so experiment. They will all taste good.)

When potatoes are cooked and parsley is wilted onto the potatoes, add butter. Stir over low heat until butter is completely melted. Remove from heat, add white pepper, stir 1 more minute, then cover and let sit for 5 minutes before serving.

Yield: 8 servings

Ham and Broccoli Bake with Parmesan Streusel

- 2 cups chopped cooked ham
- 2 cups fresh broccoli florets
- 3 cups frozen O'Brien potatoes (from 28-ounce bag), thawed
- 2 cups shredded Cheddar cheese (8 ounces)
- 8 eggs
- 1 cup milk
- 8 ounces sour cream
- 1 teaspoon salt
- ¼ teaspoon pepper
- ¾ cup Gold Medal all-purpose flour
- ¼ cup grated Parmesan cheese
- ½ stick butter or margarine, softened
- 2 tablespoons chopped fresh parsley

Preheat oven to 350°F.

In a 13 x 9-inch (3-quart) glass baking dish, combine ham, broccoli, potatoes, and Cheddar cheese. In a large bowl, beat eggs, milk, sour cream, salt, and pepper with wire whisk. Pour egg mixture over ham mixture. Bake for 45 to 50 minutes or until center is almost set. (If desired, cover and refrigerate casserole at this point up to 8 hours or overnight.)

Meanwhile, in a small bowl, stir together flour, Parmesan, butter, and parsley with a fork until crumbly. Sprinkle crumb mixture on a cookie sheet. Bake on lower oven rack for another 20 minutes stirring once. Sprinkle parsley over casserole before serving.

Yield: 12 servings

Foley House Inn
14 West Hull Street
Chippewa Square
Savannah, Georgia 31401
912-232-6622
www.foleyinn.com

THE ELEGANT FOLEY HOUSE Inn, ensconced within two lavishly renovated town-park mansions, is distinguished both by its location and historic prominence. The luxurious, romantic bed-and-breakfast mansion hotel is located in the exact center of historic Savannah. Cuisine at the Foley House Inn includes a hearty gourmet breakfast, an afternoon selection of sweets and savories, complimentary wine in the afternoon, and an evening port served by firelight in the inn's double parlors.

Reagan's Queen Anne Bed and Breakfast

313 North Fifth Street
Hannibal, Missouri 63401
573-221-0774
www.reagansqueenanne.com

ORE THAN 115 YEARS ago, Wilson B. Pettibone, a wealthy lumber baron and banker, who is known as one of Hannibal's greatest philanthropists, built this Victorian jewel for his wife, Laura. Mr. Pettibone felt it fitting to use many of his fine woods to grace the foyer, parlors, dining room, library, and staircase. The woodwork is ornate and original, as are the Rockwood fireplace tiles, stained glass windows, and gas/electric light fixtures. The Reagans have decorated with numerous antiques, period furnishings, and heirlooms, to allow guests the opportunity to experience a bit of the Victorian era. A celebrated stop along the banks of the Mississippi River, this quaint village draws its fame from the writings of humorist and author, Mark Twain.

Hash Brown Haystacks

8   cups frozen shredded hash browns (we use Dell's)
    Riley's Salt-Free Seasoning to taste (may substitute
      Mrs. Dash or salt and pepper)
8   butter pats, sliced diagonally in half
¾   cup shredded Cheddar cheese
¾   cup Sargento Bistro Mozzarella Blend with basil and
      sun-dried tomatoes (can substitute Monterey Jack)
    Crisco spray
    Fresh parsley

Preheat oven to 350°F. Generously spray a jumbo muffin tin with nonstick spray.

Place frozen hash browns in a microwave-safe bowl and thaw in microwave on 50% power (could take 5 to 6 minutes). Place about ½ inch of hash browns in the bottom of each muffin cup. Lightly sprinkle with Riley's seasoning or salt and pepper. Top hash browns with half a butter pat. Sprinkle each of the cheeses evenly in each muffin cup on top of butter. Cover each evenly with remaining hash browns. Place half a butter pat on top and lightly sprinkle with more seasoning.

Bake on middle rack for 45 to 50 minutes or until golden brown on top. Remove from oven and loosen well with a small spatula. Place cookie sheet on top of tin and flip haystacks upside down onto cookie sheet. Leave muffin tin on haystacks until ready to plate. Remove tin and flip stack over to serving plate (so the top is up) and garnish with parsley.

Yield: 8 servings

Note: Can be prepared the night before and refrigerated.

Indian Kedgeree

½ cup butter
1½ cups boned and flaked salmon
2½ cups cooked rice
2 or 3 hard-boiled eggs, chopped
1 teaspoon salt
¼ teaspoon pepper
½ teaspoon curry powder
Raisins, chopped coconut, and lime wedges

Melt butter in a frying pan until bubbling. Mix in fish, rice, eggs, salt, pepper, and curry powder. Stir with a wooden fork to keep from sticking to pan. Cook slowly until thoroughly heated. Garnish with raisins, chopped coconut, and a lime wedge.

Yield: 3 to 4 servings

Alma del Monte
372 Hondo Seco Road
P.O. Box 617
Taos, New Mexico 87571
505-776-2721
www.almaspirit.com

ALMA DEL MONTE IS A modern hacienda that wraps you in romance, luxury, and privacy. Casual elegance and warm hospitality await guests behind the hand-carved doors of this inviting bed-and-breakfast. *Alma* means "spirit" in Spanish, and you can refresh your spirit with the fresh mountain air, pure artesian well water, and amazing endless skies that are the hallmarks of Taos, New Mexico. Guests rave about Alma's signature organic breakfast offerings. Every morning brings a three-course extravaganza of taste, texture, and color. Wake to birdsong and the sun rising over Taos Mountain. Watch the sun disappear behind Pedernal Mountain as the sky turns fiery. Experience the serenity of Taos's wide-open spaces. Make a wish upon the Milky Way.

The Geneva Inn
N 2009 South Lake Shore Drive
Lake Geneva, Wisconsin 53147
262-248-5680
www.genevainn.com

EXPERIENCE DISTINCTIVE European charm and exceptional luxury at the Geneva Inn, located directly on the shores of Geneva Lake—a premier recreation area in Wisconsin. Discover a truly relaxed, unrestrained style of comfort, intimate accommodations, breathtaking lake views, and uncommon architectural craftsmanship. Enjoy the private marina, the exercise facility, and the spectacular cuisine at the renowned Grandview Restaurant. Guests will find seclusion and comfort in the peaceful atmosphere of this traditional English inn. Common areas of the inn include a three-story atrium with raised-hearth fireplace, piano lounge, landscaped terrace, and patio. Boat owners can tie up at the inn's private marina.

Italian Vegetables with Kale

2 carrots, diced
6 stalks celery, diced
1 onion, diced
6 cloves garlic, minced
4 ounces fresh thyme, minced
2 ounces fresh oregano, minced
2 ounces fresh basil, minced
2 cups peeled tomatoes
2 gallons chicken stock
1 quart beef stock
2 large bunches kale, chopped
Salt and black pepper

Sauté carrots, celery, onion, and garlic in large stockpot until onion is translucent. Add thyme, oregano, and basil and continue to sauté for approximately 4 minutes. Next add tomatoes, stirring with a wooden spoon to deglaze and combine all flavors from bottom of pot. Add beef and chicken stock and simmer for 1 hour. Add kale and continue to simmer for 30 minutes. Adjust salt and pepper to taste.

Yield: 20 servings

Lemon-Basil Carrots

    1   pound carrots, julienned
    2   tablespoons butter
    1   tablespoon lemon juice
    1   clove garlic, minced
        Salt
        Dash of pepper
   1/2 teaspoon crushed dried basil

Cook carrots in a small amount of water for 20 minutes. In a
different saucepan, melt butter. Stir in lemon juice, garlic, salt,
pepper, and basil. Add carrots and toss.

Yield: 4 servings

The Keeper's House
P. O. Box 26
Isle au Haut, Maine 04645
207-367-2261
www.keepershouse.com

THERE IS NO SUCH THING as a one-time visitor to the Keeper's House, a delightful island lighthouse inn boasting a magnificent setting on the rockbound coast of Maine. Guests return over and over again. Delicious goodies flow from innkeeper Judith Burke's aromatic kitchen. The inn is reachable only by mail boat and beckons the adventurous to this wilderness annex of Acadia National Park. The Keeper's House is surrounded by spruce wilderness and island panoramas. From the walkway to the lighthouse, you will see four other lighthouses winking through the night. By day, vast ocean stretches are cut only by the sails of windjammers and the backs of porpoises and seals.

Washington School Inn

543 Park Avenue
P. O. Box 536
Park City, Utah 84060
435-649-3800
www.washingtonschoolinn.com

WASHINGTON SCHOOL INN is a perfect example of what preservationists call adaptive use. A schoolhouse built in 1889, the building was fully restored as an inn, opening in June, 1985. Its location in the old town of Park City, Utah, puts it close to the magnificent skiing opportunities for which this area is noted. The inn offers its visitors deliciously prepared food, and afternoon goodies are always available to hungry skiers returning from the slopes.

Mexican Corn Pie

18	large eggs
6	cups cream-style corn
2	cups finely chopped green onions
2	cups yellow cornmeal
6	cups sour cream
1½	pounds Monterey Jack cheese, cut into ½-inch cubes
1½	pounds sharp Cheddar cheese, cut into ½-inch cubes
3	cups chopped mild green chilies
3	teaspoons salt
2	teaspoons Worcestershire sauce

Preheat oven to 350°F. Grease four 10-inch pie plates with vegetable spray.

Mix all ingredients thoroughly in a large container. Pour into pie plates and bake for 1 hour. Serve with salsa and sour cream. Pies store well and freeze well.

Yield: 25 servings

The Great Country Inns of America Cookbook

Parmesan-Artichoke Casserole

8 eggs
½ cup flour
1 teaspoon baking powder
1 teaspoon garlic pepper
12 ounces Monterey Jack cheese, shredded
1½ cups cottage cheese
2 small cans green chilies
½ can artichoke hearts, quartered
1 cup fresh Parmesan cheese, grated

Preheat oven to 350°F. Grease a 9 x 12-inch casserole dish.

In a large bowl, beat eggs for 4 minutes. Add remaining ingredients and mix together. Pour into casserole. Arrange artichoke hearts on top of casserole and then sprinkle with Parmesan cheese. Bake for 50 minutes.

Yield: 6 to 9 servings

Carriage Way Bed & Breakfast
70 Cuna Street
St. Augustine, Florida 32084
904-829-2467
www.carriageway.com

CARRIAGE WAY IS A TRADITIONAL Victorian-style building constructed between 1883 and 1885 by Edward and Rosalie Masters. Just imagine walking down the quaint, narrow streets of the oldest city in the United States. Then imagine walking up to a beautiful 120-year-old Victorian home in the heart of the historic district. Your eyes capture the soft, warm colors of the home. Then you see the two verandas. The white wicker chairs and a porch swing call out to you to sit, relax, and reflect on your day. As you enter the front door, the friendly atmosphere is evident. You feel the warmth, which seems to say "welcome home."

SUN MOUNTAIN LODGE

Sun Mountain Lodge
604 Patterson Lake Road
Winthrop, Washington 98862
1-800-572-0493
509-996-2211
www.sunmountainlodge.com

*S*UN MOUNTAIN LODGE has achieved international acclaim with awards for its hotel, guest rooms, cuisine, and wine list. The greatest compliments, however, come from the guests who return again and again. Set on 3,000 acres, Sun Mountain has a combination of privacy, tranquility, and serenity balanced by the highest standard of excellence in service and guest amenities that makes this an unmatched experience. Wander through the wildflowers on over 200 kilometers of trails, or see them from a horse or mountain bike. Or simply bask in the sun by the pools. Sun Mountain is glorious in winter as well, with 175 kilometers of groomed cross-country ski trails. Whether you're visiting to remove yourself from the routine or to try your hand at the lodge's long list of activities, the staff will make your visit a peak experience. There is a cafe, room service, and a full-service dining room serving northwest cuisine.

Pistachio-Orange Basmati Rice Pilaf

½	cup extra-virgin olive oil
3	cups basmati rice, washed and drained
	Zest of 1 orange
	Large pinch of saffron
5½	cups cold water
	Pinch of salt
½	cup chopped pistachio nuts

Heat olive oil over medium-high heat. Add rice and sauté for 2 minutes until lightly toasted. Add orange zest, saffron, water, and salt. Bring mixture to a boil, then reduce to a simmer. Cover and cook until rice is done. Cool. Finish rice with pistachios.

Yield: 9 servings

Potato-Onion Provençal

6 large Yukon Gold potatoes
3 large yellow onions
1 tablespoon fresh thyme
1 teaspoon lavender
1 cup grated Parmesan
1 stick butter, cut into pieces
¼ cup fresh chopped herbs
  Salt and pepper

Peel and slice potatoes into ⅛-inch rounds; set aside. Peel, halve, and julienne the onions and caramelize them along with the thyme and lavender in a large stockpot. Once onions are caramelized, you can begin to assemble the dish.

Preheat oven to 375°F. Butter a 9 x 11-inch baking dish.

Cover bottom of baking dish with a layer of overlapping potatoes. Spread a layer of caramelized onions over potatoes and season with herbs and salt and pepper to taste. Sprinkle with a thin layer of Parmesan and top with a few pieces of butter. Repeat this process until you have five layers of potatoes. Cover with aluminum foil. Bake for 1 hour or until a knife goes in with ease.

Once potatoes are fully cooked, cover with plastic wrap, press with a weighted-down baking dish, and refrigerate. When completely chilled, turn out potatoes on a cutting board and portion. To serve, reheat on a buttered cookie sheet until hot.

Yield: 8 servings

Applewood Inn
13555 Highway 116
Guerneville, California 95446
1-800-555-8509
www.applewoodinn.com

THE APPLEWOOD INN, WITH its acclaimed wine-country restaurant, is a popular Sonoma County destination for food and wine enthusiasts. This historic inn is an ideal starting point for excursions into every corner of Sonoma County's wine country as well as neighboring Napa Valley. Each guest room boasts fine Italian linens and European down comforters, as well as soothing garden or forest views. A stay at the Applewood includes a full country breakfast.

National Hotel
211 Broad Street
Nevada City, California 95959
530-265-4551

TRAVELERS ENJOY OLD-fashioned comfort and luxury at this the oldest operating hotel west of the Rocky Mountains. Upon arrival, one steps back into the Victorian era with sumptuous suites furnished with antiques from the Gold Rush days. Hospitality comes naturally here; the National has had more than 140 years of experience in making guests feel welcome. The cocktail hour is enhanced by the ornate back bar, which was originally the dining-room buffet in the Spreckels mansion in San Francisco. In the Victorian dining room, tables are softly lighted with coal-oil lamps.

Potatoes Supreme

4½ pounds potatoes (any kind)
1¼ pounds sharp Cheddar cheese, cut into ½-inch cubes
  1 cup chopped green onions
  2 pints sour cream
  3 teaspoons salt
  1 teaspoon white pepper

Boil potatoes until done (approximately 45 minutes).

Preheat oven to 300°F.

Grate potatoes into large mixing bowl (do not mash). Blend in cheese, green onions, sour cream, salt, and white pepper. Transfer mixture to large deep baking dish. Bake for 45 minutes.

Yield: 10 to 12 servings

Savory Pumpkin-Bacon Tart with Parmesan Crust

Five Gables Inn
Murray Hill Road
P. O. Box 335
East Boothbay, Maine 04544
207-633-4551
www.fivegablesinn.com

1   recipe Parmigiano-Reggiano Tart Dough (recipe follows)
8   ounces bacon, cut into ¼-inch strips
1   large white onion, diced
½   cup chicken stock
16 ounces canned pumpkin purée
¼   cup finely grated Parmigiano-Reggiano cheese
    Salt and pepper
¼   cup brown sugar
1   large egg
2   tablespoons freshly chopped thyme leaves

MIKE AND DE KENNEDY are the owners/ innkeepers of this wonderful hillside inn, which affords stunning views of Linekin Bay. Built in 1896, it has enjoyed a long tradition of hospitality. Fifteen of its 16 rooms have an ocean view. A wraparound veranda with plenty of comfortable seats is the perfect spot to view the magnificent bay and distant islands. The dining room offers chef Mike Kennedy's gourmet creations. Chef Kennedy is a graduate of the Culinary Institute of America. He shares a favorite with us here.

Divide dough in two and roll out to ⅛-inch between well-floured parchment paper. Line two 9-inch, greased tart pans with the dough. Prick bottom with a fork and bake for 8 to 12 minutes, or until edges are lightly browned. Cool to room temperature and remove from pans.

Heat a sauté pan over medium heat. Add bacon and cook for 5 minutes or until crisp. Remove with a slotted spoon and transfer to a plate lined with paper towels. Add onion to bacon fat and cook for 5 minutes, stirring often, until onion is well caramelized. Add chicken stock and stir vigorously against the pan bottom with a wooden spoon to release caramelized juices. Continue to cook until pan is nearly dry, then remove pan from heat and allow onions to cool.

Preheat oven to 350°F.

Recipe continued on next page

Combine pumpkin purée, cheese, salt, pepper, and sugar in the bowl of a food processor and mix thoroughly. Add egg and mix thoroughly. Distribute filling between cooled tart shells and top with caramelized onion, bacon, and thyme. Bake for 12 to 15 minutes or until filling is set. Cool 5 minutes before serving.

PARMIGIANO-REGGIANO TART DOUGH

- 2 **sticks butter, cut into cubes**
- ¼ **cup finely grated Parmigiano-Reggiano cheese**
- 2 **cups flour**
- ⅛ **cup sugar**
- ½ **teaspoon salt**
- 6 **tablespoons ice water**

Refrigerate butter and all dry ingredients for 1 hour before making dough. When cold, combine butter, cheese, flour, sugar, and salt in bowl of food processor and pulse until mixture is the consistency of cornmeal. Add water and pulse together just until mixed. Compact dough together and refrigerate for ½ hour before rolling out.

Yield: 2 (9-inch) tarts or 16 servings

Red Cabbage

5 large or 10 small bay leaves
1¼ teaspoons allspice
    Peppercorns
5 cups distilled white vinegar
5 tablespoons sugar
5 teaspoons salt (or to taste)
5 heads red cabbage, cut into pieces
¾ cup plus 3 tablespoons water
10 apples, peeled, cored, and sliced
5 onions, sliced
5 tablespoons bacon fat
5 teaspoons cornstarch
    Cheesecloth

Wrap bay leaves, allspice, and peppercorns in cheesecloth to make a spice bag. Mix vinegar, sugar, and salt. Add to cabbage. Add water. Then add apples, onion, and spice bag. Stir and cook for 15 minutes. Add bacon fat and continue to cook 15 minutes longer. Mix cornstarch with a little of the juice and return to thicken. Stir often.

Yield: 20 to 30 servings

Lowell Inn
102 North Second Street
Stillwater, Minnesota 55082
651-439-1100
www.lowellinn.com

THIS GREAT INN STANDS ON the site of the stately Sawyer House, erected in 1848, some ten years before Minnesota achieved statehood. The Sawyer House of that long-ago day brought the civilized East to the frontier. But as more and more of the East's modernity came to the West, the Sawyer House became an anachronism and fell to the wrecker's bar in 1924. A new Williamsburg-style hotel, the Lowell Inn, rose in its place. Today the inn recreates the aura of a long-ago and gracious era with fine antiques, linens, tableware, and glassware. The food service is simple but exquisite. The menu consists of Escargot Bourguignonne, Fondue Bourguignonne, Grapes Florentine or Devonshire, and a four-course wine service featuring wines from the family-owned mountain vineyards in Switzerland.

Wickwood Country Inn

510 Butler Street
Saugatuck, Michigan 49453
269-857-1465
www.wickwoodinn.com

TO ENTER THE WICKWOOD IS to be transported to another place in time. Bill Miller and Julee Rosso have created a retreat of coziness, privacy, and calm. Wickwood Country Inn is a small inn located in the beautiful village of Saugatuck, Michigan, often called the Cape Cod of the Midwest. Wickwood is filled with French and English antiques, Oriental rugs, over-stuffed chairs, vases of flowers, candlelight, a library of books, and eclectic music. There's generally a crackling fire in the living room fireplace and an aroma that floats through the air from the kitchen.

Roasted Asparagus

Asparagus
Extra-virgin olive oil
Cracked black pepper
Sea salt

Preheat oven to 400°F.

Spread asparagus in one layer on a baking sheet. Lightly drizzle with extra-virgin olive oil in a zigzag pattern. Sprinkle generously with cracked black pepper and lightly with sea salt. Bake for 15 to 30 minutes (usually about 20) depending on the thickness of asparagus and desired doneness. Serve immediately.

Yield: According to amount prepared

Oven-Roasted
Rosemary Potatoes

2	large sweet potatoes, peeled and cut into 1-inch chunks
5 or 6	medium red potatoes or russet potatoes, unpeeled, scrubbed, and cut into 1-inch chunks (peel if skin is green)
3 to 4	tablespoons olive oil
	Chopped fresh rosemary to taste (about 1 to 2 tablespoons)
½	teaspoon salt
½	teaspoon pepper (or more)

Preheat oven to 450°F. Spray a jellyroll pan with cooking spray.

Mix all ingredients in a large mixing bowl. Spread potato mixture in pan. Bake for 30 to 40 minutes or until browned. Stir once halfway through the baking time.

Yield: 8 to 12 servings

Old Mulberry Inn
Bed and Breakfast
209 Jefferson Street
Jefferson, Texas 75657
1-800-263-5319
www.oldmulberryinn.com/
main.htm

NAMED FOR THE OLDEST mulberry tree in Jefferson and situated on more than an acre, Old Mulberry Inn Bed and Breakfast is just a few doors from the home where Lady Bird Johnson lived as a teenager. She may well have plucked mulberries from the century-old tree that dominates the inn's parklike grounds. The inn has been featured in *Southern Living*, the *Los Angeles Times Magazine*, and the travel section of major Texas newspapers. Guests appreciate spotless rooms, pressed linens, sparkling-clean bathrooms, attentive service, and memorable breakfasts. If you like old houses but dislike the dust and musty odors that may accompany an older structure, this inn is the place to stay in Jefferson.

Golden Pheasant Inn

763 River Road (Route 32)
Erwinna, Pennsylvania 18920
610-294-9595
1-800-830-4474
www.goldenpheasant.com

THE GOLDEN PHEASANT INN is situated on the eastern boundary of Tinicum Township in a section of Bucks County that was called Manor of Highlands. In 1699, the 7,500 acres were purchased from William Penn by the London Company. With the completion of the northern leg of the Delaware Canal in 1832, oases sprang up along the route to serve the canal men on their runs from Easton to Bristol. Railroads, trucking, and oil heating all contributed to the abandonment of the canal in 1931. The tavern that faced the now-empty canal suffered hard times until 1967 when it was purchased by Ralph Schneider, who named it the Golden Pheasant Inn. Built of local fieldstone, the inn features wood-burning fireplaces, exposed stone walls, recessed windows, beamed ceilings, and an original tap room.

Saffron Rice

1   stick butter
1   cup finely chopped onion
4   cups water
4   teaspoons chicken base
    Freshly ground black pepper
8   saffron threads (optional)
2   cups short grain rice, rinsed
1   cup chopped thin green beans
1   cup frozen peas

Preheat oven to 375°F.

Melt butter in a saucepan. Add onion and cook until softened. Add water and chicken base (4 cups chicken stock may be substituted). Add pepper and saffron. Stir. Bring to boil. Add rice. Stir. Add beans and peas. Stir. Cover. Bake for 20 minutes.

Yield: 8 servings

Cheesy Scalloped Potatoes

8   medium potatoes, unpeeled
2   medium onions, diced
1½   sticks butter
¼   pound Velveeta cheese
1   pint whipping cream
1   tablespoon dried chives
    Dried parsley
    Pepper
    Paprika

Slice, boil, and drain potatoes. While potatoes are cooking, braise onions in 1 stick of butter until edges are lightly browned. Lower heat. Add cheese, cream, and chives. Stir several minutes until cheese starts to melt; remove from heat. Add remaining ½ stick of melted butter to serving container. Add potatoes to serving container. Drizzle onion-cheese mixture over potatoes. Garnish with diagonal sprinkled rows of dried parsley, pepper, and paprika.

Yield: 10 to 12 servings

Heritage Manor
33 Heritage Road
Aline, Oklahoma 73716
580-463-2563
www.1aj.org

THIS INN PROVIDES A WAY TO enjoy and experience the ambience of the early 1900s. Explore and relax in the inn's peaceful gardens and 80-acre wildlife habitat. Watch songbirds, butterflies, long-haired cattle, donkeys, llamas, and ostriches. The inn invites visitors to enjoy its more than 5,000-volume library and more than 100 channels on Dish TV. Guests can walk the suspension bridge to two rooftop decks and a widow's walk to view the stars and sunsets. There is also an outdoor hot tub for soaking. Dine in the parlor, gazebo, courtyard, or treetop-level deck, where the choice of time and menu is entirely up to the guest.

Maison Louisiane Historic Bed and Breakfast Inn

332 Jefferson Street
Natchitoches, Louisiana 71457
1-800-264-8991; 318-352-1900
www.maisonlouisiane.com

ECENTLY RESTORED TO its original luster, this circa 1898 beauty has been described as "one of the best examples of the Queen Anne style in Natchitoches." Listed on the National Register of Historic Places, Maison Louisiane is perfectly situated in the heart of the historic district, within easy walking distance of downtown shopping and dining. Four well-appointed bedrooms are in the main house, each with private bath. The Garden Suite is perfect for families or an extended stay. A full French-style gourmet breakfast is served each morning in the formal dining room. Romantic gardens surround the mansion, a perfect setting for weddings and special events.

Smothered Cottage Fries

6   medium potatoes
    Oil for frying
4   tablespoons butter
2   tablespoons Tony Chachere's Cajun Seasoning (available in most supermarkets)
1   tablespoon garlic powder

Chop potatoes into ¼-inch pieces that are about ¼-inch thick. Deep-fry potatoes until golden brown. Remove from oil and place in a large bowl with butter and seasonings. Toss until well mixed. If butter does not melt right away, place bowl in 250°F oven for 10 minutes and then toss again. Serve and enjoy.

Yield: 6 to 8 servings

Southern Grits

1	cup coarse stone-ground grits (we use Falls Mills)
4	cups water
2 to 4	teaspoons chicken base paste
2 to 4	teaspoons butter
	Half-and-half

Combine grits, water, chicken base, and butter in a saucepan. Cook over low heat for an hour, stirring occasionally. Cover and refrigerate overnight. Resume cooking the next morning, adding half-and-half as needed to thicken. Continue to cook for another hour.

Yield: 10 to 12 servings

The Rhett House Inn
1009 Craven Street
Beaufort, South Carolina 29902
1-888-480-9530
843-524-9030
www.rhetthouseinn.com

*L*OCATED IN HISTORIC Beaufort, the Rhett House Inn is a beautifully restored 1820s plantation house, with English and American antiques, Oriental rugs, fireplaces, and spacious verandas. Lush gardens provide the perfect setting for weddings and parties. Beaufort was the film site for *Forrest Gump*, *Prince of Tides*, *The Big Chill*, and *White Squall*. Elegant antebellum-era-inspired decor and live orchids create a warm ambience throughout the inn. The personalized service afforded by the staff makes the Rhett House Inn the finest accommodations Beaufort has to offer. Cuisine includes breakfast, afternoon tea, evening hors d'oeuvres, picnic baskets, and desserts.

The Victorian Villa
601 North Broadway Street
Union City, Michigan 49094
517-741-7383
www.avictorianvilla.com

THE VICTORIAN VILLA IS situated in a quaint and charming 19th-century river village, on an acre of peacefully landscaped Victorian gardens and grounds, where you can relax and sip the gentler side of life. It's a place where you can enjoy an afternoon tea in the gingerbread gazebo, share a bottle of wine and stretch out on the jewel-green lawn, unwind by the goldfish pond, and pass the day listening to a century-old fountain play its familiar bubbling refrain. And in the evening, enjoy a relaxing and elegant seven-course champagne dinner for two in the Villa's gourmet restaurant, Victoria's.

Steamed Brussels Sprouts with Fresh Parmesan and Toasted Almonds

3 pints Brussels sprouts or 2 (16-ounce) packages
   frozen Brussels sprouts
1/3 cup coarsely shredded Parmesan cheese
1/4 cup slivered almonds, toasted
   Butter or margarine
   Salt and pepper

Trim stems from Brussels sprouts. Remove wilted leaves, then rinse under cool running water. Cut any large sprouts in half lengthwise. Place Brussels sprouts in a steamer basket. Place basket over, but not touching, boiling water. Reduce heat. Cover. Steam 15 to 20 minutes or until just tender. Place Brussels sprouts in a serving bowl and sprinkle with cheese and almonds. Dot with butter. Season to taste with salt and pepper.

Yield: 8 servings

Sweet Potato Crisp

POTATO MIXTURE
8 ounces cream cheese, softened
1 (40-ounce) can sweet potatoes, drained
¼ cup brown sugar, packed
¼ teaspoon ground cinnamon
1 cup coarsely chopped apples
½ cup dried cranberries (or craisins)

TOPPING
½ cup flour
½ cup brown sugar, packed
½ cup quick-cooking oats
½ cup butter, softened
¼ cup chopped pecans

Preheat oven to 350°F. Grease a 1½-quart casserole dish or
10 x 6-inch baking dish.

Beat cream cheese, sweet potatoes, ¼ cup brown sugar, and
cinnamon in bowl with a mixer until well blended. Spoon
mixture into casserole. Sprinkle apples and cranberries over
the top.

For topping, stir together flour, brown sugar, and oats in a small
bowl. Cut in butter, then stir in pecans. Sprinkle topping
mixture evenly over potatoes. Bake for 35 to 40 minutes, until
edges bubble. Serve hot.

Yield: 8 to 12 servings

7 Gables Inn and Suites
4312 Birch Lane
Fairbanks, Alaska 99709
907-479-0751
www.7gablesinn.com

THE 7 GABLES INN FEATURES
20-foot cathedral
ceilings, an indoor
waterfall, and an attached greenhouse.
Despite the massiveness of the
building, inside you'll find a warm
welcome. Guests can explore the
meandering salmon river across the
street in one of the inn's complimentary canoes. If the fish aren't biting, you
can stop at some of the finest restaurants in Fairbanks as you enjoy a
progressive dinner, deck-to-deck and
dock-to-dock under the midnight sun.
A full gourmet breakfast is served daily,
featuring international themes.

Snowbird Mountain Lodge

4633 Santeetlah Road
Robbinsville, North Carolna 28771
1-800-941-9290
828-479-3433
www.snowbirdlodge.com

*H*IGH UP IN SANTEETLAH Gap, on the southern border of the Great Smoky Mountain National Park, lies this secluded, rustic yet elegant, historic lodge built of stone and huge chestnut logs. The view from the porch is one of the best in the mountains. An excellent library, huge stone fireplaces, and award-winning gourmet cuisine make this lodge an exceptional retreat from the pressures of the world. Whether you like fly-fishing, hiking, biking, or just relaxing in front of the fire, the innkeepers/owners, Karen and Robert Rankin, can make your trip to the mountains picture perfect.

Sweet Potato, Country Bacon, and Leek Gratin

3½ pounds sweet potatoes, peeled and sliced thin
2 to 3 medium leeks, cut into half-moons, washed thoroughly
½ pound country bacon, diced small, cooked until just crispy
3 to 4 cups heavy cream
Salt and black pepper

Preheat oven to 350°F. Grease a 9 x 11-inch casserole dish.

Sweat leeks in a bit of butter until softened; set aside. Put three layers of sweet potatoes in the casserole, seasoning each layer with salt and pepper to taste. The fourth layer should be half of the leeks and bacon. Add two or three more layers of sweet potatoes, seasoning in between. Add remaining leeks and bacon and then finish with sweet potatoes. Pour cream over sweet potatoes, allowing it to soak through. Press down on casserole to compact layers. Add enough cream so that the cream level comes to top of casserole.

Bake for 90 minutes to 2 hours. Use a paring knife to check for doneness. There should be no resistance. If casserole is getting too dark before it is done, cover with aluminum foil. Serve hot.

Yield: 12 servings

Tomato Pie

CRUST
1¾ cups flour
1 teaspoon milk powder
¼ teaspoon salt
1½ sticks plus 1 tablespoon cold unsalted butter, cut into bits
1 large egg, lightly mixed

FILLING
¼ cup Dijon-style mustard
¼ pound Gruyère cheese, grated
3 large ripe tomatoes, peeled and sliced
2 tablespoons parsley, minced
1 teaspoon tarragon (may substitute thyme or oregano)
1 tablespoon garlic, finely chopped
¼ cup olive oil

To make the crust: Combine butter, flour, milk powder, and salt in a bowl. Mix until coarse like cornmeal. Stir in egg. Press dough into an 11-inch tart pan. Chill 30 minutes.

Preheat oven to 400°F.

Spread mustard into tart shell and sprinkle cheese over. Arrange tomatoes in one layer over cheese. Bake for 40 minutes. Mix parsley, tarragon, garlic, and oil and pour over pie.

Yield: 8 servings

The Checkerberry Inn
62644 County Road 37
Goshen, Indiana 46528
574-642-0198
www.checkerberryinn.com

AT THE CHECKERBERRY Inn, the visitor will find a unique atmosphere, unlike anywhere else in the Midwest. The individually decorated rooms and suites will please even the most discerning guests. Every room has a breathtaking view of the unspoiled rolling countryside. A top-rated restaurant serves only the freshest food, using herbs and other ingredients from the local countryside.

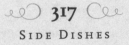

Lyons' Victorian Mansion Bed & Breakfast & Spa

742 South National
Fort Scott, Kansas 66701
1-800-78-GUEST
www.LyonsMansion.com

*H*ERE IS FORT SCOTT'S landmark Victorian residence, circa 1876, a luxurious destination bed-and-breakfast and spa tucked quietly in America's heartland. There is much here to tickle your fancy, including seven guest rooms, each with king bed, TV, phone, high-speed and wireless Internet, refreshments, mini-refrigerator stocked with beverages, coffee service, and private bath. Favored gathering places include the big front porches with swings, the gardens and pond with a soothing waterfall, and the enclosed, starlit hot tubs. Private refined dining is offered in the magnificent dining rooms of the mansion, and impeccable service and hospitality provided by hostesses is attired in early 1900s costumes.

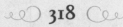
Wild Rice Casserole

3 (6-ounce) boxes Uncle Ben's Original Long Grain and Wild Rice
24 ounces real sour cream
2 sticks butter
2 cans sliced water chestnuts, drained
4 cups shredded Colby/Monterey Jack cheese
Sliced almonds

Preheat oven to 350°F. Grease a 9 x 13-inch pan.

Prepare rice according to package directions. Mix in remaining ingredients. Pour into pan. Bake for 25 minutes. Top with raw sliced almonds and continue to cook 10 minutes baking time to allow the almonds to toast as the casserole bakes. You may prefer to sauté the sliced almonds in a skillet with butter to toast a little first, then scatter them on the top of the casserole to finish 10 minutes in the oven.

Yield: 15 servings

DESSERTS

The Cornerstone Victorian
Bed & Breakfast

3921 Main Street
Warrensburg, New York 12885
518-623-3308
www.cornerstonevictorian.com

THE CORNERSTONE VICTORIAN Bed & Breakfast is nestled in the Adirondack Mountains in the charming village of Warrensburg. This stunning Queen Anne–Victorian home was built by Lewis Thomson in 1904 and features stained-glass windows, terra-cotta fireplaces, exquisite woodwork, and a grand staircase. Today the inn is a welcome place for guests desiring the warmth and hospitality often forgotten in our fast-paced world. Nearby you will find hiking, antiquing, boating, golfing, biking, skiing, and whitewater rafting, just to name a few activities. At the Cornerstone Victorian hospitality is a way of life. Indulge yourselves in a romantic retreat where you will be pampered with the splendors of times past.

Almond-Filled Cookie Cake

CRUST

2²/₃ **cups flour**
1¹/₂ **cups sugar**
1¹/₃ **cups butter**
¹/₂ **teaspoon salt**
1 **egg**

FILLING
Marzipan-almond paste
Slivered almonds

Preheat oven to 325°F. Grease a 9-inch springform pan.

Blend all crust ingredients at low speed until dough forms. Divide dough in half. Spread half in bottom of pan. Spread a ¹/₄-inch-thick layer of marzipan on dough. Press the remaining dough into a 9-inch circle between two sheets of wax paper. Place this circle of dough over the marzipan filling. Garnish with almonds. Bake for 55 to 60 minutes.

Yield: 12 servings

Almond Tart with Fresh Berries

DOUGH

4½	cups flour
1	pound butter, softened
2	cups sugar
2	pinches salt
4	large eggs

Make dough by hand or mixer. Sift flour into large mixing bowl. Gradually add butter to flour until mixture resembles cornmeal. Add sugar, salt, and eggs. Mix thoroughly without overmixing until you have a soft but solid dough. Pat dough into two thick circles; do not overwork. Cover the dough and chill at least 3 hours. While dough chills, make almond crème.

ALMOND CRÈME

12	large eggs
1	pound sugar
2	pounds almonds, processed in food processor until a fine powder
2	sticks butter, melted

Whisk eggs and sugar together by hand until light and creamy. Add almond powder and melted butter to egg-and-sugar mixture. Whisk again *slowly* until all ingredients are blended. Chill for 2 to 3 hours.

To make tart shells: Preheat oven to 375°F. Remove dough from refrigerator to counter. Roll each circle of dough into large thin circles. Place into two tart pans. Bake for 5 to 10 minutes, just until pastry is lightly browned. Remove from oven; let cool.

Recipe continued on next page

Birches Inn
233 W. Shore Road
New Preston, Connecticut 06777
203-868-1735
www.thebirchesinn.com

THIS ELEGANT COUNTRY inn overlooks Lake Waramaug. There are 12 individually appointed guest rooms and suites, all with private bathrooms, telephones, and televisions. Some rooms have whirlpool tubs and decks with lakefront views. There is a private beach, canoeing, and bicycling. The inn also features a highly acclaimed restaurant.

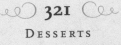

Add chilled almond crème to cooled tart shells. Spread half of crème in even layer to edges of both shells. Return filled tarts to oven. Bake for 20 minutes. Remove. Let tarts cool completely.

TOPPING
- 2 **pints fresh raspberries**
- 2 **pints fresh strawberries, halved**
- 1 **pint fresh blueberries**
- 1 **kiwi, peeled and cut into ¼-inch slices**
  Orange marmalade, as needed

Beginning at outer edges of tart shells, place raspberries in a circle on the crème. Place a circle of blueberries next to the raspberries. Place a circle of strawberries, cut side down, next to the blueberries Place another circle of blueberries next to the strawberries. In the center, overlap slices of kiwi so that no filling is visible.

Heat marmalade over low heat until thick and syrupy. Using a small pastry brush, brush marmalade over the tarts, being careful to glaze all fruit. Chill tarts for 30 minutes to set glaze.

Yield: 2 tarts, 20 servings

Apple Brownies

3   eggs
1¼ cups vegetable oil
2   cups sugar
1   teaspoon vanilla extract
3   cups flour
1   teaspoon baking soda
1   teaspoon cinnamon
3   cups chopped apples
½   cup chopped nuts

Preheat oven to 350°F.

Whisk eggs until blended; add oil and whisk again. Stir in vanilla, add flour, baking soda, and cinnamon. Fold in apples and nuts. Transfer batter to a 10 x 15-inch pan. Bake for 45 minutes.

Yield: About 24 brownies

The Old Mystic Inn
52 Main Street
Old Mystic, Connecticut 06372
860-572-9422
www.oldmystic.com

BUILT IN 1784, THE MAIN house of the Old Mystic Inn is a picturesque country colonial tucked away in the quiet hamlet of Old Mystic, Connecticut. The carriage house is located just behind the main house and was built in 1988. Located just three miles north of historic downtown Mystic, the inn offers rest and relaxation while being only a short distance to local attractions, scenic views, shopping, and dining. With its huge maple trees, gazebo, and white picket fence, the inn lends itself to the restful atmosphere often found in quaint New England towns.

1884 Bridgeford House

263 Spring Street
Eureka Springs, Arkansas 72632
479-253-7853
www.bridgefordhouse.com

SOUTHERN HOSPITALITY combined with Victorian charm awaits you at this beautiful home. 1884 Bridgeford House is nestled in a quiet neighborhood at the very heart of Eureka Springs. This Arkansas bed-and-breakfast provides a beautiful view of the surrounding mountains and the famous springs. Guests will feel at ease immediately with the smiling faces, kind words, and Southern hospitality. Complimentary cinnamon scones or other treats await guests in their rooms.

Apple Crunch Bake

3 tablespoons butter
½ cup light brown sugar
1 (21-ounce) can apple pie filling
2 teaspoons cinnamon
1½ teaspoons pure vanilla extract
1 (12-ounce) can refrigerated biscuits
½ cup chopped nuts

Preheat oven to 350°F.

In a saucepan, melt butter and stir in brown sugar, pie filling, cinnamon, and vanilla. Spread half of apple mixture in a 2-quart shallow baking dish. Separate biscuits and cut each into quarters. Arrange pieces, points up, over apple mixture. Spoon remaining mixture over biscuits and sprinkle with nuts. Bake for 35 to 40 minutes. Let stand 5 minutes. Serve warm.

Yield: 8 servings

Apple-Rhubarb Crisp

FILLING

8 large apples, peeled, cored, and sliced
2 cups rhubarb, cut into 1-inch pieces
2 tablespoons tapioca
1 cup sugar
1 teaspoon cinnamon

Mix filling ingredients together. Transfer to a greased 9 x 13-inch pan.

TOPPING

¾ cup flour
½ teaspoon salt
¾ cup brown sugar
½ teaspoon baking soda
⅓ cup butter
¾ cup oatmeal

Preheat oven to 350°F.

Mix flour, salt, brown sugar, and baking soda together. Cut in butter. Add oatmeal. Sprinkle over apples and rhubarb and pat down lightly. Bake at for 45 minutes.

Yield: 10 servings

Iron Horse Inn
526 Marie Avenue
South Cle Elum, Washington 98943
509-674-5939
www.ironhorseinnbb.com

ESTLED IN THE CASCADE Mountain foothills of central Washington, the Iron Horse Inn was originally constructed in 1909 by the Chicago, Milwaukee, & St. Paul Pacific Railroad and served until 1974 as temporary housing for men who had the job of getting trains over some of the most hazardous tracks in the country. Now featuring an extensive collection of history photographs, artifacts, and railroad memorabilia, the lovingly renovated inn has been placed on the National Register of Historic Places.

Gazebo Country Inn

507 East Third Street
Salida, Colorado 81201
719-539-7806
1-800-565-7806
www.gazebocountryinn.com

THE GAZEBO COUNTRY INN is just a few blocks from historic downtown Salida, Colorado's headwaters of adventure. A. T. and Clara Hathaway designed and built this charming Victorian-era home in 1901 to stand out among the smaller, quaint Victorian homes in this quiet neighborhood. Over the last 12 years the bed-and-breakfast has been carefully updated with the guest's every need in mind. This can be your home away from home. The hosts welcome families interested in renting the entire house for special family gatherings, such as reunions, weddings, or holidays. Breakfast is served at your door or in the inn dining room as space allows. The garden hot tub, gazebo, and spacious second-floor deck are available for all to enjoy while taking in views of the mountains or the peaceful neighborhood and gardens.

Applesauce Cake

1   stick softened butter
2   cups sugar
1½ cups applesauce
2   eggs
1   teaspoon baking soda
½   teaspoon salt
    Spices to taste, such as grated nutmeg, 1 teaspoon cinnamon, ½ teaspoon cloves
1   cup dried apricots
1   cup dried cranraisins

Preheat oven to 350°F. Grease a Bundt pan.

Mix all ingredients together and pour batter into pan. Bake for 60 minutes until done. Cool, slice, dust with powdered sugar or frost with cream-cheese frosting.

Yield: 16 to 20 servings

Note: You can cut this cake in half, wrap each half in plastic wrap and freeze in ziplock bags for up to a month. It stays moist and delicious.

Baked Fudge

8 eggs
4 cups sugar
1 cup flour
1 cup cocoa
4 sticks margarine or butter, melted
2 cups chopped pecans
3½ teaspoons vanilla extract
½ teaspoon salt

Preheat oven to 325°F.

Beat eggs until lemon colored. Add sugar, flour, and cocoa and mix until well blended. Add margarine. Stir in pecans, vanilla, and salt. Pour into a 15 x 10-inch pan. Set pan in larger pan of water. Bake for 45 to 50 minutes or until set like custard. Serve warm with whipped cream or ice cream.

Yield: 20 servings

Clayton Country Inn
Route 1, Box 8
Clayton, Oklahoma 74536
918-569-4165
www.claytoncountryinn.com

CLAYTON COUNTRY INN IS located in the heart of Oklahoma's beautiful Kiamichi Mountain Country—easily accessible from Tulsa, Oklahoma City, and Dallas. There are nine large, comfortable guest rooms or a duplex guest cottage with living room, bedroom, equipped kitchenette, and fireplace. The great room in the inn is maintained for the pleasure of guests; its high, log-beamed ceiling, natural rock fireplace, easy chairs and big sofas, television, and the wide windows with a view of the mountains and river all create a restful setting for games, reading, or just plain loafing. The knotty pine and fireplace theme is carried from the great room into the dining room, where guests will enjoy excellent food prepared with the utmost care.

The Logging Camp Ranch

5705 151st Avenue SW
Bowman, North Dakota 58623
701-279-5501
www.loggingcampranch.com

ABOVE THE RIVER, IN THE pines, there is a North Dakota few have experienced. Several generations of Hansons have owned and operated the 10,000-acre Logging Camp Ranch. This is not a dude ranch. It is a real, live, working ranch, much as it was in the 1880s. What it offers is as simple—and as complex—as the nature around it: wilderness, wildlife, and wonder. Log cabins with showers and bathrooms are provided for overnight guests, who share bountiful meals with the owners and workers. Seven different unspoiled ecological systems, including North Dakota's only ponderosa pine forest, are part of the land owned by the ranch.

Best in the West Brownies

BROWNIES

2 cups flour
2 cups sugar
2 sticks margarine
1 cup water
3½ tablespoons unsweetened cocoa powder
1 teaspoon baking soda
½ cup buttermilk
2 eggs, beaten well
1 teaspoon vanilla extract
Pinch of salt

Preheat oven to 325°F.

Combine flour and sugar; set aside. In a saucepan, combine margarine, water, and cocoa. Heat until mixture comes to a boil. Pour over the flour-sugar mixture. In a small bowl, add baking soda to buttermilk and add to batter. Add eggs, vanilla, and salt. Mix with a wire whisk (do not use an electric beater). Bake for 20 to 30 minutes. Let cool, frost, and cut in squares.

FROSTING

6 tablespoons margarine
6 tablespoons milk
1⅓ cups sugar
½ cup semisweet chocolate chips

Combine margarine, milk, and sugar in a saucepan. Bring to boil and boil for 1 minute. Remove from heat; add chocolate chips, and stir until chips are melted. Cool before frosting the cooled brownies.

Yield: 20 to 24 brownies

Black-Bottom Banana Cream Pie

- 1 (9-inch) pastry crust
- 3 tablespoons cornstarch, divided
- ½ cup plus 2 tablespoons sugar, divided
- 2 tablespoons unsweetened cocoa
- ¼ teaspoon plus a dash of salt, divided
- 1⅓ cups 1% milk, divided
- 1 ounce semisweet chocolate, chopped
- 2 large eggs
- 1 tablespoon butter
- 2 teaspoons vanilla extract
- 2 ounces block-style cream cheese, softened
- 2 cups sliced ripe bananas
- 1½ cups frozen whipped topping, thawed

Bake pastry crust according to package directions; cool on a wire rack. In a small, heavy saucepan combine 1 tablespoon of the cornstarch, 2 tablespoons of the sugar, the cocoa, and a dash of salt. Gradually whisk in ⅓ cup of the milk. Cook for 2 minutes over medium-low heat. Stir in chocolate; bring to boil over medium heat. Reduce to low and cook 1 minute, stirring constantly. Spread chocolate mixture into bottom of prepared crust.

Combine remaining 2 tablespoons cornstarch, remaining ½ cup sugar, ¼ teaspoon salt, eggs, remaining 1 cup milk, and butter in a heavy saucepan over medium heat, whisking constantly. Bring to boil. Reduce heat to low and cook 30 seconds or until thick. Remove from heat. Add vanilla. Beat cream cheese until light (about 30 seconds). Add ¼ cup hot custard to cream cheese, and beat just until blended. Stir in remaining custard.

Recipe continued on next page

Big Bay Point Lighthouse
#3 Lighthouse Road
Big Bay, Michigan 49808
906-345-9957
www.BigBayLighthouse.com

HIGH ATOP A CLIFF JUTTING into the clear, deep waters of Lake Superior, the Big Bay Point Lighthouse beckons adults in search of a secluded retreat from modern life. This unique bed-and-breakfast inn is one of the few surviving resident lighthouses in the country and is listed on the National Register of Historic Places. For over a century, mariners have relied on Big Bay Point's light to guide them along this remote and rocky stretch of Michigan coastline. Sit before the fire in the living room and recount the lighthouses you have seen and plan to see. Hike, bike, ski, or snowshoe along the shore or on the many trails in the area. Experience the deep solitude and unspoiled beauty of nature at the lighthouse inn.

Arrange banana slices on top of chocolate layer; spoon custard over bananas. Press plastic wrap onto surface of custard. Chill for 4 hours. Remove plastic wrap. Spread whipped topping evenly over custard. Garnish with chocolate curls; chill until ready to serve.

Yield: 8 servings

Black-Bottom Chess Pie

1½ cups sugar
1 stick butter, melted
1 tablespoon plus 1 teaspoon cornmeal
1 tablespoon white vinegar
1 teaspoon vanilla extract
3 eggs, beaten
1 unbaked 8-inch pie shell
5 ounces good-quality bittersweet chocolate, chopped

Preheat oven to 350°F.

In a bowl, combine sugar, butter, cornmeal, vinegar, and vanilla. Add eggs and mix well. Melt chocolate in a glass bowl in microwave for 1 minute, then stir until smooth. Drizzle over bottom of pie shell. Then slowly pour filling into pie shell. Bake for 50 minutes. You can also use a 9-inch pan and bake for 40 minutes.

Yield: 8 servings

Inn at Woodhaven
401 South Hubbards Lane
Louisville, Kentucky 40207
502-895-1011
1-888-895-1011
www.innatwoodhaven.com

SPACIOUS ACCOMMODA-tions and hearty breakfasts are staples at this historical bed-and-breakfast inn. Featuring elaborately carved woodwork, winding staircases, and spacious rooms tastefully decorated with antiques, the inn offers romance and relaxation. Rest, relax, read, and enjoy the many porches and gardens. Take a stroll around the grounds or Brown Park and the Beargrass Nature Preserve, both only a block away. Make yourself at home in the common areas, where you will find books, magazines, and after-dinner liqueurs.

The Elms Inn

84 Elm Street
Camden, Maine 04843
1-800-388-6000
207-236-6060
www.elmsinn.net/about.html

THE ELMS IS A RESTORED, circa 1806 Colonial that recaptures the rich heritage of early America. Built in the seafaring town of Camden nearly 200 years ago, the Elms is a stately and elegant home with original wide pine floors and period furnishings. Once the home of Captain Calvin Curtis and his family, it is now the home of your hosts, Jim and Cyndi Ostrowski. While your surroundings may be stately and elegant, you soon sense a casual warmth reflected by your hosts. Experience their love for lighthouses and the sea through the extensive artwork, books, and collectibles exhibited throughout the inn. Relax in one of the six guest rooms, all with private baths. Breakfast is a shared experience and features freshly prepared and beautifully presented entrées such as puffed peach pancakes or baked havarti eggs accompanied by fresh-fruit cups and home-baked treats.

*The Great Country Inns
of America Cookbook*

Blueberry Buckle Coffee Cake

CAKE

2	cups all-purpose flour
3/4	cup sugar
2 1/2	teaspoons baking powder
3/4	teaspoon salt
1/4	cup shortening
3/4	cup milk
1	egg
2	cups fresh or frozen blueberries (if frozen, thaw and drain)

CRUMB TOPPING

1/3	cup all-purpose flour
1/2	cup sugar
1/2	teaspoon cinnamon
1/2	stick butter or margarine, softened

GLAZE

1/2	cup confectioners' sugar
1/4	teaspoon vanilla extract
1 1/2 to 2	teaspoons hot water

Preheat oven to 375°F. Grease a square 9 x 9 x 2 or round 9 x 1½-inch pan.

In a bowl, blend flour, sugar, baking powder, salt, shortening, milk, and egg. Beat for 30 seconds. Carefully stir in blueberries. Spread batter in pan. Mix together topping ingredients and sprinkle topping over batter. Bake for 45 to 50 minutes or until a wooden pick inserted in center comes out clean. Stir glaze ingredients together and drizzle over the cake.

Yield: 9 servings

Squire Miller's Toasted Blueberry Buttery Pound Cake

1 stick butter
1 stick margarine
1 cup shortening
2 cups sugar
6 eggs
2 cups all-purpose flour
1 tablespoon almond extract
1 pint blueberries
Confectioners' sugar

Preheat oven to 325°F. Grease and flour a 16-inch long loaf pan.

In a large bowl, cream butter, margarine, and shortening with sugar until smooth. Alternately add eggs and flour. Beat well while adding almond extract. Stir in blueberries. Pour batter into pan. Bake for 1½ hours or until tester inserted in center comes out clean. Let cake cool. Before serving, cut into bread-sized slices and toast. Sprinkle with confectioners' sugar. Serve with butter, preserves, or apple butter.

Yield: 1 (16-inch) loaf

Fairville Inn
506 Kennett Pike (Route 52)
Chadds Ford, Pennsylvania 19317
1-877-285-7772
610-388-5900
www.fairvilleinn.com

LOCATED IN THE HEART OF the Brandywine Valley, the Fairville Inn, listed on the National Register of Historic Places, echoes the pastoral scenes of the Wyeth family paintings. Accented with barn wood, beams, and cathedral ceilings, the inn is the embodiment of elegant comfort. There are 15 rooms and suites in the main house, carriage house, and springhouse. Most rooms feature rear decks/balconies overlooking acres of gentle grassy meadows rolling toward a serene pond.

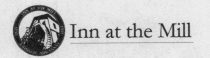 Inn at the Mill

Inn at the Mill

3906 Greathouse Springs Road
Johnson, Arkansas 72741
479-443-1800
www.innatthemill.com

THE INN AT THE MILL features eight uniquely designed suites and an additional 30 beautiful rooms connected to the original mill by a walkway. The interior of the mill was opened to create a three-level lobby. The top-level suites have internal balconies, which view the entire three-story space through a structural grid of black walnut posts and beams. The Inn at the Mill's stately waterwheel is powered by four million gallons of fresh spring water daily, rushing down the falls and into a beautiful pool filled with koi. Upon your arrival, you are greeted with a choice of coffee, tea, or wine. A complimentary continental breakfast will be served in your room, the parlor of the historic mill, or the inn's deck overlooking the mill pond and waterwheel. Additional touches include a nightly turn-down service with a daily-baked Inn at the Mill cookie by your bedside.

Bourbon-Pecan Pie

DOUGH

- 1 pound butter, cut into 1-ounce cubes
- 3 tablespoons sugar
- 6 cups all-purpose flour
- 1/2 teaspoon salt
- 4 egg yolks
- 1/2 cup ice water

In a bowl, cut butter, sugar, flour and salt. Mix egg yolks and water until almost combined. Remove and knead on floured surface. Refrigerate and roll to desired thickness.

PIE FILLING

- 2 sticks butter, cut into cubes
- 3 1/2 cups sugar
- 16 eggs
- 3/4 cup flour
- 8 cups pecan pieces
- 6 cups dark corn syrup (Karo brand)
- 3 tablespoons vanilla extract
- 1 cup bourbon

Preheat oven to 350°F (325°F. for convection oven).

In a bowl, cream butter and sugar. Mix in eggs. Add flour and mix. Add pecans and mix. Add remaining ingredients and mix. Place dough in pie pan and fill to rim with filling. Bake for about 35 to 40 minutes (20 minutes for convection oven), or until crust is golden. Serve with your favorite ice cream.

Yield: 6 to 8 servings

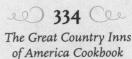

Grandmother's Old-Fashioned Bread Pudding

3 eggs, beaten
½ cup sugar
Dash of salt
1 teaspoon cinnamon
2 cups milk
2 teaspoons vanilla extract
¼ cup butter, melted
4 cups ½-inch cubes of bread, muffins, coffee cake, croissants, etc.
¼ cup raisins
¼ cup dried cranberries, cherries, apricots, and/ or blueberries

Preheat oven to 350°F. Grease an 8-inch, round baking dish.

Combine eggs, sugar, salt, cinnamon, milk, vanilla, butter, bread cubes, raisins, and dried fruit in large mixing bowl. Pour into baking dish. Set dish into a larger pan filled with ½ inch of hot water. Bake for 45 to 55 minutes until golden brown.

Yield: 8 servings

**Cook's Cottage and Suites
Bed and Breakfast**
703 West Austin Street
Fredericksburg, Texas 78624
210-493-5101
210-273-6471
www.bedandbreakfast.com/texas/
cooks-cottage-and-suites.html

*L*OCATED IN THE HISTORIC district of Fredericksburg, Texas, this nationally recognized bed-and-breakfast offers complete privacy, romance, amenities, and exceptional cuisine. Rated as one of the "Top 25 Most Romantic Inns in America" by *Travel + Leisure* magazine, the inn offers the ultimate in relaxation, rejuvenation, and romance in the heart of the beautiful Fredericksburg, Texas Hill Country. The inn is noted for aromatherapy, breakfast-in-bed baskets, herbal wraps, massage therapy, special-occasion baskets, special packages, antiques, décor, and wonderful gourmet food. Your gracious innkeeper, Patsy Swendson, welcome you and will do all she can to provide you with an experience you will always remember.

Vieh's Bed and Breakfast

18413 Landrum Park Road
(Highway 675)
San Benito, Texas 78586
956-425-4651
www.vieh.com/bb.htm

EXPERIENCE THE FRIENDLY hospitality of south Texas in this comfortable ranch-style home on 15 acres just 3 miles from Old Mexico (centrally located between Brownsville, Santa Ana, and Laguna Atascosa). A 10-acre pond across the back of the property provides the opportunity to encounter a variety of local wildlife. Five guest rooms are available: one with a king-size bed or twin beds, two with queen-size beds, and one with twin beds. There is also a cottage with a king bed or twin beds and two small couches that make into twin beds. Included is a home-style breakfast and other meals by prior request. Hosts Charlie and Lana are happy to accommodate special dietary needs. They would be pleased to help make your visit an enjoyable one. They hope that though you arrive as a guest, you will leave as a new friend.

Brownies with Hot Fudge Sauce

- ½ cup flour
- 1 cup sugar
- ¼ cup cocoa
- ½ teaspoon salt
- ¼ cup canola oil
- 2 eggs
- 1 teaspoon vanilla extract
- ½ cup chopped pecans

Preheat oven to 350°F. Butter a 9 x 9-inch glass baking dish.

In a mixing bowl, sift flour, sugar, cocoa, and salt. Add oil, eggs, and vanilla and mix well; add pecans. Pour batter into baking dish. Bake for 25 minutes. Test to see if a wooden toothpick inserted in the center comes out clean. To slice into squares, dip knife into glass of ice water, wipe, and slice. (A plastic knife works very well too.) Serve with hot fudge sauce (recipe follows) and Texas's Blue Bell ice cream.

HOT FUDGE SAUCE

- 8 tablespoons cocoa
- 2 cups sugar
- Pinch of salt
- ⅔ cup milk
- 2 tablespoons butter
- 1 teaspoon vanilla extract

Combine cocoa, sugar, salt, milk, and butter in a heavy quart saucepan (we use cast iron). Bring to boil and let boil 6 minutes without stirring. Remove from heat and add vanilla.

Yield: 20 brownies, 1½ cups sauce

Buster Bar Dessert

1 cup crushed Oreo Cookies
½ cup butter, melted
1½ cups peanuts
½ gallon vanilla ice cream, softened
1 can evaporated milk
1 cup confectioners' sugar
⅔ cup semisweet chocolate chips
1 tablespoon vanilla extract
1 carton Cool Whip
Chocolate shavings

Mix butter and cookie crumbs together. Press into a 9 x 13-inch pan. Spread peanuts over crumb mixture. Spread ice cream over nuts. Freeze.

In a saucepan, mix together evaporated milk, confectioners' sugar, chips, and vanilla. Bring to a boil and boil gently for 8 minutes. Cool completely. Spread over ice cream and return to freezer. When ready to serve top with Cool Whip and chocolate shavings.

Yield: 12 to 15 servings

Savannah House
336 North Main
Kingman, Kansas 67068
620-532-3979
www.savannahhousebb.com

RICK AND CAROL FRANCIS have worked diligently to develop Savannah House since they first purchased it in 1996. While developing the Savannah House, they put their home in Kingman up for sale and were surprised to sell it long before their new residence was finished. "We had our walls sheetrocked but that was about it," Carol explained. "But I didn't want to pay rent anywhere," she laughed. They have their living quarters on the north side of Savannah House. A door from their kitchen leads into the public dining room, where guests sip their morning coffee and enjoy the atmosphere. On the southwest corner of the building is the multimedia room, complete with large television and comfy furniture. It is called the Bear's Den, named after one of the earlier owners whose last name was Bear.

W ALNUT STREET INN INVITES you to take a step back in time to capture the warmth and elegance of a Queen Anne–Victorian inn. It was voted best bed-and-breakfast in the Ozarks by the readers of the *Springfield News Leader* four years in a row. From the first glimpse of the inn, you begin to feel its charm, its personality. Hand-painted Corinthian columns frame a wide, airy veranda with an inviting porch swing. The beveled-glass front door is opened by your innkeepers, and you know that your stay will be a special, unique experience, whether you are traveling for business or for pleasure. The inn is an urban oasis for its guests, the owners Gary and Paula Blankenship, and the staff. It is in a nationally registered historic district, one block off historic Route 66. While the guest rooms are decorated with the mellow warmth of antiques, every imaginable modern amenity is unobtrusively tucked away to create an elegant, but comfortable environment.

Buttermilk Pie

$1\frac{1}{4}$	cups sugar
3	tablespoons flour
4	eggs, slightly beaten
$\frac{1}{2}$	stick butter
1	cup buttermilk
	Zest of 1 lemon
1	tablespoon freshly squeezed lemon juice
1	teaspoon pure vanilla extract
$\frac{1}{2}$	teaspoon ground nutmeg
1	(9-inch) piecrust
$\frac{1}{2}$	teaspoon ground nutmeg

Preheat oven to 425°F.

In a large mixing bowl, combine sugar and flour. Add eggs and mix well. Stir in butter and buttermilk. Stir in lemon zest and juice, vanilla and nutmeg. Pour into piecrust. Place pie in center of oven and bake for 15 minutes, then lower temperature to 350°F and continue to bake for approximately 40 minutes until filling is set.

Yield: 5 servings

Cheesecake Bars

CRUST AND TOPPING

- ²/₃ cup butter
- ²/₃ cup brown sugar
- 2 cups flour
- 1 cup walnuts, finely ground

FILLING

- ½ cup sugar
- 16 ounces cream cheese
- ¼ cup milk
- 2 tablespoons lemon juice
- 2 eggs
- 2 teaspoons vanilla extract
- 1 teaspoon lemon extract

Preheat oven to 350°F. Press foil into two 8-inch square pans and grease with cooking spray.

To make the crust/topping: In a large bowl, cream together butter and brown sugar. Add flour and walnuts and mix until crumbly. Set aside 1½ cups of the mixture for the topping. Press remaining crumbs into the two pans and set aside.

To make the filling: In a bowl, cream together sugar and cream cheese. Beat until smooth, scraping the sides of bowl as needed. Add milk, lemon juice, eggs, vanilla, and lemon extract. Spread this mixture on the top of the crust. Sprinkle the remainder of the crumb mixture on top. Bake for about 30 minutes, or until set. Cool and cut into squares.

Yield: 2 dozen bars

The Woolverton Inn
6 Woolverton Road
Stockton, New Jersey 08559
609-397-0802
www.woolvertoninn.com

ENJOY THE GLORIOUS SETTING AND comfortable elegance of this 1792 stone manor, while feeling as comfortable as you would in your own home in the country. The inn provides the privacy of a classic country estate, yet countless fine restaurants, shops, and galleries are just five minutes away. The Woolverton Inn is situated on 10 park-like acres and is surrounded by 300 acres of rolling farmland and forest. Perched high above the Delaware River, guests can enjoy panoramic vistas and intimate views. Food is a passion at the Woolverton Inn. Each day, the head chef prepares an extravagant multicourse breakfast. Afternoon refreshments are served between 3 and 6 PM.

Circle S Ranch
and Country Inn
3325 Circle S Lane
Lawrence, Kansas 66044
1-800-625-2839
www.circlesranch.com

THE CIRCLE S RANCH AND Country Inn is one of America's most distinctive bed-and-breakfast destinations, offering romantic getaways, wedding packages, and corporate meeting facilities. The ranch was originally homesteaded as an 80-acre tract, purchased from a railroad company in the 1860s. It has been owned, expanded, and operated by cowgirl/innkeeper Mary Cronemeyer's family through five generations. Today the ranch encompasses more than 1,200 acres, including tall-grass prairies and picturesque stands of timber. It is home to small herds of bison, longhorns, Herefords, and Angus cattle, as well as indigenous wildlife.

Cherry Cobbler

1	stick butter
1	cup sugar
1	cup flour
1½	teaspoons baking powder
¼	teaspoon salt
¾	cup milk
2	cups cherries
½	cup sugar

Preheat oven to 350°F.

Melt butter in an 8 x 8-inch pan. Mix sugar, flour, baking powder, salt, and milk until smooth. Pour over butter in pan. Pour cherries on top of batter, then sprinkle sugar on the very top. Bake for 30 minutes.

Yield: 4 to 6 servings

Chocolate Chess Pie

2 sticks unsalted butter

4 ounces bittersweet chocolate

1 cup sugar

4 eggs

1 teaspoon vanilla extract

2 tablespoons stone-ground cornmeal

1 unbaked 9-inch pie shell

Preheat oven to 350°F.

In a double boiler, melt butter and chocolate together until smooth. In a large mixing bowl, lightly beat eggs and then beat in the sugar. Stir in butter-chocolate mixture, cornmeal, and vanilla extract until smooth. Pour into pie shell. Bake for 45 minutes or until set. Chill before serving.

Yield: 8 to 10 servings

Snowbird Mountain Lodge
4633 Santeetlah Road
Robbinsville, North Carolina 28771
1-800-941-9290
828-479-3433
www.snowbirdlodge.com

*H*igh up in Santeetlah Gap, on the southern border of the Great Smoky Mountain National Park, lies this secluded, rustic yet elegant, historic lodge built of stone and huge chestnut logs. The view from the porch is one of the best in the mountains. An excellent library, huge stone fireplaces and award-winning gourmet cuisine make this lodge an exceptional retreat from the pressures of the world. Whether you like fly-fishing, hiking, biking, or just relaxing in front of the fire, the innkeepers/owners, Karen and Robert Rankin, can make your trip to the mountains picture perfect.

The Silvermine Tavern
194 Perry Avenue
Norwalk, Connecticut 06850
1-888-693-9967
203-847-4558
www.silverminetavern.com

*Y*OU ARE ALWAYS WELCOME at the Silvermine Tavern, which is celebrating more than 75 years of hospitality. From its creaky wooden floors and venerable ancestor paintings to its traditional New England cuisine and antique canopy beds, the Silvermine Tavern is everything a country inn should be— warm, friendly, inviting, and brimming with charm. You're invited to stay the night, the weekend, or longer in one of the cozy, romantic guest rooms, each with its own private bath. Furnished with genuine American antiques and individually decorated, the rooms have either one double bed (some with canopies), one queen canopy bed, or two single beds. The Mill Pond Suite is a two-room suite at the water's edge, with a private deck and queen canopy bed. The Silvermine Tavern is the place for holiday celebrations; a seasonal menu and the comfort of a great old inn are just the thing.

Chocolate Chip–Pecan Pie

4 eggs
1 cup plus 2 tablespoons sugar
1/4 cup plus 2 tablespoons melted butter
1 1/2 cups dark corn syrup (Blue Label)
1 1/2 cups pecan halves
1/2 cup chocolate chips
1/4 teaspoon vanilla extract
1 deep-dish pie shell

Preheat oven to 325°F.

Beat eggs until they turn a light lemon yellow color. Slowly mix in sugar. Continue mixing and add melted butter, corn syrup, and vanilla. Put the pecans and chocolate chips in pie shell. Pour filling on top to fill pie shell. Bake for 1 hour. Serve at room temperature or warmed. (Do not serve cold directly from the refrigerator.)

Yield: 1 pie

Chocolate-Zucchini-Rum Coffee Cake

1½ sticks butter, at room temperature
2   cups sugar
3   large eggs
2½ cups flour
½   cup unsweetened cocoa
1½ teaspoons baking soda
1   teaspoon salt
1   teaspoon cinnamon
¼   cup milk
⅓   cup rum
3   cups shredded zucchini
1   cup chocolate chips
½   cup chopped pecans
¼   cup milk

Preheat oven to 350°F. Spray a Bundt pan with cooking spray.

In a large bowl, beat butter and sugar until fluffy. Add eggs one at a time. Add flour, cocoa, soda, salt, cinnamon, milk, and rum. Beat until well mixed. Add zucchini, chips, and nuts. Once again, mix well. Pour batter into Bundt pan. Bake for 50 to 55 minutes.

Yield: 1 cake

The Inn at Monticello
1188 Scottsville Road
(Route 20 South)
Charlottesville, Virginia 22902
434-979-3593
www.innatmonticello.com

A CHARMING COUNTRY manor house built in the mid-1800s, the Inn at Monticello sits cradled in the valley at the foot of Thomas Jefferson's own Monticello Mountain. Dogwoods grace the landscape; boxwoods and azaleas ornament the grounds. The inn serves a full gourmet breakfast. The aroma of freshly brewed coffee awaits you as you begin your day. Many find the inn a quiet place to curl up on the sofa in front of a crackling fire and read that long-awaited book. Others take pleasure in rocking-chair conversation, while sitting on the porch on a breezy summer day. Some enjoy a stroll to nearby Willow Lake or walk on the Thomas Jefferson walking trail to Monticello.

Captain Lord Mansion

6 Pleasant Street
P. O. Box 800
Kennebunkport, Maine 04046
207-967-3141
www.captainlord.com

HIS SPLENDID MANSION,
built by Captain
Nathaniel Lord, began
as a joyful place where his family and
descendants shared relaxing times
and created warm memories. When
the inn was established, the owners
endeavored to preserve the gracious
atmosphere that typified life there
throughout the Lord family's time.
During the latest restoration, the
original wallpaper in two of the rooms
was preserved. There are blown-glass
windows throughout the mansion.
Visitors enjoy climbing the four-story
spiral staircase to view the historic
neighborhood from the octagonal
cupola. Delicious food is served in the
lovely dining room.

The Captain's Chocolate Cake

1 (18.25-ounce) package plain devil's food chocolate cake mix
1 (3.9-ounce) package chocolate instant pudding mix
4 large eggs
1 cup sour cream
½ cup warm water
½ cup vegetable oil—canola, corn, or sunflower
1½ cups Nestle Toll House milk chocolate and caramel morsels

Preheat oven to 350°F. Spray a 12-cup Bundt pan with cooking spray and dust with flour.

Combine cake mix, pudding mix, eggs, sour cream, warm water, and oil in a large mixing bowl. Blend with an electric mixer on low speed for 1 minute. Stop mixer and scrape bowl. Continue blending on medium speed for 3 minutes, scraping sides as needed. Batter should look thick and well combined. Fold in morsels, distributing evenly throughout the batter. Pour batter into prepared pan, smoothing with a rubber spatula. Bake for 50 minutes; cake should spring back when lightly pressed and sides should just start to pull away from the pan.

Cool for 20 minutes on wire rack in pan. Invert pan onto wire rack and continue to cool for 20 minutes more. Slice and serve warm.

Yield: 1 cake

Triple-Chocolate Mousse Parfait

- 2¼ cups whipping cream
- 6 large egg yolks
- 1 tablespoon sugar
- 4 ounces white-chocolate, chopped
- 6 tablespoons unsalted butter, cut in tablespoon-size pieces,(at room temperature), divided
- 4 ounces milk-chocolate, chopped
- 4 ounces bittersweet-chocolate, chopped
  White-chocolate curls or leaves for garnish

Refrigerate 1¾ cups of the whipping cream. Whisk egg yolks with sugar and remaining ½ cup cream in a metal bowl set in a pan of simmering water. Whisk constantly while heating until mixture reaches 160°F on a candy thermometer. Remove from heat and whip with electric mixer until cool. Melt white chocolate in a medium bowl over simmering water; stir until smooth. Remove from heat and add 3 tablespoons of the butter; stir to blend. Add ⅓ cup of yolk mixture and blend in thoroughly.

Melt milk chocolate over simmering water, remove from heat, add 2 tablespoons of the butter, and stir until smooth. Add ⅓ cup of yolk mixture and stir until blended. Melt bittersweet-chocolate in medium bowl over simmering water; stir until smooth. Remove from heat and add remaining butter and half of remaining yolk mixture.

In a large bowl, whip chilled cream until stiff. Fold 1⅓ cups cream into white-chocolate mixture. Divide white-chocolate mousse among 6 wine glasses or other suitable 1 cup glasses,

Recipe continued on next page

The Seven Sisters Inn
820 SE Fort King Street
Ocala, Florida 34471
352-867-1170
www.sevensistersinn.com

BUILT IN 1888, THIS QUEEN Anne–style Victorian bed-and-breakfast has been lovingly restored to its original stately elegance with beautiful period furnishings. The Inn was judged "Best Restoration Project" and is listed on the National Register of Historic Places. Faux paintings and murals, plus carved doors from Indonesia, begin an artistic expedition that reaches the four corners of the globe. World travelers can experience lighthouses of Cape Cod, a Safari Bengal room, gilded treasures and Egyptian artifacts, stone spa showers, a sultan's bed from mysterious India, fabrics imported from Paris, and the Zen-like harmony of the Orient. Jacuzzis, Victorian soaking tubs, spa showers, fireplaces, and heated towel bars are available in most rooms. Gourmet breakfast and afternoon tea are included.

using about ⅓ cup mousse for each. Refrigerate about 15 minutes or freeze 10 minutes until top is partially set.

Fold 1⅓ cups whipped cream into milk-chocolate mixture.

Gently spoon milk-chocolate mousse over white mousse in glasses in even layers. Refrigerate for an additional 15 minutes.

Fold remaining whipped cream into bittersweet-chocolate mixture. Gently spoon dark-chocolate mousse into the glasses. Refrigerate about 2 hours or until set. Cover with plastic wrap when set. Dessert can be kept 2 days in refrigerator. Garnish with white-chocolate curls or leaves.

Yield: 6 servings

Chocolate Pâté
with White Chocolate Sauce

8 ounces bittersweet chocolate
1 stick butter
4 whole eggs plus 1 egg yolk
2 egg whites

Preheat oven to 325°F. Butter a 9-inch loaf pan.

Melt chocolate and butter in a double boiler. Let cool. Warm eggs and egg yolk over boiling water (but do not overheat), whipping constantly once eggs are warm. Beat in mixer until eggs fall off beaters in a ribboning fashion. Fold cooled chocolate into eggs.

Beat egg whites until stiff peaks form. Fold into chocolate mixture and pour into loaf pan. Bake in a hot-water bath for 45 minutes or until knife inserted in center comes out clean. Refrigerate overnight before serving.

WHITE CHOCOLATE SAUCE
5 ounces white chocolate
2½ ounces heavy cream, at room temperature

Melt white chocolate and cool to room temperature. Stir in cream. Both ingredients should be at room temperature when you mix them.

To serve: Slice pâté as you would a loaf of bread. Serve slightly warmed, with warm white chocolate sauce and an edible flower (such as nasturtium or pansy) for garnish.

Yield: 8 servings

The Darby Field Inn
185 Chase Hill Road
Albany, New Hampshire 03818
1-800-426-4147
603-447-2181
www.darbyfield.com

ONLY 6 MILES FROM NORTH Conway, yet right in the middle of nowhere, overlooking the Mt. Washington Valley and White Mountains of New Hampshire, is the Darby Field Inn. The inn quietly surprises and delights wanderers adventurous enough to leave the beaten path. It is a romantic bed-and-breakfast with fireplace and Jacuzzi rooms and suites, candlelight gourmet dining, a sophisticated wine list, and moonlit sleigh rides. The inn also has private nature trails for cross-country skiing, snowshoeing, mountain biking, or just walking. And, if that's not enough, how about a nice therapeutic massage or a rejuvenating yoga class? Whether you are looking for romance, relaxation, or a more active adventure, the Darby Field Inn has it all.

The Inn at Levelfields

The Inn at Levelfields
10155 Mary Ball Road
Lancaster, Virginia 22503
804-435-6887
www.innatlevelfields.com

CHARACTERIZED BY AN IMPRESSIVE double-tiered portico on the south front and by massive chimneys, Levelfields is one of the last antebellum mansions to be built in the Commonwealth and represents the final expression of the authentic hip-roofed Georgian Colonial style. The inn has been completely refurbished and filled with family antiques and Oriental rugs. It offers spacious rooms, king- and queen-size poster beds, and pretty fabrics, In the summer a cool drink by the pool after a busy day of sightseeing will refresh the mind and spirit. On cooler days, guest can select a book from the library and curl up by the fire.

Chocolate-Pecan Pie

1 (9-inch) piecrust, unbaked
1 cup semisweet chocolate chips
2 cups pecan halves
½ cup firmly packed brown sugar
½ cup dark corn syrup
3 eggs
1 teaspoon vanilla extract
  Whipped cream
  Additional chocolate chips, melted

Preheat oven to 375°F.

Prepare piecrust and place in a 9-inch pie plate. Sprinkle chocolate chips over bottom of crust; top with pecan halves. In a small bowl, combine brown sugar, corn syrup, eggs, and vanilla; beat well. Pour over pecans. Bake for 25 to 35 minutes or until top is deep golden brown and pie is done. Cool. Store in refrigerator. For garnish, melt approximately ½ cup chocolate chips in double boiler. Place in ziplock bag. Snip one corner (carefully, keeping hole small). Drizzle chocolate over whipped cream topping.

Yield: 8 servings

Triple-Threat Coffee Cake

 1 package yellow cake mix
 1 (20-ounce) can apple or cherry pie filling
 1 egg
 1½ sticks butter, melted, divided
 ¼ cup plus 1 teaspoon sugar

Preheat oven to 350°F. Grease a 9 x 13-inch pan.

Measure 1 cup of cake mix and set aside. Pour remaining cake mix into large bowl and combine with ½ cup of the melted butter and egg. Mix well and spread into pan. Top with pie filling and set aside. In a small bowl, combine reserved cake mix, remaining ¼ cup melted butter, and sugar. Sprinkle over pie filling. Bake for 45 minutes. Cut into 12 (3-inch) squares.

Yield: 12 servings

**Agave Grove
Bed & Breakfast Inn**
800 West Panorama Road
Tucson, Arizona 85704
520-887-9487
agavebb@earthlink.net

Agave Grove Bed & Breakfast Inn is an oasis away from home, with stress-free casual elegance that captures the serenity and magic of the desert. Highly private, yet easily accessible to Tucson's bounty, this is the perfect setting for romantic getaways or peaceful retreats to renew the spirit. Agave Grove is located on 2½ acres of lush, natural desert grounds with spectacular mountain views. A large courtyard and shaded patios are ideal for outdoor dining and relaxation, as are the waterfall-fed pool and soothing in-ground spa, putting green, and spacious gazebo-styled ramada. Agave Grove Bed & Breakfast Inn is appointed in a Southwestern décor with many family heirlooms and antiques. A full hearty breakfast with home-baked goods awaits guests in the dining room, or guests may dine casually in their suites.

LA POSADA DE Albuquerque was opened in 1939 by New Mexico native Conrad Hilton, who honeymooned here with bride Zsa Zsa Gabor. Capturing the essence of the Southwest, the hotel features an elaborate Moorish brass and mosaic-tiled fountain, handcrafted circular balcony, and Native American war-dance murals. La Posada is Albuquerque's only hotel listed on the National Register of Historic Places. Come embrace La Posada de Albuquerque's special ambience, a blend of historical elegance, quiet efficiency, and personalized service.

Flan de Café

CARAMEL

¾ cup sugar

Place sugar in saucepan and heat on high flame until sugar melts (careful not to burn). Remove when caramel color appears.

CUSTARD

1 quart milk
½ cup sugar
½ teaspoon vanilla extract
2 tablespoons instant coffee
4 whole eggs
2 egg yolks

Preheat oven to 375°F.

Mix milk, sugar, vanilla, instant coffee, eggs, and egg yolks thoroughly. Pour caramel into 6 dessert cups. Pour custard mixture on top of caramel. Place cups in a pan with water and cover. Bake for 1 to 1½ hours.

Yield: 6 servings

Fresh Apple Cake

CAKE

1½ cups salad oil
2 cups sugar
3 eggs
2 teaspoons vanilla extract
3 cups self-rising flour, sifted
3 cups chopped raw apples (any kind)
1 cup chopped nuts

Preheat oven to 325°F. Grease and flour a large pan.

Cream oil, sugar, eggs, and vanilla together in a large bowl. Add flour. Add nuts and apples. Bake for 1 hour and 25 minutes.

FROSTING

1½ sticks margarine
½ cup brown sugar
¼ cup evaporated milk

Combine frosting ingredients in a saucepan and bring to a boil. Boil for 2½ minutes. Pour over cake.

Yield: 1 large cake

The Waverly Inn
783 North Main Street
Hendersonville,
North Carolina 28792
1-800-537-8195
828-693-9193
www.waverlyinn.com

LOCATED IN THE BEAUTIFUL Blue Ridge Mountains of western North Carolina, the inn is a short drive from the Biltmore Estate, the Blue Ridge Parkway, Dupont State Forest, Chimney Rock Park, and the Flat Rock Playhouse. Cited in national publications such as *The New York Times* and *Southern Living*, the inn received high praise in *Vogue Magazine* for its "southern breakfast" with choice of omelets, French toast, pancakes with real maple syrup, grits, meats, fresh fruit, eggs and egg substitutes. Special touches include 300-thread-count sheets, Egyptian-cotton towels, robes, data ports, wireless Internet access, and cable TV. The inn is within walking distance of the Mast General Store, several fine restaurants, and exceptional shopping and antiquing. Two porches with rocking chairs await you. Come experience hospitality as it was meant to be.

The Governor's House
Bed and Breakfast

500 Meadowlake Lane
Talladega, Alabama 35160
205-763-2186
priscilla0706@aol.com

MIDWAY BETWEEN Birmingham and Anniston, The Governor's House overlooks Logan Martin Lake on Meadowlake Farm in east-central Alabama. Built in 1850 by former Alabama governor Lewis Parsons, the house was originally located in Talladega. The Governor's House is surrounded by a beautifully manicured and expansive front lawn. Antiques, quilts, and accessories from the Shaw-Gaines families provide a homey atmosphere throughout the interior. Guests are greeted with sweets and fruit upon arrival. A wonderful full-country breakfast with tasty homemade breads and jellies awaits you in the morning. Coffee and tea are served in the afternoon, and snacks are whipped up in the evening.

Diane's Fresh Fruit Cobbler

- 1 stick butter
- 2 cups sugar
- 2 cups water
- 1/2 cup Crisco shortening
- 1 1/2 cups self-rising flour
- 1/3 cup milk
- 2 cups fresh fruit
- 1 teaspoon cinnamon

Preheat oven to 350°F.

Melt butter in a 13 x 9 x 2-inch baking dish. Mix sugar and water and stir until sugar melts. Set aside.

Cut shortening into flour until the mixture resembles fine crumbs. Add milk and stir with fork until dough leaves the side of the bowl. Turn out onto a lightly floured board; knead just until smooth. Roll dough out into a rectangle about 1/4 inch thick. Sprinkle fruit evenly over dough, then sprinkle cinnamon over fruit. Roll up dough like a jelly roll. Cut roll into about 16 slices. Place slices in a dish with melted butter. Pour sugar syrup over the rolls (use all the syrup—this may look like too much liquid, but it's not). Bake for 45 to 55 minutes.

Yield: 8 to 10 servings

Ginger-Pear Coffee Cake

   3 tablespoons butter
   2 fresh pears, peeled, cored, and sliced
   1 tablespoon Fruit Fresh
  ⅓ cup brown sugar
1½ teaspoons ginger
   1 teaspoon grated lemon zest
   1 teaspoon grated orange zest
   1 egg, beaten
  ¼ cup melted butter
  ½ cup milk
1½ cups flour
  ½ cup sugar
1½ teaspoons baking powder
  ¼ teaspoon salt

Preheat oven to 350°F.

Place 3 tablespoons butter in a 9-inch cake pan and melt.
Arrange pear slices in bottom of pan in a spiral pattern. In a
bowl, mix brown sugar, ginger, lemon and orange zest; set aside.
Beat egg, melted butter, and milk together. In a separate bowl,
sift together flour, sugar, baking powder, and salt. Stir egg and
flour mixtures together until well blended. Pour batter over
pears and spread evenly. Sprinkle brown sugar mixture over top.
Cut through batter with a knife to marble cake. Bake for 25 to 30
minutes. Let stand for 5 minutes. Invert cake onto serving plate.

Yield: 1 cake

El Farolito Bed & Breakfast Inn
514 Gelisteo Street
Santa Fe, New Mexico 87501
1-888-634-8782
505-988-1631
www.farolito.com

SURROUND YOURSELF WITH
the richness of Santa
Fe's art, culture, and
history in an authentic adobe
compound. The inn offers you award-
winning private *casitas*, showcasing
exquisite, original Southwestern art
and handcrafted furnishings. The
rooms are decorated in styles relevant
to Santa Fe's rich cultural heritage of
Native American, Spanish, and Anglo
inhabitants. The inn is conveniently
located in the downtown historic
district, a short walk to numerous
galleries, shops, museums, fine dining,
and the central plaza. In the warm
sunshine, savor a leisurely breakfast
on the back porch and relax on your
garden patio. In the winter, enjoy a
fireside breakfast in the brightly
decorated dining room or the coziness
of your room.

Chico Hot Springs Resort

Highway 89 South
P. O. Box 134
Pray, Montana 59065
406-333-4933
www.chicohotsprings.com

L OCATED IN SOUTH-central Montana's Paradise Valley, Chico Hot Springs Resort is high country at its best. The Absaroka mountain range defines the eastern skyline, the Gallatin range the west, and the famous Yellowstone River runs between the two. Chico's history centers on its hot pools, whose "restorative" powers have been put to use for over a century. The water in the pools is between 100 and 104°F and includes no chlorine or other chemicals. The food at the resort is absolutely wonderful.

Grand Marnier Crème Brûlée

2 cups heavy whipping cream
⅓ cup sugar
5 egg yolks, at room temperature
½ tablespoon pure vanilla extract
¼ cup Grand Marnier, brandy, or other liqueur
6 teaspoons sugar

Preheat oven to 325°F.

Heat cream and sugar in a heavy saucepan until just boiling. Slowly whisk in egg yolks. Add vanilla and Grand Marnier. Pour mixture into 6 ramekins or small oven-safe bowls. Place in a 9 x 13-inch baking dish and fill with a hot-water bath three-quarters of the way up the outside of the bowls. Bake in oven for about 40 minutes or until set; the brûlée should not jiggle in the center. Remove from oven and let cool in the water bath. Cover with plastic wrap and refrigerate for at least 2 hours or up to two days.

When ready to serve, sprinkle a teaspoon of sugar on top of each custard. With a small, handheld butane torch, caramelize the sugar until dark brown and bubbly. The result is a hot, delicate crust over a cool, creamy middle. (Handheld butane torches are available at most cooking shops.) You can also caramelize the sugar in the oven by placing the custards under the broiler and watching carefully until sugar is dark brown and bubbly; this will heat the bowl completely and result in a soupy texture. Either way, let the sugar harden before serving.

Yield: 6 servings

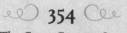

Heath Brunch Coffee Cake

CAKE

- 1 stick butter, softened
- 2 cups flour
- 1 cup brown sugar
- ½ cup granulated sugar
- 1 cup buttermilk
- 1 teaspoon baking soda
- 1 egg
- 1 teaspoon vanilla extract

TOPPING

- ½ cup Heath or Skor English toffee, finely crushed
- ¼ cup pecans or almonds, finely crushed

To make cake: Preheat oven to 350°F. Grease and flour a 9 x 9-inch cake pan.

In a bowl, blend flour, butter, and sugars. Take out ½ cup of mixture and set aside. Add buttermilk, baking soda, egg, and vanilla to remaining butter-flour mixture in bowl. Blend well. Pour batter into cake pan.

To make topping: Mix toffee and pecans into reserved butter-flour mixture. Sprinkle over top of batter.

Bake for 45 minutes.

Yield: 16 servings

Chichester-McKee House
800 Spring Street
Placerville, California 95667
530-626-1882
info@innlover.com

D. W. CHICHESTER BUILT THIS gracious home for his wife, Caroline, in 1892. Lovngly restored in 2000, the original beauty lives on. Beneath the Victorian dining room was once a pioneer gold mine. Guests will marvel at the wood and stained glass. It is an inspiration to come into this charming home, to find warm hospitality, and to remember an earlier time. A delightful breakfast is served in the dining room. The menu changes daily and features main-course egg specialties, such as ham and asparagus crepes, eggs Benedict, or Doreen's quiche. Bill's blend of coffee, fine tea, hot chocolate, juice, fruit dishes, and baked pastries are included.

Knoll's Country Inn
Bed & Breakfast

6132 South Range Road
North Platte, Nebraska 69101
308-368-5634
www.bbonline.com/ne/knolls/

*T*HE WELCOME MAT IS OUT. If it's peace, quiet, and solitude you're looking for, this inn is away from the noise of cars, trucks. and trains. Enjoy a morning or evening walk along the canal; you may be treated to a spectacular sunrise or sunset. You will be taken away from uncomfortable beds, noisy motels, and routine restaurant food. Instead you'll find queen-size beds, country quiet, and wholesome home cooking. For the ultimate in relaxation and enjoyment, there is a whirlpool tub inside. And if you are looking for a little fun and a special time under the stars, try the outside hot tub. Accommodations include five guest rooms, two with private baths. One of the delights of your stay will be a scrumptious homemade breakfast.

Hot Fudge Cake

1	cup flour
3/4	cup sugar
6	tablespoons unsweetened cocoa powder
2	teaspoons baking powder
1/4	teaspoon salt
1/2	cup milk
2	tablespoons vegetable oil
1	teaspoon vanilla extract
1	cup brown sugar, packed
1 3/4	cups hot water
	Whipped cream or ice cream

Preheat oven to 350°F.

In a medium bowl, combine flour, sugar, 2 tablespoons of the cocoa, baking powder, and salt. Stir in milk, oil, and vanilla until smooth. Spread in an ungreased 9-inch-square baking pan. Combine brown sugar and remaining 4 tablespoons cocoa; sprinkle over batter. Pour hot water over all, but *do not stir.* Bake for 35 to 40 minutes. When done, the pudding is on the bottom. Serve warm with whipped cream or vanilla ice cream.

Yield: 9 servings

Italian Cream Cake

CAKE

- 2 cups sugar
- ½ cup shortening
- 1 stick margarine
- 5 eggs, separated
- 1 teaspoon vanilla extract
- 2 cups flour, sifted
- 1 teaspoon baking soda
- ½ teaspoon salt
- 1 cup buttermilk
- 2 cups flaked coconut
- 1 cup pecans, chopped

Preheat oven to 325°F.

In a bowl, cream the sugar, shortening, and margarine. Add egg yolks one at a time, beating well after each. Add vanilla. Mix flour, baking soda, and salt together. Add to batter. Beat egg whites until stiff, then fold into batter. Divide batter among 3 cake pans. Bake for 40 minutes.

ICING

- 1 stick margarine
- 8 ounces cream cheese
- 1 tablespoon vanilla extract
- 1 pound powdered sugar

In a bowl, cream margarine and cream cheese. Add vanilla and sugar and blend. Spread icing on warm cake.

Yield: 1 large cake

Note: This cake is beautiful baked in heart-shaped pans.

Back in Thyme
1100 South 130th Street
Bonner Springs, Kansas 66012
913-422-5207
www.backnthyme.com

YOU WILL LOVE BEING A guest in this "new-old" Queen Anne, which boasts all the modern conveniences, as well as the comforts of another era. A wraparound veranda, spacious second-floor accommodations, antique leaded glass, and unique fixtures are tastefully integrated into this peaceful retreat. Enjoy your first cup of coffee in the privacy of your room or take it with you as you stroll through the herb garden and by the pond. Pause a moment at the arbor swing to watch the ducks and other wildlife. After allowing time to awaken to a fresh Kansas morning, you will want to satisfy your appetite. The French doors of the sunroom are open to invite you to a hearty breakfast. This beautiful room, which overlooks the kitchen herb garden, features towering stacked windows and a 12-foot-high tin ceiling.

Curry Mansion Inn

511 Caroline Street
Key West, Florida 33040
305-294-5349
www.currymansion.com

THIS MANSION IS ALSO AN intriguing museum listed on the National Register of Historic Places. A prime example of Key West's heritage of elegance, the mansion was built by Florida's first millionaire family. Nestled alongside the original 1899 Curry Mansion, the inn offers elegant, romantic rooms, with most opening onto a sparkling pool surrounded by the lush foliage of the Curry Estate. Guests enjoy the finest amenities, including a full deluxe breakfast, daily open bar, and cocktail parties.

Aunt Sally's Key Lime Pie

Key lime pie was first created in this house by Aunt Sally, a cook who worked for the Curry family in 1894.

> 4   eggs, separated
> ½   cup key lime juice
> 1   (14-ounce) can sweetened condensed milk
>   Cream of tartar
> ⅓   cup sugar
> 1   (8-inch) graham cracker crust

Preheat oven to 350°F.

Beat egg yolks until light and thick. Blend in lime juice, then condensed milk, stirring until mixture thickens. Pour mixture into crust. Beat egg whites with cream of tartar until stiff. Gradually beat in sugar, beating until glossy peaks form. Spread egg whites over surface of pie to edge of crust. Bake until golden brown, about 20 minutes. Chill before serving.

Yield: 1 pie

Lemon Bars

- 1 cup plus ½ tablespoon all-purpose flour
- 1 stick butter
- ¼ cup confectioners' sugar
- 1 cup sugar
- ½ teaspoon baking powder
- 2 tablespoons lemon juice
- 2 eggs, beaten

Preheat oven to 350°F. Grease a 9-inch-square pan.

In a small bowl, blend 1 cup of the flour, butter, and confectioners' sugar together. Press into prepared pan. Bake for 20 minutes.

In a bowl, combine sugar, baking powder, lemon juice, eggs, and remaining ½ tablespoon flour. Pour over baked crust. Bake for 25 minutes. Cool and cut into bars.

Yield: 9 to 12 bars

**1833 Umpleby House
Bed & Breakfast Inn**
111 West Bridge Street
New Hope, Pennsylvania 18938
215-862-3936
www.1833umplebyhouse.com

New Hope's Umpleby House is a luxurious and upscale bed-and-breakfast inn. This circa 1833 Classic Revival plaster-over-stone manor house is situated on two private parklike acres. The inn is conveniently located in the historic district, just steps from the picturesque riverside village square. Umpleby House is on the National Register of Historic Places and a member of the 1870 Wedgwood Collection of Historic Inns. With its award-winning gardens, gracious antique furnishings, hand-painted interiors, luxury amenities, and personalized attention, Umpleby House creates the perfect setting for either business or pleasure. Days begin with a complimentary home-baked breakfast served on Wedgwood china in the dining room (at individual tables), on the Victorian porch, or in the privacy of your room.

**The Cornerstone Mansion
Bed & Breakfast**
140 North 39th Street
Omaha, Nebraska 68131
402-558-7600
1-888-883-7745
www.bbonline.com/ne/cornerstone/

THE CORNERSTONE MANSION is historically known as the Offutt house. It is a focal point of Omaha's historic Gold Coast, popular with the wealthy of Omaha in the early 1900s. No expense was spared when prominent Omahans Charles and Bertha Offutt built the 14-room, 10,200-square-foot home in 1894. Offutt Air Force Base was named for their son Jarvis. The mansion began serving as a bed-and-breakfast in the mid-1980s. Today, innkeepers Mark O'Leary and Julie Mierau invite guests to enjoy the surroundings, which are reminiscent of a bygone era.

Julie's Chocolate-Oatmeal Bars

    2 sticks plus 2 tablespoons butter, softened
    2 cups packed brown sugar
    2 eggs
    2 teaspoons vanilla extract
 2½ cups flour
    1 teaspoon baking soda
    3 cups uncooked oatmeal
 1½ cups semisweet chocolate chips
    1 (14-ounce) can sweetened condensed milk (no
       substitutions)

Preheat oven to 325°F. Lightly grease 13 x 9-inch baking pan.

Beat 2 sticks butter and brown sugar in a large bowl until blended. Add eggs and beat until light. Blend in vanilla. Combine flour and baking soda in medium bowl; stir into butter mixture. Stir in oatmeal. Spread ¾ of oatmeal mixture evenly in prepared pan.

Combine chocolate chips, milk, and remaining 2 tablespoons butter in a heavy saucepan. Stir over low heat until chocolate is melted. Pour mixture evenly over oatmeal mixture. Dot with remaining oatmeal mixture. Bake for 20 to 25 minutes or until edges are browned. Cool on a wire rack until chocolate center is firm. Cut into bars once center is firmly set.

Yield: 16 bars

Lemon-Pear Tart
with Meringue

2 cups flour
1 stick butter
½ cup ground walnuts
3 eggs, separated
½ cup granulated sugar
2 fresh pears
   Grated zest of 1 lemon
1 cup confectioners' sugar
1 teaspoon lemon juice
⅛ teaspoon cream of tartar

Greenbriar Inn
315 East Wallace Avenue
Coeur d'Alene, Idaho 83814
208-667-9660

Preheat oven to 325°F.

In a bowl, combine flour, butter, walnuts, egg yolks, and granulated sugar to form pastry base. Press into a 10-inch fluted tart pan and press crust 1 inch up the sides.

Peel and poach pears. Cut pears into thin slices and lay them on crust in a circular or fan fashion. Sprinkle with lemon zest. Bake for 15 minutes. Remove.

In a bowl, beat egg whites, slowly adding confectioners' sugar, lemon juice, and cream of tartar until stiff. Place meringue in a piping bag. Pipe meringue onto tart in cross-hatch fashion. Return to oven and bake until meringue is lightly browned.

Yield: 8 servings

BUILT IN 1908, THE Greenbriar is Coeur d'Alene's only nationally registered historic mansion. During most of its history, the structure was used as a boardinghouse. The third floor, with its gracefully arched windows, was once a dance hall. A four-course gourmet breakfast is served to houseguests, and a dining facility has been added for both guests and the public to enjoy.

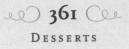

Sherwood Inn

26 West Genesee Street
Skaneateles, New York 13152
1-800-374-3796
315-685-3405
www.thesherwoodinn.com

THE SHERWOOD INN IS situated in the heart of the historic village of Skaneateles, New York, which is known as the eastern gateway to the Finger Lakes. The inn is located on the north shore of Skaneateles Lake, one of the most beautiful and cleanest bodies of water in the world. Built as a stagecoach stop in 1807, the inn has always been a favorite resting place for travelers. The handsome lobby with fireplace, gift shop, antiques, and Oriental rugs offer a warm reception. Each room has been restored to the beauty of a bygone era to create a relaxing harmony away from everyday cares. The extensive menu offers American cooking with a Continental touch, accompanied by an impressive wine list. The Old Tavern serves traditional American fare in a relaxed atmosphere.

Lemon Crème Pie

1½ cups sugar
½ cup cornstarch
2 cups half-and- half
1 stick butter
½ cup fresh lemon juice
    Zest of 1 lemon
6 egg yolks
1½ cups sour cream
    Baked pie shell

In a saucepan, mix sugar, cornstarch, half-and-half, butter, lemon juice and zest, and egg yolks. Stir over medium heat until mixture thickens and boils. Remove from heat. Add sour cream and mix well. Pour filling into pie shell. Cover with plastic wrap and cool at room temperature until set.

Yield: 8 to 10 servings

Maple-Nut Tart

⅓ cup butter, melted
1 egg, beaten
2 tablespoons whole milk
½ cup pure maple syrup
1 teaspoon vanilla extract
1 cup maple-sugar-coated pecans or walnuts,
   coarsely chopped
1 (9-inch) unbaked tart shell or pie shell
   Whipped cream
   Fresh mint leaves

Preheat oven to 350°F.

In a bowl, combine melted butter, beaten egg, maple syrup, and vanilla. Add nuts. Gently pour into tart shell. Sprinkle with extra nuts (optional). Bake for 20 to 30 minutes until top is puffed and crust is beginning to brown. Cool on a rack for 20 minutes before removing from tart pan. Serve warm or at room temperature. Garnish with a dollop of whipped cream and a fresh mint leaf.

Yield: 1 tart

The Buttonwood Inn on Mt. Surprise

Mt. Surprise Road
P. O. Box 1817
North Conway,
New Hampshire 03860
1-800-258-2625
603-356-2625
www.buttonwoodinn.com

ENJOY THE PEACEFUL SURROUNDings of this 1820s inn, which hugs the base of Mt. Surprise. Air-conditioned guest chambers feature wide pine floors, stenciling, and antiques. Deluxe rooms offer fireplaces, or a fireplace and Jacuzzi for two. Common living rooms with wood-burning fireplaces welcome you home to afternoon tea and treats. Relax by the outdoor pool, surrounded by memorable perennial gardens while spying on ruby-throated hummingbirds. Revisit favorite hiking trails and ski slopes, or discover new ones. Plan adventures to the Cog Railway or the Flume Gorge. A full breakfast is provided, and different entrées are served daily at individual tables.

Casa de las Chimeneas

405 Cordoba Road
Taos, New Mexico 87571
1-877-758-4777
www.visit-taos.com

INNKEEPER SUSAN VERNON has created an oasis behind the walls of Casa de las Chimeneas in Taos, New Mexico. The inn is tucked just a few blocks off of the Taos plaza. Its name, aptly, means "house of chimneys," and each of the eight guest rooms has its own fireplace. The inn is known for its food, and for good reason. The day starts with a sumptuous and large breakfast, featuring treats like homemade muffins, baked pears, Southwest strata, and a signature fruit frappe. The room rate also includes a light buffet supper, served each evening.

Mexican Chocolate Cake

CAKE

1¼ cups flour
¾ cup sugar
¼ cup cornstarch
½ teaspoon salt
1 teaspoon cinnamon
½ teaspoon baking soda
3 tablespoon cocoa
⅓ cup oil
1 teaspoon vanilla
1 tablespoon vinegar
1 cup cold water (for added interest, substitute ¼ cup brandy, ¾ cup water)

Preheat oven to 350°F

Lightly grease a baking pan, either an 8 x 9-inch square or round.

In a bowl, sift flour, sugar, cornstarch, salt, cinnamon, baking soda, and cocoa. In a blender, mix oil, vanilla, vinegar, and water. Mix the wet ingredients into the dry ingredients until thoroughly blended. Pour batter into pan. Bake for 30 to 35 minutes or until pick inserted in center comes out clean. Cool and cover with glaze (recipe follows).

CHOCOLATE GLAZE

- 2 tablespoons cocoa
- 1 tablespoon corn syrup
- 1 tablespoon oil
- ½ teaspoon cinnamon
- 2 tablespoons plus 1 teaspoon water (or 1 tablespoon Kahlúa plus 1 teaspoon water)
- 1 cup confectioners' sugar

Combine all glaze ingredients except confectioners' sugar in a small saucepan. Stir over medium heat until smooth and shiny. Glaze the cake over a cooling rack to allow the edges to be smooth. Dust with confectioners' sugar.

Yield: 1 cake

Glen-Ella Springs Inn
1789 Bear Gap Road
Clarkesville, Georgia 30523
706-754-7295
www.glenella.com

THIS INN REMAINS MUCH AS it was in the late 1800s, when people visited it for the health benefits of the nearby springs. Barri and Bobby Aycock have renovated the inn completely to make it a comfortable respite for today's travelers. Glen-Ella Springs Inn is a special place where people come to relax and escape the stress of urban living. Located on 17 acres only 90 miles northeast of Atlanta, Georgia, the inn offers first-class dining and personal service in an atmosphere of casual elegance. Glen-Ella Springs Inn is listed on the National Register of Historic Places.

Molten Chocolate Cake

- ½ **pound bittersweet chocolate, chopped**
- 2 **sticks unsalted butter**
- 4 **eggs**
- 4 **egg yolks**
- ½ **cup sugar**
- 7 **tablespoons all-purpose flour**
  Confectioners sugar

Preheat oven to 325°F. Butter and flour eight (5- to-6-ounce) ovenproof custard cups or ramekins.

Melt chocolate and butter over hot water in a double boiler. Let cool slightly. In a bowl, beat whole eggs, yolks, and sugar with electric mixer on medium-high until pale yellow (about 10 minutes). Reduce speed and add flour gradually. Add melted chocolate and beat until glossy (about 5 minutes). Pour batter evenly into prepared cups. Bake for 12 minutes or until set around edges but centers still move slightly. Serve warm in the same dishes or turn out upside down onto individual plates. Dust with confectioners' sugar before serving.

Yield: 8 servings

Note: To make ahead, fill ramekins and refrigerate up to six hours; add about 5 more minutes to baking time.

Orange-Strawberry Soufflé

SOUFFLE

9 large eggs, separated
11 tablespoons sugar
9 egg yolks
¾ cup orange juice
3 tablespoons all-purpose flour
6 tablespoons butter

SERVING SAUCE

2 tablespoons butter
2 tablespoons sugar
½ cup orange juice
4 cups sliced strawberries

Preheat oven to 350°F.

To make the soufflé: In a large bowl, beat the egg whites until foamy. Add 9 tablespoons sugar and beat until the whites hold stiff peaks. Do not overbeat. In a separate bowl, beat together the egg yolks, ¼ cup orange juice, and flour until well mixed. Gently fold into egg whites.

In a 10- to 12-inch oval baking dish, melt butter. Add remaining ½ cup orange juice and remaining 2 tablespoons sugar. Remove from heat when bubbly. Gently slide large spoonfuls of egg mixture into the heated sauce. Bake in oven for 13 to 15 minutes, until the center juggles only slightly.

To make the sauce: In a 10 to 12-inch frying pan, melt butter. Stir in sugar and orange juice. When bubbling stir in the sliced strawberries. Just warm, do not cook.

Yield: 6 servings

Hint: Assemble the sauce ingredients up to an hour ahead, separate eggs and prepare the berries. Beat the eggs just before baking. Have your guests seated when you bring the dish to the table.

**Bewitched and Bedazzled
Bed and Breakfast**
65–67 & 71 Lake Avenue
Rehoboth Beach, Delaware 19971
302-226-9482
www.bewitchedbandb.com

AT BEWITCHED AND Bedazzled bed-and-breakfast you will enjoy an informal, 1960s atmosphere that is also playfully elegant. Guests share the cozy compound, where they can appreciate each of the unique properties. There is a wonderful 1225-square-foot private deck with a sunken outdoor hot tub that is open year-round and a garden area with a double swing, and guests have access to the wonderful spa services located outside in the Private Spa deck or inside the spa room at the Manor. A complete extended continental breakfast is served each morning. Guests can enjoy their breakfast on the bistro tables on the deck or on the Bewitched sun porch.

The Cliveden Inn
709 Columbia Avenue
Cape May, New Jersey 08204
1-800-884-2420
www.cliveden.com

UILT IN 1884, THE CLIVEDEN is a fully restored Victorian cottage with elegant rooms, a wraparound porch, and beautifully decorated parlor. In addition, the Victorian carriage house is big enough for a family of six and features its own living room, dining room, and fireplace. Ideally located in Cape May's primary historic district, the inn is just two blocks from the beach and four blocks from Cape May's Victorian Mall.

Peach Cobbler

- 1 stick butter
- ¾ cup flour
- 2 teaspoons baking powder
- 1 cup sugar
- ¼ teaspoon salt
- ¾ cup milk
- 2 cups sliced peaches

Preheat oven to 350°F.

Put butter in bottom of baking dish and set in oven to melt. In a bowl, mix together flour, baking powder, sugar, salt, and milk. Pour batter over melted butter; do not stir. Arrange peaches on top of batter; do not stir. Bake until crust is light brown and puffy, approximately 35 to 45 minutes.

Yield: 8 servings

Peak to Peak

2½ tablespoons butter
1¼ cups milk
¾ cup flour
3 eggs
⅓ cup sugar
¼ teaspoon salt
¼ teaspoon pure vanilla extract
Confectioners' sugar
Fresh berries: raspberries, strawberries, blueberries, blackberries
Hot maple syrup
Whipped vanilla cream

Preheat oven to 425°F.

Place butter into a 9-inch glass pie dish and melt in microwave. In a blender, combine milk, flour, eggs, sugar, salt, and vanilla and process until smooth. Pour batter into pie pan. Bake for 20 minutes. Reduce oven temperature to 325°F and bake 8 to 10 minutes longer. Remove from oven and slide onto serving platter. Sprinkle with powdered sugar and serve with fresh berries, whipped cream, and maple syrup.

Yield: 6 to 8 servings

Cali Cochitta Bed & Breakfast
110 South 200 East
Moab, Utah 84532
435-259-4961
www.moabdreaminn.com

LOCATED IN THE HEART of spectacular "Red Rock Country"—a wonderland of breathtaking panoramas—is Cali Cochitta (Aztec meaning "House of Dreams"). One of the first homes built in Moab, Cali Cochitta is a late 1800s Victorian, restored and renovated to its original classic style. At least one morning during your stay, you are urged to wake early, sit on the front porch with a cup of fresh-ground coffee, tea, or freshly squeezed juice and enjoy a southern Utah sunrise. It's a sensory experience you'll not soon forget. The inn has eye-pleasing, upscale décor and accommodations that are comfortable, clean, and relaxing. Beautiful gardens and porches surround the home with lots of trees, porch swings, and rockers.

**The Blue Belle Inn
Bed & Breakfast**

513 West 4th Street
St. Ansgar, Iowa 50472
877-713-3113
www.bluebelleinn.com

*L*OCATED IN ST. ANSGAR, Iowa, "the best little hometown in Iowa," the Blue Belle Inn awaits you! Rediscover the romance of the 1890s while enjoying the comfort and convenience of the new millennium. The interior of this Queen Anne Victorian is highlighted by fireplaces, wood floors, tin ceilings with ornate moldings, and 8-foot maple pocket doors. Leaded glass, stained glass, and crystal chandeliers set in bay windows create a shimmering interplay of light and color. Candlelight, lace-covered tables, heirloom china, and German, English, French Italian, Scandinavian, or American country cuisines provide an unforgettable dining experience for weekend guests and local patrons alike.

Pear Pie (Creamy Pear Puff)

 1 unbaked pie shell or puff pastry squares
¾ cup sugar
 3 tablespoons cornstarch
 1 cup cream or evaporated milk
    Cinnamon
 6 ripe pear halves, peeled (may use canned pears)

Preheat oven to 400°F.

Lay pears cut side up in pie shell with narrow ends pointed towards the center, or center each pear half (cut side up) in a custard cup sprayed with cooking spray and lined with squares of puff pastry. Mix sugar and cornstarch. Stir into cream. Heat cream mixture in a saucepan over medium heat until hot and slightly thick. Pour over pears. Sprinkle with cinnamon. Bake at 400°F for 15 minutes, then lower temperature to 350°F and bake until set. The pie will take longer to set than the puffs.

Yield: 1 pie or 6 puffs

Pound Cake

3 sticks butter
6 eggs
3 cups sugar
2 tablespoons lemon extract
1 tablespoon vanilla
3 cups flour
1 teaspoon baking powder
1 cup milk

Place butter, eggs, sugar, lemon, and vanilla in mixer bowl. Beat on medium speed for 20 minutes until creamy. Add baking powder to flour and add to creamed mixture. Blend just until mixed. Add milk and mix until blended.

Pour into greased and floured tube pan. Bake at 350°F for 1 hour 10 min or until golden brown. Note: Oven temperatures vary, so check after 1 hour.

Yield: 1 pound cake

Hilda Crockett's Chesapeake House

P. O. Box 232
Tangier, Virginia 23440
757-891-2331
www.tangierisland-va.com

HERE IS A CONVERTED private home more than 100 years old. Delightful meals are prepared from old family recipes by a kitchen staff of island homemakers. The word "commercial" could never be applied to the food here, since everything is prepared from scratch. This unusual and famous hotel is the only one gracing the island, which is reached only by mail boat. The ride is an adventure in itself; the sky is full of ducks and geese or seagulls, depending upon the season. There is definitely an "I would like to stay forever" atmosphere about this wonderful place.

Barrow House Inn
524 Royal Street
P. O. Box 1461
St. Francisville, Louisiana 70775
225-635-4791
www.topteninn.com

HADED BY A 200-YEAR-old live oak, Barrow House stands in the heart of the quaint town of St. Francisville. The original house was a saltbox structure built in 1809, and a Greek Revival wing added just before the Civil War. A large screened porch is the place to be for coffee in the morning and drinks in the evening. Rooms are furnished in antiques dating from 1840 to 1870. The inn's candlelight dinners, featuring New Orleans–style food, are well known in the area. Six plantations (open to the public) are close by.

Praline Parfait

PRALINE SAUCE
1½   **sticks butter or margarine**
1   **cup sugar**
2   **cups (packed) light-brown sugar**
½   **cup heavy cream**
1   **cup milk**
2½   **cups chopped pecans**

Melt butter or margarine in a large pot. Add sugars and cream, then cook for 1 minute while stirring. Add milk and 1¼ cups of the pecans and cook 4 minutes, stirring occasionally. Reduce heat to medium and cook another 15 to 20 minutes. Cool and refrigerate.

PARFAITS
Vanilla ice cream
Whipped cream
Chopped pecans

Reheat praline sauce. Place 1 scoop of vanilla ice cream in a footed glass. Pour 2 tablespoons hot praline sauce on top. Decorate with a spoonful of whipped cream and chopped pecans.

Yield: 25 servings of sauce

Raisin Cream Pie

- 1 baked piecrust
- 1 cup raisins (packed), washed, drained and patted dry
- ½ cup plus 2 tablespoons sugar (or more if you like a sweeter pie)
- ¼ teaspoon salt
- ½ teaspoon cinnamon
- 1 cup sour cream
- 3 eggs, separated
- ½ teaspoon baking soda
- ½ teaspoon cornstarch

Preheat oven to 400°F.

In a saucepan, mix together the raisins, ½ cup sugar, salt, cinnamon, and sour cream and let boil slowly about 20 minutes. Remove from heat and add 3 egg yolks (beaten) and cook until yolks are thick. Remove from heat again and add baking soda. Let cool, then pour into piecrust. Beat egg whites; add the remaining 2 tablespoons of sugar and cornstarch. Spread on pie and bake just long enough to brown meringue. Watch constantly and remove from oven as soon as pie is a beautiful light brown.

Yield: 1 pie

Historic Anderson House
333 Main Street West
Wabasha, Minnesota 55981
651-565-2500
www.historicandersonhouse.com

THE HISTORIC ANDERSON House is a true step back into yesterday. Most of the furniture dates back to the inn's opening in 1856. This is the oldest operating country inn west of the Mississippi. The present innkeepers, Teresa and Mike Smith, are keeping Grandma Anderson's personality and plans in place, though it has been years since she purchased and ran the hotel. Her remarkable knowledge of food is still the cornerstone of the inn's success. The ever-filled cookie jar is still present at the front desk. Grandma's famous chicken noodle soup, Dutch cinnamon rolls, and chicken and dumplings still lend great interest and excitement to the daily menus. As in Grandma's day, shoes left outside the door are meticulously shined. Cold feet will produce a hot brick for your bed, carefully presented in a quilted envelope.

Gustavus Inn at Glacier Bay
P. O. Box 60
Gustavus, Alaska 99826
907-697-2254
www.gustavusinn.com

THE GUSTAVUS INN RESTS IN the grassy Salmon River meadow and has an ocean view of Icy Strait. The cozy hearth room, the naturalist library, and family-style dining invite conversation and new friendships. A variety of locally brewed beers and wine are served at the six-stool bar. Family-style meals served in the original homestead dining room will highlight your visit. Start your morning with a hearty breakfast, which can include homemade granola and rhubarb sauce, spruce-tip syrup on sourdough pancakes, or homemade bread and preserves. Then enjoy the noonday meal or make your day more flexible with a generous Alaskan picnic lunch. Dinner is its own adventure; just-picked garden and native edibles share the table with the freshest of salmon, halibut, and Dungeness crab plucked from Icy Strait, and a choice of desserts made just for you.

Rhubarb Crisp

- 1 cup flour
- 2 cups rolled oats
- 1 cup brown sugar
- 1 teaspoon cinnamon
- 1 cup granulated sugar
- 3 tablespoons cornstarch
- 1 cup cold water
- 8 cups chopped rhubarb

Preheat oven to 325°F.

Mix together flour, oats, brown sugar, and cinnamon; set aside.

In a saucepan, whisk together the granulated sugar, cornstarch, and water. Bring to a boil, whisking constantly. Pour thickened sauce over rhubarb and mix thoroughly.

Pack down half the oat mixture on the bottom of a baking pan. Place rhubarb mixture on top and sprinkle the rest of the oat mixture on top. Bake for at least 1 hour or until bubbly. Serve with ice cream or whipped cream.

Yield: 4 servings

Marcia's Rice Pudding

6 cups milk

¾ cup long-grain rice

1 cup heavy cream

¾ cup sugar (slightly less is better)

3 egg yolks, beaten

2 teaspoons vanilla extract

¼ teaspoon salt

1 teaspoon cinnamon

In a nonstick pot (a 3-quart pot works fine), bring milk to a boil over medium heat. Stir in rice; return to a boil. Reduce heat and simmer uncovered until rice is tender, about 55 minutes. Meanwhile, in a small bowl, combine cream, sugar, egg yolks, vanilla, and salt. Set aside. When rice is tender, stir in cream mixture until completely combined. Bring to a boil again. Remove from heat. Sprinkle with cinnamon. Chill for 4 hours.

Yield: 12 (½-cup) servings

**Honeysuckle Hill
Bed & Breakfast**
591 Old King's Highway Historic 6A
West Barnstable,
Massachusetts 02668
508-362-8418
1-866-444-5522
www.honeysucklehill.com

LOCATED ON THE EDGE OF the small village of West Barnstable, the Honeysuckle Hill Bed & Breakfast has been welcoming guests for generations. Listed on the National Register of Historic Places, this enchanting seaside cottage offers comfortably elegant rooms and graciously served breakfasts. Built around 1810 by the Fish and Goodspeed families, the Queen Anne–style inn is surrounded by lush, green lawns and colorful gardens.

*S*PENDING THE NIGHT AT historic Shaker Village of Pleasant Hill is truly a restful experience. Shaker Village is one of only three properties in Kentucky listed in the current *Zagat Survey of the Top U. S. Hotels, Resorts and Spas.* The historic setting in the heart of bluegrass country is a "don't miss experience." Dine on hearty Kentucky foods and Shaker recipes at the Shaker Village Trustees' Office Dining Room, where breakfast, lunch, and dinner are served daily. The menu includes a hearty country breakfast and changing selection for midday lunch. At dinner there is a choice of meats, salads, relishes, and vegetables with breads fresh from the oven, home-baked pies and cakes, tarts, or a special dessert from the bakery.

Shawnee Run Jam Cake with Caramel Frosting

- 2 sticks butter
- 2 cups light brown sugar, sifted
- 3 eggs, separated
- 1 cup jam with seeds
- ¾ cup chopped nuts
- 1 cup raisins
- 1 tablespoon cocoa
- 1 teaspoon cinnamon
- 1 teaspoon ground cloves
- 3½ cups flour, sifted
- 2 teaspoons baking soda
- 2 cups buttermilk
  Cinnamon
  Simple Caramel Frosting (recipe follows)

Preheat oven to 250°F. Butter a 9-inch tube pan (or two loaf pans); line with brown paper or waxed paper.

In a bowl, cream butter and add brown sugar. Beat egg yolks, add to butter-sugar mixture, and beat well. Fold in jam. Roll nuts and raisins in ¼ cup flour. Add cocoa and spices to remaining flour and sift again. Dissolve soda in buttermilk. Beginning and ending with flour, alternately add buttermilk and flour mixture. Add raisins and nuts. Beat egg whites until stiff; fold into batter. Turn batter into pan and bake until cake leaves side of pan. Turn out of pan and frost with Simple Caramel Frosting.

SIMPLE CARAMEL FROSTING

1½ **sticks butter**
1½ **cups brown sugar**
¼ **cup plus 2 tablespoons milk**
3 **cups confectioners' sugar**
1 **teaspoon vanilla extract**

Melt butter and add brown sugar in a saucepan. Add milk and bring to boil. Take off stove and let cool. Add confectioners' sugar and vanilla and beat until creamy and smooth.

Yield: 16 servings

Note: this cake can be made in a Bundt pan. Place an apple core in the middle of the cake and then frost the cake. The cake will remain moist.

Inn at Starlight Lake
P. O. Box 27
Starlight, Pennsylvania 18461
1-800-248-2519
570-798-2519
www.innatstarlightlake.com

SINCE 1909, GUESTS HAVE been drawn to this classic country inn on a clear lake in the rolling hills of northeastern Pennsylvania. The atmosphere is warm, congenial, and informal. Enjoy breakfast, lunch, and dinner in a spacious and informal lakeside dining room or order a packed picnic lunch. The restaurant serves fresh vegetables and seafood, vegetarian entrées, and pasta. Award-winning pastry chef, Mary Reyes bakes all of the bread, pastries, pies, and cakes served at the inn. She makes the delicious ice creams and sorbets on the menu and fresh pasta for the popular Wednesday-night pasta dinner.

Sour Cream Apple Pie

TOPPING
- ²/₃ cup brown sugar
- ²/₃ cup flour
- 2 teaspoons cinnamon
- ½ stick softened butter

FILLING
- ¼ cup flour
- ¼ teaspoon salt
- 1¹/₃ cups sugar
- 2 eggs, beaten
- 2 cups sour cream
- 1 teaspoon vanilla extract
- ½ teaspoon nutmeg
- 6 medium apples, peeled and shredded
- 1 (10-inch) deep-dish pie shell

Preheat oven to 375°F.

To make the topping: Mix ingredients together in a small bowl. Set aside.

To make the filling: Mix flour, salt, and sugar in a bowl. Add eggs, sour cream, and vanilla and stir. Fold in apples. Place filling in pie shell. Bake for approximately 40 to 45 minutes until firm, then place topping on pie and bake 5 minutes more. For a smaller pie tin, reduce recipe ingredients by about ⅓.

Yield: 1 pie

Sour Cream Coffee Cake

2   sticks sweet butter
2½ cups sugar
2   eggs, beaten
2   cups sour cream
1   tablespoon vanilla extract
1   cup wheat flour
1   cup white flour
1   tablespoon baking powder
¼   teaspoon salt
2   cups finely chopped pecans
1½ teaspoons cinnamon

Preheat oven to 350°F. Grease and flour a Bundt pan.

In a bowl, cream butter and 2 cups of the sugar. Add eggs and mix well. Add sour cream and vanilla. In separate bowl, sift together the flours, baking powder, and salt. Add to creamed mixture until just blended, *being careful not to overbeat*. Mix together remaining ½ cup sugar with pecans and cinnamon. Pour half of batter into Bundt pan. Sprinkle with half the pecan and sugar mixture. Add remaining batter and top with remaining pecan mixture. Bake for 1 hour. Serve warm or at room temperature.

Yield: 12 servings

Four Sisters Inns
P. O. Box 3073
Monterey, California 93942
1-800-234-1425
www.foursisters.com

*I*T ALL BEGAN IN 1976 WHEN the Post family opened their home, the spectacular Green Gables Inn on the shores of Monterey Bay, to the public. Taken by the warmth of innkeeping, the family refined hospitality to an art, carefully selecting inns for its collection. Each inn had to be very special in architecture, history, location, and privacy. From city to country, the inns became havens for their guests. Over time, the family created standards that helped define Four Sisters Inns. Today, with locations in California and Washington, each inn combines an elegant décor with exceptional service and amenities.

Art of Inner Peace
P.O. Box 821
Anahola, Hawaii 96703
808-823-0705
www.islandenchatment.com

ENTRALLY LOCATED IN ANAHOLA on the east coast of Kauai, Art of Inner Peace is close to hidden subtropical beaches, as well as a beautiful river, jungle, and mountain walks. The riverfront rooms have a private French-door entry off the lanai, a queen-size bed, and are appointed island style. This Kauai vacation retreat, a beautiful island-style home, rests in a lush tropical setting. Birds splash in the river as it flows by, and mountain peaks rise close behind. The sound of ocean waves calls you to an uncrowded beach just a five-minute drive away. Guests enjoy complimentary breakfasts or catered meals while looking out on the gently flowing river, coconut and papaya trees, and exotic tropical plants and flowers. Healthy meals are prepared with care using fresh organic ingredients from local farmers.

Sweet Treat Balls

1   cup raisins or dates
1   cup coconut, grated
1   cup walnuts
1   cup almonds
1   cup sunflower/flax/pumpkin seeds
    Pinch of saffron
1/4   teaspoon nutmeg
1/4   teaspoon cinnamon
1/4   teaspoon cardamom

Put all ingredients in a food processor and process until thick and sticky enough to roll into balls. You might have to keep shaking the mixing bowl when it gets sticky; if you really need to, add a little water to make the mixture turn. When ground to a lumpy paste, take a handful of the mixture and roll it into a ball (the size of a golf ball or smaller) between your palms. You can roll the balls in extra grated coconut if you like. Refrigerate the balls. Take out of the refrigerator at least 1 hour before eating.

Yield: 8 dozen balls

Note: These balls are a healthy, highly nutritious snack or dessert. Children love them!

Toffee Treats

12 whole graham crackers
2 sticks butter
1 cup brown sugar
1 cup slivered almonds

Preheat oven to 400°F.

Place graham crackers in a foil-lined pan. Melt butter and brown sugar together until bubbly. Pour over crackers and top with almonds. Bake for 10 minutes. Cool and cut.

Yield: 48 treats

Sundance Inn
135 West Broadway
P. O. Box 1
Jackson, Wyoming 83001
307-733-3444
www.sundanceinnjackson.com

THE SUNDANCE INN OFFERS cozy, friendly lodging to travelers exploring the town of Jackson and its surrounding area. The newly remodeled inn, built in the early 1950s and once called the Ideal Lodge, really is an ideal place to stay. There are a variety of outings to satisfy any desire, from river rafting the Snake River in the summer, to dog sledding, to visiting Granite Hot Springs for a quick dip. Since trapper David Jackson discovered the "Hole" more than 170 years ago, travelers have stopped to rest and wonder at the spectacular beauty of the valley and surrounding mountains.

Hermann Hill
Vineyard & Inn

**Hermann Hill
Vineyard & Inn**
711 Wein Street
P. O. Box 555
Hermann, Missouri 65041
573-486-4455
www.hermannhill.com

NJOY THE ULTIMATE COUNTRY-INN experience. Located on a bluff and surrounded by a vineyard, the inn's backdrop is the ever-changing panorama of Hermann and the Missouri River Valley. Sleep late, have breakfast in bed, walk to a nearby winery, explore a quiet old river town, or simply relax and contemplate the view. Later, as the day wanes, enjoy the late afternoon on your private balcony/patio and revel in the luxury that is Hermann Hill's specialty.

A note from the innkeeper: "At 10 in the evening, we deliver two heart-shaped cookies and a small dish of vanilla ice cream with some of our own port-chocolate-raspberry sauce to the door of each of our guests. It's a nice way to say good night to our guests and they look forward to it . . . even to the point of declining dessert at the restaurant. 'Oh, you must be staying at Hermann Hill,' their waiter says."

Vintage Vanilla Ice Cream

5 cups milk
4 cups heavy cream
3 cups sugar
2 tablespoons vanilla extract

In a large bowl, combine ingredients, stirring until thoroughly blended. Pour mixture into ice-cream freezer and follow your model's directions.

Yield: 1 gallon

Velvet Hammer Dessert

- 1 quart rich coffee ice cream
- 3 tablespoons crème de cacao
- 6 tablespoons Scotch whiskey
- ½ cup canned chestnuts, drained and chopped

Let ice cream soften but not melt. Place in a blender and add the crème de cacao and the Scotch. Blend at high speed until smooth (about 15 seconds). Stir in chestnuts. Pour into individual dishes or an ice-cube tray. Freeze until ice crystals form around the edge. Beat ice cream mixture until smooth again. Cover with aluminum foil and refreeze overnight.

Yield: 6 to 8 servings

Lovett's Inn
1474 Profile Road
Franconia, New Hampshire 03580
1-800-356-3802
www.lovettsinn.com

HERE IS A 200-YEAR-OLD country inn that has pretty well accommodated itself to the White Mountains of New Hampshire, truly a traditional New England setting. You won't find a better table or cellar in the North Country. There are trout streams on the grounds, a mountain pond for hardy swimmers, plus a splendid solar-heated pool, brooks, ponds, stone walls, beamed ceilings, fireplaces, and birch and pine woods. At this magnificent establishment, everything is of extremely high quality.

White Chocolate Cheesecake

- 2 cups sugar
- 4 pounds cream cheese, at room temperature
- 2 teaspoons vanilla extract
- 8 eggs
- 16 ounces white chocolate, melted

Preheat oven to 450°F.

Cream sugar and cream cheese together in a bowl. Add vanilla.
Beat eggs in one at a time. Blend in chocolate. Bake in two
springform pans in water baths for 20 minutes. Reduce heat to
250°F and continue to bake for 1 hour or until firm. Cool
thoroughly, overnight, before removing from pans. Serve with
puréed raspberries sweetened to taste with honey or sugar. This
cake can be served at breakfast.

Yield: 20 servings

*The Great Country Inns
of America Cookbook*

Kahlúa Crème Brûlée

2 cups heavy cream
4 egg yolks
2½ tablespoons granulated sugar
3 tablespoons Kahlúa
1 teaspoon pure vanilla extract
¼ cup sifted light brown sugar

Preheat oven to 325°F.

Heat cream in double boiler. With a mixer, beat egg yolks,
gradually adding granulated sugar. Remove cream from heat,
and slowly pour into egg mixture, stirring constantly. Add vanilla
and Kahlúa. Pour mixture into six 3½-inch ramekins and set
ramekins in a pan of warm water. Bake for 50 minutes. When
custard is set, remove from oven, sprinkle with brown sugar,
and place under broiler for about 2 minutes until sugar is
caramelized. Chill at least four hours before serving.

Yield: 6 servings

Richmont Inn
220 Winterberry Lane
Townsend, Tennessee 37882
866-267-7086
www.richmontinn.com

LOCATED ON A FORESTED
mountain in the
Smoky Mountains,
the Richmont Inn is fashioned in the
architectural style of the Appalachian
cantilever barn. The inn offers scenic
views of towering Rich Mountain.
Richmont is decorated with 18th-
century English antiques and offers
fine gourmet meals. Guests have
access to an Appalachian garden of
native wildflowers. The entrance to
Great Smoky Mountains National Park
is only 10 minutes away.

Romantic RiverSong,
A Bed & Breakfast Inn
1765 Lower Broadview Road
P. O. Box 1910
Estes Park, Colorado 80517
970-586-4666
www.romanticriversong.com

RiverSong is a small country inn at the foot of Giant Track Mountain in Estes Park, Colorado. Once a luxurious summer home of the wealthy, RiverSong is now a very special and inviting bed-and-breakfast inn. The inn is at the end of a country lane on 27 wooded acres and offers a rushing trout stream, a rustic gazebo reflected in the inn's own pond, and gentle hiking trails with rock benches to enjoy the breathtaking panorama of snow-capped peaks in adjacent Rocky Mountain National Park.

Kicking Kiwi Pastry

1	box puff pastry
8	ounces cream cheese
2 to 3	cups confectioners' sugar
1	teaspoon lemon juice
7 or 8	kiwis

Preheat oven to 350°F.

Thaw puff pastries, then cut into 2 to 3-inch squares. Place on greased baking sheets; bake for about 10 minutes, until edges are golden. Let cool. Beat together cream cheese, confectioners' sugar, and lemon juice until smooth. Set aside. Peel and cut kiwis into medium slices. Frost each pastry with 2 tablespoons of cream cheese mixture, and top with 3 or 4 kiwi slices. Sprinkle with confectioners' sugar.

Yield: 10 servings

COOKIES

Rabbit Hill Inn
48 Lower Waterford Road
Lower Waterford, Vermont 05848
802-748-5168
www.rabbithillinn.com

THIS WHITE CLAPBOARD INN was built in 1827 as a home with a small shop fashioning sleighs and winnow mills (a device that separates dust from grain). After several additions, the inn started its long history of nourishing weary travelers in 1840. In its early days, it served the area's logging community. The marks of the drovers' and lumberjacks' spiked boots can still be seen on the floors. Lower Waterford is the most photographed town in Vermont and is nicknamed "the white village" for its 10 post-Revolutionary white houses, of which Rabbit Hill Inn is the focal point. The two connecting dining rooms are famed throughout the area for relaxing, unhurried meals, genuine home-cooked food, and an extensive wine list to please the connoisseur. Rabbit Hill Inn is a wonderful place to be.

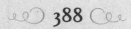*The Great Country Inns
of America Cookbook*

Apple and Nut-Filled Cookies

FILLING
4 apples, chopped
2 teaspoons lemon juice
1 teaspoon cinnamon
½ teaspoon nutmeg
½ teaspoon ground ginger
½ cup raisins
½ cup finely chopped nuts
2 tablespoons butter
1 teaspoon cornstarch
2/3 cup sugar
¼ cup water

Combine all ingredients in a saucepan and cook over low heat until mixture is thick but apples are still firm (not mushy). Cool filling in refrigerator.

DOUGH
1 stick butter
1 cup sugar
1 egg
2 teaspoons baking powder
¼ teaspoon salt
1 teaspoon vanilla extract
3 cups flour
½ cup milk

In a large bowl, beat butter and sugar together until fluffy. Add egg, baking powder, salt, and vanilla. Gradually add flour and milk alternately until soft dough is formed. Refrigerate for about 20 minutes.

Preheat oven to 350°F.

Roll out dough and cut 2-inch rounds with a cookie or biscuit cutter. Place almost a teaspoon of cold filling in center of each round. Wet edges with water and place another cookie round on top. Prick cookies around edges with a floured fork to seal. Bake for 10 to 12 minutes.

Yield: 16 cookies

COOKIES

Desert Dove Bed & Breakfast
11707 East Old Spanish Trail
Tucson, Arizona 85730
520-722-6879
www.desertdovebb.com

THE DESERT DOVE BED-AND-breakfast offers serene comfort in the desert. Guests will feel right at home in this natural, sun-baked adobe bed-and-breakfast. Its great porches; polished, colored concrete floors; and open trusses in the great room, along with the antiques and collectibles give this bed-and-breakfast its unique ambience. A 1927 wood-burning cook stove in the delightful country kitchen invites guests to a time long past. Gourmet breakfasts are served on vintage tableware. Guests are invited to have afternoon treats and relax in a serene desert setting. The hydrotherapy spa is a great place to unwind at the end of the day. Take in the beautiful sunsets and stars, hiking and biking trails, horseback riding, and bird-watching locations all in the great Arizona Sonoran desert.

Betty's B&B Cookies

         2 sticks butter
         1 cup granulated sugar
         1 cup brown sugar
         2 eggs
         1 teaspoon vanilla extract
         2 cups flour
      2½ cups blended oatmeal (measure oatmeal and blend in blender to a fine powder)
        ½ teaspoon salt
         1 tablespoon wheat germ
         1 teaspoon baking powder
         1 teaspoon baking soda
       12 ounces chocolate chips
         1 cup (or half a bag) English toffee bits
      1½ cups nuts (we like pecans best)

Preheat oven to 375°F.

In a bowl, cream butter with both sugars. Add eggs and vanilla. In another large bowl, mix together flour, oatmeal, salt, wheat germ, baking powder, and baking soda. Blend both mixtures. Add chips, toffee bits, and nuts. Place 2 inches apart on cookie sheet (or baking stone). Bake for 7 to 10 minutes.

Yield: 56 cookies

Chocolate-Zucchini Cookies for a Crowd

~~~~~~~~

½ cup milk

1 teaspoon lemon juice or 1 teaspoon vinegar

1 stick margarine, softened

½ cup vegetable oil

1¾ cups sugar

2 eggs

½ teaspoon vanilla extract

4 cups flour

¼ cup cocoa

½ teaspoon baking powder

1 teaspoon baking soda

½ teaspoon cinnamon

½ teaspoon ground cloves

2 cups finely diced zucchini

12 ounces semisweet chocolate chips

Preheat oven to 350°F. Grease cookie sheets.

In a large bowl, combine milk and lemon juice. Let stand for 5 minutes to sour. In another bowl, cream together margarine, oil, and sugar. Add eggs and vanilla and combine thoroughly. Beat sour milk into margarine mixture. In another bowl, mix flour, cocoa, baking powder, baking soda, cinnamon, and cloves until well combined. Add this to the creamed mixture and beat very well. Fold in zucchini and chocolate chips. Using a teaspoon, drop dough onto cookie sheets. Bake for about 12 minutes. (Cookies have a cakelike texture and do not spread much.)

Yield: 12 dozen small cookies

The Sanders, Helena's Bed and Breakfast
328 North Ewing
Helena, Montana 59601
406-442-3309
www.sandersbb.com

HERE IS AN INN NATIONally acclaimed as one of the best bed-and-breakfasts in the United States and Canada. Over the years, Bobbi Uecker and Rock Ringling have greeted world travelers, business folks, anglers, hikers, families on grand tours of national parks, and countless other guests. For each guest, individual needs and comforts come first. You are invited to come and enjoy it all: seven guest rooms with elegant furnishings, comfortable beds, and private baths; afternoon refreshments in the parlor; a full-course breakfast; a great location near downtown Helena and the state capitol area; and the extras like a summer afternoon on the front porch, a walk downtown, or a hike up Mount Helena.

Gingerbread Mansion

400 Berding Street
Ferndale, California 95536
707-786-4000
www.gingerbread-mansion.com

WELL KNOWN AS ONE OF northern California's most photographed inns, the Gingerbread Mansion is a spectacular example of Victorian splendor, both inside and out. The exterior boasts spindlework, turrets, and gables, as well as a formal English garden. Inside are four parlors and eleven romantic guest rooms, all decorated with antiques. The Gingerbread Mansion is strategically located in the heart of the Redwood Empire, minutes from majestic state parks with magnificent groves of giant redwoods, breathtaking ocean views, secluded beaches, and endless hiking and walking tours.

Coconut Macaroons

¾	cup water
4½	cups sugar
12	egg whites
1	teaspoon vanilla extract
1	teaspoon salt
1½	cups shredded coconut
	Maraschino cherries, sectioned

In a small saucepan, combine water and 3 cups of the sugar. Bring to boil over medium heat. Brush sides of pan occasionally with water to prevent crystallization. Cook to 242°F on a candy thermometer. Remove from heat.

While sugar is cooking, beat egg whites until frothy; using low mixer speed, gradually beat in remaining 1½ cups sugar until stiff peaks form. Still on low speed, gradually beat in hot sugar mixture. Add vanilla and salt. Set aside to cool.

Preheat oven to 350°F. Line insulated baking sheets with parchment paper.

When sugar mixture is cool, gently fold in coconut. Scoop dough into balls and place on baking sheets. Put a piece of maraschino cherry on top of each macaroon before baking. Bake for 15 minutes or until golden. Store in an airtight container.

Yield: 3 dozen cookies

Dried Pear and Walnut Biscotti

- 3 eggs
- 1 cup sugar
- ½ melted butter
- ½ cup dried snipped pears
- 1 cup chopped walnuts
- ¼ teaspoon walnut flavoring
- 3½ cups white flour
- ⅓ cup corn flour
- 1½ teaspoons baking powder

Preheat the oven to 350°F. Line a baking sheet with parchment paper.

In a large bowl, beat the eggs with the sugar until thickened and pale yellow. Fold butter into the batter. Fold in the pears, nuts, and walnut flavoring. Combine flours and baking powder. Fold the flour mixture into the egg mixture one quarter at a time (the dough will be very thick) and mix until well incorporated.

Divide the dough in half and form each half into a cylinder 1½ inches in diameter and 8 to 10 inches long. Place on baking sheet and bake for 15 to 20 minutes, until golden. Remove from the oven and cut into ½-inch slices. Place the cut slices on the baking sheet. Bake for an additional 8 to 10 minutes, until the slices no longer look wet in the middle and are crisp.

Yield: 30 to 36 cookies

Steamboat Inn
42705 North Umpqua Highway
Steamboat, Oregon 97447-9703
1-800-840-8825
541-498-2230
www.thesteamboatinn.com

THE STEAMBOAT INN IS located 38 scenic miles east of Roseburg, Oregon, on Highway 138. It commands a breathtaking view of the North Umpqua River. Nestled among the towering firs of the Umpqua National Forest, the inn is a perfect lodging base for the numerous nearby attractions, such as Crater Lake National Park, Diamond Lake, excellent wineries, and a wildlife safari park. Fishing at its most challenging, trails for hikers, and swimming are all within minutes of the inn. The inn's cafe offers a menu featuring homemade soups, pies, breads, and other delicious treats available for breakfast and lunch. The inn is small enough to allow groups the exclusive use of the entire facility during the winter months.

Gaston's White River Resort

1777 River Road
Lakeview, Arkansas 72642
870-431-5202
www.gastons.com

GASTON'S WHITE RIVER RESORT
began in 1958 when Al
Gaston, Jim Gaston's father,
purchased 20 acres of White River
frontage with six small cottages and six
boats. Now the resort covers over 400
acres with 2 miles of river frontage and
has 79 cottages ranging in size from
two double beds and a bathroom to a
two-story cottage with 10 private
bedrooms. As the premier trout-fishing
resort in America, Gaston's has caught
and cooked a lot of trout. Over the
years, it has developed what may be
the world's largest collection of
recipes—brought together from many
sources, including the Gaston family
and the finest restaurants. You will
never find a more magnificent view
than the one from our restaurant.
Almost rivaling the tranquil beauty of
the river view is the cozy atmosphere
created by the collection of old tools,
antiques, and historic photography.

Hillbilly Cookies

1 cup dark brown sugar, firmly packed
1 cup granulated sugar
2 sticks margarine
2 eggs
1 teaspoon baking soda
½ teaspoon baking powder
1 teaspoon vanilla extract
½ teaspoon salt
2 cups unsifted flour
1 (6-ounce) package chocolate chips
1 cup chopped pecans
2 cups rolled oats

Preheat oven to 350°F.

Cream together both sugars and margarine using an electric mixer or food processor. Add eggs and beat well. Add baking soda, baking powder, vanilla, and salt; mix well. Stir in flour. At low speed, mix in chocolate chips, nuts, and oatmeal. Spoon batter onto cookie sheet and bake for about 12 minutes. If chewy cookies are desired, bake a few minutes less.

Yield: 3 dozen cookies

Lemon-Iced Cookies

- 2 sticks butter
- 2 cups sugar
- 2 eggs
- 3 cups flour
- 1 teaspoon baking soda
- 1 teaspoon baking powder
- 1 cup buttermilk
  Juice and grated zest of 1 orange
- 2 cups confectioners' sugar
  Juice and grated zest of 2 lemons

Preheat oven to 400°F. Line cookie sheets with parchment paper.

In a large bowl, cream butter and sugar until fluff;, add eggs. In another bowl, combine flour, baking soda, and baking powder. Alternately add dry ingredients and buttermilk to creamed mixture. Add orange juice and zest. Drop batter by teaspoons onto cookie sheets. Bake for approximately 12 minutes.

Mix confectioners' sugar with the lemon juice and lemon zest. Ice cookies while hot.

Yield: 5 dozen cookies

1785 Inn
P. O. Box 1785
North Conway,
New Hampshire 03860
603-356-9025
www.the1785inn.com

A VISIT TO THE 1785 INN in the Mt. Washington Valley of New Hampshire is an experience you'll long remember. From the charm and beauty of its original colonial construction to the cheerful, welcoming atmosphere of its Victorian lounge, this classic New England country inn has a tradition of friendly, Yankee hospotality. Every season brings recreational activities galore. The dining room is renowned for its quality of service and cuisine, and the wine list has been called one of the finest in the world.

Fairville Inn

506 Kennett Pike (Route 52)
Chadds Ford, Pennsylvania 19317
1-877-285-7772
610-388-5900
www.fairvilleinn.com

*L*OCATED IN THE HEART OF the Brandywine Valley, the Fairville Inn, listed on the National Register of Historic Places, echoes the pastoral scenes of the Wyeth family paintings. Accented with barn wood, beams, and cathedral ceilings, the inn is the embodiment of elegant comfort. Fresh flowers gracefully welcome you. Your room has all the comforts of a country inn. The cuisine is delicious and there are meals for special diets are available upon request. The inn is especially suited for adult family gatherings.

White-Chip Island Macadamia Cookies

1 2/3	cups all-purpose flour
3/4	teaspoon baking powder
1/2	teaspoon baking soda
1/2	teaspoon salt
1 1/2	sticks butter, softened
3/4	cup packed brown sugar
1/3	cup granulated sugar
1	teaspoon vanilla extract
1	large egg
2	cups (12-ounce package) Nestle white morsels
1	cup flaked coconut, toasted if desired
3/4	cup macadamia nuts

Preheat oven to 375°F

Combine flour, baking powder, baking soda, and salt in small bowl. In a large mixer bowl, beat butter, brown sugar, granulated sugar, and vanilla until creamy. Beat in egg. Gradually beat in flour mixture. Stir in morsels, coconut, and nuts. Drop by rounded tablespoons onto greased cookies sheets. Bake for 8 to 10 minutes or until edges are lightly browned. Do not overbake. Cool on baking sheets for 2 minutes. Transfer cookies to wire racks to cool completely. (These freeze well for up to a month if wrapped airtight in heavy foil.)

Yield: About 3 dozen cookies

Dark Molasses Cookies

1½ sticks butter or margarine
1¼ cup granulated sugar
¼ cup molasses
1 egg
½ teaspoon salt
1 tablespoon ground ginger
2 teaspoon baking soda
1 teaspoon cinnamon
2 cups all-purpose flour

Preheat oven to 350°F.

In a large bowl, cream butter and 1 cup of the sugar until fluffy. Add molasses and egg. In a separate bowl, whisk together remaining ingredients. Add ½ cup at a time to molasses mixture, mixing well between each addition. Form dough into balls (about 1 inch in diameter) and roll them in the remaining ¼ cup granulated sugar. Place on cookie sheets. Bake for about 10 to 12 minutes.

Yield: 4 dozen cookies

Front 30 Ranch Guest House
198 Cedar Mills Road
Gordonville, Texas 76245
903-523-5982
www.front30ranch.com

IF YOU ARE LOOKING FOR Lake Texoma lodging or a Lake Texoma resort, the Front 30 Ranch Guest House provides outstanding bed-and-breakfast accommodations. Refresh your spirit, relax, and enjoy the tranquil setting of this working cattle ranch. Take advantage of authentic Texas hospitality with an impressive choice of amenities. Lodging at this bed-and-breakfast represents the best Texoma has to offer. Located in north Texas, with southern Oklahoma, Thousand Trails, and Cedar Mills Marina just minutes away, the Guest House sets a high standard for a bed-and-breakfast.

White Lace Inn
16 North 5th Avenue
Sturgeon Bay, Wisconsin 54235
920-743-743-1105
www.whitelaceinn.com

THIS VICTORIAN INN IN famous Door County, Wisconsin, offers 15 very special guest rooms in three historic structures. Every room is complete with the comforts expected at a fine inn. At windows, on dressers, over a bed, or in a frame, you will find the lace from which the White Lace Inn takes its name.

Oatmeal Chocolate–Heath Bar Cookies

2	sticks butter (or use half butter, half margarine)
2	cups granulated sugar
2	cups brown sugar
4	eggs
3	teaspoons vanilla extract
4½	cups flour
2	teaspoons baking powder
2	teaspoons baking soda
7	cups Quaker Oats old-fashioned oatmeal
1	(7-ounce) Hershey's milk chocolate candy bar, chopped into large pieces
6	Heath candy bars, chopped

Preheat oven to 375°F.

In a large bowl, cream together butter, granulated sugar, and brown sugar. Beat in eggs and vanilla. Set aside. Mix together flour, baking powder, and baking soda. Fold this into butter mixture. Add the oatmeal and candy bars. Make large cookies and bake for 8 to 10 minutes (it is best to underbake a little).

Yield: 4 dozen large cookies

Oatmeal Cookies

- 1 cup shortening
- 2 sticks butter
- 4 eggs
- 3 cups brown sugar
- 1 cup half-and-half
- 3½ cups flour
- 2 teaspoons baking soda
- 2 teaspoons baking powder
- 1 tablespoon cinnamon
- 1 tablespoon ground nutmeg
- 6 cups raw oats
- 1 (12-ounce) box raisins

Preheat oven to 350°F.

In a large bowl, mix shortening, butter, eggs, brown sugar, and half-and-half. In another bowl, mix flour, baking soda, baking powder, cinnamon, nutmeg, oats, and raisins. Add wet ingredients to dry ingredients. Roll dough and cut into 48 cookies. Place on cookie sheets. Bake for 35 minutes.

Yield: 4 dozen cookies

Inn at Ellis River
P. O. Box 656
Jackson, New Hampshire 03846
1-800-233-8309
603-383-9339
www.innatellisriver.com

THE 20 ROOMS AND THE separate cottage, all named after local waterfalls, are beautifully appointed with period antiques and a wide variety of traditional and modern amenities. The inn is located in the quaint village of Jackson, which lies at the edge of the 750,000-acre White Mountain National Forest, surrounded by spectacular natural beauty. It nestles in a landscape of covered bridges, white steepled churches, rolling farmland, mountain grandeur, and cascading waterfalls. Bring back the romance of life, and let the serenity of the inn, the river, and the mountains create cherished memories. Come and rejuvenate at the Inn at Ellis River.

Inn at Occidental

3657 Church Street
P.O. Box 857
Occidental, California 95465
707-874-1047
www.innatoccidental.com

THIS AWARD-WINNING INN IS nestled in the heart of Sonoma County, in the valley and town of Occidental, where vineyards, redwoods, and coastal scenery provide unparalleled beauty. From the moment you walk through the front door, you'll know this is not just another wine-country inn. The bold, vibrant walls and whimsical folk art will grab your eye and elicit a smile. A selection of hors d'oeuvres and local wines are served in the late afternoon. A wonderful Sonoma-harvest breakfast is served each day to delight your senses and awaken your taste buds.

The Great Country Inns of America Cookbook

Sasquatch Cookies

1½ cups packed light-brown sugar
1⅓ cups granulated sugar
1½ teaspoons salt
1½ teaspoons baking soda
2 sticks butter
1 cup shortening
5 eggs
6½ cups sifted cake flour
24 ounces semisweet chocolate chips

Preheat oven to 360°F. Line baking sheets with parchment paper.

In a large bowl, cream together sugars, salt, baking soda, butter, and shortening; beat well. Add eggs, one at a time, beating well. Add flour 1 cup at a time, mixing well after each cup. Add chocolate chips. Drop the dough, using a small ice-cream scoop, onto baking sheets. Bake for 10 to 12 minutes. Cool 5 minutes on sheets before transferring cookies to a cooling rack.

Yield: 7 dozen cookies

Grandma's Sesame Seed Cookies

2½   cups flour
½   teaspoon baking powder
⅛   teaspoon salt
1   cup sugar
2   sticks butter, softened
2   egg yolks
1   teaspoon vanilla
    Sesame seeds

Sift together flour, baking powder, salt, and sugar. Cut in butter. Add egg yolks and vanilla and blend well. Chill dough for 2 hours.

Preheat oven to 400°F.

On a floured board, roll dough out to ⅛-inch thickness. Cut into 2 x 1½-inch rectangles. Put cookies on a baking sheet and sprinkle with sesame seeds. Bake for 8 minutes, being careful not to burn.

Yield: 4 dozen cookies

**The Carleton House
Bed & Breakfast**
803 North Main
Bonham, Texas 75418
903-583-2779
1-800-382-8033
www.carletonhouse.com

LOCATED IN THE HEART of historic downtown Bonham, just one hour northeast of Dallas, is the historic Carleton House Bed & Breakfast. This newly renovated three-story Victorian, listed on the National Register of Historic Places, features a large entrance hall, a parlor, a dining room with ceiling mural, and a music room. Each room includes a comfortable bed, special antiques, lacy touches, reading materials, and a private bathroom equipped with an claw-foot tub.

Hotel Manning

100 Van Buren Street
Keosauqua, Iowa 52565
319-293-3232
www.showcase.netins.net/
web/manning/

EDWIN MANNING CAME chugging up the Des Moines River in 1837 on a side-wheel riverboat, disembarking at a romantic bend of the river where he founded the town of Keosauqua. The first floor of what is now the hotel was built in 1854 as a general store. Manning added the second and third stories in the late 1890s and turned the building into a hotel and restaurant serving the riverboat trade. It immediately became famous for its food and warm hospitality and remains famous to this day.

Sugar Cookies

1 pound margarine
1 cup granulated sugar
1 cup confectioners' sugar
2 eggs
1 teaspoon vanilla extract
4 cups flour
1 teaspoon cream of tartar
1 teaspoon baking soda
Sugar

Preheat oven to 350°F.

In a large bowl, mix the margarine, sugars, eggs, and vanilla. In another bowl, combine flour, cream of tartar, and baking soda, and add to the butter-sugar mixture, stirring to blend. Roll the dough into balls, dip in sugar, and flatten with a glass. Bake for just 12 minutes. Do not overbake.

Yield: 3 dozen cookies

Wedding Cookies

- ½ cup confectioners' sugar plus extra for rolling cookies
- 2 sticks butter or margarine, softened
- 2 cups all-purpose flour
- ⅛ teaspoon salt
- ½ teaspoon vanilla extract

Preheat oven to 400°F.

In a large bowl, combine sugar and butter and mix until smooth. Add flour, salt, and vanilla; cream together. Mixture should be stiff. Roll dough into balls. Place on baking sheets. Bake for 10 to 12 minutes. Roll cookies in confectioners' sugar before cooling.

Yield: 2 dozen cookies

1870 Wedgwood Inn
111 West Bridge Street
New Hope, Pennsylvania 18938
215-862-2570
www.wedgwoodinn.com

THIS GRACIOUS TWO-AND-A-half story Victorian structure with a gabled hip roof has been offering lodging since 1950. Surrounded by manicured landscaping, including a gazebo, the building features a large veranda with scrolled wood brackets, turned posts, and a *porte cochere*. Hardwood floors, lofty windows, and antique furnishings create a comfortable 19th-century feeling in each of the bedrooms. The inn is filled with Wedgwood pottery, original art, handmade quilts, and fresh flowers. Delicious food is served in the sun porch, the gazebo, or in one's bedroom.

BEVERAGES

The Historic Taos Inn
125 Paseo del Pueblo Norte
Taos, New Mexico 87571
505-758-2233
www.taosinn.com

EXPERIENCE SOUTHWESTERN charm and history in this quintessential New Mexico inn in the heart of Taos's historic district. Acclaimed by *National Geographic Traveler* as one of America's great inns, it is listed on the national and New Mexico registers of historic places. Since 1936, the Historic Taos Inn has welcomed famous folks like Greta Garbo, D. H. Lawrence, and Pawnee Bill. More recently, celebrities like Robert Redford and Jessica Lange have been spotted sipping margaritas in the lobby. The inn was founded on a rich legacy of excellence. Guests are eager to sample the atmosphere of old Taos, yet expect modern amenities. So the inn's goal is to deliver just that—to provide the finest personal services and warm, relaxed surroundings.

Adobe Bar Classic Margarita

1 ounce Cuervo Gold tequila
1½ ounces sweet-and-sour mix
¼ ounce Cointreau
Splash of fresh lime juice

Shake all ingredients with ice in cocktail shaker. Pour into margarita glass.

Yield: 1 serving

Coco-Loco

4 ounces coconut milk
4 ounces fresh lime juice
2 ounces rum

Blend all ingredients.

Yield: 1 serving

La Posada de Albuquerque

La Posada de Albuquerque

125 Second Street NW
Albuquerque, New Mexico 87102
1-800-777-5732
505-242-9090
www.laposadaalbuquerque.com

Follow in the footsteps of the giants like John F. Kennedy, Jimmy Stewart, Bill Gates, Lucille Ball, Spencer Tracy, and Al Gore, who have all signed the guest registry at the historic La Posada de Albuquerque. This charming Spanish Colonial hotel is located just steps from the convention center and the Route 66 Entertainment corridor. La Posada de Albuquerque was opened in 1939 by New Mexico native Conrad Hilton, who honeymooned here with bride Zsa Zsa Gabor. Capturing the essence of the Southwest, the hotel features an elaborate Moorish brass and mosaic-tiled fountain, a handcrafted circular balcony, and Native American war-dance murals. La Posada is Albuquerque is the only hotel listed on the National Register of Historic Places.

**Murphy's House
Bed and Breakfast**
2020 5th Avenue North
Great Falls, Montana 59401
406-452-3598

URPHY'S HOUSE IS A friendly bed-and-breakfast that serves a full breakfast of fresh fruit in season, farm-fresh eggs, bacon, and sourdough pancakes. It is furnished with lots of antiques and collectibles and has the distinction of being the oldest bed-and-breakfast in Great Falls.

Wedding Punch

2 (12-ounce) cans frozen lemonade concentrate
2 (12-ounce) cans frozen pineapple juice concentrate
1 quart water
1 liter ginger ale
1 liter sparkling water
1 large bottle sparkling white grape juice or champagne
   Fresh strawberries
   Mint leaves

Combine juices and water in a large punch bowl; mix well. Right before serving, add ginger ale, sparkling water, and juice/champagne. Stir to blend. Garnish glasses with fresh strawberries and a sprig of mint.

Yield: 50 (4-ounce) servings

Note: You can freeze some of the juice mixture in a pretty mold and add it to the punch bowl to keep the drink cool without diluting flavors.

Fresh Fruit Smoothie

¼ of a cantaloupe, peeled and cut into 1-inch cubes
¼ of a honeydew melon, peeled and cut into 1-inch cubes
1 pint strawberries, washed and sliced
1 cup seedless red grapes, washed and stemmed
1 banana, peeled and cut into 1-inch pieces
2 (6-ounce) containers fruit-flavored yogurt

Combine all the fruit in a covered freezer container and freeze overnight. About 1 hour before serving, remove fruit from freezer and allow to soften slightly. Place yogurt and fruit into a blender and process until smooth. Serve immediately.

Yield: 4 servings

Shiloh Morning Inn
2179 Ponderosa Road
Ardmore, Oklahoma 73401
1-888-554-7674
www.shilohmorning.com

Welcome to one of Oklahoma's premier bed-and-breakfasts, Shiloh Morning Inn, a romantic, secluded getaway, conveniently located halfway between Dallas and Oklahoma City, just minutes off I-35. This country inn is an oasis, where you can leave your cares behind as you enjoy the rural Oklahoma countryside, soak in a private hot tub, stroll on the resort's 73 acres of peace and quiet, and enjoy life as it was meant to be. With five suites in the main house and two very private cottages, all featuring king-size beds, fireplaces, TV/VCR, mini-fridges, and either whirlpool tubs for two or a private hot tub, Shiloh Morning Inn bed-and-breakfast will prove to be your own little piece of heaven on earth.

Izaak Walton Inn
290 Izaak Walton Inn Road
Essex, Montana 59916
406-888-5700
www.izaakwaltoninn.com

THE IZAAK WALTON INN IS A rail buff's haven. Helper engines idle in the yard, 100 feet from the inn's front door, waiting to push the next train over Marias Pass. Snowsheds, trestles, and tunnels with majestic mountain scenery provide unmatched photography opportunities. Great fly-fishing and exciting river rafting are among several fun-filled activities available. The Signal Room is the perfect place for planning sessions. Relax and let your ideas develop in an uninterrupted atmosphere. Winter brings a new kind of life to the Izaak; there are over 30 kilometers of groomed ski trails as well as guided ski tours into Glacier National Park. The awe-inspiring peaks are a hiker's dream. After years of tireless and faithful service, the cabooses now nestle among the grandeur of the mountains, atop a hill overlooking the inn and Glacier National Park,—the perfect setting for your mountain-cabin getaway.

Hot Buttered Rum

5	cups brown sugar
8	cups powdered sugar
2	pounds butter
2	quarts vanilla ice cream
4	tablespoons cinnamon
2	tablespoons nutmeg
24	shots dark rum

After mixing the first five ingredients, freeze batter. When ready to use, mix 1 shot of dark rum with 2 tablespoons of batter per serving. Fill rest of cup with hot water.

Yield: 24 servings

Mint Julep

Handful of fresh mint
Southern Comfort or bourbon of choice
Amber Bacardi Rum
Sugar
Angostura aromatic bitters
Lemon

Boil mint until water turns green. Strain the mint from the water and put water in a glass pitcher. Add 1 cup sugar for each quart hot water to create a mint syrup. Mint syrup can be kept refrigerated for three days.

Fill a silver mint julep cup with ice, add 1 ounce of bourbon and ½ ounce of rum. Stir in mint syrup to fill the cup. Add 2 drops of bitters and garnish with lemon and fresh mint.

The 1842 Inn
353 College Street
Macon, Georgia 31201
1-877-452-6599
www.the1842inn.com

As the name implies, the inn was built in 1842. It was the home of the former mayor of Macon. The 1842 Inn blends the amenities of a grand hotel and the ambience of a country inn. The guest rooms and public areas dwell within a Greek Revival antebellum house and an adjoining Victorian house that share a quaint courtyard and gardens. The 19 guest rooms, the parlors, and the library are tastefully designed with fine English antiques and paintings, Oriental carpets, tapestries, and elaborate draperies. The inn features a complimentary full breakfast served to guests, along with the morning newspaper, in their choice of three locations: their room, the parlor, or the courtyard.

Deerpark Country Inn
P. O. Box 817
Buckhannon, West Virginia 26201
1-800-296-8430
304-472-8400
www.deerparkcountryinn.com

*L*IZ AND PATRICK HAYNES invite you to surround yourself with 100 acres of rejuvenating country ambience that reflects a bygone era. The inn includes an 18th-century log cabin, a post–Civil War farmhouse, and a newly constructed Victorian wing. Detailed period architecture is featured throughout. About 400 feet from the inn is the two-story lodge— a 19th-century log cabin with an attached wing, offering three gracious bedrooms, a fireplace as large as a man is tall, and French doors that open onto two wraparound porches perfect for watching fireflies, shooting stars or snowflakes falling on deep pine forests. All the rooms and suites of both buildings are richly furnished with fine antiques and collectibles, ferns and fresh flowers, and crisp cotton linens; each has its own personality as well as central air, a private bath, and other amenities. Mist rises from the pond that invites you to fish under the watchful eye of resident mallards and clannishly arrogant geese.

Orchard Peach Smoothie

1 cup low-fat peach yogurt
1 ripe peach
1 cup fresh pineapple
3 cups ice
1 cup Dole Orange-Pineapple juice
Mint for garnish

Pulse ingredients in a blender until smooth. Serve in a large-globe red-wine glass. Place fresh mint on top.

Yield: 4 servings

Sparkling Peach Schnapps

2 teaspoons peach schnapps, chilled
4 ounces chilled sparkling wine
   Fresh peach slices

Spoon the schnapps into a chilled champagne flute. Fill with
sparkling wine. Garnish with peach slice.

Yield: 1 serving

**Cook's Cottage and Suites
Bed and Breakfast**
703 West Austin Street
Fredericksburg, Texas 78624
210-493-5101
www.bed-inn-breakfast-tx.com

LOCATED IN THE HISTORIC
district of Fredericks-
burg, this widely
recognized bed-and-breakfast offers
the ultimate in relaxation, rejuvenation,
and romance in the heart of the beautiful Texas Hill Country. Innkeeper
Patsy Bynum Swendson is a nationally
recognized authority on Southwest
cuisine who has authored 49
cookbooks and appeared on television
for over 20 years. A German farmer's
breakfast is included with your stay.

Redstone Inn

82 Redstone Boulevard
Redstone, Colorado 81623
970-963-2526
www.redstoneinn.com

WHEN YOU COME UPON Redstone, Colorado, a tiny mountain village hidden beneath massive red cliffs, you might not expect to find a first-class hotel and resort.

The Redstone Inn is the focal point of this 100-year-old Arts and Crafts town. All of it was created by mine owner John Osgood as a utopian community for his workers and their families. Open every day of the year, the Redstone Inn treats you to early 20th-century style at reasonable rates. After a day of hiking, tennis, horseback riding or fishing, there's nothing like a soak in the pool or hot tub. Whether you're planning a wedding, a special dinner to thank your employees, or a week-long conference, the creative Redstone Inn staff will do the work for you. You'll find everyday dining an event in itself at the Redstone Inn. People come from all over the state to enjoy the versatile cuisine. And the Redstone is easily accessible, even in winter. Colorado Highway 133 (designated as a scenic byway) is kept clear and safe year round. The Redstone is the perfect hub from which to explore the Colorado Rockies.

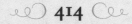
Redstone Colada

- ½ ounce banana liqueur
- ½ ounce coconut rum
- 2 ounces half-and-half
- ½ cup fresh or frozen strawberries
- 2 scoops ice cubes
  Whipped cream
  Grenadine
- 1 fresh whole strawberry

Combine liqueur, rum, half-and-half, strawberries, and ice cubes in blender and blend well. Top with dollop of whipped cream, drizzle with grenadine, and garnish with a fresh strawberry.

Yield: 1 serving

Sunshine Punch

- 1 (6-ounce) can frozen orange juice concentrate
- 1 (6-ounce) can frozen lemonade concentrate
- 1 (6-ounce) can frozen lime concentrate
- 4 cups cold water
- 1 (28-ounce) bottle 7-Up chilled
  Lemon or lime sherbet (optional)

In a large pitcher or punch bowl, combine all ingredients except sherbet. Stir until juices are thawed and blended. Top with scoops of sherbet, if desired.

Yield: 18 servings

Hickory Bridge Farm
96 Hickory Bridge Road
Orrtanna, Pennsylvania 17353
1-800-642-1766
717-642-5261
www.hickorybridgefarm.com

HICKORY BRIDGE FARM is a quaint country retreat with accommodations in a 5-bedroom farmhouse (circa 1750s) and four private cottages with fireplaces. Dinner is served in a beautiful restored Pennsylvania barn decorated with hundreds of antiques. All meals are farm fresh and bountiful. Full breakfast is offered to overnight guests at the farmhouse and is delivered to their cottages on Sunday morning. The farm is located 9 miles west of Gettysburg, Pennsylvania, on 75 beautiful acres—a wonderful place to relax while visiting Gettysburg or antiquing in the area.

The Wildflower Inn
3725 Teton Village Road
Jackson, Wyoming 83001
307-733-4710
www.jacksonholewildflower.com

THE WILDFLOWER INN IS where you will experience Jackson Hole as it is meant to be. The beautiful log-country inn is located on 3 quiet acres surrounded by aspens, ponds, and mountain views. The Wildflower Inn is located within minutes of Grand Teton and Yellowstone national parks, the Jackson Hole Mountain Resort, and the town of Jackson. Wonderful restaurants, golfing, tennis, fishing, and bike paths are located nearby. The Wildflower Inn is famous for its gorgeous setting, beautiful decor, luxurious guest rooms, incredible breakfasts, and the warm, personal attention offered to each and every guest.

Teton Tea

4 cups cranberry juice
2-inch stick of cinnamon
2 cups orange juice
¼ cup lemon juice
½ cup sugar or to taste

Simmer cranberry juice and cinnamon in a large, non-aluminum pan for about 20 minutes. Add orange juice, lemon juice, and sugar. Heat until sugar is dissolved and drink is hot. This is a very special drink for a cold winter day and is beautiful at Christmas time.

Yields 4 to 6 servings

POTPOURRI

Tunnel Mountain
Bed and Breakfast
Route 1, Box 59-1
Elkins, West Virginia 26241
304-636-1684
www.bbonline.com/wv/tunnel/

Tunnel Mountain Bed and Breakfast is a charming three-story fieldstone home nestled on the side of Tunnel Mountain (part of Cheat Mountain), on 5 private wooded acres surrounded by scenic peaks, lush forests, and sparkling rivers. Named for the 1890 railroad tunnel that passes under the hillside, this bed-and-breakfast is a romantic country retreat. The interior is finished in pine and rare wormy chestnut woodwork. Tastefully decorated throughout with antiques, collectibles and crafts, it extends a warm and friendly atmosphere where guests can feel at home. Just down the road from Tunnel Mountain Bed and Breakfast is the 998,000-acre Monongahela National Forest, which offers wonderful hiking and cross-country skiing opportunities.

Apple Compote

   5 large, firm, slightly tart apples, peeled and sliced
   1 (15-ounce) can Mandarin oranges
   3 cups water
  12 pitted prunes, cut in half
 1/3 cup raisins
   2 tablespoons cornstarch
   1 teaspoon cinnamon
 1/2 teaspoon nutmeg
   1 (20-ounce) can pineapple tidbits

Place apples, oranges (with juice), raisins, prunes and 2½ cups of the water in a large pot. Cook at low boil for 10 minutes, stirring occasionally. Mix cornstarch in remaining ½ cup water and add to apple mixture with cinnamon and nutmeg. Cook for 2 minutes. Turn off heat and stir in pineapple. Serve hot or refrigerate and serve cold in summer. Great over pancakes, waffles, or ice cream.

Yield: 6 to 8 servings

Avocado-Lime Vinaigrette

4	avocados, halved, seeded, and scooped out
½	cup lime juice
¼ to ½	cup honey
2	tablespoons ground coriander
1	tablespoon minced garlic
1	cup extra-virgin olive oil
	Salt and pepper

Combine all ingredients except olive oil in a food processor and purée until smooth. Emulsify the oil into the mixture. Strain through a sieve. Season with salt and pepper to taste. Thin with water if desired. Can add more lime, honey, or spice to personal liking.

Yield: 4 cups

The Greyfield Inn
Cumberland Island, Georgia 32035
904-261-6408
www.greyfieldinn.com

THE GREYFIELD INN ON Cumberland Island is a luxurious, romantic oceanfront mansion built in 1900 and furnished today as it was then. In true Southern fashion, the Greyfield takes great pride in dining. Each morning, guests awaken to a full and satisfying breakfast that includes one of the chef's specialties. The day's island explorations are accompanied by a satisfying picnic lunch. During the cocktail hour each evening, hors d'oeuvres are served in the oceanfront bar. Dinner is a casually elegant affair, served in the glow of candlelight. It features fresh and creative cuisine, accompanied by selections from the inn's wine cellar.

1823 Historic Rose Hill Inn

Rose Hill Inn
233 Rose Hill Avenue
Versailles, Kentucky 40383
859-873-5947
www.rosehillinn.com

UILT IN THE EARLY 1800S, Rose Hill was one of the original estates in Versailles, Kentucky. The inn is located 15 minutes west of Lexington, close to horse farms, Keeneland, and the Kentucky Horse Park. Seven guest rooms are available. Freshly baked cookies await you when you check into your room. Everything is baked from scratch on the premises . Breakfast can be delivered to your room, or you can join other guests in the main dining room.

Better 'n Purchased Salsa

2	(28-ounce) cans whole tomatoes
	Juice of 1 lemon
2 or 3	jalapeños (less if you want mild), seeded and chopped
2	medium onions, coarsely chopped
6	cloves garlic, minced
8	green onions, chopped
1	cup coarsely chopped fresh cilantro, or 3 tablespoons dried
¼	teaspoon Italian seasoning
1	teaspoon salt
¼	teaspoon cayenne pepper

Put all ingredients in blender and pulse just a few times until the ingredients look chopped. Salsa will taste better if it has a little time to sit, but keeps well in refrigerator for a couple of weeks.

Yield: 20 servings

Casket Mountain Chilies

1 (27-ounce) can whole green chilies or
    6 (4-ounce) cans, drained
1½ pounds Monterey Jack cheese
3 cups milk
¾ cup flour
3 eggs
1½ teaspoons salt
    Chili powder to taste (optional)

Preheat oven to 350°F. Spray a 9 x 13-pan with cooking spray.

Cut 1 strip of cheese for every chilie and stuff each chilie. Arrange stuffed chilies in pan. Grate remaining cheese. In a bowl, mix milk, flour, eggs, and salt together and pour over chilies. Bake for 45 minutes to 1 hour. Let stand for 10 to 15 minutes. To serve, cut into 9 squares. Serve with tomato slices marinated in tequila-lime vinegar, sweet cornbread, and sausage patties.

Yield: 9 servings

Note: You can stuff chilies the night before and cover pan and refrigerate. This is a big time-saver in the morning.

Old Schoolhouse Bed & Breakfast

P. O. Box 1221
Fort Davis, Texas 79734
432-426-2050
www.schoolhousebnb.com

NESTLED AT THE FOOT of Sleeping Lion Mountain, this historic adobe home is a true lesson in West Texas hospitality. The perfect mix of old-time tranquility and modern comfort, the Old Schoolhouse Bed & Breakfast is the ideal escape for any guest. Built in 1904, the spacious adobe building served as the schoolhouse for Fort Davis children until the 1930s. Guests enjoy a large, shady deck, and full breakfast, while rooms are equipped with ice makers, refrigerators, and ceiling fans. It is located three blocks from local attractions and downtown shopping, and biking and birding are available nearby.

The Historic Taos Inn

125 Paseo del Pueblo Norte
Taos, New Mexico 87571
505-758-2233
www.taosinn.com

THIS HISTORIC ADOBE building is nestled in the heart of Taos's historic district. Thirty-three rooms and three suites are graced with Spanish colonial antiques, whimsical handmade furniture, and hand-woven Oaxacan bedspreads. The Adobe Bar and Doc Martin's Restaurant are award winners.

Doc's Chilies Rellenos

25	Anaheim chilies
	Oil

FILLING

2	pounds Monterey Jack cheese, shredded
2	pounds Cheddar cheese, shredded
1	red onion, finely diced
1	bunch cilantro, chopped
¼	cup cumin

BATTER

2½	cups blue corn flour
1½	cups all-purpose flour
2	eggs
2	beers
1	bag plain tortilla chips

Fry chilies in oil until skins turn white. Transfer to a glass container; cover with plastic wrap to steam. When chilies cool, peel, split one side, and seed, leaving stem intact.

To make the filling: Combine cheeses, onion, cilantro, and cumin in a mixer with paddle attachment on low speed until it forms a ball.

Shape cheese mixture into the shape of a chilie and stuff the chilies. Squeeze chilie around cheese, making sure seam ends come together. Refrigerate for 1 hour.

To make the batter: Whisk together flours, eggs, and beer in a mixing bowl until smooth. Batter should be the consistency of heavy cream. Adjust if necessary with water. In a food processor fitted with a double blade, crush tortilla chips.

Dip stuffed chilies in batter and let excess drip off, then dredge in tortilla chips. Deep fry in 350°F oil until outside is brown and inside is melted. Serve with green chilie, salsa fresca, sour cream, goat cheese, and toasted pumpkin seeds.

Yield: 12 servings

The Captain Freeman Inn

15 Breakwater Road
Brewster, Massachusetts 02631
1-800-843-4664
www.captainfreemaninn.com

THE CAPTAIN FREEMAN INN invites you to return to an earlier era and experience the romance and history of the sea any time of the year. Sleep in an elegant canopy bed surrounded by antiques and fresh-cut flowers. Relax in your own private bath. Soak up the warmth of a private whirlpool spa. Stretch out in front of your own fireplace. Smell the early morning coffee and come down for a cup. Enjoy a sumptuous full breakfast, served poolside on the porch in warm weather, or fireside in the cozy Cape Cod dining room. Every day, breakfast includes fresh-squeezed juice, fruit, and the innkeeper's special menu choice for the day. A short stroll down the old packet landing road leads you to Breakwater Beach on beautiful Cape Cod Bay.

Easy Hollandaise

2 egg yolks
2 tablespoons cold unsalted butter plus 1 cup unsalted butter, room temperature and cut into several pieces
3 tablespoons freshly squeezed lemon juice
2 tablespoons freshly squeezed lime juice
5 drops Tabasco sauce

In a heavy-bottomed saucepan over low heat, whisk egg yolks with the 2 tablespoons cold butter and lemon and lime juices. Continue to whisk until butter melts and mixture begins to thicken and coats back of a spoon. Immediately remove pan from heat and begin adding room-temperature butter, ¼ cup at a time, returning pan to heat and whisking until each addition is incorporated. Add Tabasco and stir well. Sauce will thicken as you work. Final product is pale yellow and silky with the consistency of a milk shake. Use the sauce immediately.

Yield: 1 cup

Nicky's Enchiladas

12 corn tortillas
½ cup oil
2 packages grated Monterrey Jack cheese
1 chicken, cooked, boned, and diced (or same amount of cooked turkey)
¾ cup chopped onion
½ stick butter
¼ cup flour
2 cups chicken broth
1 cup sour cream
1 (4-ounce) can jalapeños or green chilies, sliced

Preheat oven to 350°F.

Dip tortillas in hot oil until soft. On each tortilla, place 2 tablespoons of the cheese, 1½ tablespoons chicken, and 1 tablespoon onion. Roll up tortillas and place seam-side down in a shallow 9- x 13-inch ovenproof casserole dish.

Melt butter in a saucepan. Blend in the flour, then add broth and cook, stirring constantly, until thick and bubbly. Stir in sour cream and peppers. Cook until heated through, but *do not boil*. Pour sauce over tortillas. Bake for about 30 minutes, then sprinkle remaining cheese on top. Bake another few minutes until cheese is melted. Serve hot.

Yield: 6 servings

Mayan Ranch
P. O. Box 577
Bandera, Texas 78003
830-796-3312
www.mayanranch.com

THE INTERNATIONALLY renowned Mayan Ranch is by far the most popular ranch in the famous Texas Hill Country (also known as LBJ Country). There are a wide variety of activities, culinary and otherwise, from cowboy breakfasts cooked out on the trail to steak fries and barbecues. The Mexican-style food surpasses that of any in Texas. Owner Judy Hicks has her own cookbook, *Miss Judy's Wild Western Recipes*, from which this recipe was taken.

Sampson Eagon Inn

238 East Beverley Street
Staunton, Virginia 24401
1-800-597-9722
www.eagoninn.com

*T*REAT YOURSELF TO something truly special. Be pampered by the personal attention and warm hospitality of your hosts, Frank and Laura Mattingly. Enjoy the relaxing atmosphere and comfort of this beautifully restored antebellum mansion. Wake from a restful night's sleep in your canopied bed to a gourmet "skip-lunch" breakfast. Experience Staunton's history and its variety of shops and restaurants just steps from the inn's doors. The inn is also a convenient home base for sightseeing, antiquing, and the varied outdoor activities of the Shenandoah Valley and nearby Blue Ridge and Allegheny mountains.

Fine Herb Cheese Soufflés

   1 dozen eggs
   4 cups finely shredded cheese (Cheddar, Gouda, Swiss, Monterey Jack; combination of two or more is best)
   ½ cup all-purpose unbleached flour, sifted with 1½ teaspoons baking powder
  16 ounces small-curd cottage cheese
   ¼ cup melted butter
   ¼ cup finely chopped fresh herbs (combination of parsley, chives, and thyme is great)

Preheat oven to 350°F. Butter 10 jumbo nonstick muffin cups.

Beat eggs until very frothy and pale lemon in color. In a large mixing bowl, toss cheese with the flour mixture and herbs. Fold in cottage cheese. Gently fold in eggs. Fill buttered muffin cups to top with batter. Bake for 30 to 35 minutes. Remove when puffed and golden brown. Allow soufflés to rest in pan a few minutes to make removal easier.

Yield: 10 servings

Notes: Leftovers freeze very well. However, the soufflés should be thawed first, then heated in the microwave for about 1 minute or so; overheating will give the cheese a rubbery texture. Do not add salt! If desired, a bit of spice, such as dry mustard, cayenne, freshly ground white pepper, or Tabasco, can be added to taste. Nice additions to this basic recipe are drained steamed broccoli or asparagus.

French Dressing

2 teaspoons salt
2 teaspoons black pepper
1 teaspoon chili powder
1½ teaspoons dry mustard
1 cup sugar
1 cup salad oil
1 cup white vinegar
½ cup diced onion
1 (13-ounce) can tomato soup
Garlic powder to taste

Mix well. Refrigerate. Dressing will keep in the refrigerator for 1 week.

Yield: 8 servings

Whitestone Country Inn
1200 Paint Rock Road
Kingston, Tennessee 37763
1-888-247-2464
www.whitestoneinn.com

WHITESTONE IS DESIGNED to resemble a small New England village. Accommodations are in five different buildings, all within a short walk of each other. With a casual style, Whitestone specializes in bountiful regional-country cooking, featuring locally grown vegetables and fruit in season, old-fashioned desserts, farm-raised beef, and hot biscuits and gravy. Your dining experience will be memorable. Linger over breakfast in the large breakfast room, surrounded on three sides by windows providing incredible views of meadows, lakes, and mountains. Dinner is served with unpretentious elegance and candle-light, soft music, and fresh flowers.

Evergreen Inn
1109 South Main Street
Anderson, South Carolina 29624
864-225-1109
864-375-9064
www.spa-it.com

THIS BEAUTIFUL INN IS IN the oldest home in Anderson, built in 1834 by the Ackers-Broyle families. Magnificent, huge oaks and unusual pines, along with one of the largest crepe myrtle trees in the South, surround the inn and restaurant. The spa and restaurant building, located next to the inn, was built in 1906 as a wedding gift for an Ackers-Broyle granddaughter. The inn's present owners are Peter and Myrna Ryter. Peter, originally from Switzerland, has been the chef in many fine restaurants in California, including his own in Redondo Beach. He was named one of the "Top 100 chefs in America for the 20th Century" by the International Restaurant Association.

Warm Goat Cheese Soufflé

10	ounces cream cheese
5	ounces goat cheese
4	egg yolks
1	cup heavy cream
½	cup bread crumbs
½	cup melted butter
	Salt and white pepper

Preheat oven to 385°F. Butter 8 ramekins.

Let cream cheese and goat cheese soften in a food processor. Mix in cheese and eggs (one at a time), then cream. Blend well. Add salt and pepper to taste. Sprinkle bread crumbs on bottom of ramekins. Fill ramekins with batter. Bake for 35 minutes. Refrigerate and serve later with mango chutney on the side.

Yield: 8 servings

Gourmet Chutney

  3 pounds ripe peaches, peeled, pitted, and diced
  1 pound ripe mangoes, peeled, pitted, and diced
  2 quarts cider vinegar
  2 pounds sugar
  2 tablespoons yellow mustard seed
  1 tablespoon ground red chile powder
1½ cups golden raisins
  1 medium onion, diced
  1 clove garlic, diced
  1 clove garlic, minced
  8 ounces candied ginger, boiled with ½ cup water
     until soft and syrupy

In a medium saucepan, combine peaches, mangoes, and 1 quart of the vinegar. Bring to boil, then simmer over medium heat 20 minutes. Set aside.

In a medium saucepan, combine sugar and remaining 1 quart vinegar; boil until thick and syrupy. Drain liquid from fruit into sugar-vinegar mixture. Boil until thick. Stir in fruit, mustard seed, chile powder, raisins, onion, and garlic and cook for 45 minutes. Add ginger and its syrup. Cook another 30 minutes. Pour into hot, sterilized canning jars and seal. This chutney should age at least 1 week for best flavor.

Yield: About 6 pints

Grant Corner Inn
122 Grant Avenue
Santa Fe, New Mexico 87501
505-983-6678
www.grantcornerinn.com

*H*ERE IS AN EXQUISITE colonial-manor inn in the heart of Santa Fe. With an ideal location just two blocks from the historic plaza, Grant Corner is nestled among intriguing shops and galleries. Built in the early 1900s as a home for the Windsors, a wealthy New Mexican ranching family, the inn boasts charming guest rooms, each appointed with antiques and treasures from around the world.

Good Medicine Lodge

537 Wisconsin Avenue
Whitefish, Montana 59937
406-862-5488
www.goodmedicinelodge.com

*S*ITUATED IN WHITEFISH, Montana, in the heart of America's greatest outdoor-recreation region, Good Medicine Lodge is only a few turns from the Big Mountain, a short hike from Glacier National Park, a paddle away from Whitefish River and Lake, and a nine iron from the Flathead Valley's nine golf courses. Six spacious rooms and three suites, most with balconies and mountain views, have private baths, vaulted wood ceilings, and custom-made lodgepole pine or iron beds. Decorated in a Western motif, the roomy interiors are punctuated by crackling fireplaces, solid wood furnishings, and fabrics influenced by Native American textiles. The lodge was named one of *Travel America* magazine's "10 Most Romantic Inns."

Granola

4½ cups old-fashioned rolled oats
 2 cups shredded coconut
 1 cup brown sugar
 ¾ cup chopped pecans
 ¾ cup sliced almonds
 5 tablespoons vegetable oil
 5 tablespoons honey
 ½ cup raisins
 ½ cup dried cranberries
 ½ cup dried berries (blueberries, cherries, strawberries, raspberries)

Preheat oven to 350°F.

In a large bowl, combine oats, coconut, brown sugar, pecans, and almonds. Heat oil and honey in a saucepan until warm and pour over oat mixture; stir to coat. Spread mixture evenly in a rimmed cookie sheet. Bake until coconut and nuts are golden, about 20 minutes, stirring occasionally. Let cool, stirring frequently while cooling. Add dried fruits and stir to combine. Store in an airtight container at room temperature.

Yield: 10 cups

Pineapple Soufflé

2 (16-ounce) cans crushed pineapple (do not drain)
¾ cup flour
1 cup sugar
2 eggs
White bread, crusts cut off
Melted butter

Preheat oven to 350°F.

In a bowl, whisk together pineapple, flour, sugar, and eggs. Pour batter into a shallow casserole dish. Top with small squares of white bread dipped in melted butter. Bake for 45 minutes to 1 hour, until lightly browned. Excellent served with any type of pork: ham, pork chops, tenderloin, you name it!

Yield: 8 servings

Crystal River Inn
326 West Hopkins
San Marcos, Texas 78666
512-396-3739
www.crystalriverinn.com

THE CRYSTAL RIVER INN IS located on the major highway connecting Austin and San Antonio in the lovely little riverside town of San Marcos. The crystal-clear headwaters of the San Marcos River are here, along with two theme parks, a major university, and four unusually beautiful historic districts. The inn is located in one of these districts, shaded by pecan trees. It is an 1883 Victorian, with fireplaces in many of the guest rooms, designer décor, antiques, a wicker-strewn veranda, a fountain courtyard, and many special touches. Guests enjoy brandy and chocolates at bedtime, fresh flowers, and, of course, delicious food—fast becoming legendary in central Texas.

Country Homestead
Bed and Breakfast

22133 Larpenteur Memorial Road
Turin, Iowa 51059
712-353-6772
1-888-563-7455
www.country-homestead.com

THE HISTORIC COUNTRY Homestead is nestled in the beautiful Loess Hills of western Iowa, overlooking the Missouri River Valley, in the midst of what was once a tall-grass prairie. The house was built by R. T. Reese and his family after they homesteaded the farm in 1855. It has been enlarged by succeeding generations and is now open as a bed-and-breakfast inn by the fourth generation, David and Lin Zahrt. Amenities include two guest rooms upstairs, with king or queen bed and private bath. Included is a full breakfast with wholesome food. Out the back door are 450 acres of Loess Hills and 1,062 miles of quiet, paved Monona County roads.

Homemade Yogurt

 2 cups nonfat powdered milk
 1 teaspoon live yogurt culture
 3 cups 98°F water (body temperature)
 1 quart jar with a lid
 1 insulated picnic cooler

Combine powdered milk, yogurt culture, and water in the jar. Stir until well mixed. Fill the jar to the top with warm water. Place lid on jar. Place jar in cooler and add water bath (temperature of 100 to 110°F.) to the level of the jar neck. Place lid on the cooler and allow yogurt to thicken for 8 hours. Refrigerate.

Yield: 4 cups

Jalapeño-Cheddar Pie

- 1 cup bread crumbs
- ¼ cup grated Parmesan cheese
- ¼ cup melted butter
- 2 pounds cream cheese
- 5 whole eggs plus 3 egg yolks, beaten together
- ¼ cup flour
- 2 teaspoons minced garlic
- ½ cup minced onion
- 3 cups grated Cheddar cheese
- 2 tablespoons chopped fresh herbs
- 2 minced jalapeños
- ½ cup beer (optional)

In a small bowl, combine bread crumbs, Parmesan cheese, and butter; set aside. In a large bowl, beat together cream cheese, eggs, and flour until well blended. In another bowl, combine remaining ingredients and fold into the cream-cheese mixture. Grease a 10-inch springform pan. Line bottom of pan with the bread crumb mixture. Pour batter into pan and let stand in refrigerator for 24 hours.

Preheat oven to 325°F.

Place pan in water bath and bake for 1½ hours or until a knife inserted in the middle comes out clean. Refrigerate until well chilled. Remove from pan and portion accordingly.

Yield: 1 pie

Rabbit Hill Inn
48 Lower Waterford Road
Lower Waterford, Vermont 05848
802-748-5168
www.rabbithillinn.com

THIS WHITE CLAPBOARD INN was built in 1827 as a home with a small shop fashioning sleighs and winnow mills (a device that separates dust from grain). After several additions, the inn started its long history of nourishing weary travelers in 1840. In its early days, it served the area's logging community. The marks of the drovers' and lumberjacks' spiked boots can still be seen on the floors. Lower Waterford is the most photographed town in Vermont and is nicknamed "the white village" for its 10 post-Revolutionary white houses, of which Rabbit Hill Inn is the focal point. The two connecting dining rooms are famed throughout the area for relaxing, unhurried meals, genuine home-cooked food, and an extensive wine list to please the connoisseur. Rabbit Hill Inn is a wonderful place to be.

The Leadville Country Inn

127 East Eighth Street
Leadville, Colorado 80461
719-486-2354
www.leadvillebednbreakfast.com

MINING HISTORY GIVES the town and inn their names. These days Leadville is a year-round paradise for outdoor enthusiasts, history buffs, and antiquers. The inn has made a mark for its cuisine; as one previous guest put it, "The aromas from the kitchen remind me of my grandmother's house." All of the little touches in the decorating and restoration make you feel as if you are the honored guest of a very good friend. The inn is renowned for its quiet, peaceful setting—the perfect place for a romantic getaway.

John Wayne Casserole

  3 tablespoons butter
  2 large onions, chopped chunky style
  1 large red bell pepper, chopped chunky style
  2 green chilies (Anaheims are good), chopped chunky style
  2 cloves garlic, minced
  1 jalapeño pepper, minced
 12 eggs, separated
 ½ cup milk
 ¾ cup all-purpose flour
  2 tablespoons ground black pepper
 32 ounces sour cream
  3 cups Cheddar cheese, grated or shredded
 ¾ cup blue corn tortilla chips
  2 teaspoons Dijon-style mustard
  2 tablespoons sugar
    Sour cream
    Chopped chives
    Chopped tomatoes

Preheat oven to 350°F. Grease two 9 x 13-inch baking dishes

In a large frying pan, combine the butter, onions, green chilies, and bell pepper. Add garlic and jalapeño. Sauté lightly and remove from heat. In a large mixing bowl, combine egg yolks, milk, flour, and pepper. Add sour cream, cheese, tortilla chips, mustard, sugar, and the cooled sautéed mixture. Mix until well combined. Beat egg whites until they are stiff then fold into the mixture. Dividebetween baking dishes.

Bake for approximately 1 hour. The casserole is done when top is a little crusty and starts to crack. Serve with a little sour cream on the side, sprinkled with chopped chives and chopped fresh tomatoes.

Yield: 18 to 20 servings

Orange-Flower Jelly

1½ cups strained freshly squeezed orange juice
2 tablespoons orange flower water (available at gourmet specialty shops or health-food stores)
3½ cups sugar
1 (3-ounce) container liquid fruit pectin

In a large pan, combine orange juice, orange-flower water, and sugar. Bring to a boil over high heat, stirring to dissolve sugar. Immediately add pectin. Return to a full boil that cannot be stirred down. Boil and stir for 1 minute. Remove from heat and ladle into jars. Store in refrigerator.

Yield: 3 to 4 servings

Cook's Cottage and Suites Bed and Breakfast

703 West Austin Street
Fredericksburg, Texas 78624
210-493-5101
210-273-6471
www.bedandbreakfast.com/texas/
cooks-cottage-and-suites.html

*L*OCATED IN THE HISTORIC district of Fredericksburg, Texas, this nationally recognized bed-and-breakfast offers complete privacy, romance, amenities and exceptional cuisine. Rated as one of the "Top 25 Most Romantic Inns in America" by *Travel + Leisure* magazine, the inn offers the ultimate in relaxation, rejuvenation and romance in the heart of the beautiful Fredericksburg, Texas Hill Country. The inn is noted for aromatherapy, breakfast-in-bed baskets, herbal wraps, massage therapy, special-occasion baskets, special packages, antiques, décor, and wonderful gourmet food. Your gracious innkeeper, Patsy Swendson, will welcome you and do all she can to provide you with an experience you will always remember.

Hope-Bosworth House
Bed & Breakfast Inn

21238 Geyserville Avenue;
P. O. Box 42
Geyserville, California 95441
1-800-825-4233
707-857-3356
www.hope-inns.com

THE HOPE-BOSWORTH House is a charming Queen Anne–Craftsman-style Victorian built in 1904 by an early Geyserville pioneer and settler, George M. Bosworth. The house, built entirely of heart redwood, is a "pattern-book house." The house was built with day labor, and all the milling for the custom shiplap siding was done on the site under the direction of Mr. Bosworth. During the 1906 earthquake, the brick chimneys toppled to the ground and plaster fell from the walls, but the house withstood the quake. All of the rooms are a step into the past. The original oak-grained woodwork is evident throughout the house, from the large sliding doors in the hallway to the upstairs tower bedroom. Polished fir floors and antique light fixtures enhance the period furnishings, completing the comfortable décor.

Pasta Soufflé

3 dozen ravioli of your choice
1/2 stick butter
1/4 cup flour
3 cups milk
Salt and pepper to taste
4 large eggs, separated
1 cup shredded Swiss cheese

Preheat oven to 400°F.

Cook the ravioli in boiling water until barely done and still firm. Drain, rinse, and drain again. Melt butter in small saucepan. Add flour and stir until smooth. Add milk, salt, and pepper, and cook over medium heat until thickened. Add egg yolks and Swiss cheese to sauce and mix well. Whip the egg whites into peaks and fold into the sauce. Place ravioli in a soufflé dish and pour sauce over. Fold together gently. Bake for 45 minutes.

Yield: 6 servings

Civil War Peanut Brittle

1 cup sugar
2 tablespoons butter
¾ cup peanuts (or choice of nut)

In a medium skillet, mix together sugar and butter until mixture begins to thicken and turns dark tan. Drop a teaspoon of the mixture into cold water. When it hardens, it is done. Remove from heat and immediately mix in peanuts. Let cool. Break apart to serve.

Yield: 1 large candy bar

Fairville Inn
506 Kennett Pike (Route 52)
Chadds Ford, Pennsylvania 19317
1-877-285-7772; 610-388-5900
www.fairvilleinn.com

OCATED IN THE HEART OF the Brandywine Valley, the Fairville Inn, listed on the National Register of Historic Places, echoes the pastoral scenes of the Wyeth family paintings. Accented with barn wood, beams, and cathedral ceilings, the inn is the embodiment of elegant comfort. There are 15 rooms and suites in the main house, carriage house, and springhouse. Most rooms feature rear decks/balconies overlooking acres of gentle grassy meadows rolling toward a serene pond.

The Red Coach Inn

Two Buffalo Avenue
Niagara Falls, New York 14303
716-282-1459
1-800-282-1459
www.redcoach.com

*M*ODELED AFTER THE OLD Bell Inn in Finedon, England, the Red Coach Inn has been welcoming guests to Niagara Falls, New York, since 1923. Overlooking the spectacular Upper Rapids and just 1,500 feet from the American Falls, the bed-and-breakfast is Niagara Falls' most distinctive historic structure, with its English Tudor exterior and its warm English-country ambience. The inn offers meeting space for business conferences, family reunions, or small wedding receptions. The Red Coach Inn was chosen as a "Top Ten Getaway" by *Fortune* magazine.

Grilled Vegetable Crepes with Smoked Tomato Coulis

VEGETABLE CREPES

- 1 zucchini, cut lengthwise into ¼-inch thick slices
- 1 yellow squash, cut lengthwise into ¼-inch-thick slices
- 1 portabella mushroom, stem removed
- 1 red bell pepper, halved and seeded
- 4 tomatoes, halved and seeded
- ½ cup olive oil, divided
- 1 teaspoon salt, divided
- 1 teaspoon ground black pepper, divided
- ½ teaspoon mesquite seasoning
- ½ teaspoon roasted garlic spice
- 6 tablespoons heavy cream
- 1 teaspoon liquid smoke
- 2 scallions, coarsely chopped
- 12 prepared crepes

To make the crepes: Toss vegetables, 2 tablespoons of the olive oil, ½ teaspoon of the salt, and ½ teaspoon of the pepper in a mixing bowl. Grill vegetables until tender. Set tomatoes aside.

Reheat the grilled vegetables in a sauté pan with 2 tablespoons olive oil, scallions, mesquite seasoning, roasted garlic spice, remaining ½ teaspoon salt, remaining ½ teaspoon pepper, cream, and liquid smoke. Heat in small saucepan prior to serving.

    4 **tomatoes, grilled and set aside from above**
    1 **teaspoon liquid smoke (mesquite flavored)**
    1 **tablespoon olive oil**
2 to 3 **cloves garlic**
        Salt and pepper

To make the sauce: Place all ingredients in a blender. Pulse to desired consistency. Heat in small saucepan prior to serving.

To serve: Divide vegetables among crepes and roll them, using 3 crepes on each plate in a tiered effect. Pour heated sauce over the crepes. Serve with wild rice and spring mix with raspberry vinaigrette.

Yield: 4 servings

The Crocker House
Country Inn

967 Point Road
Hancock Point, Maine 04640
1-877-715-6017
207-422-6806
www.crockerhouse.com

THE CROCKER HOUSE Country Inn is tucked away on the peninsula of Hancock Point. Its quiet, out-of-the-way location, fine cuisine, and individually appointed guest rooms all combine to make the Crocker House a refreshing and memorable destination. The restaurant, open to the public, continues to draw guests from distant places for its extraordinary cuisine and live piano on Friday and Saturday nights.

Port Wine and Stilton Vinaigrette

    1   egg
    ¼   cup sugar
    1   tablespoon Dijon-style mustard
    ⅓   cup raspberry vinegar
    ⅓   cup port wine
    ½   teaspoon salt
    3   tablespoons chopped onion
    1   tablespoon dry Good Seasons Italian Dressing mix
    2   cups oil (we use a corn/olive blend)
    2   ounces Stilton cheese

In a food processor, combine egg, sugar, mustard, vinegar, wine, salt, onion, and Italian dressing mix. Process 1 to 2 minutes. *slowly* dribble in the oil and add 1½ ounces of the Stilton. When all the oil is used, check for taste. Add remaining Stilton if you like a stronger blue-cheese flavor. The slower you process the oil, the creamier the dressing becomes. This dressing is excellent tossed with fresh greens, grape halves, walnuts, and chunks of Stilton.

Yield: 1 quart

Refrigerator Pickles

6 cups sliced cucumbers
1 cup sliced onion
1 cup sliced green bell pepper
1 cup vinegar
2 cups plus 1 tablespoon sugar
1 tablespoon celery seed

Stir ingredients together until sugar is dissolved. Store in refrigerator. Great with meat dishes or on sandwiches, as pickles are very crisp.

Yield: 2 quarts

Audrie's B&B
23029 Thunderhead Falls Road
Rapid City, South Dakota 57702
605-342-7788
www.audriesbb.com

THE ULTIMATE IN CHARM AND Old-World hospitality, Audrie's B&B offers spacious suites and cottages that are furnished with comfortable European antiques. All lodgings feature a private entrance, private bath, patio, hot tub and Black Hills–style breakfast. Each room provides you with a setting that quiets your heart and says, "Breathe deep, you have all the time in the world." This country home and 7-acre estate is surrounded by thousands of acres of national forest in a secluded Black Hills setting. This is the area's first and finest bed-and-breakfast establishment.

Red Creek Inn,
Vineyard and Racing Stables
7416 Red Creek Road
Long Beach, Mississippi 39560
228-452-3080
www.redcreekinn.com

THIS CIRCA 1899 INN IS located on 11 beautiful acres of magnolias and ancient oaks. It is a three-story raised French cottage with a 64-foot front porch. There are six elegant fireplaces and wonderful antiques for the visitor's enjoyment. Located on the Mississippi Gulf Coast, about an hour east of Louisiana, the house was originally built by a retired Italian sea captain to entice his young bride away from her family's home in New Orleans. The owner describes the long porch as a spot "where I can eat boiled shrimp and crabs in the shade of magnolias, or just swing to my heart's content, enjoying a tall drink and a thick novel." Delicious cuisine is served in the elegant dining room.

Rémoulade Sauce

1	cup mayonnaise
4	hard-boiled eggs, finely chopped
1	teaspoon dry mustard
2	tablespoons finely chopped fresh parsley
1	tablespoon finely chopped green bell pepper
1	teaspoon finely chopped garlic
1	tablespoon anchovy paste
1	teaspoon Worcestershire sauce
6	finely chopped olives
	White pepper to taste
1	tablespoon finely chopped capers
1	tablespoon finely chopped fresh chervil
1	tablespoon finely chopped fresh tarragon
1	tablespoon finely chopped gherkins

Place mayonnaise in a bowl. Add remaining ingredients and mix well. Serve with shrimp, crab, or other seafood.

Yield: 1½ cups

Sausage, Gravy, and Biscuits

- 1 pound country-flavored bulk pork sausage
- 2 tablespoons finely chopped onion
- 6 tablespoons all-purpose flour
- 1 quart milk
- 1/2 teaspoon poultry seasoning
- 1/2 teaspoon ground nutmeg
- 1/4 teaspoon salt
  Dash of Worcestershire sauce
  Dash of Tabasco sauce

Brown sausage in large skillet over medium-low heat. Add onion; cook and stir until transparent. Drain, discarding all but 2 tablespoons of grease. Stir in flour; cook over medium-low heat until mixture bubbles and turns golden. Stir in milk. Add seasonings and cook until thickened, stirring constantly. Serve over halved Bisquick biscuits.

Yield: 6 servings

Spahn's Big Horn Mountain Bed and Breakfast
70 Upper Hideaway
Big Horn, Wyoming 82833
307-674-8150
www.bighorn-wyoming.com

HIGH ON THE SIDE OF THE Bighorn Mountains, in a whispering pine forest, you will find this rustic lodge built by Ron Spahn, a former Yellowstone Park ranger. It is at the edge of the one-million-acre Bighorn National Forest. Deer, moose, eagles, and turkeys are commonplace, and even elusive bear and mountain lions are never far away. Hearty food is served on a deck with a 100-mile view. Western-style supper cookouts followed by evening wildlife safaris are a tradition at the lodge.

**Manor House
Bed and Breakfast**
612 Hughes Street
Cape May, New Jersey 08204
609-884-4710
www.manorhouse.net

ANOR HOUSE, A BED-
and-breakfast inn, is
located on Hughes
Street, often called the prettiest street
in Cape May. Though the inn is nestled
in a very quiet residential neighborhood, all of the wonderful restaurants
and attractions that Cape May has to
offer are only a short walk away. The
Manor House features a wraparound
front porch with comfortable rocking
chairs, along with a secluded English-
style garden that encourages relaxation
and savoring afternoon treats and
refreshments.

Soft Pretzels

$\frac{1}{8}$ cup hot water (105 to 115°F)
1 package dry yeast
1$\frac{1}{3}$ cups warm water
$\frac{1}{2}$ cup brown sugar
5 cups flour
Coarse salt
Baking soda

Preheat oven to 400°F. Grease 3 cookie sheets well and sprinkle
with salt.

Stir hot water and yeast together in a bowl. Stir in warm water
and brown sugar. Slowly add flour, stirring constantly until
dough is smooth and doesn't stick to bowl. Transfer dough to
lightly floured board and knead until smooth and stretchy. Set
aside.

Pinch off dough the size of golf balls and roll each piece into a
14-inch-long rope. Shape into a pretzel. Fill a frying pan with
water and for each cup of water add 1 tablespoon baking soda.
Bring to a gentle boil. Add pretzels and cook for 30 seconds,
then transfer to cookie sheets. Sprinkle pretzels with salt and
bake until golden, about 10 minutes. Serve with mustard.

Yield: about 2$\frac{1}{2}$ dozen pretzels

Southwestern Casserole

1 pound ground pork sausage
4 scallions, diced, reserving ²/₃ of the diced green tops
2 (7-ounce) cans diced mild green chilies
6 slices (approximately) sourdough French bread
1½ cups Colby-Jack cheese
1 small Roma tomato, skin only, diced into ¼-inch dice
10 eggs
1 cup half-and-half

Fry sausage until browned and almost cooked through. Add scallion bottoms along with ⅓ of the green tops and cook until meat is thoroughly cooked. Turn off heat and add chilies. Mix well.

Spray a 9 x 13-inch baking dish with cooking spray. Place the bread slices into the dish to cover bottom. Pour sausage mixture evenly over bread. Spread cheese evenly over sausage. Sprinkle reserved diced green scallion tops and tomato skin over cheese. In a separate bowl, beat eggs and add half-and-half. Pour over casserole. Cover with plastic wrap and refrigerate overnight.

Preheat oven to 350°F. Bake casserole for 35 minutes. Cover with aluminum foil and continue to bake another 15 minutes.

Remove from oven and let stand for 5 minutes before serving.

Yield: 6 to 8 servings

Pecan Street Inn Bed & Breakfast
1010 Pecan Street
Bastrop, Texas 78602
512-321-3315
www.pecanstreetinn.com

VOTED "BEST BED-AND-BREAK-fast in Bastrop County" 2004 and 2005, the Pecan Street Inn is an elegant early 1900s Victorian home. It is listed on the National Register of Historic Places and is designated a City of Bastrop landmark. Nestled under a grove of native pecan trees, the eclectically styled Carpenter Gothic/Queen Anne has been lovingly restored over the last 15 years by innkeepers Shawn and Bill Pletsch. Signature gourmet, sit-down breakfasts are served at the guests' discretion, and include stellar main dishes, such as pecan waffles with strawberries Grand Marnier, fruit, and baked goods. All are served on china with silver and crystal in one of the two dining rooms.

Creekside Inn and Resort

16180 Neeley Road
Guerneville, California 95446
707-869-3623
www.creeksideinn.com

CREEKSIDE INN AND RESORT IS A warm and welcoming inn nestled among the redwoods in the Russian River Valley in the heart of Sonoma County's Great Northwest. This delightful bed-and-breakfast has an assortment of charming cottages, sunny decks, a pool, picnic areas, and a casual attitude. A generous breakfast is served in the inn's dining room each morning.

Strata with Roasted Red Pepper, Provolone Cheese, and White Corn

2 slices white bread, crust removed
    Butter
1 red bell pepper, roasted and peeled
½ ounce Provolone cheese
12 frozen white or yellow corn kernels
1 egg
⅓ cup milk

Oil the inside of small ramekin. Butter 1 slice bread and place in ramekin, buttered side down. Fill with approximately ¼ roasted bell pepper, cheese, and corn kernels. Butter the second slice of bread, place on top, buttered side up. Mix egg with milk and pour into ramekin. Cover and refrigerate overnight.

Preheat oven to 350°F.

Place ramekin in a water bath and bake for about 45 minutes until puffy and golden brown on top. At Creekside, we serve in the ramekin with fruit and salsa.

Yield: 1 serving

Swiss Cheese Pie

        1 piecrust
8 to 12 ounces shredded Swiss cheese
           Nutmeg
        2 large eggs
    1¹/₃ cups milk

Preheat oven to 475°F. Spray a pie pan with cooking spray or grease lightly with butter.

Spread piecrust into pan. Fill crust with cheese (more for a denser consistency, less for a more delicate consistency; we use about 12 ounces). Sprinkle with nutmeg. Bake for 10 to 12 minutes (until piecrust starts to brown). Turn oven temperature down to 375°F. Bake for about 20 more minutes. Allow to sit for a couple of minutes to set before serving. We serve the pie with sautéed cherry or grape tomatoes and bacon for breakfast or with salad for lunch.

Yield: 1 pie

Samuel Durfee House
352 Spring Street
Newport, Rhode Island 02840
401-847-1652
1-877-696-2374
www.samueldurfeehouse.com

THE SAMUEL DURFEE HOUSE is a Newport, Rhode Island, bed-and-breakfast inn built in 1803 by banker Samuel Durfee of Providence. It is conveniently located in Newport's Yachting Village, just a block from the harbor and the restaurants and shops on Thames Street. It is 1½ blocks from Bellevue Avenue with its mansions, shops, and the Tennis Hall of Fame. Enjoy a delicious gourmet breakfast each morning in the parlor or back patios. Specialties of the house include Portuguese sweet-bread, French toast, coddled eggs, eggs frittata, and baked stuffed French toast.

The Bucksville House

4501 Durham Rd.
Kintnersville, Pennsylvania 18930
610-847-8948
www.bucksvillehouse.com

THE BUCKSVILLE HOUSE bed-and-breakfast, a registered Bucks County historical landmark, provides the visitor not only with country charm, but also with over 200 years of Pennsylvania history. Built in 1795, the Bucksville House has had several lifetimes and expansions as an 1830s hotel, a tavern, speakeasy during the Prohibition period, and a private residence. Innkeepers Barbara and Joe Szollosi purchased the Bucksville House as an "ultimate handyman's special" in 1984 and began welcoming guests a year later. The house's décor reflects its 1790s to 1840s origin. Period reproductions include four-poster beds, a country kitchen table and cabinet, desk, bureau, and backgammon set. Restored 19th-century pieces, antique collectibles, original art, and nearly 100 quilts (the earliest homespun quilt dates to the 1800s) can be found throughout the bed-and-breakfast.

Wine Jelly

2 cups red wine
6 cups sugar
1 (1¾ ounce) box fruit pectin

In a saucepan, combine wine and sugar over medium heat until sugar dissolves, stirring constantly. Increase to a boil and add pectin. Stir, bring to a rolling boil, and boil for 1 minute longer. Skim off foam and fill jars or wine glasses ⅔ full. Store in refrigerator.

Yield: 2 pints

INDEX

The Great Country Inns
of America Cookbook

The Great Country Inns of America Cookbook